ETHICS IN ETHNOGRAPHY

ETHNOGRAPHER'S TOOLKIT
Second Edition

Jean J. Schensul, Institute for Community Research, Hartford, Connecticut
Margaret D. LeCompte, University of Colorado, Boulder

PURPOSE OF THE ETHNOGRAPHER'S TOOLKIT

The second edition of the **Ethnographer's Toolkit** is designed with the novice field researcher in mind. In this revised and updated version, the authors of the **Toolkit** take the reader through a series of seven books that spell out the steps involved in doing ethnographic research in community and institutional settings. Using simple, reader-friendly language, the **Toolkit** includes case studies, examples, illustrations, checklists, key points, and additional resources, all designed to help the reader fully understand each and every step of the ethnographic process. Eschewing a formulaic approach, the authors explain how to develop research questions, create research designs and models, decide which data collection methods to use, and how to analyze and interpret data. Two new books take the reader through ethical decision-making and protocols specific for protection of individual and group participants in qualitative research, and ways of applying qualitative and ethnographic research to practical program development, evaluation, and systems change efforts. The **Toolkit** is the perfect starting point for students and faculty in the social sciences, public health, education, environmental studies, allied health, and nursing, who may be new to ethnographic research. It also introduces professionals from diverse fields to the use of observation, assessment, and evaluation for practical ways to improve programs and achieve better service outcomes.

1. *Designing and Conducting Ethnographic Research: An Introduction, Second Edition*, by Margaret D. LeCompte and Jean J. Schensul

2. *Initiating Ethnographic Research: A Mixed Methods Approach,* by Stephen L. Schensul, Jean J. Schensul, and Margaret D. LeCompte

3. *Essential Ethnographic Methods: A Mixed Methods Approach, Second Edition*, by Jean J. Schensul and Margaret D. LeCompte

4. *Specialized Ethnographic Methods: A Mixed Methods Approach*, edited by Jean J. Schensul and Margaret D. LeCompte

5. *Analysis and Interpretation of Ethnographic Data: A Mixed Methods Approach, Second Edition*, by Margaret D. LeCompte and Jean J. Schensul

6. *Ethics in Ethnography: A Mixed Methods Approach*, by Margaret D. LeCompte and Jean J. Schensul

7. *Ethnography in Practice: A Mixed Methods Approach*, by Jean J. Schensul and Margaret D. LeCompte

ETHICS IN ETHNOGRAPHY
A Mixed Methods Approach

Margaret D. LeCompte and Jean J. Schensul

ALTAMIRA
PRESS

A division of
ROWMAN & LITTLEFIELD
Lanham • Boulder • New York • London

Published by AltaMira Press
A division of Rowman & Littlefield
A wholly owned subsidiary of The Rowman & Littlefield Publishing Group, Inc.
4501 Forbes Boulevard, Suite 200, Lanham, Maryland 20706
www.rowman.com

Unit A, Whitacre Mews, 26-34 Stannary Street, London SE11 4AB, United Kingdom

British Library Cataloguing in Publication Information Available

Library of Congress Cataloging-in-Publication Data

LeCompte, Margaret Diane.
 Ethics in ethnography : a mixed methods approach / Margaret D. LeCompte and Jean J.
Schensul.
     pages cm. — (Ethnographer's toolkit, second edition Book 6)
   Includes bibliographical references and index.
   ISBN 978-0-7591-2209-3 (pbk. : alk. paper) — ISBN 978-0-7591-2210-9 (electronic)
 1. Ethnology—Methodology. 2. Ethnology—Research. 3. Ethnology—Moral and ethical
aspects. I. Schensul, Jean J. II. Title.
   GN345.L424 2015
   305.8001—dc23

                                                          2014043349

Printed in the United States of America

CONTENTS

List of Examples   ix
Introduction to the *Ethnographer's Toolkit*   xv

Chapter 1   Ethics and Ethnography   1
Introduction   1
What Are Ethics?   2
What Are Research Ethics?   3
Ethics in Social Science Research   5
What Is a Human Subject?   8
Ethics and Epistemology: Do Ethnographers Face Greater
    Ethical Challenges Than Other Types of Researchers?   17
Confronting the Stereotype of Scientific Neutrality   19
Formal Research Ethics and Everyday Research Ethics   26
Summary   32

**Chapter 2   The Evolution of Formal Concerns about and Ethical
Principles Governing Human Research**   35
The Origins of Formal Oversight   35
Medical Research and Risk to Human Subjects   35
Social Science Research and Risks to Human Subjects   45
Disciplinary Codes of Ethics and the Problems
    of Enforcement   49
The Belmont Report 1978   50
The Belmont Principles   51
Summary   71

Chapter 3   Formal and Semiformal Responsibilities   73
Introduction   73
Semiformal Responsibilities   73
Formal Contractual Responsibilities   89
When Is IRB or IEC Approval Necessary?   96
Issues of Particular Concern to IRBs and IECs   97

Levels of Review   98
Components of an IRB Proposal   101
The Power of Institutional Review Boards and
    Institutional Ethics Committees   104
Coping with Multiple IRBs   108
Summary   112

Chapter 4   **Informal Ethics: The Implications of Researcher Roles**
             and Characteristics   113
             Introduction   113
             The Embedded Contexts and Multiple Roles of
                 Ethnographic Work   116
             Being a Learner   120
             Creating a Field Identity   126
             Coping with Relationships in the Field:
                 Personal Characteristics, Asymmetrical
                 Relationships, and Positionality   136
             Personal Friendships in the Field   156
             Summary   158

Chapter 5   **Informal Ethics: Long-Term Relationships and**
             Reasonable Responsibilities   159
             Introduction: Feasible and Possible Responsibilities   159
             Coping with Associations in the Field: Affiliations
                 and Sponsorships   162
             Maintaining Good Relationships   165
             Coresearchers and Research Partners   169
             Negotiating an Exit and Leaving the Field   172
             Reciprocity and Feedback   175
             Dissemination and Disposition of Data   177
             Assuring Program Continuation   178
             Summary   178

Chapter 6   **Ethical Issues in Ethnographic Teamwork and**
             Community-Based Research   179
             Introduction   179
             Ethical Considerations in Intrateam Interactions   180
             Ethical Considerations in Team Interaction with
                 Study Communities/Sites and Participants   192
             Protecting the Study Community   196
             Summary   201

Chapter 7 **Going Beyond Belmont: New Issues and Challenges** 203
Introduction 203
Challenges to IRB "Surveillance" and Control 205
Contesting Western Epistemological and
    Ontological Hegemony 215
Redefining Key Terms in the Twenty-First Century 216
Obtaining Consent 217
Exposure to Risks and New Forms of Vulnerability 224
Technology and Retrievability of Information 234
Ethics and the Consequences of Interpretation 236
Summary 250

Chapter 8 **The Role of Reflection in Ethnographic Research** 251
Introduction: What Is Reflection? 251
Identifying Subjectivities 255
Positionality and Power 262
The Risks of the "Other" 263
Taking Stock 264
Summary 264

Appendix A: IRB Proposals 267
Appendix B: Consent Forms and Assent Forms 317
References 343
Index 357
About the Authors 375

LIST OF EXAMPLES

Example 1.1: When is the research "human research"? The TOR network   8

Example 1.2: What is a "live" human being?   9

Example 1.3: A "live" human subject   9

Example 1.4: When is a river a person?   13

Example 1.5: Should a forest be granted personhood?   14

Example 1.6: Experiencing a different reality: Disrupting the spirits of the dead   16

Example 1.7: Building rapport and understanding by sharing experiences and roles   23

Example 1.8: Police raid in a high-risk site   28

Example 1.9: What to do when a key informant for illegal activities is arrested   29

Example 2.1: The yellow fever studies of Walter Reed, 1905   37

Example 2.2: The Tuskegee Syphilis Study, 1932–1972   37

Example 2.3: Syphilis experiments in Guatemala   40

Example 2.4: The Willowbrook hepatitis study: 1963–1966   41

Example 2.5: "Outsourcing" research to investigate how to brainwash individuals so as to improve military interrogation techniques   41

Example 2.6: Study of lead abatement in Baltimore   43

Example 2.7: Conducting risky studies in poor countries when conducting them in the United States is impossible   44

Example 2.8: Obedience to Authority Experiments, Stanley Milgram, 1962   46

Example 2.9: The Stanford Prison Experiment, Philip Zimbardo, 1971   47

Example 2.10: The Tearoom Trade   48

Example 2.11: Studying inmates in a prison school   59

Example 2.12: Obtaining consents for a study of middle school children   60

Example 2.13: Studying how being infected by the HIV virus affects the work of artists   63

Example 2.14: The sensitivity involved in linking DNA data to individuals' sex and math scores   64

Example 2.15: Pregnancy and parenting as disincentives to high school graduation for Latinas   64

Example 2.16: Levels of confidentiality required for a study of domestic abuse   66

Example 2.17: Professor McIntyre assesses his own instruction   67

Example 2:18: Obtaining anonymous/de-identified data on sensitive topics in a sensitive town   70

Example 3.1: When researchers cannot agree on research results   78

Example 3.2: A publications agreement from the Institute for Community Research   79

Example 3.3: Working with reporters to improve accuracy of reporting   83

Example 3.4: Failure to maintain records   104

Example 3.5: Deliberate violation of formal rules regarding research conduct   106

Example 3.6: When IRBs disagree   109

Example 4.1: How being perceived as someone "in the know" impedes data collection   121

Example 4.2: Bridging class differences in the field   122

Example 4.3: Creating a field identity in Short Grass   128

Example 4.4: Creating a field identity that avoided being viewed as a "narc"   128

Example 4.5: Creating a field identity that uses people's partial
understandings about researchers   130

Example 4.6: When participants misunderstand the researcher's topic
and act abnormally because the initial script is poorly related to the
research question   130

Example 4.7: Juggling fieldwork requirements with requirements
of roles acquired in the field site   132

Example 4.8: Conducting research on community understanding
of Alzheimer's disease   133

Example 4.9: Why Navajos only visited the ethnographer at night   137

Example 4.10: When teen action researchers wouldn't take researchers
to visit their neighborhood   137

Example 4.11: Social distance between male researchers and female
residents in Short Grass   138

Example 4.12: Reducing status differences to improve communication
about behavior too intimate to describe to male researchers   139

Example 4.13: Using same-sex researchers to run focus groups
on sexual behavior in Sri Lanka   139

Example 4.14: Confusing attentive ethnographic listening with
sexual interest   140

Example 4.15: Avoiding unwanted sexual attention   141

Example 4.16: How a team member's romance destroyed a research project 142

Example 4.17: Equating physical characteristics with moral characteristics
or competence   147

Example 4.18: Where is fat considered to be attractive? Differences in
beauty between the United States and Somalia   148

Example 4.19: Protecting a fieldworker from racism   149

Example 4.20: Interviewing young women in Mauritius: Whether to
match interviewers to respondents or not   150

Example 4.21: Altering data collection strategies in a youth-led
participatory action research project to better elicit sensitive information 151

Example 4.22: Race as an impediment to researcher access   152

Example 4.23: How ethnic prejudice creates social distance   152

Example 4.24: When to avoid looking like a "hippie"   153

Example 4.25: The impropriety of "going native": When to avoid imitating research participants   154

Example 4.26: Class differences in approaches to dental care   155

Example 4.27: Class and ethnic differences in ways to "relax"   156

Example 4.28: The danger of being associated with marginal groups in a community   157

Example 4.29: Avoiding negative roles and maintaining open communication   157

Example 5.1: Establishing boundaries between "reasonable" and "impossible" informant requests   160

Example 5.2: When perceptions influence hiring decisions   162

Example 5.3: Dressing to contradict negative stereotypes   163

Example 5.4: When the wounds of history won't heal: Working with an intractable stereotype   164

Example 5.5: When informants think researchers' prior affiliations are beneficial   165

Example 5.6: Proving one's chops in traditional drinking competitions   166

Example 5.7: "Tests" that place researchers in physical and legal danger   167

Example 5.8: Deciding not to publish a story so as to preserve good relationships   168

Example 5.9: When a team member shows good judgment in taking protective action   169

Example 5.10: When a team member blows the whistle   170

Example 5.11: Taking action in a crisis   171

Example 5.12: Taking a drunken man home   172

Example 6.1: Team research on alcohol use and sexual risk in India   184

Example 6.2: When staff members do not realize that they lack knowledge and training or when they are in need of supervision   186

Example 6.3: Responding to the disclosure of work-related stress
in a team member 187

Example 6.4: Staying safe in high-risk research sites 188

Example 6.5: Keeping female fieldworkers safe in India 188

Example 6.6: Reporting on activities that placed a team member at risk 189

Example 6.7: Deciding where to eat and sleep 191

Example 7.1: Problems arising when oversight for clinical trials is lacking 210

Example 7.2: Making lemonade out of a sour requirement to perform
professional service to the university 214

Example 7.3: Establishing a new IRB at the University of Connecticut
Health Center 215

Example 7.4: Implementing and evaluating a needle exchange program
in Hartford, Connecticut 221

Example 7.5: Obtaining informed consent from Indian women in a
study about gender inequality and marital intimacy 221

Example 7.6: Creating vulnerability by using a particular data
collection technique 225

Example 7.7: Situational and informational risks 226

Example 7.8: The dangers posed by inexperienced researchers in
revolutionary societies 229

Example 7.9: Risk incurred by a group because studies revealed
characteristics possessed or experiences had by some members
of the group 232

Example 7.10: Cultural and physical risks associated with the environment 232

Example 7.11: Multiple realities in search of a single story 239

Example 7.12: Two stories, same data 243

Example 8.1: Sacred mountains versus enormous telescopes 254

Example 8.2: Discovering a "cold spot" 256

INTRODUCTION

INTRODUCTION TO THE *ETHNOGRAPHER'S TOOLKIT*

The *Ethnographer's Toolkit*, a mixed methods approach to ethnography, is a series of seven texts on how to plan, design, carry out, and use the results of applied ethnographic research. While ethnography as an approach to research may be unfamiliar to people accustomed to more traditional forms of research, we believe that ethnography will not only prove congenial but also essential to many researchers and practitioners. Many of the investigative or evaluative questions that arise in the course of answering basic questions about ongoing events in a community or school setting or in the context of program planning and evaluation cannot be answered very well with other approaches to research, such as controlled experiments or the collection of quantifiable data alone. Often there are no data available to quantify or programs whose effectiveness needs to be assessed. Sometimes, indeed, the research problem or issue to be addressed is not yet clearly identified and must be discovered. In such cases, mixed methods ethnographic research provides a valid and important way to find out what *is* happening and to help research-practice teams plan their activities.

NEW IN THE SECOND EDITION OF THE *ETHNOGRAPHER'S TOOLKIT*

In this second edition of the *Toolkit*, we have updated many sections of the books and, based on feedback from our colleagues, we have clarified many of the concepts and techniques. Book 1 of the *Ethnographer's Toolkit, Designing and Conducting Ethnographic Research: An Introduction*, remains an introduction and primer, but it includes new material on data collection, definition, and analysis as well as new chapters on research partnerships and using ethnography for a variety of applied purposes. In Book 1 we define what ethnographic research is, when it should be used, and how it can be used to identify and solve complex social problems, especially those not readily amenable to traditional quantitative or experimental research methods alone. Book 2, *Initiating Ethnographic Research: A Mixed Methods Approach*, now is devoted to the process of developing a conceptual basis for research studies and to more detailed questions of research design, modeling, and preparing for the field experience. Books 1 through 4 emphasize the fact that ethnography is a peculiarly human endeavor; many of its practitioners have commented that, unlike other approaches to research, the *researcher* is the primary tool for collecting primary data. Book 3, *Essential Ethnographic Methods: A Mixed Methods Approach*, demonstrates that ethnography's principal database is amassed in the course of human interaction: direct observation, face-to-face interviewing and elicitation, audiovisual recording, and mapping the networks, times, and places in which human interactions occur. Further, the personal characteristics and activities of researchers as human beings and as scientists become salient in ethnography in ways not applicable in research that permits the investigator to maintain a more social and conceptual distance from the persons and phenomena under study. Interpretation of ethnographic research results emerges only from the process of engaging researcher understanding with direct, face-to-face experience.

Book 4, *Specialized Ethnographic Methods: A Mixed Methods Approach*, is a collection of ten individually authored chapters that includes new chapters on cutting-edge approaches to ethnography as well as chapters on hidden populations, analyzing artifacts, and using secondary data, photovoice, and GIS systems. Book 5, *Analysis and Interpretation of Ethnographic Data: A Mixed Methods Approach*, has been updated and linked more closely to the theoretical and conceptual approaches outlined in Books 2 and 3, and it includes new examples.

Book 6, *Ethics in Ethnography: A Mixed Methods Approach*, and Book 7, *Ethnography in Practice: A Mixed Methods Approach*, are entirely new to the *Toolkit*. The former provides extensive detail on the burgeoning field of formal and informal research ethics, includes chapters that address the special considerations needed for ethical procedures in team and collaborative research, and examines the way that the environment for research has changed in ways that mandate new procedures for complying with ethical principles. Book 7 discusses innovative applications of participatory community-based ethnographic research in design, interventions, evaluation, dissemination, instruction/teaching, and ethics.

We have designed the *Toolkit* for educators, service professionals, professors of applied students in the fields of teaching, social sciences, social and health services, medicine, communications, engineering, the environment, and business, advanced undergraduate and graduate students, and professionals working in applied settings who are interested in field research and mixed methods ethnographic research. The examples we include throughout the books are drawn from these fields as well as our own research projects and those of our colleagues. We also believe that the *Ethnographer's Toolkit* will be useful to any researcher, whether novice, apprentice, or expert, who desires to learn how to, or more about how to, carry out high-quality ethnographic and mixed methods research.

INTRODUCTION TO BOOK 6

Ethics in Ethnography: A Mixed Methods Approach begins by defining what ethics and ethics in research are. In an approach important for ethnographers, it goes far beyond the normal—and formal—concern in research ethics for the procedures outlined in federal requirements for the ethical treatment of human subjects. It treats in detail as well what we have called informal or everyday ethics, those that govern daily interactions between researchers and individuals in the field. Book 6 takes the position that all research is subject to the same ethical considerations as is ethnography; no particular research design is more or less prone to generate ethical issues for researchers or the people they study. It also defines the focus of ethnographic research—human beings—and includes what kinds of nonhuman "beings" might be considered foci of research in non-Western societies. Chapter 1 initiates the discussion by raising concerns about narrow definitions both of ethical principles and what constitutes "good" research practice in the twenty-first century.

Chapter 2 presents a short history of the development of formal oversight of research practices, and it outlines the abuses that led to their regulation. It highlights the problems of enforcement of the ethical treatment of human participants in research, and it discusses how the Belmont Report of 1978 defined the guiding principles for research ethics and developed an enforcement mechanism for them. Chapter 3 is devoted to a detailed discussion of formal and semiformal responsibilities incumbent on researchers studying human beings. It includes a discussion of Institutional Review Boards and their procedures, and shows how the Belmont Principles are translated into concern for informed consent, vulnerable subjects, risks and benefits of research, and confidentiality and protection of private information elicited from research participants. It also addresses the ethics involved in formal contractual relationships with sponsors, organizational research partners, coinvestigators, community residents, and research participants.

Chapters 4 and 5 move to the realm of more informal or everyday ethics and address how researchers' roles and personal characteristics affect their daily interactions in the field, from initial entry into the field until the researcher concludes his or her study and takes leave of the research site. Chapter 6 recognizes that, increasingly, ethnographers work in teams that can include other researchers, community partners, and consultants. Doing fieldwork and writing up research in teams creates many complexities, not the least of which are those involving how to manage the ethics of joint work and publication and creating consensus on procedures and how to work with human participants so as to be consistent in not affecting them negatively.

Throughout Book 6, references are made to dramatic changes in the world in which researchers now operate both in terms of its diversity and in the stance that researchers must adopt where increasingly they must share power, insights, and credit for research with participants who demand a say in how they are portrayed and in the risks they are willing to undergo. Chapter 7 summarizes these references and goes "beyond Belmont" in examining new challenges and issues researchers face in dealing with IRBs and in redefining procedures so as to be congruent with new field realities. It also includes a section on the ethics of interpretation of research results, a topic that heretofore has been little dealt with in the literature. Finally, chapter 8 makes explicit the important role that reflection places in research, both in terms of assessing the quality of the research practice and in evaluating the degree to which researchers have adhered to their own personal, as well as formal and informal, ethical principles.

1 ❦❦❦

ETHICS AND ETHNOGRAPHY

Introduction

What Are Ethics?

What Are
Research Ethics?

Ethics in Social
Science Research

What Is a Human
Subject?

Ethics and
Epistemology: Do
Ethnographers
Face Greater
Ethical
Challenges Than
Other Types of
Researchers?

Confronting
the Stereotype
of Scientific
Neutrality

Formal Research
Ethics and
Everyday
Research Ethics

Summary

INTRODUCTION

This book presents the range of ethical concerns that ethnographers face while planning for and doing their work
in the field, in interpreting their analyzed data, and in
handling the dissemination of their results once they have
completed their work. Some of these concerns are formally
codified and must be addressed prior to gaining approval to
begin a research project; others involve the informal rules
and norms that govern everyday interaction with people
in the field and on research teams. All of them require an
understanding of the multiple—and sometimes conflicting—histories, cultures, and value systems in which these
ethics are embedded—professional disciplinary cultures,
the culture of funding agencies and regulatory bodies, the
culture of the communities under study, and their relationships and conflicts with the cultures in which they are
embedded. In this book, we move beyond a simple discussion of the codified requirements of regulatory bodies and
look at the more complex twenty-first-century interplay
of ethical considerations and decisions as acted out by
researchers as they cope with power relationships and competing discourses in the field.

In this chapter we define what ethics and ethics in
research are, and we point out some common misconceptions about the relationship between research designs and

1

consideration of their ethics. These clarifications will help when we get into deeper discussion of how ethnographers address ethics in the field. We also confront what we believe to be a bias in most discussions of research ethics toward rather narrowly drawn definitions and procedures. This bias derives from the focus in ethics on notions of individual rights, agency, and personhood embedded in Western culture and jurisprudence. We also bring up some as yet unclear areas that derive from the differences between such Western notions and those often quite different conceptions embedded in many of the cultures researchers may wish to study. We then distinguish between formal research ethics informed by national and disciplinary guidelines, and the informal ethics of everyday life interactions between researchers and the people and communities they study.

WHAT ARE ETHICS?

Ethics are principles that govern interactions between and among people and with regard to their relationship with their surroundings. Ethics underpin the values, norms, and rules that dictate how people should act so as not to be harmful to others. They are enshrined in religious documents, the common law, codified legal treatises, and cultural norms, and are informed by philosophies that support varying rationales for their existence and implementation (Deyhle, Hess, and LeCompte, 1992; Gubrium, Hill, and Flicker, 2013; Levine, 1988; Mikesell, Bromley, and Khodyakov, 2013). All behavior is governed to some degree by the ethical principles extant in people's cultures, including the behavior of researchers in the field. Researcher behavior increasingly is shaped by requirements that investigators act in ways that do as little harm as possible to the individual people, groups, and even animals that they study. If they are physical scientists, that harm applies to the living world and environmental systems in which the results of their studies are applied, and if they are archeologists, they are enjoined to do as little damage as possible to the historical and prehistorical record. Social researchers, including ethnographers, are also encouraged not only to minimize harm but also to "do good," if possible, including returning research results to study sites and other efforts as appropriate. They are also required to consider issues of confidentiality and to ensure that the people with whom they are conducting research have agreed voluntarily to participate with full understanding of the nature of the research, its importance to society, and its implications for them.

Ethnographers, in particular, work directly with people, and consequently cannot do their work without understanding how to address these considerations in the context of what constitutes appropriate behavior both in their own culture and in the culture and setting being studied. Since the mid-twentieth century, they also have had to abide by more formal procedures similar to those required of medical researchers, including obtaining consent, reducing harm, and informing participants about the conduct of their research and the risks attendant to it. Research ethics, then, consist of principles having to do with how researchers conduct their work so as to do as much good for and as little harm to the people they are studying, to make sure that they do not reveal confidential information either to people in the setting or other researchers, and to confirm that the people whom they select for their research are willing collaborators and participants who have a clear understanding of the research and what it will mean to them.

WHAT ARE RESEARCH ETHICS?

Initially, research ethics had to do with whether or not the research conducted was done competently, according to disciplinary tenets, and by qualified investigators. Scientists were trusted to "do the right thing," or the best thing, and basically, ethical research was research well and rigorously done, without a careful consideration of whether the individuals under study might experience harm. Voluntary participation was not a priority, or at least was a considerably less important priority than the scientific community's need for advances in knowledge. Further, the voice of the people studied was more or less irrelevant; the authoritative voice was that of the researcher, who unearthed the "true" story using empirical means; participants' thoughts and meanings paled in the face of the researchers' more objective authority. In fact, too much apparent closeness to the people studied, it was believed, could leave a researcher vulnerable to charges of violating positivistic canons for rigor, including being biased, creating subjective results, and "going native."

From the 1800s up until the mid-1900s, ethnographers wrote about the communities they studied pretty much with impunity as to what they said, since their results were considered to be "objective" facts. Even though many of the results might now be called opinions, the mostly nonformally educated people portrayed, who did not have access to researchers' publications or representations, never questioned, critiqued, or contradicted them, nor, for the most part, were researchers critiqued by their peers. Other early ethnographies also tended to create frozen portraits of living people, written in the present tense (the so-called ethnographic presence), with the authorial voice of the ethnographer receding as an "absent presence" (Marcus and Fischer, 1986) in the text. Readers tended to think that the practices portrayed were the "real" or "true" representations of the culture, and that any deviation from those portraits indicated a loss of traditional culture (cf. Freeman, 1983; Buchholz, 1984; Shankman, 2009). Community and indigenous voices were neither heard nor considered important because much early ethnography, whether by travelers, religious workers, or anthropologists, took place in colonial environments where "natives" were simply documented, rather than included (although there were exceptions [cf. Rylko-Bauer et al., 2006]). Further, given how North American and European anthropologists tended to romanticize so-called traditional ways as more pure and authentic than anything "modern," cultural change was defined as cultural loss, a degeneration of culture, rather than as the normal evolution of dynamic human groups. It was difficult, therefore, for people who had once been studied by an anthropologist ever to legitimately differ from the portrait that anthropologists or other writers established without being labeled as having "lost" their culture, or worse, having their cultural practices labeled as primitive, violent, or disgusting (Borofsky, 2005). In these ways, ethnographic portraits silenced the voice of researched communities and fossilized a portrayal of them over which they had little control.

These representational practices began to change, however, as anthropologists revisited their own or the sites of earlier researchers and began to realize how dynamic cultures actually are and how "change" did not mean "loss" of a way of life but instead a complex, rich, and creative set of adaptations to constantly changing contexts and circumstances. Further, the critique of representation, with its privileging of indigenous voices and representations, may be as one-sided as the representations of outside researchers. What is important to recognize, given the perspective we take in this book, is that every community articulates a number of voices or perspectives about what happens there. Only a representation that takes all of these perspectives into account can pretend to approximate a balanced and full portrait of that community.

ETHICS IN SOCIAL SCIENCE RESEARCH

Like researchers in the hard sciences, the primary ethical concern of social scientists and qualitative researchers in earlier eras had to do with how to avoid violating positivistic canons of objectivity. This meant that their principal preoccupation involved avoiding interaction with participants that could contaminate the "natural" behavior they wished to study in its daily settings. Tensions existed between this dictate and interaction with interviewees, especially key informants, since close relationships with such individuals were necessary. Nonetheless, though convinced that their more intimate and engaged approach was appropriate, ethnographers still worried about critiques by other social scientists about the degree to which their involvement and intimacy with participants in the field would alter their behavior, skew research results, and generate charges of researcher subjectivity.

Some scholars, however, began to argue that it was unethical to write up research as though one were a member of their culture (see for example, the title of one classic work, *We, the Tikopia*, written by the very non-Tikopian anthropologist, Raymond Firth [1936]). Ultimately, speaking "for" a group of which one was not a part was defined as potentially harmful to the people studied. Examples abounded (see Geertz, 1989–1990); some ethnographic portrayals were egregiously one-sided, representing not a dispassionate description but more clearly the subjective reactions of a researcher to an ahistorical and atypical situation in which the studied community found itself. This was the case with Colin Turnbull's *The Mountain People* (1987). In Turnbull's presentation, the status of the Ik, an African tribe, had deteriorated in fewer than three generations from being prosperous hunters to scattered bands of hostile, starving people. Turnbull's description portrayed the Ik as amoral and even sociopathic. What Turnbull failed to describe sufficiently was the cause of the Ik's distress; in fact, they were victims of an environmental crisis that Turnbull did not consider. Flooding from a dam had required that the Ik be moved to a new area that was too small and infertile to support the community, and the people were dying of hunger. However, Turnbull's ethnography remains the primary source of information about the Ik, including its devastatingly negative portrayal and its violation of canons for good research methodology.

In the late twentieth century, a lively discussion emerged over whether or not researchers could or should speak *for*, or *about*, or *in the voice of* the people being studied. Contemporary scholars, particularly those from outside the Western mainstream, vigorously criticized the earlier literature, arguing that anthropologists had no right to "speak for" or portray the "other" with such certitude (Said, 1978, 1989, 1994; Spivak, 1988). Others have been applauded for taking stands against the mistreatment by others of groups they have studied—for example, Donna Deyhle, for the treatment of Navajo and Ute people who were denied appropriate schooling and disenfranchised by local white communities, as well as cheated out of oil and gas royalties by the US federal government (Deyhle, 2009), and Barbara Rose Johnston and Holly M. Barker (2008) for writing and speaking out publicly about the fate of island peoples displaced by nuclear testing in the Pacific. Still others have argued in favor of advocacy *with* rather than advocacy *on behalf of* marginalized groups in the United States (Schensul and Schensul, 1978). Notwithstanding, other researchers have felt that their professional ethics prevented them from becoming advocates for "their" people at least until long after they left their research site.

These critiques have changed the focus of ethics in research from one linked primarily to technical exactitude and performative rigor to one in which a *valid* (and still rigorous) portrayal of the people under study becomes paramount, as does the obligation of the researcher to negotiate, include, and at times to privilege the perspective of participants in their results and interpretations. Further, interpretive and postmodern theorists as well as members of the community investigate, increasingly ask, or even require researchers to present all sides of issues under study. They also expect that researchers will help study participants and their communities to seek redress when they are faced with mistreatment or various forms of injustice. This approach to portraying communities and research results requires a change in researcher stance vis-à-vis participants from one of distance to one of inclusion. We have argued that the kind of collaborative and participatory research illustrated throughout the *Ethnographer's Toolkit*, and that we have advocated in Book 6, chapter 6, and Book 7, provides at least one important form of considerable constraint on inappropriate representations of communities and cultures, as the participants being studied often play a role in the research as well. Their presence is an ongoing validity check on the questions researchers explore, what they find, and how the findings are interpreted and presented, and even with whom they are shared. Further, it provides communities the research skills to represent themselves and their situations in their own way.

Even when the researchers are not precisely collaborators with the community, a principal question is whether

Definition: A human subject of research is a living human individual about whom an investigator conducting research obtains identifiable private information (or data) through intervention or interaction with that individual (or other participants in the research project)

Definition: Private or personal identifiable information is information that research participants would not want to be disclosed publically and which could be linked to them in ways that would reveal their identity

or not the research is of value to the community or individuals of study. Thus, it is important for research to be of value not only to researchers and to "science" or the research enterprise in general but also to community members. That value can be assessed in terms of its utility or its capacity to produce a valued result such as the capacity of a community to advocate for a need or a right, the positive result of an intervention, an appropriate representation of the community to the world, or even self-reflection by the researcher.

WHAT IS A HUMAN SUBJECT?

Ethics govern human behavior, and social scientists study those humans. Humans *are* the focus for social science research. Thus, though what "humans" are may seem quite straightforward, the matter bears some discussion. Normally, a **human subject** is a living individual with whom an investigator engages through intervention or interaction to obtain data that consists of **identifiable private information** about that individual (or other participants in the research project). Private or personal information is information participants provide to researchers voluntarily that they would not want to be disclosed to the public and which could be linked to them such that their identity could be revealed.

EXAMPLE 1.1

WHEN IS THE RESEARCH "HUMAN RESEARCH"? THE TOR NETWORK

Researchers from several institutions became interested in the way dissidents from various countries communicated secretly among themselves using anonymous computers linked to the Internet via a web called the TOR network. They presented their study at a conference in Amsterdam, and the news network, CNN, picked up the story. Given CNN's reporting, other researchers reported the study to the Institutional Review Board (IRB) at the original authors' university, arguing that the study should be quashed because the researchers had not sought IRB approval. The researchers argued that they had not needed such approval because theirs was not human research. They were only examining the "traffic" on the network, or the number of messages from specific countries. They could not access the content of the messages, and they did not know the names, locations, or even the identification

numbers or passwords of the participants in the TOR network, given that passwords were changed every few seconds. Thus they were not collecting information directly from or about human beings, they could not determine the content of messages being sent, and they could not trace the messages to any particular user. After long and heated debate, their IRB ruled that the research was not research involving human subjects directly, and therefore did not require IRB approval.

One problem that remained, however, was that the country of origin could be identified, and given a high volume of "traffic" from that country, that information could alert authorities of dissident or undesirable communications that the government might want to squash. This issue, however, did not affect the IRB's decision about this particular research project because it did not reveal the identity of any specific human subject.

 **EXAMPLE 1.2**

WHAT IS A "LIVE" HUMAN BEING?

By contrast, while archeological studies generally are not considered to be studies of live human beings, in one case, forensic archeology did involve a living human— Professor Dennis Van Gerven at the University of Colorado—who volunteered a cheek swab and his DNA for comparison against that of a long-buried historical figure who might have been a murder victim. While the focus of the investigation was not a live human being, the study did require DNA from someone who was alive and who matched the ethnicity and sex of the corpse, and the research thus qualified as "human research." Van Gerven's DNA also helped to prevent the misidentification of the corpse's remains as those of very long-deceased Native Americans, whose remains also had been found in the area.

EXAMPLE 1.3

A "LIVE" HUMAN SUBJECT

In a study conducted by youth with adult support, and with Institutional Review Board approval, on ways of "hustling" or selling recycled, stolen, pirated music or videos, or illegal goods, youth conducted anonymous or non-identified surveys and brief, de-identified interviews with teens who were selling such items in different areas of their city. In the process one young man offered to do a videotaped interview about his life as a "hustler." Once the interview was conducted, the young man had the opportunity to view it, and he decided that it could be shown to the public with the proviso that his face be blurred. He was comfortable with the fact that his voice as well as his story might identify him to some people, but he also felt that the content of the story did not reveal anything threatening to him personally and conveyed an important message to others.

      This young man was a "live" human subject, protected by human subject regulations and able to make decisions about his participation and representation of self in the context of a methodologically rigorous study. While the collection of oral histories, myths, and stories about a culture does involve interviewing live human beings, insofar as the research involves collecting only "cultural" material that is widely known in the community, it usually does not involve the collection of "personal and identifiable information that an individual would not want disclosed" and does not require special scrutiny by an IRB, at least from the perspective of protection of "human subjects." In much the same way, a great deal of historical research usually does not require live human beings for subjects because it relies on analysis of documents and secondary sources. To the extent that it uses these sources alone, historical research is not technically "human research." Thus, research is not "human research" if no data are obtained from "live human beings" with whom interactions should be governed by ethical considerations. Research using sensitive data that are drawn from live human beings but are completely de-identified so that their sources cannot be traced—even to the group from which they are drawn—also is not usually considered research on human subjects for purposes of ethical consideration because the data cannot be traced to their source, which thus cannot be revealed. There are, for example, hundreds of national, state, and study-based de-identified databases, even including de-identified qualitative databases that do not require human subjects review prior to use because no individual humans can be identified in the databases. The only consideration that might cause a researcher to pause is when the de-identified data come from an entire group, such that every person in that group would be known or presumed to possess whatever negative, stigmatized, or otherwise suspect characteristics had been revealed. In such a case, the researcher might consider protecting the *group* through de-identification.

In contemporary research, however, researchers now encounter new and complex problems with regard to what constitutes a "human" or a "living" being. Doing ethical research also requires understanding what is considered to be *living*. By this we mean that humans and their cultural reference groups attribute to *perceived "living"* entities the same deep cultural meaning as to living beings. Examples of things or groups *perceived to be living* might be human remains in archeological sites, animals, stone totems, or spirits. Researchers who study groups that hold such beliefs must be aware that they have ethical responsibilities toward these so-called nonliving entities, even though their training might not have prepared them for such eventualities. A simple example involves human remains found in archeological sites. Previously viewed as objects of study by archeologists and other scientists, human remains found in such sites in the United States now are accorded legal protection by the Native American Graves Protection and Repatriation Act (NAGPRA). They must be repatriated to the living people most closely related to them, and reinterred according to the customs of those people. Often, the indigenous people who claim them consider that even making them available for study prior to burial is a violation of cultural ethics. That is, such human remains, even though no longer living, have been accorded legal rights because they are now viewed as human based on the claims of Native American advocates, whereas before they were perceived as nonhuman objects of study by researchers who were not Native American.

In some cultures family and community members who are deceased (e.g., ancestors or ancestral spirits) are considered to be the equivalent of living humans. In these cultures, ancestors enjoy many of the same rights (and in turn, have obligations) as do people who are not deceased. While learning about the process of communicating with and paying proper respect to the deceased may seem strange, uncomfortable, or even bizarre to Westerners, doing so may be a crucial part of eliciting a complete portrayal of a community as well as understanding how families function.

Another example of an entity not ordinarily thought of as "human" recently has emerged in US jurisprudence, that of "corporate personhood." Under the law, corporations now are counted as individuals, with the same rights to free speech and belief as human beings (*Citizens United, Appellant v. Federal Election Commission*, 2010). This issue currently is being hotly debated in the United States in controversies over who can contribute financial support for political campaigns, who must pay taxes, and who is responsible for providing health care. The decision also raises questions relevant to research. Researchers now must ask themselves what ethical stance should be taken toward such corporate individuals, and how or if they should obtain corporate consent to be investigated. If corporations are persons, do researchers have the same ethical responsibilities toward them as they do to individual human persons? Who grants permission for study, or can individuals belonging to the corporation be contacted without permission from the head of the corporation? Can the corporate individual grant consent for all its component human individuals? Can it compel them to participate? While these questions would apply to research in any corporate or organizational setting, they also could generate unique legal implications if as-yet-unspecified requirements are not met. If considered to be "persons," could corporations sue for misrepresentation or invasion of privacy or ethical issues involving consent if researchers did not have their permission to conduct research? Can they also attempt to control the contents of publications, as happened in a recent court case (cf. Briody et al. 2012)? While not unfamiliar in principle, such situations may require unconventional solutions, since the aggrieved "party" is not an individual human being.

Less familiar forms of personhood arise when the scope of "human research" is broadened beyond a Western-oriented and biomedically influenced definition of human beings.

EXAMPLE 1.4

WHEN IS A RIVER A PERSON?

In New Zealand, the Whanganui Iwi people consider the Whanganui River that runs through their land to be as integral a part of their culture survival and sustenance as any given human or set of human beings (Kennedy, 2012). The Whanganui Iwi hold that their duty toward the river is to "increase its value" by collectively preserving, conserving, augmenting, and enhancing it over time for the security of future generations. However, Crown law holds that holding a title to a property establishes a regime of rights to capture, to exclude, to develop, and to keep. The Whanganui Iwi value the river's resources for its contribution to their survival as a group; without it, they die. Western law values it for the profit to be made by treating it as a resource to be exploited, dammed, shared, subdivided, and even alienated from the tribal people who depend on it. In order to protect the river properly, the Whanganui Iwi were able to make their view of the river as a living integrated whole prevail; it is declared a "person" under Commonwealth law. This legal entity is protected by guardians appointed from a collective of the Whanganui Iwi, members who possess the chiefly power to make decisions about it and who act together for the benefit of the river. It no longer is viewed either legally or by the public simply as a natural resource. The river now cannot be harmed by diversion, pollution, excess fishing, and other kinds of exploitation, or a myriad of other acts that would endanger it and the people with whom it is inextricably linked.

Researchers studying this community would have to determine what ethical stance should be taken toward a river-as-person, who would speak for it, and how.

Many indigenous peoples accord a kind of personhood to the Earth (e.g. Mother Earth, Gaia), reverencing it and caring for it and its resources as the fundamental basis of their survival as a people. However, Western thought does not have the same perspective on the natural environment, and the case of the Whanganui River is rare. As indigenous peoples increasingly face Western and global corporate exploitation of their plants, animals, forests, mineral resources, mountains, air, and water for profit, the very Mother Earth upon which they depend is endangered in ways that threaten their existence and, over time, the existence of all humans. Their cultures will not survive the loss of its environmental basis. Interestingly, with growing concern over global climate change and its effects on planetary life and health, Western scientists, especially those with concern for health and social well-being, are slowly shifting to a more globalized view of health as a planetary concern (Friel, Marmot, McMichael, Kjellstrom, and Vågerö, 2008; Horton et al., 2014; McMichael, 1995). Indigenous and scientific perspectives appear to be converging as life on this planet is threatened.

The notion of *free, prior, and informed consent* (FPIC) is an attempt to provide some protection for indigenous natural resources. Enshrined in the International Labour Organization Convention 169 (ILO 169) and Article 32 of the UN Declaration on the Rights of Indigenous Peoples, FPIC gives indigenous people the right to determine and develop priorities and strategies for use and development of their own land and other resources. It also requires states to negotiate in good faith with indigenous peoples, to obtain their uncoerced prior informed consent regarding any use of their lands or resources, and to provide redress for any adverse impact on indigenous peoples as a consequence of such development (https://www.culturalsurvival.org/node/10635).

EXAMPLE 1.5

SHOULD A FOREST BE GRANTED PERSONHOOD?

The Kuy people of Cambodia live in the Prey Lang forest, which covers large parts of Cambodia. This forest is the home of their tree-living spirits, the place where dead are buried, and the source of food, medicines, and other materials for living. However, the Cambodian government is leasing the entire forest to corporations for industrial plantations of cashew, rubber, and acacia trees, and has ignored attempts by the Kuy to seek restitution through Free Prior Informed Consent (FPIC) or to negotiate for protection of their lands (Keating, 2012).

Indigenous people have begun to demand free, prior, and informed consent from multinational corporations and governments prior to any resource extraction or exploitation. The example of the Whanganui River may provide a model for achieving legal protection—that is, personhood and the gaining of "human" rights—for forests and other environmental features that people feel are an integral part of the community. The enforcement of such agreements is, however, poorly carried out, easily circumvented, and often ignored by wildcat operations, poachers, and other illegal activities. Even with proper legal protection, exploitation can continue, requiring constant monitoring and surveillance by indigenous or local people as well as regulatory bodies.

While the notion of free, prior, and informed consent most often is associated with relationships between indigenous peoples and corporations wishing to mine, dam, cultivate, or otherwise alienate land from its virgin uses, its provisions resemble the principles of the Belmont Report, discussed in the next chapter, which was written to protect human subjects of research. Thus, FPIC also has relevance for researchers who may find it useful as a way of understanding connections between a people and their Earth, as well as objects that Western thought defines as inanimate. For example, the burgeoning use of hydraulic fracturing, which injects chemicals and wastewater deep into the earth to break up oil- and gas-bearing shales and rock formations, does in fact produce energy fuels. It also produces earthquakes in seismically quiet areas, pollutes air and aquifers, and causes tap water to burst into methane-fueled flames. Some indigenous people on whose ancestral land fracking is being carried out view fracking as injecting poisons into the body of Mother Earth, and they attribute the adverse impacts to the consequences of poisoning their mother. Sherpas in Nepal are coming to believe that the many and increasing number of deaths on Mt. Everest can be explained by the sacred mountain's anger at being exploited for profit in mountain climbing adventures for amateurs. Damming rivers creates electricity and diverts water for irrigation, but it also causes the death of river currents and the plants and animals—including humans—that depend on them. By absorbing the sun's energy, fields of solar collectors steal that energy from the ground beneath them, and from the plants and animals living there. In the belief of the Paiute people of the Southwestern United States, such theft is illegitimate, and could be dangerous to all living things. While we do not present solutions to how ethnographers might address these ethical issues, we call attention to them as emblematic of how the world of research—and the ethics attendant to conducting it—are changing, and why good researchers ignore these changes and the power relationships at play in the communities they study at their peril. We also note that understanding these issues and differences can mean literally entering into and embracing a different reality.

EXAMPLE 1.6

EXPERIENCING A DIFFERENT REALITY: DISRUPTING THE SPIRITS OF THE DEAD

Early in her research in the Navajo Nation, LeCompte went camping with several informants and some archeologist friends in the Canyonlands of the US Southwest. Picking a high bluff overlooking the San Juan River, the group pitched their sleeping bags and settled in for the night. LeCompte did not sleep well; not only were her companions snoring loudly, but she had "waking" nightmares. Figurative images kept scrolling across her field of vision, even when her eyes were closed. The next morning, she described the images—tall, thin, humanlike figures—to her friends. "Skinwalkers!!!" exclaimed one. LeCompte had never heard the term. Her friends explained that skinwalkers are malevolent witches who either are themselves, or are associated with, the spirits of the dead. They are shape shifters, capable of transforming themselves into any animal and then assuming the speed, strength, and cunning of that animal. They are able to use mind control to cause their victims to hurt themselves and others, and as witches, they can cast spells. LeCompte's description of her nightmares exactly described representations of skinwalkers—but until that moment, LeCompte had never seen or heard of those descriptions, or even of skinwalkers. Later that morning, while exploring their campsite, the group discovered that they had been camping nearly on top of an ancient burial ground—exactly the kind of place that skinwalkers were said to inhabit.

LeCompte herself still did not believe in skinwalkers, but she had to give credence to the possibility that they did exist, at least in Navajo country, and that whether or not they did exist, knowing that Navajos believed in them was an important part of understanding Navajo culture and acting appropriately within it. It was important to avoid violating Navajo graves by visiting them and consequently disrupting the spirits. LeCompte used that knowledge in assigning Navajo field assistants to work in places where they would not be in danger of violating taboos about the association with death, dead people, and places where dead people might be located.

Cross Reference:
See Example 10.4, Book 1

ETHICS AND EPISTEMOLOGY: DO ETHNOGRAPHERS FACE GREATER ETHICAL CHALLENGES THAN OTHER TYPES OF RESEARCHERS?

Another issue to be addressed is whether or not ethnography as a research design is more ethically problematic than other kinds of research. It is certainly true that qualitative or mixed methods researchers usually have considerably more social contact with the people they study than researchers who only engage in quantitative and experimental studies. As a consequence, they have more opportunities to encounter social situations with ethical valence. These are the types of situations that raise issues of everyday ethics. Qualitative/field researchers also experience increased face-to-face exposure to the personalities and cultures of research participants, exposure that is likely to help them develop greater sensitivity to cultural issues than quantitative researchers have and therefore to enable them to be more attuned to local ethical issues. That said, both qualitative and quantitative researchers must pay attention to, and exercise vigilant concern over, the adherence to ethical standards in their interpersonal interactions.

In past eras, the sole ethical responsibility of researchers was to conduct high-quality research that generated findings that were credible within disciplinary guidelines and to professional peers. Viewed this way, researchers first and foremost owed ethical allegiance to their discipline or to science in general. Such a concern foregrounds the overall methodological rigor with which studies were conducted and the integrity of the researcher. Unethical research, then, was research that was poorly conducted or falsified; it compromised the truth value not only of that particular investigation, but of science in general. In the twentieth century, however, the focus of ethical considerations began to shift. While disciplinary *integrity* and scientific rigor still were the gold standard for good research, adherence to impeccable discipline-based scientific *practice* no longer provided the *principal* guideline for ethical research. Over and above disciplinary rigor, the prevention of physical harm to human research participants began to assume greater and greater importance in response to horrific scientific harms discovered after World War II in Germany and in the United States. Concern for human subjects of research focused initially on medical research and the harm it could do to the living beings upon which experimentation was conducted. (For further information, see the Office of Human Research Protection website archives at http://search.hhs.gov/search ?q=unethical+historical+studies.)

A better way of thinking about the real differences in research type and their designs, however, may be to consider the nature of the data they use. Quantitative research generates "hard" or easily measurable numeric data because it is concerned with directly observable or reportable phenomena: how many of what kinds of units do how many things, or how many units possess what degree of a specific characteristic. Data that are, by contrast, concerned with phenomena that can only be measured indirectly are considered to be "softer." The presence or absence of such phenomena can only be identified by assessing their *impact* on empirically observable phenomena, which requires defining them in such a way that their manifestations can be observed. Observing its manifestations, rather than a phenomenon itself, can lead to accusations that the investigations lack rigor, or raise questions from researchers not familiar with qualitative investigations, such as "Do the indicators chosen to represent a phenomenon actually measure them?" "Does the fact that researchers invent indirect measures for a phenomenon raise questions about researcher subjectivity?" "What if the researcher simply lacks knowledge of how phenomena might be made manifest?" While the hard/soft distinction between types of data is, indeed, an accurate portrayal of data characteristics and whether they are based on direct or indirect

 Key point measurement, *the hard/soft distinction does not constitute a real dichotomy with regard to fundamental differences in research designs. This is because all quantitative*

research begins with qualitative evidence that has been transformed into numeric information or numbers that do not reflect "real" quantities (LeCompte and Schensul, 2010; Schensul, Schensul, and LeCompte, 2013; Schensul and LeCompte, 2013). For example, Likert scales generate data that resemble numbers, but they actually represent *ranges of qualities*, not real quantities. Similarly, math, science, and language test scores look like the most quantitative of data, but they are based upon qualities and degrees of more intangible factors, for which the scores are taken as indicators or proxies in a process of operationalization. They are not "real" measurements of a fixed quantity. So-called quantitative measures still are based upon specific understandings and interpretations held by researchers as to what exists, what is worth studying, and how it might be operationalized and rendered observable. *Ethics, then, consist in taking exquisite care in operationalization, assuring that the meanings attached to measures are understood and considered valid by the people under study, and then adhering to the tenets of formal and informal ethics as discussed throughout this volume—regardless of whether the research is considered to be qualitative or quantitative. In fact, the difference in research approaches is minuscule with regard to ethics.* Further, in quantitative research we often develop "latent" variables that are also not directly measured but are composites of other variables that are. The most important points are that qualitative, quantitative, and mixed methods research needs to be as rigorous, as understandable, and if appropriate, as replicable as possible within the tenets of its own traditions, and that ethical procedures, formal and informal, are followed in planning, in field interactions, and in analysis, interpretation, representation, and dissemination.

 Key point

CONFRONTING THE STEREOTYPE OF SCIENTIFIC NEUTRALITY

Some quite common—and totally antiquated—stereotypes about science and researchers still affect how lay people and even ethnographers think about science and scientists. The conventional stereotype depicts researchers as solitary white males in starched white lab coats, diligently running experiments on small mammals, mixing chemicals in laboratory test tubes, or administering tests to people in clinical settings. Occasionally the stereotype involves a team effort, in which the lone scientists are replaced by a chief of research, who authoritatively administers a hierarchical team of underlings whose status is denoted by their different lab coat colors and often their gender. The researcher's role is simple: find the truth and report it to the awaiting community of scholars. With respect to the people or phenomena under study, a similar simple obligation exists: do not get involved with the subjects and maintain a detached and neutral stance toward results and their consequences. The stereotype also portrays scientists as able to control all—or at least most—of their personal biases about the outcomes of the research and at least most of the variation that exists in human life, the better to get at the single root causes of specific events.

The roots of the conventional stereotype can be found in the philosophy of positivism and the methods of experimental research. Positivism required that a conceptual distance be maintained between the researcher and the outcomes of research, a distance labeled "objectivity." Maintaining objectivity required a disinterested stance by researchers, such that their actions or prior beliefs would not influence the results. Laboratory-based experimental research, with its rigid controls, adapts well to such strictures, but it never has had much applicability in most social science research, and especially ethnographic research, that is based in community or organizational settings and not in controlled laboratories. First of all, ethnographers never wear white lab coats (they get dirty in the field); they are more often dressed in some approximation of what local people wear, adapted for comfort and including comfortable shoes—unless, of course, the field of observation actually is a laboratory whose personnel wear white lab coats! Ethnographers also cannot maintain continuous conceptual, social, and spatial distance from people among whom they live and with whom they interact daily, in all sorts of funny, dire, delightful, and uncomfortable circumstances. Finally, ethnographers have little, if any, control over events in the field. In fact, like naturalistic biologists, they are specifically enjoined to observe naturally occurring events—even in intervention studies—so as to understand what people normally do as a baseline. On the other hand, ethnographers have been perceived as "lone wolf" researchers, working alone with their "informants" in the field. As we have seen throughout the *Ethnographer's Toolkit*, this stereotype also no longer holds. Thus, the conventional stereotypes not only do not characterize, but are inappropriate for, the kind of applied and critical ethnography described in the *Ethnographer's Toolkit*.

LIMITATIONS OF THE CONVENTIONAL STEREOTYPE

- Little, if any, ethnographic research takes place in controlled laboratory settings or other settings in which some measure of technical, procedural, or design control over the course of events to be studied is possible. Some exceptions are ethnographic research and interventions based in schools or clinic/hospital settings where some factors can be controlled or modified systematically. One analogy to laboratory studies involves controlled comparison of case studies, in which "cases" are compared in terms of the presence or absence of specific "variables" (for example, the Whiting and Whiting studies of childhood in six cultures [Whiting and Whiting, 1963], cross-site studies of educational innovation in the 1970s, or Ragin's [2014] sociological qualitative comparative analyses of small samples of countries as cases). However, these cases are naturalistic studies, and no researcher controls were implemented in them.
- The stereotype usually omits discussion of many steps in the research process: planning and design; assembling research teams; gaining access to the field; analyzing, debating about interpretations of, and writing up data; and disseminating results to a broad public.

- It ignores the human relationships that are crucial to the success of any ethnography.
- It minimizes the impact of human characteristics of the researcher, including his or her personal tastes, personality, and training, which are important during problem definition, data collection, and choice of frameworks for interpretation of research results.
- It treats researchers as if it were possible for them to control completely or withhold their opinions or biases.
- It tends to regard human subjects of research and their problems as objects of study, rather than as complex individuals with needs and interests, ideas, and contributions to consider.
- It gives limited consideration to the issue of the researcher's audience above and beyond scientific peers, and when, to whom, and how results of research should be reported.
- The stereotype also does not reflect the gender, ethnic, class, occupational, religious, and educational diversity found in the contemporary scientific community.

Cross Reference:
See Book 1 for a discussion of positivistic tenets

Cross Reference:
Note the discussion of Institutional Review Boards in Books 1, 3, and later in this book

The conventional stereotype has been increasingly discredited, in large part because it now is clear that no scientists, especially ethnographers, can maintain the detachment that it calls for. In fact, it is impossible for *any* researcher to set aside all biases, if only because some of them involve issues of which researchers are unaware or find beyond their control. It may also be *unwise* to attempt to remain entirely neutral, since many of the hunches or ideas that researchers have about what they observe and what they use to begin analysis and interpretation of results do, in fact, come from their own personal interests, values, and preferences, as well as from their theoretical perspectives. Further, the principal tenet of participant observation—an essential data collection strategy used by ethnographers—is that ethnographers come to understand

Cross Reference:
See Book 2 on sources of research questions

the people whom they study *through engagement with them*. People are much more likely to talk freely about their experiences if they feel that the researcher can share in and empathize with the difficulties and joys attendant to those experiences. Empathy, after all, is a critical dimension of participant observation as well as in-depth interviewing, another very important ethnographic method. People being studied are much more likely to feel that the researcher's feelings of empathy are authentic if they know that researchers have had similar experiences themselves, as Example 1.7 below, demonstrates.

Cross Reference: See Book 3 for discussions of participant observation and in-depth interviewing

EXAMPLE 1.7

BUILDING RAPPORT AND UNDERSTANDING BY SHARING EXPERIENCES AND ROLES

Margaret LeCompte found that her past experience as a school administrator helped the school staff for whom she was conducting a study of school reform feel more comfortable confiding in her. She, too, they agreed, had been "in the trenches" as they were. Those confidences greatly facilitated collecting data on the difficulties and agonies of institutional change, even though some disclosures were more cathartic than enlightening, and several made the ethnographer privy to information to which she was not legally entitled. During an informal conversation with the ethnographer, a frustrated school principal suddenly pulled out the records of one teacher who was suspected of sexual abuse and another who had been accused of drug abuse by a group of very religious parents. As confidential records, all these documents were supposed to be excluded from the ethnographer's scrutiny. "I suspect that the first teacher *might be* an abuser. And although it isn't pleasant, I know I'll have to confront him. But the second teacher is just being made the victim of parents who don't agree with her particular philosophy of teaching. She isn't a very good teacher"—here he pulled out the teacher's evaluation record—"but she isn't an addict. The problem is, the parents who don't like her are powerful in this community." The ethnographer was left knowing information that wasn't relevant to her study and wasn't her "right to know," but that the principal needed to talk about. He chose the ethnographer as a trusted neutral confidant.

For many years, anthropologists have argued not only that maintaining positivistic neutrality is impossible to achieve but also that it constitutes poor research practice. Increasingly, critical theorists have joined them. These

researchers hold that it is impossible to develop the rapport necessary for good ethnographic understanding and data collection if social distance is maintained between researchers and informants. A hallmark of anthropology as a discipline always has been its dedication to understanding the perspective of the people living in the communities under study; the search for such "local meanings" is called an **emic approach**. The word *emic* comes from "phonemic," or the meaning of sounds. Emic approaches, which characterize all ethnographic research, seek to understand the meaning of people's lives, as they themselves define them. Accurate recording of local meanings and understandings requires intensive observations and in-depth interviews (see LeCompte and Preissle, 1993; Bernard, 1995; Pelto and Pelto, 1978); specific subfields of the social sciences, including cognitive anthropology and sociological studies of the social construction of reality, are especially committed to the development of methods that assess how people think and believe (Werner and Schoepfle, 1987; Weller and Romney, 1988).

Definition: The term *emic* comes from "phonemic," or the meaning of sounds. Emic approaches seek to understand the meaning of people's lives, as they themselves define them

For ethnographers, working to create such understanding and rapport can produce dilemmas, especially when the ethnographer is trying to understand and develop empathy for practices and beliefs that are foreign to or even antithetical to their own. Anthropologists have long coped with these kinds of conflicts by adhering to a position of *cultural relativism*, which permits them to argue that while the practices and beliefs may not be shared by, or are even valid for, the ethnographer, they can be legitimately studied and understood as shared by and valid for the people under study. Thus, while ethnographers may not be neutral at all regarding how the practices are viewed *outside of the field site*, within the field site, and even in the presentation of the data outside the field site, the ethnographer is constrained by principles that forbid criticizing what the informants do or believe in comparison with what ethnographers have been trained to do or believe. This position is important to basic ethnography, but it is not necessarily held to strictly in application because ethnographers may wish to be involved in or to introduce change strategies with supportive elements in a community that are not endorsed by everyone, that counter positions that ethnographers and some community members do not agree with, and thus at times may be unpopular.

The stance of neutrality often has been interpreted as mandating that researchers must never intervene in or try to change the lives of the people they study. However, many applied ethnographers are able to apply their research theories and methods specifically because study populations desire change and feel that research results can help bring this about. Applied ethnographers often enter a field setting with specific change strategies in mind, and they identify partners interested in working on those strategies. Introducing change can help to reveal cultural and structural nuances that were not otherwise apparent, thus improving the research. Further, most public health researchers, critical theorists, and some feminists argue that unless the research helps the people under study more fully understand the conditions in which they live and even, perhaps, improve them, it has no validity (Brydon-Miller et al., 2003; Frisby et al., 2009; Lather, 1986; Minkler and Wallerstein, 2010; Israel et al., 2013; Langhout, 2011; Laska and Peterson, 2011). Similarly, all feminists argue that the particular life experiences of women and the way these experiences differ from those of males are sufficient to mandate an approach to research that is cognizant both of the "standpoint" (Harding, 2004; Hartsock, 1983; Nielson 1990) of the researcher and of the impact that the research will have on the persons studied. Critical theorists argue that one's standpoint derives from one's relative position of economic and social privilege within the social structure of a society; it is affected also by the relative advantage one enjoys by virtue of one's particular race, gender, regional origins, religious affiliation, gender orientation, or a wide range of other factors that are used to discriminate among groups in a society. Feminists and transformational action researchers alike (see Schensul and Schensul, 1978; Schensul et al., 2014) argue that standpoints affect both the kinds of questions researchers find interesting and the interpretations they apply to data once they are collected. They mandate a careful analysis of one's standpoint and the blind spots or

Cross Reference:
See Book 7, chapters 1 and 2

Cross Reference:
See Book 1 for a more extensive discussion of critical and postmodern theories

Cross Reference: See Book 1, chapter 3, for a discussion of research paradigms

Cross Reference: See Book 2 on the importance of self-identification in entering the field

biases that it creates not only before research begins but also throughout one's career as an investigator. Specific value orientations underpin the theoretical paradigms we have outlined in Book 1; researchers generally will select a paradigm that matches both the field situation and the ethnographer's own values. Finally, feminist and critical researchers argue that it is dishonest and unethical not to make clear to research participants what one's background and ideological commitments are (Roman, 1992, 1993). Thus, contemporary applied ethnography tends to advocate an "in the trenches" and transformational stance regarding interaction with research participants.

FORMAL RESEARCH ETHICS AND EVERYDAY RESEARCH ETHICS

In this book, we distinguish between procedural or formal ethics and everyday, ordinary, or informal ethics (Lambek, 2010). We also confront the rather ethnocentric stance of many current guidelines whose unit of ethical focus remains the single individual unfettered by community norms or the community itself. The current research climate demands a change in approach to considering ethical issues generated in the study of both individuals *and* entire groups and communities. We also provide practical suggestions for addressing these issues and case examples illustrating how ethnographers have handled them.

Formal Ethics

Formal ethical research issues are those that address institutional rules governing the care of human subjects and the procedures that researchers are required to follow to assure the respectful, beneficent, socially just, and non-oppressive treatment of living subjects of research —especially human beings. Governmental monitoring has arisen in response to the past cruel, unnecessary, and often egregious mistreatment of experimental subjects, especially in medical research. The development and institutionalization of these monitoring processes is described in chapter 2.

The focus of formal ethics primarily has been on *how* research is done, *by whom, for what reasons,* and *what happens* to individuals as a consequence of their being studied in a research project. The focus is on the protection of the individual from harms perpetrated by the research, either directly or indirectly. Formal ethical principles also govern legal contractual research relationships, what happens to data after they are collected, how they are interpreted, and how those interpretations are used (LeCompte, 2015).

Formal ethical considerations also govern protection of research staff from harm in field settings. The need to protect research staff and to build such protections into ethical procedures formalized for a specific study has arisen as ethnographers have become involved in field research on HIV risk behavior, ethnographic research in war zones, and other situations in which both the researchers and the study participants may be at risk, or may put each other at risk.

Finally, because so much of ethnographic research concerns vulnerable populations, formal ethical considerations require attention to the management of emotional crises, exposure to abuses, mention of interpersonal violence, suicide threats, depression, or other pleas for help. Now most researchers are required to identify how such instances will be addressed and to specify the referral networks and services available to study participants in advance of the study.

Informal Ethics

Informal ethics govern daily interactions with people in the field (Lambek, 2010). Researchers who have little need to interact with their study participants confront fewer informal ethical dilemmas than do qualitative researchers and ethnographers, as we have pointed out above. The nature of ethnographic research mandates an ongoing presence in a field site and relying on relationships forged with people in the field site. Presence requires ethnographers to understand cultural norms and values and appropriate interactive behaviors with the population in general. This means learning the rules of politeness and intimacy, correct linguistic expressions, and ways of pro-

Definition:
People who have deep knowledge of their own culture and the unique ability to stand somewhat outside it so as to explain it to others

Cross Reference:
See Book 3 on identifying key informants and key informant interviewing

Key point

viding social and emotional support. Meeting and establishing relationships are especially important with special individuals called **key informants or community experts**. Key informants/community experts are so important to fieldwork that Oswald Werner and Mark Schoepfle have referred to them as cultural "consultants" (Werner and Schoepfle, 1987); many books have been written describing the invaluable contribution that such people have made to investigations (Burgess, 1985; Liebow, 2003; Whyte, 1991, 2012; Aronson et al., 2007). Such relationships extend beyond the research endeavor; they can and often do evolve into friendships and colleague-ships in which ideas are exchanged, social interactions enjoyed, and life experiences shared. Key informants/community experts also can become partners in the data collection and interpretation process. *However, the deep and personal relationships that ethnographic researchers establish with their informants can lead to many of the ethical dilemmas that arise in the course of ethnographic field research.*

Ethnographers have described the occasionally fraught moments that they experienced with their key informants, especially when researchers have failed to understand cultural norms, political dynamics, or interpersonal peculiarities, and informants have had to set them straight.

EXAMPLE 1.8

POLICE RAID IN A HIGH-RISK SITE

An Institute for Community Research (ICR) study headed by anthropologist Margaret Weeks investigated how drug users who injected drugs placed themselves and others at risk of exposure to HIV in different physical locations. The purpose of the study was to explore whether some sites created environments that placed drug users at higher risk than others. Researchers with experience in the collection of such data met active drug users who were willing to act as key informants, taking them around to the sites that they used and introducing them to other drug users. After this preliminary phase, the researchers began to interview networks of drug users at different sites and to ask them to test for HIV infection. The results of the HIV testing were not de-identified to the research team, and researchers knew which participants were infected in accordance with prior IRB approval.

While accompanied by a key informant-guide, one of the researchers observed a known-to-be-infected drug user passing his used syringe to another who was not infected. The researcher's first inclination was to intervene. However, the guide interfered and refused to allow the researcher to do so, noting that interfering with the moment of exchange was always dangerous since it could produce a violent response. The researcher also recognized that taking this step could violate confidentiality, an ethical mandate, and could endanger the study by revealing that the researcher had privileged and confidential knowledge about an individual. Though in considerable conflict about failing to prevent an action that might cause HIV infection, the researcher followed the instructions of the key informant.

Key informants also can be caught between conflicting demands of their life in their communities and their responsibilities to and deep feelings for the researchers' work. Thus, relationships with key informants and people in the field, while critical to the research process, also may lead to contradictions between the needs and requests of key informants and ethical principles and demands of the research endeavor.

   **EXAMPLE 1.9**

WHAT TO DO WHEN A KEY INFORMANT FOR ILLEGAL ACTIVITIES IS ARRESTED

In a study of lifestyle and substance use among young adults, a member of an ICR research team befriended a young man in the study community about her age who had had years of experience in selling drugs. He had organized a trusted citywide network of lower-level distributors across the city and an efficiently functioning infrastructure for the distribution and sale of marijuana and for regular return of the money. He recounted to the researcher details of how he had created the infrastructure and managed to remain connected to drug supplies and his "staff" while still remaining in a regular job and making a full salary. The study was ensured by a Federal Certificate of Confidentiality that protected participants engaged in illegal activity from subpoena by the police. However, one day, he was arrested on a minor offense. He approached the researcher for assistance in obtaining bail. She discussed the question of whether or not she and the study team should help him. After reflection on his situation, the potential liability of the study investigator and grantee institution, and her own responsibility to him as a key informant and a friend, she made a decision independent of the study to help him to raise the money for bail. He was eventually released with the requirement that he provide some number of days of community service. Since IRB reviews of studies that place vulnerable populations at risk (pregnant women, children, people with

mental health problems, and prisoners) require representatives of the study population, he did his community service, as a representative for an IRB, reviewing
protections in place for people like himself in studies that placed young substance
users and sellers at risk. This solution enabled him to continue to act as a key
informant while providing guidance to other researchers.

All of these factors produce ethical concerns in everyday
life. In addition, researchers are held to formal requirements regarding the ethical conduct of research and treatment of the people being studied; these are enforced by
contractual relationships and governmental agencies.

One area affecting both everyday and formal ethics involves confidentiality. Researchers are required
to respect the privacy of the people they study, holding
what is said and observed in confidence and not identifying specifically from whom or how information has been
obtained. Some kinds of research make this very easy; the
data are collected, for example, by anonymous or de-identified surveys, and analysis is conducted on the collective
body of data. However, as attentive listeners and skillful
interlocutors who spend long periods of time in the field
and have many opportunities to interact informally with
participants, ethnographers often are told many things
that people ordinarily would not disclose. Similarly, disclosures and personal information emerge in in-depth
interviews. Thus, ethnographers can become privy to
much personal, private, and often very sensitive information. In these situations researchers must be very careful
not to reveal such information about others, even to their
friends in the study community who might know the
person and misuse the information in some unpredictable way. Even and perhaps especially among researchers
and their key informant friends, it is necessary to maintain secrecy with respect to such information. Nevertheless, ethnographers have a story to tell. How much of the
information they collect should remain confidential and
not just "de-identified," and in what ways?

Compensation of informants is another thorny ethical
issue. What kind of reciprocity is both appropriate as com-

pensation for research participants and still not unethical? Though it is considered unethical to pay research participants for *information* on the grounds that doing so could lead to coercive pressure to reveal information that individuals really do not want to, or should not, reveal, it is not unethical to pay participants for the *time* that they have spent, especially for long, in-depth interviews, translations, and other services rendered while working with researchers. If paying people for information is inappropriate, what other forms of reciprocity *are* appropriate? At what point does reciprocity—exchange of money, goods, and services for access to information—become a fee for service or potential bribery or coercion? Is it even ethical to use information that has been in some way bought? Are data obtained through purchase or bribery less likely to be accurate or to be interpreted accurately?

As we have indicated above, yet another—and quite current—ethical issue has to do with changes in perceptions regarding who has the right to tell the story of, portray, or otherwise to "represent" a given people's culture, lifestyle, and concerns. When friends tell stories about one another, contradictions can be confronted by others in the neighborhood, and gossip can be counteracted. However, in the past, the books and articles in which ethnographers' views and descriptions were contained were rarely accessed or challenged either by colleagues or key informants. Only occasionally did two ethnographers separately enter the same field to investigate the same phenomenon. When they did, it was usually at two different time points, which made it impossible to disaggregate the effects of time and history from the separate interpretations of the ethnographers themselves (Critchfield, 1978; Redfield, 1956; Lewis, 1966; Mead, 1928; Freeman, 1983; Shankman, 2009). Furthermore, most of the people in the communities described by ethnographers were not literate, and key informants seldom could read materials written about them. Thus, they were not in a position to discuss, debate, or contradict the research findings (cf. Clifford and Marcus, 1986).

Other, more local, checks on researcher violations of ethics now exist. The individuals and communities ethnographers study are increasingly literate, well connected, and

Cross Reference: The issue of representation is discussed in detail in Book 1, chapter 3, and Book 7, chapter 1

educated. Community leaders, educational administrators, and target populations—all participants in research ventures—also are increasingly politicized (Brosted et al., 1985; Whyte, 1991; Greaves, 1994; Manderson et al., 1998; Schensul et al., 1999; Schensul, 2002). They have learned that they have the right to question research results, and that research, if conducted properly, can work to their advantage. They also have something to say about how best to carry out aspects of the research since they know their constituents better than the researchers do. The Internet offers communities from one end of the globe to the other the power of instant communication and access to information never before available. It is not surprising then, that while ethnographers seek research partners, they also turn to their research partners to validate and verify, and even to help them represent research results. There is a growing body of literature that cuts across disciplines and suggests approaches ranging from co-construction of ethnographies to participatory representation through performance ethnography for addressing ethical considerations in representation (Denzin and Lincoln, 2011; Henry-Waring, 2004; Mahon, 2000; Voithofer, 2005).

Thus, the past practice of framing ethical concerns as one-way interactions, *from* the researcher *to* those being studied, has become obsolete, even though the perspective it reflects still dominates research methods texts and the practices of regulatory agencies and does not fully reflect the dynamics of current community-based research or research that is approved and monitored by groups from the participant communities themselves.

SUMMARY

In this chapter, we introduced the notion of formal and informal ethics in research, and as well, we discussed some new and ongoing challenges to the ethical nature of what ethnographers do. In the next two chapters, we discuss the evolution and implementation of formal ethical requirements. We then describe how the personal characteristics and institutional affiliations of the researcher have an impact on the kinds of interactions and ethical issues researchers face in the field and present a more detailed discussion of informal or everyday ethics. The final chapters include a presentation of special concerns attendant to team and collaborative research, a discussion of ethical concerns that have arisen as ethnographers more and more frequently need to be cognizant of and guided by the ethical concerns of groups they hope to study, especially those from non-Western communities, and a chapter on the role of reflection as both a guide to interpretation and a check on ethical ethnographer behavior.

2 ━●━●━●━

The Origins of
Formal Oversight

Medical Research
and Risk to
Human Subjects

Social Science
Research
and Risks to
Human Subjects

Disciplinary
Codes of Ethics
and the Problem
of Enforcement

The Belmont
Report 1978

The Belmont
Principles

Summary

THE EVOLUTION OF FORMAL CONCERNS ABOUT AND ETHICAL PRINCIPLES GOVERNING HUMAN RESEARCH

THE ORIGINS OF FORMAL OVERSIGHT

In the previous chapter, we outlined the types of formal and informal ethics that influence the conduct of ethnographic research. In this chapter, we address the evolution of formal ethical oversight for human research. Here we discuss why formal oversight over human research is needed, and show how the principles governing ethical treatment developed, along with agencies to enforce those principles. We also look at how the definitions of risk have been expanded beyond those of medical research to address how reputational harm can come from research designed to describe a group's behavior, rather than intervene in it. Finally, the principles that inform formal ethical monitoring of research by governmental bodies are discussed in detail.

MEDICAL RESEARCH AND RISK TO HUMAN SUBJECTS

When people think of the mistreatment of human subjects of research, their most frequent referent usually is to Nazi doctors' treatment of concentration camp prisoners during World War II. And indeed, for many years, concerns over ethics mainly focused on experimental medical research because some of the most horrific examples of unethical behavior have derived from medical and biological investigations. From 1941–1945, Nazi doctors conducted so-called medical experiments on prisoners, for which research subjects not only did not give their consent but also were unwitting or unwilling subjects of horrific experimentation. The numerous experiments included sterilization; exposure to typhus, malaria, and other diseases; exposure to high altitude, low pressure, and freezing; transplantation of bone, tissues, and organs; and burns by phosphorus. Most were performed in barbaric conditions, without anesthesia or appropriate sanitation. For the most part, these experiments added nothing to scientific knowledge and can only be attributed to exercises in sadism (Annas and Grodin, 1992; Baumslag, 2005). The Nuremburg War Crimes Tribunal, convened to document and try perpetrators of crimes against humanity inflicted by the Nazi regime, found the behavior of many Nazi concentration camp doctors to be particularly heinous. The outrage stimulated by their behavior led in 1947 to the creation of the Nuremberg Code, which was among the first documents to codify the ethical conditions for the conduct of research involving human subjects. It emphasized the absolute requirement that participants render voluntary consent prior to participating in research projects. Promulgated by the United Nations in 1964, the Declaration of Helsinki (DoH) (World Medical Association, 2015) went further, making the rules for conduct of medical research more and more stringent. The DoH not only provided ethical guidelines for physicians engaged in research but also required that there be an independent review of research protocols to assure that the research proposals followed ethical guidelines established by both of these documents, and to ensure consent by legal guardians in the case of minor children or the mentally incompetent. The International Ethical Guidelines for Biomedical Research Involving Human Subjects reinforced these standards.

However, the Nazis were not the only perpetrators of abuse upon human research subjects. As we describe in the pages to follow, much harmful research has occurred, and indeed is still being carried out, and much of it has been conducted by researchers in and from the United States. Our summary here includes only some of the more egregious cases.

EXAMPLE 2.1

THE YELLOW FEVER STUDIES OF WALTER REED, 1905

The yellow fever studies of Dr. Walter Reed in 1905 stand as a benchmark in the growth of concern for the human rights of research participants. Dr. Reed developed an experimental vaccine that he thought might prevent yellow fever, which decimated American soldiers working in tropical zones. Rather than simply impose vaccination upon the American troops under his command in Panama, Dr. Reed asked for volunteers who were willing to be injected with the new and untried vaccine. As an incentive to undergo vaccination, he told the soldiers that it probably was inevitable that they would contract the disease if they were not vaccinated, given the environment in Panama. He paid them $100 if they survived the initial vaccination and $200 if they contracted the disease despite the vaccination—a substantial incentive, and one that would be hard to turn down given soldiers' wages at the time (Pierce and Writer, 2005).

Reed's procedures were among the first to use written consent "contracts" to augment verbal consent and represented one of the first efforts to obtain consent from healthy human subjects in risky medical research. However, Reed and his associates did not fully disclose everything the soldiers might experience, and he minimized the consequences of contracting yellow fever from the vaccine—that is, the possibility of death.

EXAMPLE 2.2

THE TUSKEGEE SYPHILIS STUDY, 1932–1972

Perhaps the most famous and controversial of all studies in the United States was the Tuskegee Study of Untreated Syphilis, carried out by the US Public Health Service in collaboration with Tuskegee Institute. It was designed to observe the course of untreated syphilis to the point of death, primarily in poor, uneducated, African American men in the rural South. One purpose of the study was to answer some questions about the treatment of late and latent syphilis, which had been inadequately studied, as well as other puzzling findings: while some, though it was insufficient treatment, in the early stages of the disease could render an infected person noninfectious, it was unclear what the proper treatment of late latent syphilis was for people who had been infected for more than four years and were more than fifty years of age. Neither the standard syphilis treatment with heavy metals nor newly available penicillin seemed to result in improvements in persons with the late latent disease; these individuals most often were asymptomatic, though their blood tests showed infection. In fact, for men over the age of fifty, the standard of care was not to treat asymptomatic but infected individuals because the treatment was ineffective and often brought health risks of its own, including allergic reactions to penicillin. Morbidity and mortality statistics also showed that in many cases, people who had been treated died before those who went untreated—though the reasons for these findings also were unclear. Furthermore, those who were in the late latent stages of the disease were not very much handicapped by it. It was not until negative cardiac and other effects began to appear that the late-stage disease became problematic.

The Public Health Service, working with the Tuskegee Institute, began the study in 1932. Investigators enrolled in the study a total of six hundred impoverished, African American sharecroppers from Macon County, Alabama, 399 of whom had previously contracted syphilis before the study began and 201 without the disease. Macon County was chosen primarily because it had one of the highest rates of syphilis infection in the country; further, an association between poverty and prevalence of syphilis had been discovered, and Macon County was one of the poorest counties in the South. For their participation in the study, the men were given free medical care, meals, and free burial insurance—if they agreed to an autopsy. Some may have received heavy metal treatments (arsenicals and bismuth), the standard treatment for syphilis at the time, but few received a dose sufficient to cure the disease. The treatment that they did receive, though inadequate to cure syphilis, was sufficient to render the men noninfectious. Since one goal of public health studies at the time was to reduce the spread of syphilis, this was a salutary effect.

Critics of the TSUS argue that the men in the study were never told they had syphilis; according to the Centers for Disease Control, the men were told they were being treated for "bad blood," a local term used to describe several illnesses, including syphilis, anemia, and fatigue. Nor were they ever treated for it, even after the US Public Health Service began using penicillin in 1943. By 1947, penicillin had become the standard treatment for early-stage syphilis, and even inadequate doses of the standard treatment of penicillin rendered sufferers noninfectious. Some subjects did seem to have gotten penicillin treatment on their own from medical sources other than the CDC and for diseases other than syphilis, but such treatment was not part of the TSUS, and it is not clear that it was taken in time or in sufficient quantities to achieve a cure for their syphilis.

Given all the uncertainties about late latent syphilis, Tuskegee scientists continued the study for decades, withholding penicillin, not adequately treating the participants, and failing to give information about penicillin to the patients. The study continued under numerous US Public Health Service supervisors until 1972, when a leak to the press and subsequent accusations that the study was racially motivated eventually resulted in its termination (see Jones, 1993). The victims of the study included numerous men who died of syphilis, forty wives who contracted the disease, and children born with congenital syphilis.

The forty-year study was ethically controversial because researchers knowingly failed to treat patients with penicillin even though the drug was validated in the 1940s to be an effective cure for early-stage syphilis. The men in the TSUS, however, were in later stages of the disease, in which the effects of penicillin were unclear. In addition, given the low relative status position of the men vis-à-vis the researchers and their lack of education, race, and poverty, the men were clearly vulnerable subjects who could not understand the consequences of participating in the study and perhaps could not have objected to it. In addition, since the men were not informed of what would happen to them, they could not have truly consented to participate.

A big problem was that much of the study was not needed; the progression of the early stages of syphilis had been well documented retrospectively—though among white men—for years and thus added no new information about that period of infection. However, the disclosures by a whistleblower of the study's malfeasance led to major changes in US law and regulation on the protection of participants in clinical studies. Now studies require informed consent (with exceptions possibly for US federal agencies that can be kept secret by Executive Order), communication of diagnosis, and accurate reporting of test results. Descendants of the Tuskegee participants ultimately sued the US government for damages, and the suit was settled out of court for $10 million. President Clinton issued a formal apology for the research in 1997 (see Clinton, 1997). Investigations into syphilis did not end with the Tuskegee study, however; more recent and quite unethical studies followed.

EXAMPLE 2.3

SYPHILIS EXPERIMENTS IN GUATEMALA

In October 2010 it was revealed that US Public Health Service doctors in Guatemala went much further than they had in Tuskegee, Alabama. The TSUS had recruited only those individuals who already tested positive for syphilis and then matched them with noninfected controls. However, investigators reported that American doctors deliberately infected prisoners, soldiers, and patients in a Guatemalan mental hospital with syphilis and, in some cases, gonorrhea, from 1946 to 1948, with the cooperation of some Guatemalan health ministries and officials. The subjects of the study had sex with infected prostitutes or had abrasions on their bodies rubbed with infectious materials. As an official report of the US Centers for Disease Control states:

> According to materials in the archives, the primary purpose of the studies was to develop human models of transmission of *Treponema pallidum*, the bacteria that causes syphilis, by sexual transmission and cutaneous and mucous membrane inoculation in order to assess effectiveness of potential chemoprophylactic regimens. Additional studies were conducted to assess potential for re-infection of persons with untreated latent syphilis or of those with recent treatment of syphilis with penicillin; to compare performance of various serologic tests for syphilis; and to develop human models of transmission and chemoprophylaxis of the agents of gonorrhea (*Neisseria gonorrhoeae*) and chancroid (*Hemophilus ducreyi*).
>
> Subjects for the transmission studies included female commercial sex workers (CSWs), prisoners in the national penitentiary, patients in the national mental hospital, and soldiers. These subjects were also involved in comparative serologic studies. Transmission studies initially included sexual exposure of prisoners to female CSWs experimentally infected with either syphilis or gonorrhea. Later, subjects underwent direct inoculation, primarily of skin and mucous membranes, by viable *T. pallidum, N. gonorrhoeae, and H. ducreyi.* The design and conduct of the studies was unethical in many respects, including deliberate exposure of subjects to known serious health threats, lack of knowledge of and consent for experimental procedures by study subjects, and the use of highly vulnerable populations. (http://www.hhs.gov/1946inoculationstudy/findings.html)

A total of 696 men and women were exposed to syphilis without their knowledge or consent and more than eight hundred to the other bacteria for chancroid and gonorrhea. When the subjects contracted the disease they were given antibiotics, though it is unclear if all infected parties were cured. In October 2010, the United States formally apologized to Guatemala for conducting these experiments.

Syphilis was not the only condition in which researchers were interested and for which research vulnerable persons were recruited and sometimes coerced into participation.

 **EXAMPLE 2.4**

THE WILLOWBROOK HEPATITIS STUDY: 1963–1966

Willowbrook was an asylum for mentally ill children. At the time, hepatitis was epidemic in such institutions and researchers wanted to study the natural course of the disease. Arguing that most of the children would have acquired the infection anyway, investigators planned to infect Willowbrook's young patients with benign hepatitis. They did ask parents to consent to their children's participation, but they also told parents that failure to consent might mean that their children would no longer be welcome at Willowbrook.

Studies such as Willowbrook increased concern over the use of people who could not legally or educationally give consent because they were incapable of understanding the research and its possible consequences. They also highlighted the coercive impact of threatening to deny people services or treatment they needed if they did not consent to research procedures. Pregnant women, for example, were fed meals laced with radioactive iron to measure both the uptake of such nutrients in their own bodies and the developing fetuses and its long-term effects; the women were from low-income communities and could not otherwise afford vitamins, but at the same time, they also were not told of the dangers of radioactive elements in their diet to themselves and their babies (Hagstrom et al., 1969). Still other studies were conducted in clandestine ways, in other countries, involving many universities and researchers, some of them with collaboration of the US military and governmental intelligence agencies.

 **EXAMPLE 2.5**

"OUTSOURCING" RESEARCH TO INVESTIGATE HOW TO BRAINWASH INDIVIDUALS SO AS TO IMPROVE MILITARY INTERROGATION TECHNIQUES

In the years following the Korean War, researchers became interested in why captured American soldiers broke down and denounced the ideas of capitalism and imperialism and confessed to crimes they might not have committed. At a conference in Montreal, Canada, in the early 1950s, US and Canadian psychologists and psychiatrists discussed what they called "brainwashing"; by that they meant that the experiences the captives had had in prison must have made them so vulnerable as to replace deeply held ideas and commitments, even if only temporarily. Some of the conference attendees included officials from the US military and the Central Intelligence Agency (CIA) of the United States. One person present was a highly esteemed Scottish-born American psychiatrist, Ewen Cameron, from McGill University in Canada, who was very interested in the idea of brainwashing as a therapeutic strategy for all manner of mental illnesses. He felt that if the contents of the "diseased" brain could be erased, faulty minds could be remade and replaced with healthy ones. He was convinced that "the violent destruction of his patients' minds was the necessary first step on their journey to mental health, and therefore not a violation of the Hippocratic Oath" (Klein, 2007, 42). Beginning in the early 1950s, his work included using multiple courses of electroshock to erase the memories of mentally ill people and long periods of total isolation, extreme sensory deprivation, drug treatments, sleep deprivation, induced narcosis, and even insulin overdoses to destroy patients' original personalities and knowledge bases preparatory to intensive and repetitive reprogramming to rebuild both. Cameron had a readily available supply of potential subjects in the patients who came to his clinic for treatment. Because he was their doctor, patients readily signed standard consent forms giving Cameron absolute power to treat them, up to and including frontal lobotomies. Although they often had only minor problems—postpartum depression, episodic depression, or marital problems—Cameron's patients were treated for years in his clinic as though they had major derangements and were subjected to the full brunt of his attempts to erase brains so as to rebuild them anew. None were ever told of the overall impact of the studies or the doctor's ultimate goals, and many were rendered by the treatments unable even to engage in acts of daily living, like feeding themselves, toileting, and sleeping normally. Some experienced lifelong disruption and dysfunctionality. Nonetheless, Cameron published prolifically on his research and its importance.

Ostensibly sought out as a way to inoculate Western soldiers against the coercive treatment they might experience if they were taken hostage, Cameron's results were seen by the Central Intelligence Agency operatives at the conference instead as a way to develop "special interrogation techniques"—much more effective means of interrogating potential spies, captured soldiers, and terrorism suspects. The CIA funded his research and treatment practices for over a decade. Subsequently, the CIA published handbooks on interrogation and torture techniques based on Cameron's experiments that have formed the basis for "enhanced" interrogation strategies to the present day (CIA, 1963, 1983, cited in Klein, 2007). It is clear that the CIA sought out Dr. Cameron because of his research in Canada, research that the CIA could not conduct in the United States because his "treatments" actually constituted torture and clearly violated all manner of medical ethics. The story of Cameron's work is one among many following the revelations of Nazi medical war crimes that registered concerns in the United States about researchers failing to obtain consent from research subjects, failing to inform subjects that they were part of experimental research studies, and further harming persons who already were suffering from mental upsets. Cameron died before a group of his former patients finally discovered what had been done to them and sued McGill University, the Canadian government, and the CIA, all of which had funded Cameron's research. The CIA and the Canadian government eventually agreed to settlements which were paid to them in 1988 and 1992, respectively (Klein, 2007).

Still other studies involved exposure of young children to hazards, about which they and their parents were not fully informed.

   **EXAMPLE 2.6**

STUDY OF LEAD ABATEMENT IN BALTIMORE

In the 1990s, researchers from the Kennedy Krieger Institute in Baltimore conducted an environmental study that sought to determine if different levels of abatement of lead paint in older houses in Baltimore would affect the blood lead levels of young children living in those houses. The Institute, well respected for its work with children with disabilities, paid for abatement programs at two levels, both above local and state standards, but neither congruent with "full abatement." Families already living in the area—and hence in houses contaminated with lead—were encouraged to move into, and continue to live in the experimental houses, which at the time were perceived to be improvements in their living conditions, so that continued monitoring of the lead levels in their children could take place. The Johns Hopkins IRB approved the study, saying that the lead exposure posed "no risk" to children since they already were living in houses that were contaminated. But the study was ultimately ruled unethical because the parents were not informed about the risks of any lead exposure at all, or alternative means for reducing exposure, nor were the blood and environmental tests being administered used to reduce the health damage caused to children from lead exposure (Spriggs, 2004).

In fact, this study was further deemed unethical not only because it took advantage of low-income families who had few opportunities to live in safer houses, but because the primary beneficiaries were seen not to be the children and families who participated but the landlords who were able to improve their profits by determining the cheapest form of lead abatement they could get away with (Spriggs, 2004).

Medical Research and Formal Requirements

As formal ethical requirements in the United States increasingly mandated that researchers fully disclose to potential research subjects what participation in their studies might entail and the risks that participants might experience, some researchers tried to escape from monitoring in the United States by implementing their studies in countries whose populations were less sophisticated and literate. Especially among very poor communities, any services or compensation that researchers could offer were significant enticements that could override participant concerns about their safety. We already have described two such "runaway" studies conducted in Examples 2.3 and 2.6. A third and more recent study was conducted in Africa when the researchers' Institutional Review Board denied them approval to conduct the study in the United States.

EXAMPLE 2.7

CONDUCTING RISKY STUDIES IN POOR COUNTRIES WHEN CONDUCTING THEM IN THE UNITED STATES IS IMPOSSIBLE

Medical researchers proposed to study the impact of various treatments for HIV infection on pregnant women and their babies. By that time, the drug AZT was known to be effective in slowing the progression of HIV infection to full-blown AIDS disease, but the researchers wondered what the effect of AZT treatment would be on developing fetuses, and whether it would provide any protection from HIV infection. First, they planned to conduct pregnancy testing and HIV testing simultaneously among groups of women of child-bearing age. Women who proved to be both HIV positive and pregnant were to be recruited for the study. All of the women would get prenatal education classes, lunches during their classes, and supportive care not related to their pregnancy. They also were divided into three groups. One would get a short dose of AZT upon recruitment. A second would get ongoing AZT treatment throughout their pregnancy, and a control group would get no AZT at all. Several factors meant that the researchers could not carry out their project as

planned in the United States. First, the fact that women got both pieces of information at the same time—not only that they were pregnant, but also that they were infected with a fatal disease that could be transmitted to their babies—was considered to constitute a serious emotional risk to the participants. Second, the fact that the women were poor and uneducated meant that they were not likely to be able to understand fully all the ramifications of the study, and therefore, might be incapable of freely consenting to participation. Third, the researchers wanted to have a true control group, one that provided no real anti-HIV treatment at all. Such a control group that would deprive women of a known and effective treatment simply to create the opportunity for comparison is a violation of research ethics under any circumstances in the United States and is no excuse for denying potential participants access to the real purposes and risks of the study. The researchers were denied approval for their study in the United States, and they decided to carry out the study in Africa. At that time, US researchers were not bound by rules that required they abide by the same IRB guidelines overseas as in the United States. In the United States, the standard of care required treatment with AZT. However, in Africa, a non-treatment control group design was deemed to be ethical since local resources were not sufficiently available to treat all pregnant women who were infected, and thus lack of treatment *was* the standard of care. Though African women in the treatment group did get AZT for the duration of the study, it was not possible to sustain Western standards of care once the study had been completed—at least with study resources. This created a problem for local populations who anticipated benefiting from continued availability of AZT; they may not have understood that it would not be available after the study was over (Levine, 1998; Lurie and Wolfe, 1997).

Situations such as those described above have led to changes in the US federal regulations. Now any research carried out by investigators from US universities and institutions must follow the same guidelines and principles for protecting human subjects, though not necessarily the same procedures, that obtain in the United States, regardless of where the research site is located.

SOCIAL SCIENCE RESEARCH AND RISKS TO HUMAN SUBJECTS

Unlike medical research, investigations by social and behavioral scientists were not seen initially as involving life or death risks, or even as having the potential for causing physical or psychological harm. However, a number of key research projects helped to establish the principle that non-medical research also could involve risks and cause lasting harm to participants. Experiments by social psychologists Stanley Milgram and Philip Zimbardo revealed that serious risks to humans can be both emotional and psychological. Designed to explore why the German people colluded, consciously or not, with the Nazi regime in their plan to exterminate Jews, Romanies, homosexuals, and other people the Nazis deemed undesirable, these experiments explored how and why people in authority could induce ordinary citizens to inflict terrible punishment on other human beings. In each case, a mock experiment was set up and volunteers were recruited to participate, but they were not told what the real experiment entailed.

EXAMPLE 2.8

OBEDIENCE TO AUTHORITY EXPERIMENTS, STANLEY MILGRAM, 1962

The experiments took place in a laboratory-like office, presided over by a white-coated "scientist" who actually was a confederate of Milgram's. The volunteers were seated at a desk before a screen and told that behind the screen was an individual to whom they were to ask questions. If the answers were incorrect, they were to push a button that ostensibly administered an electric shock for punishment. What the volunteers did not know was that the "subject" was a member of the research team and that the shocks were not real. The real subjects of the study were the volunteers, and the research question involved how great an impact an authority figure could have in making people violate their principles. The volunteers were urged by the "scientist"/authority figure to continue administering shocks as instructed, despite the screams and objections of the person allegedly being interrogated and a meter that purported to show increasing levels of pain. Some of the volunteers actually administered what they thought was a lethal shock, saying that they did so because the "scientist" told them to do it (Milgram, 1963; Haney et al., 1973).

Milgram and his associates deceived the volunteer subjects about the objectives of the study, filmed them without their consent, and did not allow them to withdraw from the study, even though some begged to be allowed to leave. These experiments had a profound impact on some of the volunteers, who, even though they were afterward told that the experiment was a hoax and were allowed to meet the unharmed assistant, were horrified that they could be so influenced by somebody in a position of power as to commit murder. Some suffered lasting psychological damage (Milgram, 1963). Zimbardo's experiments tested a similar hypothesis: that people could be induced to behave in horrific ways if the context supported such behavior.

 **EXAMPLE 2.9**

THE STANFORD PRISON EXPERIMENT, PHILIP ZIMBARDO, 1971

These experiments took place in a simulated prison environment. Zimbardo acted as "superintendent of the prison." Volunteer subjects were assigned to be guards or prisoners. "Guards" were placed under no limitations as to how they treated "prisoners," except that physical violence was prohibited. Prisoners had to do what the guards ordered. The "guards" humiliated prisoners, denied them restroom "privileges," forced them to do manual labor, and subjected them to solitary confinement. The only escape for prisoners was punitive; they were offered "parole" by the guards in exchange for forfeiting the compensation they were to receive for participating in the experiment. None of the mock prisoners accepted the offer. The prisoners exhibited considerable distress; one even went on a hunger strike to be freed from participating. The experiment was stopped only after an outside observer questioned the ethics of the experiment (Hagstrom et al., 1969; Haney et al., 1973; Rothman, 1982; Krugman and Ward, 1961).

Like the Milgram experiments, Zimbardo's volunteers were put in positions of power over helpless individuals, and then encouraged to inflict disagreeable treatment on them. The psychological damage to the individuals who simulated guards was similar to that of the Milgram experiments: shame and guilt at the degree to which a "game" could induce inhuman behavior. Both sets of studies raised concern over issues of consent, voluntary participation, deceit, and failure to ameliorate the adverse impact of participation in research studies.

EXAMPLE 2.10

THE TEAROOM TRADE

Laud Humphreys' (1970) doctoral study of gay men in public places, conducted prior to the requirement that such studies be approved by Institutional Review Boards, raised another issue of risk and potential harm to subjects and highlighted the importance of maintaining privacy for research subjects engaged in stigmatized or illegal behavior. Humphreys observed men meeting in public toilets (nicknamed by users as "tearooms") for the purpose of hooking up with other gay men and having sex. He gained entry by volunteering to be the "watch queen," a person who would look for police and cough to warn tearoom participants when a police car came by. He identified himself as a scientist/researcher to some of the men, who then agreed to be interviewed. Humphreys found that those who agreed to be interviewed tended to be more affluent and educated than other tearoom participants. So a year later, to avoid social class bias, he tracked a set of other men to their homes through their license plates, posed as a health care worker, and interviewed them about their health, sexual behavior, access to services, and other topics. He collected additional information—license plates—that could link the men to behaviors that they would not have wanted disclosed. Though it could be argued that public toilets are public spaces where people can have no expectation of privacy, Humphreys' actions ultimately were considered unethical, since many of the men he observed did not know he was studying them and that they were unwitting and possibly unwilling participants in a study. Those men who were tracked to their homes were deceived by Humphreys as to his reasons for wanting to interview them. The men could have suffered considerable social, emotional, financial, or reputational harm had their illegal and stigmatized behavior been disclosed (Sieber, retrieved August 14, 2014, from http://web.missouri.edu/~bondesonw/Laud.html).

These and many other studies made it clear that harm can be social, emotional, psychological, financial, legal, reputational, or cultural. Studies of political participation can, for example, reveal which people stand in opposition to dictators and subject participants to possible punishment. Studies of school enrollments can disclose which children are undocumented or have parents who are and who might be subject to deportation. Studies that induce participants to talk about religious practices, break taboos, or to reveal their sexual identities, could, if violations of confidentiality or inappropriate reporting occurred, lead to shunning and could induce illness. Even studies as apparently benign as those involving children's activities (Adler and Adler, 1995; 1996) or teachers' notions of child development (Deyhle and LeCompte, 1994) could identify and threaten groups engaged in illegal activities such as shoplifting and smoking or stigmatize populations whose exercise patterns or ideas about age-appropriate responsibilities diverge from what is considered mainstream, and therefore acceptable, practice. These and many other studies make it clear that in most cases, researchers must take care to ensure that study participants understand the research in which they are being asked to participate, and as well, any possible risks associated with it. Participants must agree that the measures taken to protect their confidentiality are adequate, that they are not coerced in any way, subtly or otherwise, to participate in a study, and that they have access to proper resources and recourse should they experience physical or psychological harm while engaging in the study. The only exceptions to these principles are if an IRB agrees that a study that is of crucial importance for the welfare of individuals and the public at large cannot be conducted without some degree of deception.

DISCIPLINARY CODES OF ETHICS AND THE PROBLEM OF ENFORCEMENT

Professional associations for all social science disciplines have created codes of ethics regarding the avoidance of harm to human subjects to which researchers in those fields should adhere. Examples include the American Psychological Association, the American Anthropological Association, the American Sociological Association, and the Society for Applied Anthropology. The problem has been that, like the Helsinki Declaration and the Nuremberg Codes, most of the disciplinary codes lack enforcement capacity to stop unethical research. Only a few professional associations that also control licensing of their professional members, such as the American Medical Association and the American Bar Association, have the power to revoke the licenses of members who fail to abide by the code of ethics. Few other professional associations have such power, and few academic disciplines even provide licensing for its scientists and scholars. By the 1970s, it had begun to be clear that without mechanisms for addressing ethical violations in research, no matter how egregious ethical violations might be, there existed little formal incentive to halt them.

THE BELMONT REPORT 1978

Outrage in the US Congress over studies like the Tuskegee Syphilis Project and revelations of how research participants had been mistreated led the US Congress to become interested in regulating some forms of research. In 1974, Congress passed the National Research Act, which required federal monitoring of certain kinds of research. This, in turn, sparked the creation of the Commission for the Protection of Human Subjects of Biomedical and Behavioral Research, the first public national body to shape bioethics policy in the United States. The Commission sponsored the Belmont Commission, the group that produced the 1978 Belmont Report, which established a set of guidelines for the ethical conduct of all research on humans. It also instituted a mechanism for enforcing those guidelines by creating the Office of Human Research Protection (http://www.hhs.gov/ohrp/), a division of the US Department of Health and Human Services, to guide and enforce the Report's provisions, and by writing the provisions of the Belmont Report into the Code of Federal Regulations (CFR) as Title 45, Part 46 (United States Code of Federal Regulations 2001). *The Belmont Report required that researchers adhere to principles of justice, beneficence, and respect for persons. These have been translated roughly into issues of informed consent and the capacity to offer it, the avoidance of unnecessary risk to research participants, and the requirement that no single group unduly incur either the benefits or the risks of participation in research. No researcher whose institution receives funding from the United States government is exempt from the oversight of Institutional Review Boards that monitor research practice and enforce the Belmont Principles.* Furthermore, the existence of the Belmont Principles enhances the authority of codes of

 Key point

 Key point

ethics in disciplinary professional associations, since the mechanisms established by the Belmont Report (National Commission for the Protection of Human Subjects of Biomedical and Behavioral Research, http://www.hhs.gov/ohrp/humansubjects/guidance/belmont.html) provide a means for enforcing them.

Reflecting the climate of the Nuremburg Tribunal, the ethical focus in the Belmont Report echoed activities of the medical profession and its understanding of both research design and its limited definition of risk as that of physical harm: It required that researchers should seek to do no harm to research participants beyond risks experienced in everyday life, and that in any case, risks should be minimized. Further, consent to any incurred risk at all, including the mere fact of donating time for participation in a project, must be given by research participants prior to the research experience. The Belmont guidelines now are applied to the conduct of all research on human beings, including in the social and behavioral sciences and education, though their origin in medical research has come to pose some problems for social scientists whose research does not follow the same disciplinary and experimental rules of biomedical research. The remainder of this chapter discusses the specifics of the Belmont principles as they are applied in practice.

THE BELMONT PRINCIPLES

The Belmont Report was concerned with three basic principles: justice, beneficence, and respect for persons. *Justice fundamentally has to do with equity.* The principle of justice requires fairness of subject selection such that the burdens of participation in research should be distributed equitably throughout the population; no group should be studied to excess just because it is convenient. Both the burdens and the benefits of participation in research should be shared equitably, and those who bear the burden of research should be the ones who benefit from it. People should not be excluded from research unless there are scientific or safety reason for exclusion—for example, studies of pregnancy normally would not include men—and vulnerable populations must not be exploited.

Key point

Key point

Definition: Risk is defined as a degree of potential harm greater than what is encountered in everyday life

The principle of beneficence addresses the issue of risks and benefits. The researcher should seek to minimize risks to participants in research projects, and risks should be balanced by benefits. Risks include physical, social, emotional, financial, cultural, and reputational discomfort or harm. **Risks** should not be described in ways that minimize their actual severity; neither should benefits be overestimated. Benefits can accrue to a group, rather than to the specific individual, but must be so stated.

The principle of beneficence requires that researchers provide potential research participants with a full and proper assessment of risks and benefits and explain how they will be protected from harm, including how their personal, private information will be protected by confidentiality or anonymity. Finally, beneficence issues include how the research results will be disclosed and to whom. The issue of disclosure also involves a concern for the consequences of research to participants in the future, a factor that may involve some clairvoyance on the part of the researcher but one that cannot be ignored (LeCompte, 2015).

Key point

The principle of respect for persons has to do with voluntarism. Key to understanding the components of voluntarism are full disclosure; the consent process; issues of coercion; privacy; and protection for vulnerable persons. All participants in research should freely choose to participate and be able to withdraw from a study if they choose. They must be legally, linguistically, and cognitively capable of understanding what they are being asked to undergo, and they must not be placed in situations where failure to participate might subject them to retaliation or harm. They also must be able to understand completely what they will encounter during the research process and what the consequences of their participation are, and to be certain that the researcher will protect their identity and the identifiability of the information they provide. Note here that the "consenting unit" is considered to be an individual, who is unfettered by cultural ties to a community that could interfere with that individual's exercise of agency. The Belmont Principles do not consider issues of collective or group consent, and except for persons who are considered to be legally unable to give consent and who need a guardian to consent for them, the question of who can give consent is not addressed—as described earlier.

Researchers, however, usually study individuals drawn from a group and then report the results for all those individuals aggregated into a group. The results obtained from such a group of individuals can have implications for the entire group from which the individuals were drawn. Further, researchers are increasingly asked to consider the ethical implications of their work for whole communities. Often, no single individual has authority to give consent for the investigation of a community or the collective group of which he or she is a part. In other cases, risks attendant to other people involved in the study may need to be considered and their consent obtained. This might apply, for example, in field-based substance abuse or violence research, where the research ethics section of a proposal needs to describe the risks and protections for study staff as well as community residents and the community as a whole. Later in this book, we address the issues involved in who can give consent for groups, under what conditions, and for whom.

The Consent Process

Title 45, Part 46, of the US Code of Federal Regulations (CFR) codifies federal regulation of the ethical conduct of human subject research. It does so because *the US government has taken responsibility for enforcing* **Key point** *rules about informed consent to make sure that human beings do not become participants in research projects unwillingly or without their knowledge.* In addition, *people must be informed about and fully understand what* **Key point** *the research entails before consent can be considered legitimate.* People who cannot understand the research procedures cannot be well enough informed to give consent for participation legitimately, freely, and with full knowledge of the study.

Overall, the idea of consent embedded in the Belmont Report is based on the Western notion of free will. The right of individuals to control their own lives and to enter into agreements and contracts is crucial to ensuring legally

effective informed consent processes. Research participants must be legally able to give consent (i.e., they must be
adults, not under guardianship, and not in custody). Consent must be given freely and not under circumstances of
coercion or duress. Legal representation is required when a
participant is a minor, in custody, or mentally incapacitated
in ways that would prevent him or her from understanding
either what will happen to them in the course of a study or
that refusal to participate is an option. The consent process is ongoing; participants in long-term studies such as
ethnographies may have to be reminded that people whom
they have come to know well are, in fact, still researchers
collecting information on them and not simply friends.
Researchers, then, are constant participants in the consent
process, as are their assistants, the participants themselves,
and their legally authorized representatives. Initial consent
requires that participants receive:

- A description of the study and what will happen to
  them
- A description of the risks and benefits, one that
  includes the possible future consequences of the
  research
- A statement that participation is voluntary
- A description of confidentiality protections
- Contact information if they wish to discuss the study
  with those responsible for it, in their language of
  preference.

Normally, this information is contained in *consent
letters*, which must be signed to indicate consent by participants or marked with their initials and witnessed by a
person who signs to confirm consent. Examples of consent letters are provided in the appendices to this book.
However, legal guardians can give consent under certain
circumstances, and in very special circumstances, written
consent can be waived, especially if the letter of consent
serves as the only way to identify participants in sensitive
or illegal activities or if the group under study has a history of ill treatment by authorities for having signed documents. *Assent letters* also are required for minors (between

the ages of about seven and seventeen or the legal age of adulthood in the state in which the study is taking place); these include an abbreviated description of the study, and signed acknowledgment that the minor understands what the study entails and agrees voluntarily to participate in the study, assurances about privacy, and the capacity to end participation if the individual desires.

The single event—signing of consent letters—is, however, only the start of the ongoing consent process. Participants not only must understand what is involved in their participation, but they can never be allowed to forget that the relationship with a researcher is an unusual one, such that anything they disclose could end up being data for the researcher. Further, researchers must continually tell research participants about changes in the research study, unanticipated risks, and other consequences of participation. Appendices at the end of this book provide some examples of informed consent letters and the kinds of guidelines that Institutional Review Boards provide to researchers.

Risks

Research always involves certain risks and benefits; some projects may be riskier than others, and ***participation in research projects involves greater risk for certain types of people than it does for others.*** As we describe below, risks can come from many sources. They can include:

Key point

- Physical harm
- Psychological, emotional, or sociocultural harm from having to participate in activities that violate cultural norms or personal values
- Legal damage from having disclosed illegal status or activities
- Financial damage
- Harm because confidentiality is breached and private, personal information is disclosed
- Harm incurred because the research itself is risky and the study is poorly designed and/or the researcher is not qualified to carry it out

- Risks that are indirect, or at the time of the research, poorly understood or unknown

Indirect risks could include such things as research that resulted in the disclosure of a woman's undocumented immigration status, which, in turn, led to her deportation. In such a case, her children, who may or may not have been research subjects, and who may be legal residents, would experience indirect risk because their mother is gone. Or a researcher's inadvertent disclosure of the HIV status of a study participant to a friend who knows the participant, and who might reveal it to others, thereby jeopardizing the study participant's standing in the community as well as revealing information the participant would not want to be known by the public. Researchers may not know all the possible risks that involve violating cultural taboos or normative practices as a project begins; this is why the consent process must be ongoing, so that researchers can keep participants fully informed as they learn more about the community, new information emerges, and as the cultural context of the study changes. With new information, conditions with respect to risk, harm, and confidentiality may be identified and procedures modified.

Researchers must determine and Institutional Review Boards must certify that risks are minimized, and are reasonable in relation to the benefits. Benefits may accrue either to the participant or the group to which he or she belongs, or to science or society. It is certainly acceptable that much research may not benefit the participants themselves, but that fact should be made known prior to the study's initiation so that they can consent to participate in a study that does not help them directly. It also is the case that benefits should not be exaggerated. For example, some novice researchers claim as a benefit that participants may enjoy talking with a researcher about their experiences. However, such a claim can be dubious despite the fact that people often say at the end of an interview that talking through their experiences has helped them to understand themselves or reflect differently on their situation. Researchers also cannot claim that payments made to participants are benefits. Payment for information is never considered to be a benefit; rather, it is considered to be compensation for the time spent by the participant in responding to interviews or surveys. Payments also are not usually made for participating in interventions since this might be considered coercive or at the very least might influence the perceived acceptability or efficacy of the intervention. That said, compensation also should not be disproportionate to the service rendered or to rates of pay current in the community for time spent in similar research activities. Excessive compensation can be considered coercive, especially in resource-poor communities. It is important to note that the term *excessive* is context specific. In some settings, an appropriate compensation may be a $4 equivalent, or a certificate for the purchase of coffee or another desirable edible or drinkable. In other settings, interviewees may be paid up to $100 for a long, single interview depending on the "going rate" in the study setting. Researchers should be aware that participants might know each other and discuss what researchers are paying for respondent time and effort, especially if there are a number of field studies occurring in the same community. If one study pays $25 per interview and a second pays $50 per interview, this may become known in the community, and the first study will be compelled to equate payment to the level of the second in order to be perceived as compensating fairly. This has happened numerous times in HIV research in cities such as Chicago, Miami, New York, San Francisco, and especially in smaller cities such as New Haven and Hartford, Connecticut, where many studies may be ongoing at the same time.

Research that is risky can, of course, be carried out; some such research has great social and scientific value. Of crucial importance is whether or not the investigator is capable of conducting the study, the participants have agreed to participate voluntarily, and they know what they are getting into as well as what the potential future consequences of their participation might be. They must agree that the risks of the study are balanced by the benefits it would generate. In addition, it is important to assess whether or not the design of the study is rigorous enough for the results to be believable and the efforts of the researchers and the participants, both of whom are taking risks—although somewhat different ones—to be useful, valid, and respected.

Vulnerable Participants: By Definition and Situational

Vulnerable populations consist of persons who cannot truly consent freely to participation in a research project because they are too young to enter into such agreements; would incur unnecessary risks because of their health, legal, or social status; could feel coerced to participate; or be unable to understand the risks or procedures involved in participation.

Definition: Vulnerable populations consist of persons who cannot truly consent freely to participation in a research project because they are too young to enter into such agreements, would incur unnecessary risks, experience possible coercion, or be unable to understand the risks or procedures involved

Vulnerable Populations by Definition

The Code of Federal Regulations (CFR 45-46) codifies certain categories of people for whom special consideration always must be given. These include people who are not able to consent for themselves or who would be especially vulnerable to risks, and who are considered *by definition* to be **vulnerable populations**.

The categories listed below are vulnerable *by definition.*

VULNERABLE POPULATIONS AS DEFINED BY THE CODE OF FEDERAL REGULATIONS

- mentally handicapped people or people who are severely mentally ill
- children under the age of eighteen (or the legal age of adulthood in the country or state where the study takes place)
- incarcerated or institutionalized persons, including prisoners, people on probation, and the institutionalized mentally ill
- orphans
- pregnant women if the study is concerned with pregnancy

These individuals are considered vulnerable because they cannot give consent, either because they are too young to give legal consent; are in custody of others, including legal conservators who make decisions about them; have reduced mental capacity and cannot understand what is being asked of them; or might be subject to treatments that could adversely affect their pregnancy. Research that involves these vulnerable populations invites special scrutiny and call for special responsibilities on the part of the researcher regarding obtaining consent from legal guardians and protecting the privacy of information obtained. It also requires that IRBs include members who have special expertise in the area of vulnerability concern by virtue of their personal or professional experience or both, since IRBs are charged with ensuring adequate protection of such populations.

EXAMPLE 2.11

STUDYING INMATES IN A PRISON SCHOOL

Dr. James Pearson, as a new PhD in educational anthropology, landed a teaching job in the recently organized school within a federal maximum security prison south of Houston, Texas. All of the inmates at the prison had committed major felonies: murder, rape, grand theft, selling drugs. Many of them were virtually illiterate; many saw attending school as a way to escape the boredom of prison life and to earn "good time" toward parole so as to have better life chances if and when they got out. Dr. Pearson wanted to study how well the prison school fit within the structure of the prison, the functions it played within the control system in the prison, and how participants (inmates, teachers, administrators) felt about the school. To gain IRB approval, he needed not only the permission of the prison authorities to interview all individuals in the school but also the consent of each individual staff member and prisoner whom he planned to study. Consent from the inmates themselves was necessary but not legally sufficient because, as persons in custody, they no longer had the legal right to agree to participate independently and thus could not be protected from harm by signing a consent form. He also needed a prison representative or prisoner advocate in the IRB review to make sure that prisoners' rights were known and ensured (Pearson and LeCompte, 1986).

Today, Pearson also would have to have obtained an additional permission from the Office of Human Research Protection (OHRP) in Washington, which now has established a special review unit for all research involving prison inmates. In effect, the possibility of doing research on persons who are in some way under the jurisdiction of the legal system—including people on probation, in juvenile diversion programs, or awaiting trial—has become very challenging. However, it is not impossible. Researchers such as Richard Altice of Yale University, who conducts HIV research with prisoners in Connecticut, or Jemel Aguilar, of the University of St. Joseph in West Hartford, Connecticut, who has conducted work with prisoners and ex-prisoners in Texas, have managed to penetrate the bureaucratic structures of the prison institutions and the OHRP and to gain IRB reviews that protect their participants.

EXAMPLE 2.12

OBTAINING CONSENTS FOR A STUDY OF MIDDLE SCHOOL CHILDREN

Margaret LeCompte and Deborah Holloway wanted to examine the impact of participation in arts-based education on middle schoolers enrolled in an experimental Arts Focus school. Their research design involved conducting observations in teachers' meetings, classrooms, and at arts-related activities, going on field trips with students and teachers, and interviewing teachers, school administrators, parents, and their children. The three-year study included follow-up interviews of the children each year to assess change in their attitudes toward the arts, their own sense of identity, and in their career aspirations over time. Getting consent of the teachers and administrators was straightforward, but the children were another matter. The researchers couldn't include any child unless that child and his or her parent had signed consent forms. The researchers started recruitment with the sixth- through eighth-grade students, asking them to sign assent forms saying that they understood the project and wanted to be a part of it. Because school rules forbade the researchers from contacting parents directly, the children then had to take a parental consent form home for their parents or guardians to sign, indicating consent for the children to participate. Many forms never reached the parents. Some were lost in backpacks or on the way home. Other children forgot that they couldn't participate, even if they wanted to, without a parent's signature. Some parents who wanted their children in the study couldn't persuade them that the project was worth the effort.

Belmont guidelines require respecting the agency of both adults and minors to consent voluntarily to a study. If those minors are able to understand what is involved in the research project, they are able to "assent" and participate with the permission of their parents or guardians. If they do not agree to assent, they can voluntarily refuse to participate even if their parents have given permission. Since middle school children were quite capable of understanding the purpose of LeCompte's and Holloway's research and their data collection procedures, they also were deemed capable of giving *assent* to participation, which is required in addition to the parents' *consent*. It also is true that gaining assent is a useful strategy for recruitment; no middle school child can be forced to participate in something whose value they haven't been sold on in the first place! Even if they were forced into a study, their participation would not likely yield much valuable information.

Situationally Vulnerable Participants. Similar protections are required for research that could pose physical, emotional, social, cultural, or financial risk to participants, given the context, particular participant characteristics or behaviors, or the topic of the research itself. In these situations, the research could jeopardize such participants, who may be involved in behavior that is perceived to be dangerous to others (such as drug selling), or is already stigmatized (being transgender), or is considered illegal (being undocumented) in the society where the study is located. In these cases, potential participants are defined as *situationally* vulnerable. Among such categories of people are:

- women who are pregnant if the research has to do with their pregnancy
- people who are illiterate or who do not speak the dominant language of the culture or the language of the researcher
- people whose participation in a research project would expose their own illegal status or activities, and thereby cause them to risk arrest and imprisonment
- people who are ill or physically handicapped, especially if the research is concerned with their illness or condition

- people who feel pressure to participate in the research in order to receive or continue with treatment that they need or want and cannot otherwise obtain

Examples of research that could be risky, dangerous to participants, or could subject participants to coercive pressures include studies that investigate situations in which participants could be subject to coercive pressures.

- people who use drugs in a society that designates those drugs to be illegal (risk of disclosure of illegal actions)
- immigrant teen-aged dropouts, some of whom might be illegal residents subject to deportation, or whose participation in a study could reveal that their parents or siblings are illegal residents
- doctor/client interactions in an abortion clinic, where clients could feel as though failure to participate in the research project could jeopardize their ability to obtain an abortion
- doctors in a clinic where abortions are practiced, whose medical practice is being scrutinized by pro-life activists
- students in an innovative classroom, whose teacher wishes to study their reactions to a new instructional program. These students could feel that failure to participate would affect their grades.

Even the general requirement that researchers obtain signed consent forms from all participants in a research study can, in fact, endanger persons engaged in illegal or tabooed activities if the only way such persons could be identified were if the authorities seized the researcher's consent forms.

Many people who are not vulnerable by definition or given a specific context or topic will agree to participate in studies but refuse to place their signatures on consent forms because they, or people like them, have experienced past or present persecution, discrimination, class or caste

or religious differences, have learned to distrust government agents or the police, or are involved in activities in
war zones. These individuals also are vulnerable, although
they are not formally defined as such; they deserve the
same special protections as people legally defined as vulnerable. In these cases, researchers instead may seek a
waiver of signed consent and use oral consent procedures
and signatures of the researcher indicating that consenting procedures have been reviewed with the participant
and that the participant has consented.

Sensitive Topics

Many of the examples provided throughout the *Ethnographer's Toolkit* involve research on sensitive subjects
such as sexual behavior, HIV infections, mental illness, and
potentially misunderstood or stigmatizing cultural, sexual,
and social/class and caste differences. Research that explores
sensitive or difficult topics, those which can cause participants to experience distress when recalling hurtful or traumatic events or secrets, or those that can cause distress if
others discover what they have experienced or disclosed,
can pose significant risk to participants. Such research can
render them *situationally vulnerable*. Participation in various sexual acts; drug use; antisocial, illegal, or stigmatized
behavior; infection with poorly understood or stigmatized
diseases such as the Ebola virus, hepatitis C, or HIV; having
suicidal thoughts; or experiencing or witnessing traumatic
occurrences such as accidents, domestic abuse, kidnapping,
rape, imprisonment and torture, death of a loved one, war-
fare, or natural disasters—all can be sensitive or difficult.
Even people who have knowledge of others' such experiences can be traumatized, and that trauma can subject the
participants to risk.

Definition: Sensitive or difficult topics are those that can cause participants to experience distress when recalling hurtful or traumatic events or secrets, or when others discover what they have experienced or disclosed

EXAMPLE 2.13

STUDYING HOW BEING INFECTED BY THE HIV VIRUS AFFECTS THE WORK OF ARTISTS

A local artist/activist and member of the arts faculty of a university was interested
in the way that the personal lives and preoccupations of artists are reflected in their
work. She wanted to interview visual and performing artists who have HIV/AIDS to

find out how the illness has affected their work and their own social activism. The university's Institutional Review Board found that though the fact of being infected with the HIV virus was, by itself, a sensitive issue, because all of the people whom she sought to interview already had disclosed their HIV/AIDS status publicly and portrayed its impact in their artworks, the researcher's study did not put participants at any risk greater than what they ordinarily experienced.

EXAMPLE 2.14

THE SENSITIVITY INVOLVED IN LINKING DNA DATA TO INDIVIDUALS' SEX AND MATH SCORES

A university researcher interested in why boys scored higher in math than girls on standardized tests hypothesized that the quality of "maleness" would be positively related to test scores in mathematics. He proposed to examine the relationship between sex (maleness and femaleness) and mathematical ability at the genetic level, using testosterone levels as a measure of "maleness." He proposed to study male and female college juniors by collecting their SAT math scores, their GPA in math classes in high school, and their grades in math classes taken in college, as well as cheek swabs and saliva samples. The cheek swabs and saliva would be analyzed for relative levels of testosterone; the relationship between these levels and participants' sex, math scores, and testosterone levels would then be examined to explore hypotheses about the impact of "maleness" and "femaleness" on math performance. The researcher proposed to preserve the anonymity of the participants by assigning codes to them rather than using their names and reporting data only in the aggregate. However, he did promise to release to each participant his or her own individual scores. He also argued that since the proposed collection of DNA data would be relatively noninvasive, there would be little risk to participants. However, the researcher's university Institutional Review Board did not agree that the study posed little risk. Though it purported to be based on biological differences, the IRB felt that the study actually addressed cultural stereotypes of male and female performance, rather than genetics. Further, the IRB members felt that knowing their testosterone levels might actually be harmful to students whose levels were counter to what they felt to be appropriate for their sex.

EXAMPLE 2.15

PREGNANCY AND PARENTING AS DISINCENTIVES TO HIGH SCHOOL GRADUATION FOR LATINAS

Elsa Gonzalez, a doctoral student in education, wanted to study why young Latinas failed to complete high school. Knowing that pregnancy and parenting duties are key disincentives to high school graduation, she proposed to conduct a study of young Latina girls who were pregnant or who already had babies. She focused on two issues: the "push out" disincentives in schools that discourage girls from continuing their education, and the "pull in" incentives that make having a family more desirable than staying in school. Elsa planned to interview young girls about their attitudes toward school, education, feelings about having a family, differences between girls who were born in the United States and those who weren't, and the impact of family background and educational levels on the girls' plans. She planned to locate her population at a clinic serving both a low-income housing development and a trailer park housing many immigrant and seasonal migrant families.

    Elsa's project raised many questions about risks and potential coercion. First of all, the young women were minors, and therefore vulnerable by definition. They also were pregnant or new mothers, which made them situationally vulnerable since the research was relevant to their parenting status. Elsa did not know whether they were legal immigrants or not, but since she wanted to compare girls born in the United States with those born elsewhere, it would have been difficult to avoid mention of whether or not the participants themselves, or their parents and siblings, were legal residents of the United States. Disclosure of undocumented status meant participants—or their family members—could be deported. Finally, by recruiting the girls at the only clinic where they could obtain affordable health care for themselves and their babies, Elsa risked having participants agree to participate in her study for fear that refusal would cause them to be barred from obtaining needed health services.

    Studies such as Elsa's are important, and like many studies, risks notwithstanding, are worth doing. Researchers simply must design their studies to do as little harm as possible, and to make sure that consent procedures are clear. Further, mandates for special care to such vulnerable subjects warrants obtaining a Certificate of Confidentiality from the federal government. Such a certificate means that the researchers' data cannot be seized by law enforcement agencies and used to prosecute participants, even if they are engaged in illegal behavior.

EXAMPLE 2.16

LEVELS OF CONFIDENTIALITY REQUIRED FOR A STUDY OF DOMESTIC ABUSE

David Bowen was interested in why women who were abused by their domestic partners frequently refused to prosecute their abusers and often continued to live with them. He asked the director of a local shelter for battered and abused women if he could approach the shelter's clients to recruit a population to study. He had expected to need a rigorous consent process and to be required to rigidly safeguard the identity of participants because of the sensitivity of the topic. He had not, however, thought of the danger posed to women if their abusers learned of their participation in such a study. Further, asking women for detailed information about their abusers ran the risk of making the abusive partners themselves "secondary subjects" (LeCompte, 2008a) or unwitting participants in the study if the identity of the abusers themselves were disclosed. As a consequence, Bowen's study required establishing several layers of confidentiality: for the shelter and its staff, for the women themselves, and for the abusive partners.

Coercion

The Belmont Principles require that people participating in research projects must freely volunteer to do so. Consent obtained under conditions in which people feel compelled to participate, or feel *coerced*, for whatever reason, is considered unethical. Many people could be considered vulnerable because of coercion, even though they would not otherwise be vulnerable. Examples of situations that could be considered coercive include:

- People who hope for some benefit, even when it is not offered (as in students in the class of a teacher who is doing research on those students, who hope for an increase in their grade because of their participation, or prisoners who hope for award of "good time" because they were participants in a study)
- Potential participants who feel pressure to participate in a research study in order to receive, or to continue to receive, treatment that they need or want and cannot otherwise obtain, such as the clientele of a free medical clinic

- People who are offered the promise of payment for participation in a study when they really need that payment to meet expenses for the week or month
- People who feel coerced because they feel that failure to participate would result in withholding of privileges, loss of status, or deprivation of other benefits, such as students whose teacher wishes them to participate in research on a curriculum, or prisoners who believe that failure to join a research project would jeopardize their efforts to earn "good time" or reduced sentences
- People subject to the exercise of "undue influence" by significant others or persons in authority (including teachers, service providers, or mental health professionals)
- Individuals who have been identified as suitable for participation by persons who have power over them (e.g., service providers, teachers, mentors, etc.)

For example, juveniles charged with criminal behavior could agree to participate in research for fear that they would encounter reprisals if they refused the request of a supervisory social worker, probation officer, or other employee of the juvenile justice system to do so.

EXAMPLE 2.17

PROFESSOR MCINTYRE ASSESSES HIS OWN INSTRUCTION

Professor James McIntyre, who had developed a number of innovative instructional programs over the years, wanted to know what, if any, impact the programs had on his students. He proposed spending the next few semesters evaluating students in one particular class. His proposal called for administering an attitudinal questionnaire to students at the beginning of the semester and then readministering it at the end of the semester to see how student attitudes have changed. He wanted to conduct a follow-up study by readministering the questionnaire again at the end of the students' college career to see how stable the changes, if any, were over time. In addition, McIntyre wanted to collect student assignments done in his class and the journals students were required to keep about their experiences in the class.

The type of study McIntyre proposed is a familiar one for many instructors. However, it poses coercive risks to students who fear that their professor could retaliate against those who refuse to participate. Further, because professors know who the students are, their rights to privacy also cannot be guaranteed. In cases such as McIntyre's, some Institutional Review Boards have proposed having the student materials collected and held by a neutral person—even a member of the IRB—until after the semester ends and the grades are posted. At that point, issues of coercion are reduced, and the professor can contact students and ask permission to use their materials. The data from any student who refuses to participate then are discarded by the custodian of the data. Only materials from students who have consented to participate are returned to the professor/investigator.

Protection of Privacy, Exceptions, and Waivers

Researchers protect their research subjects by holding confidential the identity of the groups, communities, and individuals whom they study. They do this by using codes, pseudonyms, or altered histories and biographies. This reduces the risk of having sensitive information linked to individuals in ways that could subject them to embarrassment or harm. While researchers customarily talk about *anonymity* and *confidentiality, it is important to recognize that these terms are not identical.* **Anonymity** means that no one, not even the researcher, knows from whom specific data have come. Only surveys that are self-administered and have no identifiers on them or data that have been de-identified in other ways so as to have no codes or names on them can be anonymous. More common is the promise of **confidentiality**, which is all that ethnographers can offer, because they do in fact know who their research participants are by the very fact of interacting with, interviewing, or observing them regularly. Confidentiality means that the identity of the participants is disguised or coded in ways that prevent others from being able to identify them.

There are some exceptions to the rules about protecting identity. It is not necessary for researchers to disguise the

Definition: Anonymity means that no one, not even the researcher, knows from whom specific data have come

Definition: Confidentiality means that the identity of the participants is disguised or coded in ways that prevent others from being able to identify them

identity of specific public figures, particularly elected officials, who, it is presumed, have waived the right to anonymity at least with respect to their public actions. In certain
limited instances involving research that might disclose a
research participant's illegal activity, researchers can obtain
a Writ of Protection or a Certificate of Confidentiality from
the US Office of Human Research Protection. Such a writ
or certificate assures both the researcher and the research
subject that the information gathered by the researcher is
"privileged"; that is, the government—including agencies
such as the police—agrees that it will not subpoena or seize
the researcher's data in order to find out the identity of the
researcher's subjects. Such certificates normally are granted
only in cases where the research can be carried out in no
other way. The Certificate of Confidentiality is obtained by
preparing for submission to the federal Office for Protection from Research Risks (OPRR) a package of information
in accordance with their guidelines, including:

- a description of the target population, sample size,
  and sampling procedures
- why the writ is required, including that without
  complete privacy for participants, the research cannot be carried out
- required statements of assurance from the researcher's home institution that it reviews research in
  accordance with US government regulations
- copies of approved consent forms
- the statement of acceptance of the plan for protection of human subjects approved by the Institutional
  Review Board of the researcher's home institution,
  the grantee organization (if any), and its grant
  review committee

Researchers can ask for a waiver to the customary written consent in cases where a written consent form would
be the only way that the research participant's identity
would be known and the knowledge of that identity might
prove risky to the participants. Waivers to the requirement
for written consent also can be obtained if the population
is illiterate or if it has historical suspicions about signing

documents—as is the case with many American Indian people, for whom signing documents often meant they ended up losing their land or custody of their children, or people from rural areas of northern India, who may have limited formal education and experience-based distrust of bureaucratic procedures and government officials. In such instances, a strong case for an oral consent process can be made. This involves having the consent forms read to the potential participants and having them sign a statement indicating that they have been properly informed about the study. An alternative IRB-approved strategy that is used in other countries is for the researcher to obtain the oral agreement of nonliterate respondents who are not able to write their names, and then sign and date the data collection form assuring the veracity of the claim. The lists that these procedures create, of course, serve to identify who has participated in the research, and, as such, may need special custodial care.

Another exception to these stringent requirements involves research that uses data collected in such a way that no individuals can be identified—such as anonymous electronic or mailed surveys. Such research can even include very sensitive data if it cannot be linked to specific persons. An example might include data about the prevalence of HIV/AIDS (a stigmatized disease) obtained from blood samples (a sensitive material) taken from newborn babies (a vulnerable population), if the data associated with the samples only included the gender and race of the baby and the location of hospitals where the samples were collected. Anonymous data are often collected from individuals about sensitive topics using a variety of similar means of collecting data.

EXAMPLE 2.18

OBTAINING ANONYMOUS/DE-IDENTIFIED DATA ON SENSITIVE TOPICS IN A SENSITIVE TOWN

A recent study of parental protection of youth from exposure to substance use conducted by researchers from the Institute for Community Research in a town in central Connecticut addressed these issues. De-identified households responded to a rapid assessment protocol about whether or not they protected or locked up their prescription drugs and alcohol. Using an electronic survey, additional data were collected from parents in the community on the same topic. The de-identified survey did collect demographic information from the respondents as well as information about other household practices related to drug and tobacco use. In this instance, the data collection process was part of a collaboration with the town prevention committee. In the collaboration, the ICR collected the data and returned it after analysis in aggregate form to the sponsoring prevention committee. The committee agreed in advance, however, that though information on schools would be obtained, the analysis would not include break-outs by individual schools in order to protect the town's schools from any potential stigmatization.

It should be pointed out that all of the examples above, including those involving collecting anonymous data, still require approval by an Institutional Review Board.

SUMMARY

In this chapter, we have discussed the origin of formal concerns for ethical treatment of human participants in research, linking it to many egregious cases of mistreatment of such participants, sometimes in the interests of science, but in other instances, for little more than callous disregard for human suffering or sadism. We have suggested that despite international concern and declarations about the rights of human beings involved in research, it was not until 1974, when the US Congress passed laws creating an oversight agency within the Department of Health and Human Services and commissioned the Belmont Report, that principles governing the ethical treatment of human participants in research were codified and embedded in a monitoring and enforcement mechanism. The principles are those of justice, beneficence, and respect for persons. In practice, they involve the equitable treatment of research participants with regard to the benefits and risks of research, the right of participants to be treated in ways that do not harm them, and the right of individuals to consent to participation, and their right to be fully informed about what the research they are being asked to join involves. We also describe obtaining informed consent as a process, especially for long-term research such as ethnography, where ethnographers always know who their participants are, and we distinguish between anonymity and confidentiality. We confirm the necessity for researchers to assure the privacy of information given to them by participants.

We should point out that though violations of research still do occur, many mechanisms now exist to monitor research. These mechanisms have made a considerable dent in the frequency and level of egregiousness of violations in the past thirty years. They include thorough review of all studies by well-informed Institutional Review Boards; a description in grant proposal submissions of protection procedures for human subjects, including research staff and members of the communities in which the research takes place; the requirement to report ethical violations and adverse effects to organizational IRBs and to federal and other funders; careful review of written consent forms and other forms of consent prior to initiating the research; and reviews of both IRB performance and ethical compliance by federal regulators and monitors such as the Office of Human Research Protection (OHRP). Researchers, physicians, and public health researchers are required to take ethics courses and human subjects' protection training and to demonstrate current certificates of training completion; students take classes and workshops in the ethical conduct of research and, if conducting research themselves, must demonstrate certificates attesting to the completion of such courses. Finally, there are now opportunities through various funding agencies to study and explicate ethical issues in human research via training programs; as well, new journals on ethics in scientific research now exist to publish material on the emerging field of research ethics. In the next chapter, we elaborate on the ethical principles and concepts in this chapter by describing formal procedures for obtaining permission to conduct research and detail what researchers must do to assure conformity to formal ethical principles and practices.

3

FORMAL AND SEMIFORMAL RESPONSIBILITIES

Introduction

Semiformal Responsibilities

Formal Contractual Responsibilities

When Is IRB or IEC Approval Necessary?

Issues of Particular Concern to IRBs and IECs

Levels of Review

Components of an IRB Proposal

The Power of Institutional Review Boards and Institutional Ethics Committees

Coping with Multiple IRBs

Summary

INTRODUCTION

In the first chapters we discussed some important definitions and controversies that ethnographers face in the field. We then distinguished between formal and informal research ethics. The former involve government, contractual, and disciplinary principles that govern formal ethical comportment in research projects. The latter involve the personal characteristics and more or less informal affiliations of researchers, how these affect the way ethnographers present themselves to others, and how they are presented and represented by others in their research sites. We then provided a brief history of how formal oversight of research conduct evolved. In this chapter, we will be discussing semiformal and formal responsibilities inherent in much ethnographic research.

SEMIFORMAL RESPONSIBILITIES

Semiformal obligations include those embodied in disciplinary codes of ethics and others attendant to tacit agreements between researchers, the community, and other agencies such as the media, advisory bodies, and voluntary associations.

Definition: Semiformal obligations are those that are not legally binding but reflect disciplinary or professional codes of ethics, understood norms and standards of practice, and personal and informal surveillance of one's own ethical practices in the study setting

73

Relationships with Disciplinary Professional Associations

The codes of ethics developed by the various academic disciplines are a source of moral suasion for research scholars who are responsible for knowing and performing in accordance with the content of the ethical codes developed by their respective disciplines, the expected behaviors they imply, and how these codes might be evolving over time. However, as we have pointed out earlier, disciplinary codes of ethics often are only guidelines rather than specific sets of instructions or lists of requirements. Further, disciplines neither have the resources nor the authority to enforce these guidelines. Thus, the guidelines have no real enforcement power for scholars who violate their tenets unless violations are egregious, come to the attention of the disciplinary or wider public, and result in some form of punitive action (loss of grant funding, loss of a job, failure to grant a degree). The guidelines only identify where violations exist, and aggrieved parties can only hope that bodies with some enforcement power—such as IRBs—will take action.

Changes in the codes of ethics often are initiated by gradual changes in how research is carried out vis-à-vis participants. Some recent changes in the Code of Ethics of the American Anthropological Association, for example, address the importance of establishing relationships with groups or communities affected by research to ensure that they are protected from harm, that they agree both with the subject matter of the research and the ways in which data and results are to be managed, and that the results of the study will be disseminated to them in appropriate ways (http://ethics.aaanet.org/ethics-statement-0-preamble/)3-obtain-informed-consent-and-necessary-permissions/). The guidelines also make clear that informed consent in anthropological research may be based on oral agreements, and must be ongoing to accommodate to changes in field study conditions. This particular consideration addresses the problem of long and complex consent forms required by the IRBs of research institutions and in particular schools of medicine and education. These longer forms have been designed to protect the institution as well as participants in medical/ drug or educational studies including experiments.

A third important enhancement to the 2012 AAA guidelines is related to the obligation to be "honest and open about your work." The guidelines refer to the problem of "compartmented" research in which social scientists who are working only on part of a larger project are not fully informed about the entire project. In such cases, because they cannot ensure transparency of motivation, design, or interests of the project overall, their research is considered to be "ethically problematic." Discussions about transparency of motive and interests of all parties have become increasingly important as more social scientists work for military establishments or other institutions, including some businesses whose motives or long-range goals may be questionable in relation to vulnerable populations or whose requests to researchers may place them in violation of their individual or their disciplinary ethics (http://ethics.aaanet.org/ethics-statement-2-be -open-and-honest-regarding-your-work/).

Disciplinary associations sometimes weigh in on particular current—and sometimes highly controversial— research issues. A notable case involves the recruiting of anthropologists and other social scientists by the US military for the Human Terrain Program. To the military, *human terrain* is a code word for the human beings who live in geographic areas of concern to the military. Understanding the dynamics and characteristics of the "human terrain" is tantamount to understanding the history, culture, politics, and social and economic context of people in a particular area, and the networks of associations among the people that inhabit it. The military realized that people trained as social and behavioral scientists, and especially as anthropologists would be the most skilled at "mapping" the human terrain, and they recruited a number of them to be "embedded" with combat troops in war zones. Some of the work of these embedded social scientists was dedicated to increasing cross-cultural understanding between US soldiers and local people. However, the military also could use the information collected by anthropologists to trace networks of potential combatants in ways that necessarily would identify these individuals and put them at risk. Since it was impossible to protect the identity of such people or to safeguard the privacy of the information they produced, the AAA found such activities on the part of AAA members to be unethical. The AAA also stated that problems could arise if local people were confused as to who anthropologists were working with—their local communities or the US military. Such confusion could jeopardize the work of other anthropologists in the area and anthropologists in general because it would create distrust of the entire discipline. The AAA thus resolved to recommend that anthropologists should not cooperate with the Human Terrain Program (http://www.aaanet.org/issues/AAA-Opposes -Human-Terrain-System-Project.cfm). Responding to such concerns and deciding how to act on them constitute one form of semiformal responsibility.

Issues of Authorship and Dissemination Agreements

Another serious semiformal responsibility involves who gets authorship credit for research when it is disseminated, and how much "authorship" refers to authors of papers, presentations, blogs, and other formal communications about the work to the public. Individual researchers have fewer such responsibilities because they have no coresearchers who could be potential coauthors. Nonetheless, they may wish to share credit with funding agencies, key informants, and consultants or specific research assistants. However, even they may have to consider issues of data ownership and ways of giving appropriate credit to sponsorships.

Some sponsors or funding agencies may specify who owns the data, who has access to them, and may control the right to publish findings. The US Centers for Disease Control, for example, usually require that one or more of their scientists coauthor publications stemming from a CDC-funded contract or grant. The National Institutes of Health require that after a designated period of time, data from studies over a specific funding level be de-identified and shared with the public. This time period is specified to indicate that the investigators and others associated with the study are expected to publish main study findings in a timely fashion. Sharing arrangements must be described in the initial grant application, and are reviewed in advance of funding.

An initial agreement about ownership of data and who gets to share it is crucial to avoid the emergence of hard feelings or even lawsuits after a project is finished. This is particularly important when the research is sponsored by a corporation or other entity that views the data as proprietary, and the researchers are students or junior scholars who need to finish a degree or generate publications to enhance their careers. It also is critically important in research partnerships where all parties contribute to the study, have participated in different aspects of the study, and expect to participate in its benefits and to have use of the data for their own purposes. Yet another circumstance exists when universities and communities are partners in a study. University researchers often feel that study data are "theirs," but in these types of research partnerships, data ownership arrangements must be firmly established in prior contractual agreements between the organizations and the university to avoid arguments over "who owns the data" as well as the results of the study which may include patents or commercially valuable intellectual property. Finally, data and publishing agreements are required in international research partnerships in which institutions in partner countries want to share and use the data.

Researchers who work in teams have similar, and some even more complex, data-sharing responsibilities, since not all people involved in a project contribute equally or have equal responsibility for the work. Thus, an initial agreement should at least specify who is listed as first author, second author, and so on for the first publications, and if the order should change with subsequent works. These agreements always can be renegotiated if contributions and workloads change. Further, some thought should be given to how disagreements over the interpretation of data should be handled, especially in cases where lead investigators disagree over the content, causes, or interpretations of the phenomena studied, and yet still have to produce a single report.

EXAMPLE 3.1

WHEN RESEARCHERS CANNOT AGREE ON RESEARCH RESULTS

Margaret Gibson's initial work with the Punjabi Sikh community in central California was carried out with a coprincipal investigator from the Sikh community, a man who had a PhD, but in experimental psychology. Gibson was investigating the ways in which Punjabi Sikh immigrant children negotiated academic success in the face of ethnic discrimination in the schools while still maintaining close ties with their traditional family members and the community. Her partner, accustomed to experimental research, was not comfortable with ethnographic methods and discounted as data much of what Gibson collected. He also had linkages to constituencies in the community whose vested interests called for a particular outcome of the study, one that highlighted racism in the school. Gibson later learned that he was from a different community in the Punjab than the study participants in California. Many of the members of Gibson's study community did not like him. He also was completely unconvinced that her description of the school's dynamics and what she called "accommodation without assimilation" (1988) among the immigrant children was valid. Unable to reach agreement on the content of their final report, Gibson wrote one report to the funding agency, and he produced another, containing his own interpretation and conclusions. In retrospect, Gibson said that she should have been more aware of the impact her partner's prior training and connections would have on his ability to collaborate with ethnographers, and of his own preconceived notions about student success and failure and the ethnic dynamics in the school. Had she had more information, she might have chosen another collaborator (1985).

Gibson's experiences argue for taking as much care in choosing coinvestigators and establishing prior understandings with them as one does in developing a research question and design; care taken ahead of time makes clear that the semiformal responsibilities have a lesser likelihood of turning into seriously formal headaches.

Many journals now require a definition of the different roles that contributing authors play in contributing to a manuscript. The following agreement was established among researchers and field staff for a study on oral health. The agreement took into consideration the various important contributions of each of the coauthors and their respective roles in preparing and publishing papers and oral presentations based on the study.

 **EXAMPLE 3.2**

A PUBLICATIONS AGREEMENT FROM THE INSTITUTE FOR COMMUNITY RESEARCH

Procedures for Approval of Manuscript/Paper/Presentation Project GOH

Acquiring Topic Approval

Any individual seeking to lead author a paper or presentation from this project will need to submit a request for approval from the PIs. In this request, the following information should be provided:

- Paper topic
- Study hypotheses and expected variables or concepts to be explored
- Date of submission to PIs
- Expected authors in expected authorship order (please see Authorship Guidelines below)
- Expected journal or professional conference to which you will submit

Paper proposals will be discussed during weekly meetings of the research team. After receiving an email from PIs approving the paper proposal, the authors will sign an agreement by which they agree to the roles and responsibilities and the authorship order. This will help prevent future conflicts and delineate the level of contribution each author would be required to make toward the scientific paper/monograph.

Authorship Guidelines

Authorship and Contributorship

According to the International Committee on Medical Journal Ethics (ICMJE), an author is defined as one who has made substantial contributions to the conception and development of a manuscript. The ICMJE guidelines state that "authorship credit should be based on all of the following: 1) substantial contributions to conception and design, acquisition of data, or analysis and interpretation of data; 2) drafting the article or revising it critically for important intellectual content; and 3) final approval of the version to be published." All other contributors should be listed as acknowledgments.

This means that, while all project staff and investigators may be included as authors on any publications produced from this study, they will only be included as an author on any given publication or presentation if they meet guidelines for authors as defined by these ICMJE guidelines for authors. Otherwise, project investigators and staff, as defined above, will be listed as contributors to a given manuscript. HOWEVER, every effort will be made to involve all above listed investigators as authors on each paper produced from this project. It is the responsibility of the lead author on each given paper from this project to ensure such opportunities for involvement are given. A lead author must contact each project investigator to invite them to be an author on the paper and specify their expected role.

Authorship Order

LEAD/FIRST AUTHOR—The lead or first author of a given paper or professional presentation will lead conceptualization and writing of a given manuscript or professional presentation. He or she will also decide authorship involvement and order. All of this will be subject to approval from the principal investigators, using the procedure outlined in the Procedures for Approval of Manuscript/Paper/Presentation. It is the responsibility of the lead author to ensure that all listed authors on the paper or presentation contribute at the level submitted to and approved by the PI. Alteration of authorship order subsequent to this approval will require reapproval by the PI serving as senior author on the paper.

SECOND AUTHOR—The second author of a given paper or professional presentation will support the paper with coconceptualization and extensive writing, such as taking a leadership role on writing a section of the paper or presentation. Given the nature of partnership between the university, ICR, and NCAA, the second author should be from one of these organizations. This approach will increase the collaboration, knowledge, and perspectives offered by the paper or presentation. For lead authors with less writing experience, inclusion of a more seasoned publication writer is recommended for second authors.

SENIOR (LAST) AUTHOR—Senior authors of papers will be positioned as such due to their oversight of the paper/presentation as a whole and their ability to ensure that the paper/presentation fits within the overall study and the previous and ongoing papers and presentations developed from the initiative. As such, principal investigators-owners are in the optimal position to serve as senior author on all papers and presentations produced from their respective studies.

Role of the Lead Author to Pursue the Paper/Presentation Once Approved: As lead author of an approved paper or presentation, you have SIX MONTHS from your date of approval to submit the DRAFT paper or presentation for review. Should you not submit a paper or presentation within that SIX MONTHS time frame, you relinquish your rights to lead author this work. If you have a topic submitted for presentation, you must resubmit that topic for approval if you would like to create a paper from that work, as well. You are, however, allowed to submit a topic for both presentation and publication.

Obligations to Maintain Author Involvement on a Paper: In accordance with the guidelines of most journals, you are required to share your revisions and resubmissions with all authors at every resubmission. Nothing should be submitted to any journal or any conference without approval from all authors on the paper or presentation, unless they agree that you may submit it without their final approval. YOU MUST provide each author with a final copy of any submitted manuscript, report, or presentation for their records. You must also provide each author with a full citation of presented or published work. Make sure to include PIs.

Changing Approved Paper Topic, including Hypotheses and Expected Variables to Be Explored, Authors and Authorship Order, Journal or Conference for Submission: Any changes in information provided and approved via this topic approval process will require resubmission of the Topic Approval Form with specifications as to why these changes are needed. YOU MAY NOT ALTER THIS INFORMATION WITHOUT APPROVAL FROM THE PI AND THE SENIOR AUTHOR. In such intentions, the lead author should discuss with other authors and send an email to the PIs and get feedback on the suggested change.

The Media

Sometimes the media can be very helpful to researchers, especially for dissemination purposes. At the same time, they can be as irritating as paparazzi—looking for stories where none exist and interfering with sensitive observations. National and even international media can make stories and research results—or the adverse or negative results of a study—available to the world in a flash. Though it might be quite the opposite of the researcher's intentions, the consequences of such instant publicity can have negative implications for medical or social practice, or could permanently negatively stereotype a group of people. For these reasons, making research results public through radio or TV interviews, press conferences, and other public events requires special care, training, and practice so as to ensure the confidentiality of respondents and research sites and to avoid disclosing information that would jeopardize any respondent or study community. Universities and other institutions such as UN agencies have special communications units that help researchers practice their delivery and plan ahead for questions. With practice and training, media mistakes can be avoided.

Another challenge is the publication of early or incomplete results. The scientific process is such that the results of even the most rigorous studies often contradict the results of other studies. Controversies can erupt over such issues as whether, when, and how mammograms should be conducted or how, whether and in what ways global climate change is taking place, and whether or not hydraulic fracturing ("fracking") harms the quality of air and water or causes earthquakes. Sometimes these controversies stem from genuine differences in rigorous research results that use different technologies or are based on different populations. Occasionally debates occur because improvements in technology or longitudinal data demonstrate that a favored approach is outdated or unnecessary. At times, however, ambitious scientists report and publish results they know are erroneous in popular journals and other media simply to get publicity, advance their careers, and gain a competitive edge. Examples include the publication of research on cold fusion by University of Utah physicists that other researchers could never replicate, and the publication of work by cell biologists from South Korea who claimed that they had figured out how to make ordinary human cells transform into stem cells. Still other examples include researchers whose work demonstrates conflicts of interest; research conducted or funded by corporations or lobby groups is suspect because it is expected to support the biases or vested interests of the funder. More and more such activities that are completely unethical and misleading to the public are now being scrutinized and reported on in an effort to stem the tide of scientific fraud (http://www.scientificamerican.com/article/an-epidemic-of-false-claims/; Fang et al., 2012). Unfortunately, misleading or confusing results may provide ammunition to science "deniers," which, in the worst-case scenario, can turn an uninformed public away from science (Kalichman, 2009).

Taking precautions with the media is especially important when working with community members and youth. Often these partnerships are very attractive to reporters who want to interview residents or youth researchers at events where the results of their work are being disseminated. Community members or youth may not have experience in speaking to the press, so preparing them for such conversations by anticipating what questions reporters might want to ask is very important. In such cases, we suggest considering the following:

- Prepare a script for the press to use in reporting that identifies agencies and funders properly.
- Prepare a list of questions for reporters or other media personnel to use.
- Prepare participants in advance by discussing and practicing responses to these questions and other talking points.
- Include in preparation the topics to avoid discussing and how to avoid answering questions about topics with which the interviewee is unfamiliar.
- Ask reporters or media personnel to share their articles before they are published to avoid printing errors or misrepresentations.

In press conferences, researchers and their partners present results and convey messages over which they have control, and reporters ask questions following the presentation. However, reporters who attend special events often have little time to spend with researchers and other participants, and even less time to prepare their articles. Thus, project staff may find it impossible to see an article or video report before it is published. The newspaper articles reporters write can compete with others prepared by project staff and submitted for careful review and publication. For this reason it is best to prepare reporters as much as possible beforehand, through conversations and brief and well-written materials that highlight the main points to be emphasized.

EXAMPLE 3.3

WORKING WITH REPORTERS TO IMPROVE ACCURACY OF REPORTING

Institute for Community Research youth researchers identified underage drinking to be a problem in suburban communities. They conducted a study, and from their results they created a film that illustrated the problem and provided alternative solutions (https://www.youtube.com/watch?v=791KyBCMTxQ). The film was presented at a Town Hall meeting attended by over 150 people including parents, children, teens, and the press. The local press was anxious to interview the teens. Knowing this, ICR prepared the youth presenters, who also were actors in the film, to answer questions that the organization thought members of the press would ask. They trained youth to turn the conversation to these questions. Further, ICR staff members who had good relationships with the local press asked for the opportunity to review the reports (video and written) before they were published. The press, who were prepared in advance with written materials about the film and the campaign—Lead by Example—within which it was presented, created more or less accurate representations of youth work and audience response. Ensuring that this would happen required considerable attention on the part of ICR program staff over a several-month period before the Town Hall meeting. The end result was a request to create with the press a videoed interview with youth about the problem of underage alcohol consumption among youth in the town. This video became very popular with a variety of audiences in the community.

For all of the reasons noted above, it is a good idea whenever possible to make friends with local reporters and television personalities and gain their trust. Insofar as members of the media understand the purposes of a project and become its supporters, they can be important allies and can make valuable contributions. Invoking their understandings as a semiformal responsibility can forestall unfortunate and untimely disclosures.

Advisory Bodies

Research projects often benefit from the input and support of advisory bodies. These bodies, variously termed Community Advisory Boards (CABs), Strategic Alliances, and Technical or Scientific Advisory Groups, consist of people invited by the study leaders to contribute their time and advice/counseling to the study because of their specific knowledge and expertise related to the study topic. These contributions can be political—linking the study to important constituencies or resources; technical—providing useful research inputs such as advice on instruments or expertise on subject matter; or diplomatic—including important persons from the community whose support is desired. Advisory groups composed of

community members (CABs) can, if constituted effectively, even assist in managing disagreements or conflicts
in the community or even in the study team, should they
arise. Some examples of such advisory groups and their
functions include the following:

- Researcher Tiarney Ritchwood, from the University of North Carolina, plans to conduct a study of
  factors contributing to adolescent sexual risk in a
  rural African American community in the South.
  She is working under the umbrella of a large community health promotion coalition composed of
  service agencies and activists. She plans to invite
  interested members of the coalition and a group of
  youth to act as advisors to the study and to assist in
  the development of the measures she plans to use.
  Eventually, she hopes they will help plan and implement an intervention.

- A study to improve flu vaccination among older
  adults in senior housing in Hartford, Connecticut,
  was supported by a "vertical" alliance of stakeholders that included the State Department of Health,
  the Visiting Nurse Health System, the local Area
  Agency on Aging, vaccine experts, and geriatricians
  from the departments of medicine and aging at the
  University of Connecticut. Members of the Strategic Alliance for Vaccination Prevention contributed
  information, gap funding for vaccines, vaccination
  clinics, and participation in educational campaigns.
  They were essential in the success of the study
  (J. Schensul et al., 2009).

- An innovative study to increase the use of female
  condoms engaged a community advisory board of
  diverse women, HIV advocates, and representatives of service agencies who were familiar with the
  needs of potential users and networked with them.
  These women met regularly as a volunteer group
  for several years to create new strategies for reach-
  ing different target populations with information
  about female condoms and their benefits. When the
  project was over, the CAB shifted its base of opera-

tion to another AIDS prevention organization and continued to implement the interventions it had developed throughout the duration of the study (Weeks et al., 2010).

- A collaborative international study of the role of alcohol in contributing to HIV in India linked the Institute for Community Research and the International Institute for Population Sciences, Mumbai. The study leaders, Schensul, Singh, Gupta, and Lahiri, formed an external technical advisory group (TAG) made up of the director of the National Institute for Medical Statistics (NIMS, Mumbai), directors of several international NGOs working on men's and women's issues, and other Indian scientists leading studies related to men and HIV. The TAG met annually in Mumbai and Goa to review the study design and study results, and to help plan publications (cf. Schensul, Singh, Gupta, Bryant, and Verma, 2010) and to endorse and support two international conferences on the topic.

These advisory bodies tend to be project specific. "Best processes" for their development and maintenance over the life of a project are outlined in an overview article by Newman et al. (2011). Other advisory models are more stable and permanent; some are formally constituted as 501C3s (nonprofits) organizations. They consist of major stakeholders in health, education, and culture that may or may not include members of local communities or local advocates or community spokespersons.

A model that does not fit either of these (project-specific or stable, incorporated community bodies) is the "living alliance" described by Radda and Schensul (2011). This model describes how alliances among organizations working on specific topics or with specific demographics (in this case older adults) can be forged to support a longer-term program. The alliance evolves as the program of research evolves, bringing in new members who are specifically focused on the issues currently being addressed with the study population while retaining close working connections with others. The challenge to researchers revolves around ensuring continued commitment and connections among all the alliance members. It is important to note that these community entities, including the voluntary associations mentioned below, can offer excellent community representation to university and other research center IRBs.

Local Voluntary Organizations (LVOs)

Local voluntary organizations consist of citizen's groups in which members volunteer their time. These organizations are extremely diverse; many can persist over a long period of time. Community or local voluntary organizations include parent-teacher organizations, organizations that advocate for children with disabilities or special needs, support groups of different kinds, block clubs and neighborhood associations that monitor neighborhood block safety and maintenance, community organizing groups, prevention commissions, and other kinds of community organizations. In other countries, voluntary associations may include block clubs (as in "informal" communities or *sentimientos humanos* in Lima, Nairobi, and Manila), religious study groups or *comunidades de base* in Central America, or women's groups (*mahila mandals*) in India. The composition and membership of these organizations is voluntary, though the chairs or leaders may be elected. Their viability varies over time because they depend on volunteers who may lose interest, move elsewhere, age out, or burn out. Voluntary organizations in a community can have an important influence on a research project and its outcomes, even if they are not formally affiliated with the project. Sensitive issues such as the introduction of harm reduction programs (e.g., needle exchange vans) into neighborhoods may draw the attention of local voluntary groups representing different positions on the harm reduction spectrum. Similarly, local voluntary groups (LVOs) may form over immigration issues, arguing for and against immigration policies or natural resource exploitation, in which different groups array for and against such activities. Good ethical research practice suggests that researchers should discuss any study, especially one addressing a controversial topic, with interested LVOs, and strive to obtain their support throughout the study's duration.

Challenges in Studying Social Movements

Over the past two decades ethnographers have paid increasing attention to the study of social movements (Edelman, 2001). The *Encyclopedia Britannica* defines social movements as: "A loosely organized but sustained campaign in support of a social goal, typically either the implementation or the prevention of a change in society's structure or values. Although social movements differ in size, they are all essentially collective. That is, they result from the more or less spontaneous coming together of people whose relationships are not defined by rules and procedures but who merely share a common outlook on society" (http://www.britannica.com/EBchecked/topic/551335/social-movement). Social movements are characterized by members' passionate, emotional, and usually well-argued commitment to a designated goal. The size of social movements ranges from modest to global. Since the advent of social media, social movements often involve making connections via face-to-face and Internet-based networks and social media. Many social scientists now study social movements, both global and local. While their study and analysis can be done "from a distance," understanding the internal complexity, diversity, divergent positionalities, and emergent reality of such movements calls for participant observation (Edelman, 2001; Magaña, 2010). Some social movement research activists such as Fals Borda would argue that it is impossible to engage in participant observation and other forms of data collection to characterize a social movement without being part of it. His ethical stance was to join with peasant movements in Colombia, using his ethnographic knowledge base to facilitate organizing and advocacy (Fals Borda, 1992). He referred to this process as participatory action research. Others, like Stephen Schensul in the 1970s, engaged with the civil rights movements of the time and embedded various forms of data collection and analysis for scientific and social advocacy purposes into the process of long-term community development (Schensul, 1973; Schensul and Schensul, 1978). Burdick supports this position (1995), noting that the study of social movements can contribute to good theory, and good practice.

Many members of current social movements do not really want to be involved in participatory action research approaches. These approaches intermesh observational engagement with research so as to identify issues and strategies that would facilitate community development and enhance social justice purposes. Given a frequently stated lack of enthusiasm about participatory research on the part of movement members, the question for a researcher who wishes to study such movements anyway should be, "What should be the proper ethical stance of a social movement 'observer' with respect to others in the movement?" The emotional nature of social movements (Goodwin et al., 2009) suggests that ethnographers studying and involved with them must have a correspondingly high level of passion for and commitment at least to the goals, if not the process, of the movement they are observing. This, of course, can generate the types of biases in observation that we have described earlier, which can be counteracted by good methodological procedures and constant self-reflection or reflexivity.

FORMAL CONTRACTUAL RESPONSIBILITIES

Formal responsibilities can derive from a number of sources. Below we discuss contractual obligations spelled out in the agreements between funding and sponsoring agencies, with governmental departments and institutional review boards, and with community bodies with whom researchers create partnerships.

Contracts with Funding Agencies

Funding agencies and researchers initiate mutual responsibilities when researchers respond to proposal requests which funding agencies develop to provide the framework for investigations they see as priorities. Some funding announcements may be in the form of formal contracts, in which the specifications are spelled out in considerable detail by the funders. Applicants must describe how they will carry out the specific research requested by the funder. Other funding announcements lay out program directions and priorities that are encouraged over time (e.g., governmental Requests for Proposals [RFPs] or Program Announcements). Still others specify guidelines but are one-time applications (e.g., governmental Requests for Applications [RFAs]). Foundations also specify grant program requirements and granting priorities. In general, all of these announcements—regardless of whether they are private or public—spell out the specific areas to which the research should be addressed or programs that should be studied, the time period for which funding will be provided, the categories of individuals or groups eligible to compete or apply for funds, and how much money will be available for specific projects. They may even specify preferred research design elements—such as the use of ethnography, surveys, analyses of secondary data sources, or Internet-based social media; or studies that require experimental designs to evaluate program or intervention impact. They may specify target populations or specific sites to be investigated, partnership organizations that must be included as participants, qualifications of the researcher(s), plans for the dissemination of results, and a variety of other stipulations. Often they suggest, directly or indirectly, that the proposed research must enhance or go beyond what has already been funded. Guidelines also can call for cooperative agreements with specific organizations or groups, meaning that the funders will join forces with the researchers and can have significant influence over study design and protocols.

Proposals that respond to such requests (RFPs or RFAs) must include detailed information as to how the researcher plans to conform to these stipulations. The proposals, if accepted, are in fact legal contracts between researcher and funding agencies which delineate many or most of the responsibilities that the researcher must carry out in the course of the study. The timelines and data planning matrices found in Book 1, chapter 6, of the *Ethnographer's Toolkit* are examples of how one researcher responded systematically to one set of RFP requirements. Though the level of detail required in different grant applications to different funding agencies varies considerably, and the degree of flexibility inherent in the type of funding opportunity also varies, all grants awarded are contracts to be fulfilled, or provided with explanations as to why they can or cannot be fulfilled, or both.

Contracts with Governmental and Nongovernmental Agencies

In this section, we discuss contracts. Contracts usually involve work required by governmental agencies, businesses, or nonprofits for work rendered. The work is specifically detailed in the contract, and contractors are bound to comply with those specifications. A contract with a governmental or nongovernmental agency or a nonprofit organization is much like a contract with a funding source. Like a funding source's contract, agency contracts establish a range of responsibilities that researchers are obliged to carry out. Normally, these contracts dictate the purposes of the research, the topics or questions which the researcher is to investigate, what kind of data will be collected, how and where data will be stored, and often, where and with whom the researcher will be expected to work. They also dictate how much time the researcher has to complete the task, how and for what purposes funds will be disbursed, and to whom and when results will be disseminated.

Contracts also specify how the people who are targets of research are to be treated from an ethical standpoint and how they will be protected from undue risks or breaches of privacy stemming from their participation in the study. Often, formal researcher responsibilities include descriptions of how research results will be presented to various audiences, including requirements that the researcher provide ongoing feedback to research participants or partners while the study is in progress. They also usually specify who has permission to use the data for future publications as well as who owns the data, how publications are to be authored, and how the project is to be represented in them.

With regard to contracts, researchers can face ethical questions as to whether or not they are willing to undertake what the contract requires. Are the contract and the work to be undertaken consistent with the researchers' values and ethical principles required by IRBs and discipline?

If they aren't, to what degree can the contract be modified or negotiated? How much does the researcher really know about the kind of work involved? That is, is the work the researcher is to undertake "compartmented," or part of a larger effort that the researcher knows nothing about and which could be contrary to the researcher's beliefs and values? If so, are these broader goals even knowable? In chapter 4 of Book 1 of the *Toolkit*, "An Overview of Research Design," we spelled out a variety of ways in which researchers design investigations, and in Books 3 and 4 we discuss the methods that researchers will specify in their contractual relationships. These designs, procedures, and protocols are, in effect, blueprints for the above-described contractual relationships and responsibilities. Because researchers usually constrain their designs within very broad guidelines, they actually have a good deal of latitude in defining the responsibilities that they will be called upon to carry out in field studies, which often are exploratory and descriptive. However, in contracts, experimental research or clinical trials using protocols that have to be approved in advance, researchers may not have much flexibility in the field. In fact, however, in most grant applications researchers must spell out in advance and in considerable detail what they will be doing, even in a formative or exploratory study.

Cross Reference: See Book 1, chapter 4

Cross Reference: See Books 3 and 4 for more information on these specifications

Institutional Review Boards and Institutional Ethics Committees

Formal responsibilities and obligations also exist in the rules imposed on researchers by governments and the codes of ethics they establish that govern the appropriate behavior of researchers vis-à-vis other human beings with whom they work and interact in research settings. In the United States, the Code of Federal Regulations (CFR), which codifies all administrative regulations promulgated by agencies of the federal government, spells out in detail requirements that the Department of Health and Human Services has established for the treatment of human research subjects. Researchers should recognize that they will need to obtain a variety of formal permissions before entering the field, and they are well advised to investigate what these permissions are, from whom they must be obtained, what they entail, how to apply, and how long the process will take. Students and experienced researchers alike, regardless of whether they are based at a university or in an alternative research setting, will need the approval of Institutional Review Boards (IRBs) or Institutional Ethics Committees (IECs).

Institutional review boards are routinely established by universities, research institutions, and medical facilities; often they are found in foundations, funding agencies, school districts and other social service agencies, and indigenous communities that have a commitment to take leadership in or participate in research. There also are independent community IRBs that can be contracted with to conduct IRB reviews for organizations that do not have their own IRBs. IRBs review proposals for human subjects and research ethics concerns, regardless of where the research is to be conducted. The Code of Federal Regulations originally required that every institution carrying out research with human subjects establish an Institutional Review Board or Institutional Ethics Committee that, in turn, was required to give ethical approval of all research done by researchers who received federal funds to carry out their research at that institution. The IRB was charged with guaranteeing that research conducted by researchers from institutions in the United States was ethical, regardless of whether the work was done within or outside of the country. IRB monitoring procedures then could assure that researchers adhered to the CFR's requirements. In practice, most IRBs review all research projects that involve human subjects, whether or not the individual investigators receive federal funds. This is because most institutions housing researchers do, in fact, receive some kinds of federal subsidy or grants, and any researcher working in or with such a federally subsidized institution falls under the jurisdiction of that institution's IRB. This does not mean, of course, that all research must be reviewed by the IRB. Some forms of qualitative research, such as folklore, for example, are not considered to be subject to IRB review because the data are collected at the cultural rather than the individual level.

Cross Reference:
See Book 2, chapter 2, for a more detailed discussion of these permissions and how to obtain them

Cross Reference:
See Book 2, chapter 3, "Preparing for Challenges in the Field," which addresses applications to IRBs and similar international bodies

Cross Reference:
Recall Examples 2.3 and 2.7 in this book

It is worth mentioning that universities and other grantee organizations may have multiple IRBs, especially if the institutions are very large and conduct large numbers of social, clinical, and laboratory studies. Usually in such cases, one IRB reviews clinical/laboratory and biomedical studies and another reviews social science applications. It thus is wise to determine in advance which IRB is best for a study. Further, universities collaborate with other organizations and vice versa. IRBs can agree to waive review to another IRB or to develop a shared form and format across partner organizations. Without such agreements, an application may have to be reviewed separately by each of the partner institutions, processes which have high potential for delaying the start of a study.

IRBs are required to establish and make public their own procedures for approving research studies. Obtaining approval usually involves submitting a written proposal to the IRB, which then will review and approve or disapprove the study. Normally, research—systematic collection of data from human individuals and groups with the intent to disseminate its results—cannot begin until IRB approval is obtained. In recent years, tribal communities and other indigenous/aboriginal peoples have established their own equivalent of Institutional Review Boards; thus, researchers based in universities often are required to seek approval from and satisfy the requirements of several such boards before they will be granted access to the population and can begin their research. In international settings, and in multisite research in general, all sites where research is to take place are required to conduct an ethics review of a proposed study on an annual basis.

Cross Reference: See Example 10.3 in Book 1 for an account of events that transpired when researchers were not aware of all the individual approvals needed

While individual IRBs may vary a bit in their procedures and the requirements they establish for researchers, overall, the set of responsibilities that they oversee for researchers all are related to conformity with the Belmont Principles. Their principal concern is that people who agree to participate in research not be subject to harm unless the harm is justified by the value of the research and unless participants fully understand what they are agreeing to do. Unlike medical researchers who may be introducing new medications, technologies, or surgical procedures to patients in clinical trials, ethnographers are less likely to engage in research that is potentially dangerous to the physical health of research participants. Nevertheless, close IRB scrutiny of ethnographic research, like any research involving human subjects, is justified on the basis of the potential harm that might be done to research participants if their confidentiality, anonymity, or privacy were breached. Relationships between people in the research site and ethnographers are close and frequent. Participants are known well by the researchers and participants know the researchers equally well. Consequently, there is higher probability that a researcher inadvertently might convey a confidential piece of information to another participant in the course of everyday conversation at the supermarket.

However, community ethnographies, especially those that are entirely qualitative and based on participant observation and in-depth interviews, often receive particularly stringent scrutiny by IRBs because many IRB members are physical scientists or medical researchers and do not understand the nature of community-based research or the work of qualitative ethnographers, and also because anonymity of participants in ethnographic research can be difficult to maintain. In addition, the social dynamics in which many ethnographic descriptions are embedded include descriptions of particular individuals whose identity cannot be completely disguised. Particular unique individuals, communities, or institutions sometimes cannot be described at all without providing some markers that would clearly disclose who or what was under investigation. However, ethnographers can guard against unwanted disclosure by grouping and de-identifying data from interviews or observations, changing features of biographies and sharing them in print selectively and with the permission of the individuals, and disguising the sites where research takes place. In some cases in which ethnographers fear that the data proffered to them could put participants at risk because they are undocumented or may be involved in illegal activities, researchers can obtain a government certificate of confidentiality that protects against requisition of study data in grand jury or other legal reviews. Another issue involves that of "secondary subjects." Mixed methods

Key point

ethnographers often are involved in network research that can lead to the collection of data on "secondary subjects"— people who do not know that they are being described to researchers by others. Network research also can inadvertently involve vulnerable populations such as homeless young teenagers who are not under the protection of the state, their guardians or parents, or other responsible adults. Network research methods, critical to identifying members of important target populations, are still unfamiliar to most IRB members. It can be difficult for ethnographers working on sensitive topics to explain the value of their work and defend the adequacy of procedures to assure security and confidentiality in ways that will assure IRB approval. Later in this chapter we will discuss ways that researchers can help IRB members better understand their particular approach to investigation.

WHEN IS IRB OR IEC APPROVAL NECESSARY?

As we indicated in chapter 1, any research on live human beings must be approved by the researcher's Institutional Review Board or Institutional Ethics Committee as well as any other relevant IRB-like bodies controlling access to the population in question. *So one of the first things investigators must decide is whether or not they are engaged in* research. *Second, they must decide if the focus of their study is* live human beings. These decisions may not be as obvious as they seem on the surface.

 Key point

Definition: Research is a systematic investigation that is designed to develop or contribute to generalizable knowledge and whose results will be disseminated to others. It generally includes not only investigations, but also development of research methods, assessments and tests, and evaluation

Research is a systematic investigation that is designed to develop or contribute to generalizable knowledge; its results are intended to be disseminated to others. It generally includes not only empirical investigation but also the development of research methods, assessments and tests, and evaluation. Key to the above definition is that the investigation be *systematic, produce knowledge* that can be generalized to or inform the condition of other human populations, and that it *be disseminated* to others, whether by publication or a public presentation. Journalism generally is not considered to be scholarly research, and therefore it does not fall under the scrutiny described below. To fall under IRB jurisdiction, then, investigations must be research, the intent of which is to disseminate knowledge, and must also be conducted systematically with and on *live human beings*. As we mentioned in chapter 1, however, a factor complicating contemporary research is that some human groups treat objects of reverence and features of the environment, including rivers and mountains, as living beings. How to approach these communities and their living beings is addressed when we discuss "Beyond Belmont" later in this book.

In order to obtain approval from an IRB or IEC, researchers must submit a proposal for research to their own institution's IRB, or another institution's IRB that handles such approvals if their institution does not have an IRB. In addition, all institutions and community groups involved in the study must review the proposal or waive the review to another IRB in writing.

IRB proposals differ somewhat from research proposals developed for the conduct of the investigation or submission to a funding agency. Most IRBs are not very concerned with the theoretical or conceptual framework of the research, or even a literature review that reveals if anyone else has done similar studies, unless the fact that other people have used the same procedures without harming subjects forms the researcher's justification for a particular approach. Appendix A presents an example of the human subjects section of a proposal to an IRB.

ISSUES OF PARTICULAR CONCERN TO IRBS AND IECS

What IRBs really want to know is how researchers will treat participants. They check to assure that researchers follow the mandates for beneficence, justice, and respect for persons spelled out in the Belmont Report and other similar declarations of the rights of human subjects of research. Below are the five principal issues with which IRBs generally are concerned:

- Protection of human subjects of research against undue and unnecessary *risks* from participation in research
- Assurance that researchers have engaged in *equitable recruitment* for every research participant,

have made sure that participants have given *voluntary consent* to their participation, *understand what the researcher plans to do* with them and with the research data, and *know they can withdraw* from the study without penalty

- assurance that the *privacy of the research subject* will be protected
- a guarantee that participants in research know *who is doing the research* and how to contact them if they have questions or problems with their participation in the study
- guarantees that special care be taken when research is carried out on or among *vulnerable populations*

IRBs that review grants involving community-based research also want to know how the researchers will interact with the larger community, whether the research may place any organization or group in jeopardy in that community, and whether the study will provide feedback to the study community when the results are in.

Of special interest to IRBs are studies by researchers who engage in participant observation or interviewing in natural settings with active drug users, gang members, social movement activists, prisoners, homeless children living in difficult residential circumstances, or studies that are conducted in locations such as war zones that expose them and their research participants to the chance of physical risk.

If research is to be conducted with vulnerable people in settings that could be dangerous physically or psychologically for either the researchers or the people who are part of the study, the IRB will want to know what protections are in place to safeguard both.

LEVELS OF REVIEW

In the previous chapter we described the categories of vulnerable subjects of research, and as well, how the sensitivity of the research topic can induce vulnerability in specific groups. Deciding how vulnerable the population is is one of the first tasks researchers seeking IRB approval must tackle. Once researchers determine the degree of vulnerability of the participants, the sensitivity of topics to be addressed, and the risks posed by their data collection methods, they must choose the level of review that the proposal should undergo by the IRB. Levels of review involve rigor and comprehensiveness; they are linked to the risks the study might pose to study populations. IRBs are not required to agree with the researchers' characterization of a study; once they have done a preliminary review of the abstract, an IRB can decide that a study either needs more or less scrutiny than that asked for by the researcher.

There are three levels of review: exempt, expedited, and regular review. Each corresponds to a degree of scrutiny by the IRB. *Exempt review does not mean "exempt from review."* *All* research with human subjects must be reviewed by an IRB; the term *exempt* only means that this category of research is subject to the least amount of scrutiny because it poses the least risk to participants. *Exempt review is never appropriate for interviews/surveys with children.* Exempt review *is* the category appropriate for research involving the following:

Key point

Key point

Key point

- Interviews or surveys where:
  - Subjects' answers are anonymous, or
  - There is no risk to subjects' reputation, employ-ability, insurability, etc.
- Educational tests where
  - Subjects' answers are anonymous, or
  - There is no risk to subjects' reputation, employ-ability, insurability, etc.

Studies involving tests with children **never** *can be exempt.*

Key point

- Observation of normal educational practice or pro-cedures
  - For example, teacher training, evaluation of stan-dard curriculum where the research does not involve interviews, surveys, audiovisual documen-tation, or educational testing of children
- Analysis of existing data where
  - The data are publicly available, or
  - The data are recorded in a manner that the subjects cannot be identified, directly or through codes

Even research using what ordinarily might be considered very sensitive data, such as DNA information, could be exempt if there is no way to link the DNA information to specific individuals or the groups to which they belong. However, it is important for researchers to check with their own IRB regarding how they treat exempt reviews; not all IRBs adhere to the same definitions for exempt status. For example, some IRBs might require expedited—somewhat more rigorous—review for a study on a sensitive topic such as sexuality, even if it is anonymous. They also may require a full panel review—the most rigorous—for anonymous data collection with minors (under the age of eighteen or twenty-one).

Key point *Expedited review involves research that is somewhat more sensitive, risky, or intrusive.* It often is handled by IRB staff in consultation with members of the IRB, or with only the chair(s). It usually is a less lengthy procedure than regular review. Expedited review is appropriate for:

Definition: Minimal risk refers to risks no greater than those encountered by participants in normal everyday life

- Research that presents no more than **minimal risk** to the subjects—or no greater risk than people would experience in everyday life—and
- Research on individual or group characteristics or behavior (including, but not limited to, research on perception, cognition, motivation, identity, language, communication, cultural beliefs or practices, and social behavior) or research employing survey, interview, oral history, focus group, program evaluation, human factors evaluation, or quality assurance methodologies, and
- Research that does not involve eliciting, or the risk of disclosing, personal, identifiable information

Most research involving children will require at least expedited review. Even if it does not involve vulnerable subjects or sensitive topics, research using audio and videotapes is subject to expedited review because it reveals the identity of participants unless special care is taken to disguise identity. As noted previously, some IRBs may consider any research on a sensitive topic and/or with a vulnerable population to require a full rather than an expedited review.

Full panel "regular" review involves an examination of the proposal by the full IRB panel of faculty, nonscientists, and members of the community, convened in a regular meeting. Such a level of review is reserved for

Key point

- any proposal not meeting exempt/expedited criteria
- any proposal the expedited/exempt reviewer sends to the full panel

Typically, regular review is required for any study investigating vulnerable subjects or illegal activities, most research using videorecordings, or addressing extremely sensitive topics, such as stigmatized illness. It also is required for any study involving significant risk to participants. Undergoing regular review does not mean that studies that might be risky to participants cannot be carried out. It only means that special care must be taken to assure that all participants fully understand what they are agreeing to do, what the risks of agreement are, and have voluntarily consented to become subjects or participants.

COMPONENTS OF AN IRB PROPOSAL

While the proposals that researchers submit for approval to IRBs generally do not have to be as lengthy as those provided for other kinds of agencies, they must address the Belmont issues by providing detailed descriptions of at least the following:

COMPONENTS OF AN APPLICATION FOR IRB PROPOSAL

- The *purpose or aims* of the study
- The *population* to be studied, including population characteristics, selection criteria, sampling procedures, the number of subjects to be studied, and recruitment procedures
- The *data collection methods, and if it is an intervention, what the researcher plans to do with the*

research participants, where, and for how long. For example, the researcher might say that he or she planned to observe children in their regular classrooms and on the playgrounds for two weeks, to audiotape interviews with them, to collect the results of their standardized tests, and to ask them to role-play an imaginary interaction with their teacher that the researcher would videotape. This section includes lists of questions or topics to be asked about in interviews.

■ Most IRBs require researchers to provide *copies of any questionnaires, tests, surveys, observational protocols, or other instruments* that are to be used. Researchers should check with their IRB's requirements to make sure that they include all of the necessary documents.

■ *Copies of letters from institutions,* schools, hospitals, clinics, youth centers, or any other organization where potential subjects are to be located usually are required. Such letters indicate that the organization supports the researcher's project and agrees to provide access to the site and to the target population. This is important for any field study, but it can be especially important in the case of student research; students fail sometimes to make sure that they actually can carry out a study where they propose to work!

■ The *qualifications of the researchers* to carry out the research as well as *how to contact them* by telephone, mail, fax, email, or other means

■ *How the researcher plans to protect the identity or privacy* of the people who participate in the study and what will be done with the data when the study is complete

■ The *risks and benefits* of participation in the project

■ The researcher's plans to *ameliorate any adverse effects* experienced by participants, if risks are present

■ Copies of *consent (for adults) and assent (for minors) letters* to be sent to research participants, explaining the research study and asking for the consent of individuals whom the researcher wanted to study

All of the information listed above must be considered so that researchers can determine which level of review to ask for and the IRB can make sure that proper protective procedures are followed.

Contents of consent forms must include much of the same information that the proposal itself contains, though in abbreviated form and in language accessible to the potential participants. Contents of consent forms or letters must include:

■ A narrative detailing what will happen to participants
■ A description of all data collection procedures that participants can expect to encounter
■ Description of the topics to be covered, as well as sample questions to be asked, including examples of the most sensitive ones
■ Details about where the research will take place
■ How long the data collection procedures will take
■ Assurance that participants can refuse to answer questions or can end participation if they wish without any consequences to them
■ How they will be compensated for their time
■ A statement of risks and benefits
■ A statement of how risks will be addressed and managed
■ A description of provisions for protection of privacy of subjects (confidentiality or anonymity)
■ A description of provisions for disposal of data once the research is completed
■ Identification of the researcher and his/her sponsors, as well as contact information for the researcher and his/her supervisor

THE POWER OF INSTITUTIONAL REVIEW BOARDS
AND INSTITUTIONAL ETHICS COMMITTEES

Failure to comply with IRBs can have serious consequences for both individual researchers and their institutions. Failure to obtain IRB approval before initiating a research project, to comply with IRB rules and regulations once a project has been approved, or even failure to maintain an auditable trail of actions taken by an IRB and the researchers it supervises can bring drastic consequences. IRBs can abrogate a researcher's permission to conduct research or recommend withdrawal of degrees or funding awarded to researchers who did not follow HRC procedures. Researchers can experience loss of respect in the scholarly community, especially if their misconduct leads to federal sanctions that delay or otherwise impede the work of others. They can even be sued in court by participants who have been harmed by research participation. In the worst-case scenario, they may lose their jobs, even if they are tenured faculty.

Institutions can be punished as well. Federal monitors do audit the research records of institutions, and if they find serious violations, they can impose a variety of sanctions. IRBs can halt a single research project completely until the violation is addressed satisfactorily, as in Example 3.4.

EXAMPLE 3.4

FAILURE TO MAINTAIN RECORDS

University researchers engaged in a longitudinal study of twins were startled to find that an audit by the Office of Human Research Protection (OHRP) cited them for failure to keep adequate records of participant consent. From a study of 250 twin pairs, consent forms could not be found for thirty-two individuals. This meant that the researchers either had to find the missing consent forms, or find the participants and reconsent them before they could continue with the study. The only other alternative was to eliminate from the study those individuals without consent forms, and since each individual was part of a pair, that option would have meant deleting data from sixty-four people, or more than a fifth of the participants, from the study. Careful searches of the researchers' data unearthed some of the missing forms, as they had been misfiled. But some simply were missing or were inadequate because consent had been obtained verbally over the phone, rather than signed in person as required. The

researchers complied with the OHRP by finding as many of the people as they could and obtaining their consent again, and deleting the others from their study.

IRBs also can

- shut down all research activities at an institution until the violation has been addressed satisfactorily
- shut down all current research activities at an institution and order the re-review and recertification of all projects by the current IRB
- shut down all current research activities at an institution, disband its IRB, select and retrain an entirely new panel of IRB members, and then re-review and recertify all research projects

The latter penalties are, of course, very time consuming and can effectively put an institution and all of its researchers out of the research business for more than a year.

Many such problems are little more than matters of poor record keeping, but they are taken very seriously by the OHRP notwithstanding. Some are revealed when an "adverse event" occurs and a research participant is harmed. Some notorious cases have been those in which gene transplant experiments were tried as cures for serious illness and participants who were not fully aware of the risks that they were running were injured or died (Kimmelman, 2008), either because the researchers knew and did not tell them of risks, or because the researchers themselves did not know all the risks, or because the participants incurred serious risks in the hope that they would be cured even though they had been told of the small likelihood of that happening.

More problematic are those cases where researchers decide that getting IRB approval is a hassle they do not want to bother with and deliberately circumvent the process, or when they deliberately violate explicit or implicit government rules about what they may or may not study and what information they may disseminate. A notorious case was the research of Steven Mosher, a graduate student from Stanford University.

EXAMPLE 3.5

DELIBERATE VIOLATION OF FORMAL RULES REGARDING RESEARCH CONDUCT

For his doctoral dissertation, Steven Mosher proposed to study methods of birth control and contraception in the People's Republic of China during the late 1960s. Both Stanford University's Department of Anthropology and the government of China agreed to his project, but the Chinese government stipulated that he was not to talk about, collect data on, or explore the use of birth control techniques to select the sex of children. Most especially, Mosher was not to investigate possible instances of abortion and female infanticide. Mosher was, however, approached by American groups who were strongly opposed to the practice of abortion, and they encouraged him to expose what they believed to be the widespread occurrence of abortion-caused female infanticide in China. Mosher agreed to investigate infanticide and abortion, in violation of his agreements with Stanford and the Chinese government. Mosher also put his own informants at great risk of exposure to governmental agents enforcing population controls by publishing identifiable photographs of their faces in the Taiwan press. He did not, however, inform them of how risky being identifiable might be. His undiplomatic act of publication in Taiwan also embarrassed the Chinese government. Although a commercial press published his findings, Stanford University refused to approve his dissertation research because of the risks he created for informants, and he did not receive his PhD. His noncompliance with governmental agreements on what he could and could not study interfered with the relationship that Stanford University had with the US government and with the work of other researchers hoping to work in China.

Research Conducted Outside the United States or by Noncitizen Researchers

Constraints on or responsibilities for researcher behavior imposed by the political culture or governmental edicts at the research site often are taken for granted when researchers do their work within their own country. Most researchers in the United States, for example, are aware of guidelines for the ethical treatment of human participants in research studies to which all investigators are held responsible. However, ignorance of the rules regarding the protection of human research participants is no excuse for not following them. Researchers may, for example, be unaware of the guidelines for treatment of certain types of human subjects. The US Office for Protection from Research Risks (OPRR) requires that special protections be established for interviewing prisoners and other persons in custodial institutions, including anyone under the jurisdiction of the justice system. This can include people who are on judicial probation or parole or those engaged in punitive alternatives to incarceration. Without reading the guidelines, researchers might fail to put into place those special protections, thereby unwittingly exposing persons in custody to unwarranted risk. ***Doing research outside the United States does not exempt researchers from compliance with IRB requirements.*** Not only must such researchers comply with all the dictates of the Office of Human Research Protection in the United States, they also must seek out and comply with standards prevailing in the country where the research is to take place—even though in many countries, the rules and regulations for conduct of research are not clearly codified. This means that researchers must be particularly careful to engage in preliminary planning and fieldwork to find out what obstacles they might encounter before they embark on a project outside of their home country or with a self-governing tribal community. In particular, they must determine how they can ensure that the requirements of their own country's government for human subjects protection can be addressed in the country in which they are doing their research, and take care to describe these procedures in their proposal. In another case described in Example 10.2 in Book 1 of the *Ethnographer's Toolkit*, researcher assurances to a tribal group in the United States regarding the privacy of their DNA data were abrogated by other researchers who gained access to the information through a laboratory. This act compromised the entire study as well as the integrity of the original researchers and the trust of the tribal group. Researchers must be aware of such issues, keeping in mind that at times the requirements of their own IRBs may violate ethical considerations in the country in which they are doing their study (a case in point is requiring signatures on consent forms when people cannot write and local researchers offer them alternatives to signing their consent). Further, they must also keep in mind that their IRBs very

Key point

Cross Reference: Examples 2.3, 2.5, and 2.7 in this book detail three cases, in Africa, Guatemala, and Canada, in which researchers carried out studies that would have been forbidden in the United States

likely cannot monitor their study to see whether they have met the ethical conditions set for them, and act ethically, notwithstanding.

Institutional review boards are responsible not only for reviewing and approving new projects but also for conducting annual reviews of ongoing projects. Annual reviews require researchers to report:

- how many subjects have been recruited and studied
- whether the research procedures have changed
- whether the research has had any adverse effects on participants
- how adverse effects—if any—have been treated and what researchers have done to assure that such effects do not occur again
- what results, if any, have been obtained

 Key point

Adverse event (AE) reports normally are brief but important. *IRBs have the power to require changes in research projects to make them less risky for subjects, to disapprove new projects, to stop ongoing projects, or to prevent researchers from publishing or using data from completed projects if researchers have not obtained appropriate approvals and conformed to the general guidelines concerning ethical treatment of research participants and the specific terms of their own approval agreement negotiated with the IRB.*

IRBs also are authorized to approve or disapprove research taking place outside the United States, if the researchers are US citizens or legal residents, or even if they are noncitizens working with or under the auspices of institutions located in the United States, or non-US citizens doing research in their own countries but sponsored by a US institution.

COPING WITH MULTIPLE IRBS

In joint or collaborative projects, IRBs in each of the partner institutions will usually want to review the study independently. Some IRBs or IECs are more rigorous and detailed than others, especially those in medical schools

or clinical settings that typically review clinical trial or treatment protocols. IRBs can disagree as to the level of review needed for a study, a circumstance that Dr. Janette Klingner discovered in a project jointly sponsored by the University of Colorado, the University of Florida, and the University of Kentucky.

EXAMPLE 3.6

WHEN IRBS DISAGREE

Klingner's three-state study involved observations of regular elementary school reading classes. As the principal investigator, Klingner argued that the research should be reviewed in the exempt category, as it involved regular classroom activities, called for no intervention, and elicited no data directly from children. Her IRB in Colorado and the one in Kentucky agreed, but the Florida IRB felt that because the research involved children, it should receive an expedited review. The problem was that exempt review requires no parental consent forms, and expedited review does. Obtaining all the consent forms would have been an enormous task and certainly would delay the study considerably. Nonetheless, Klingner's study was delayed for months while a resolution was negotiated.

Cross-institutional collaborations generally involve contracts or formal permission to work together, to collect data in the institution, and to comply with institutional requirements. Other formal permissions may be required. Many Native American or First Nations groups in the United States and Canada have their own procedures for reviewing studies, establishing formal collaboration and cost sharing, and conducting ethical review.

International work may require a substantive review of a study at the national level, and as well, permission granted through the applicant country's embassy before a project will be funded. Obtaining these formal permissions requires good contacts and relationships both at the governmental and community level, and can take a long time to complete. All of these reviews and negotiations take time, often months, before they are completed, especially if more than one review committee is involved. Researchers should start early to identify the approvals needed, build their relationships, obtain the necessary approvals, and prepare and submit their studies for ethics review by the proper bodies. It is not unheard of for a researcher to be forced to wait beyond the period for which a study was funded to obtain all approvals required for initiation of the project. This situation should be avoided at all costs. Discussions with other researchers who have worked in a setting or country as well as project funders while in the development phase of a project can help to avoid such problems.

Researcher Responsibilities for Educating IRB Members

Ethnographers and other qualitative researchers often find that the members of their IRBs are unfamiliar with and distrustful of standard ethnographic procedures—in particular, the exploratory and often uncontrollable nature of the investigations (see Tolich and Fitzgerald, 2006). The guidelines that follow are designed to help researchers educate IRB members on different modalities of research that, though different from experimental and quasi-experimental designs, are no less rigorous or capable of adhering to ethical mandates. One of the most helpful strategies can be to recruit social scientists, anthropologists, and ethnographers as members of the IRB—or volunteer for service oneself. The presence of a resident ethnographer on the IRB can help translate what ethnographers do for the uninitiated. Barring that, researchers need to heed the following issues with which IRB members often struggle:

- Ethnographic research often seems vague to researchers accustomed to experimental designs.
  - Solution:
    - Educate the IRB. Explain the history of the design proposed and its appropriateness for the project to be undertaken.
    - Learn to describe the study procedures more concretely.
- Researchers may have difficulty specifying to the IRB exactly what the research problem is, as problem identification itself often is, in fact, the focus of

the study. Further, research problems may evolve or change as the research unfolds.

- Solution:
  - Describe the issue under consideration as carefully as possible.
  - Describe the observable symptoms of the unknown problem.
  - Present a study model.
  - Submit change requests as needed to conform to evolving questions.

Cross Reference: Book 2, chapter 3, on Formative Modeling

- Since ethnographic research often is exploratory or descriptive, researchers may not be able to provide the IRB with formalized instrumentation.
  - Solution: Explain the purpose of the research as carefully as possible to the IRB, indicating the originality of the approach or topic and the appropriateness of exploratory research to the project.
  - Solution: Propose the study as a pilot project, if appropriate.
  - Solution: Be as specific as possible and provide whatever information is available. For example,
    - List the topics to be addressed in informal interviews.
    - List the potential places/sites to be observed.
    - List the potential phenomena to be observed.
    - Provide preliminary observational guides, topics for interviews, and themes to be explored.
    - Indicate that additional instruments will be submitted for review when they are developed.
- Researchers may not be able to specify to the IRB exactly every single population or group that might be included because the population vectors may be unknown.
  - Solution: Be as specific as possible.
    - Specify the range of population types to be studied, with informed consent drafts for each.
    - Propose the use of network or snowball sampling if one of the purposes of the study is to identify new populations.
    - Use a change request if the original population descriptions prove inaccurate or inadequate.

- IRBs may not know exactly what "ethnographic" or "qualitative" methods are, or how long they take to carry out.
  - Solution:
    - ○ Explain methods in detail.
    - ○ Create a data matrix that displays who is being treated to what method, for how long, where, and why. This is especially useful in the human subjects sections of grants.
- Methods initially proposed to and approved by the IRB often are found to be inadequate for unanticipated new questions or circumstances.
  - Solution:
    - ○ Use a change request, asking to add a data collection strategy.
    - ○ Provide a rationale, describe the population and strategies for selection and recruitment, and append appropriate consent forms and instruments (LeCompte, 2004; Tolich and Fitzgerald, 2006).

Cross Reference:
See chapter 6 in Book 1 for examples of such matrices

SUMMARY

In this chapter, we have described the types of semiformal and formal ethical responsibilities that researchers face in the field. We also have delineated in broad strokes the requirements for constructing proposals for approval from IRBs and procedures that researchers must follow to obtain them. In the chapter that follows, we examine how the personal characteristics and roles that researchers play shape informal or everyday ethics.

4 ━●━●━●━●━

INFORMAL ETHICS: THE IMPLICATIONS OF RESEARCHER ROLES AND CHARACTERISTICS

Introdu̶

The Embedded
Contexts and
Multiple Roles
of Ethnographic
Work

Being a Learner

Creating a Field
Identity

Coping with
Relationships
in the Field:
Personal
Characteristics,
Asymmetrical
Relationships,
and Positionality

Personal
Friendships
in the Field

Summary

INTRODUCTION

Researchers may be unaware of quite real informal ethical guidelines they follow unconsciously and scrupulously because such guidelines constitute ordinary good practice within their own society. They include such things as not lying to, or stealing from, research participants, not falsifying data to make them conform to the researcher's own expectations or theories, and being sure to have plans for disseminating data. University researchers, for example, generally have research dissemination plans because publication or presentation of research results is required for career advancement. Similarly, medical researchers do not use contaminated materials in their laboratories or procedures, not only because they might contaminate research results but also because they might be harmful to participants. However, ethical practices in the field involve more than avoiding STDs—Sex, Theft, and Deceit. As we have stated repeatedly, ethnography is a peculiarly human endeavor. Access to the research setting, the key informants, and other participants who constitute the focus of the study—all depend on the appearance, presentation of

113

self, social skills, and specific behaviors of the ethnographer in the research setting. Thus, it is critically important for prospective researchers to learn ahead of time, or discover early on, the boundaries of acceptable behavior and life-style in the communities they wish to investigate. Doing so will ensure that they navigate those boundaries effectively and maintain high comfort levels for both themselves and study participants. Knowing the cultural rules in the study community will permit them to avoid depending only on their own notions of good manners and informal ethics and norms and to use those that are considered appropriate and acceptable in the community under study.

Researchers are advised to review Books 1 through 4 of the *Ethnographer's Toolkit* that describe how ethnographers learn about local culture in the course of the human interactions that facilitate amassing their principal database: direct observation, face-to-face-interviewing and elicitation, audiovisual recording, and mapping the networks, times, and places in which human interactions occur. Chapter 3 of Book 1, chapter 2 of Book 2, and chapters 2 and 3 of Book 3 all address important features of researcher positionality and power vis-à-vis participants in the research site. These affect how researchers accomplish a successful entry into the field and the ways in which their personal characteristics and background experiences affect their reception by, and the way they themselves relate to, participants, once they begin their research. The reader is advised to review the above-mentioned chapters concerning researcher characteristics first; in this chapter, we are more concerned about the ethical implications of the roles that ethnographers acquire in the field, including those that are initially self-selected, then ascribed to them in the community because of their personal characteristics and affiliations, and ultimately developed over time in the course of fieldwork. We first define what roles and multiple role enactments are. We then present a schema for understanding the complexity of these roles in figure 4.1.

In everyday life, each of us plays multiple roles. Each of these roles develops a "self" peculiar to it and framed by the responsibilities and privileges, expectations, and obligations defining that role. A woman can simultaneously be a

mother, daughter, sibling, lover or wife (or both), friend, employer/employee, student, club member, churchgoer, volunteer, recipient of public assistance, former refugee, or current immigrant. Thus, each individual inhabits multiple roles, which in turn create multiple "identities," each of which has compelling obligations, somewhat specialized functions, rights and duties, and limitations.

The influence of role obligations, responsibilities, and rights can be so compelling that people may react to a person more in terms of their role than in terms of the individual's special personal characteristics. In a sense, people actually "see" roles as clearly as they see the people who inhabit those roles. Thus, when teachers say, "We need a new English teacher, and Mr. Smith (the principal) has to hire one!" they are referring to the job responsibilities inherent in the role of principal. And when children say, "My mother has to fix our dinner every evening," they are referring to what all mothers—as mothers—are expected to do for children. However, these roles sometimes can overlap. If teachers say, "I don't care if Mr. Smith is a colleague; he's still the superintendent of schools!" they mean that Mr. Smith's authority over them—in his role as superintendent—mitigates his identity as colleague and causes him to act in an authoritative way which creates social distance between them and him in social interaction. Similarly, teenagers may assert, "My mom is my best friend!" while at the same time hiding from Mom evidence of behavior of which they know that she—in her role as parent—would disapprove.

In everyday life—and particularly in Western-European and North American life—these discrete roles or selves each carry out their functions more or less within the confines of their particular and appropriate situation. People tend to compartmentalize their many roles, restricting what they communicate to others to messages and behaviors appropriate for the situation. For example, some people may find it difficult while at work to communicate intimate details about their private lives as spouses, parents, or hobbyists. Others become skilled at identifying *when* they can cross boundaries in "normal" culturally specific situations.

Ethnographic research imposes many varied identities and special role relationships on researchers during the course of their investigations. Ethnographers not only occupy the normal roles people play in everyday life, but they also may acquire additional roles that are specific to their activities in the field. Some of these roles derive from the relationship they form in the research site; other roles derive from their personality and appearance. Still others may be required or expected of them in carrying out "participant observation," such as "taking minutes" at meetings or being the person who always has a pencil and a pad of paper when such are needed. In fact, learning the roles required to act like a member of the community studied as well as those related to research is one of the hallmarks of a good ethnographer.

Key to knowing how to carry out the multiple role responsibilities ethnographers have is understanding the impact of their personas on the research process—and the impact of the research process itself on the researchers' personas. The researcher's *person (*or *persona)* is made up of three components: the first is what we refer to as the "**role** [or *roles*] of the researcher." A role is a position within a social structure, defined both by the obligations and responsibilities assigned by the culture to that position and the expectations that other people have for how the person occupying that role should think and behave. The second component consists of the actual personal, demographic, and physical characteristics that researchers possess, regardless of their role. These may result in variation in how different individual researchers inhabit and act out their roles.

> **Definition:** A role is a position within a social structure, defined both by the obligations and responsibilities assigned by the culture to that position and the expectations that other people have for how the person occupying that role should think and behave

THE EMBEDDED CONTEXTS AND MULTIPLE ROLES OF ETHNOGRAPHIC WORK

The third component of a role is the context in which interaction takes place; it frames how researcher roles and personality intersect with the environment to produce behaviors that are perceived and interpreted by participants, and then constantly adjusted as researchers and participants observe, interact with, analyze, and evaluate each other. To clarify these multiple and overlapping responsibilities, we present figure 4.1, in which we visualize the complex and

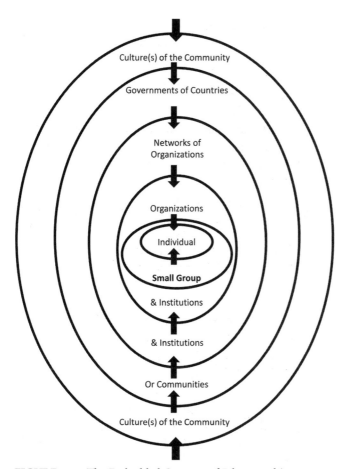

FIGURE 4.1   The Embedded Contexts of Ethnographic Research. The term *embedded contexts* is from Cole and Griffin (1987); we have adapted their scheme for more general use.

multifaceted settings of ethnographic work as a series of concentric circles in which smaller contexts are embedded within larger ones. Each of these concentric circles provides the social context for a variety of social responsibilities and obligations required of ethnographic researchers. The context constitutes the third component, framing and shaping how the researcher is viewed and behaves and what the researcher role is and is perceived to be.

As figure 4.1 indicates, the contexts in which ethnographers operate include:

- the *government of the country or community* in which the project is located and its associated regulations for and constraints on research
- the *network of institutions* collaborating in the design and execution of the project
- the *institutions or organizations*, formal and informal, operating in or constituting the research site
- the *culture of the community* in which the research project is located and the variety of ways that it is expressed in the diversity of beliefs and behaviors extant in the community
- *small groups* that are the structural components of the site, including classrooms, work groups, friendship cliques, and social networks
- *individual research participants* and their individual cultural articulations

Cross Reference: These are described in considerable detail in Book 2

Each of these contexts will have their own formal and sometimes informal ethical requirements.

Within the contexts, researchers are responsible for leadership in the following:

Cross Reference: See Book 5 for an extended discussion of analysis and interpretation

- Forming partnerships, alliances, and relationships
- Initiating, arranging, and carrying out the ongoing business of data collection and analysis during the course of the research project
- Analyzing and interpreting the data, which means determining how the masses of raw questionnaires, observational notes, interviews, tests, maps, and a variety of other raw data sources make sense, when taken as a whole, sometimes with study participants
- Helping people in the research site make sense of data in ways that not only help researchers understand them better but also result in research presentations that are meaningful to the group that requested the study in the first place

All of these responsibilities have ethical implications. These include:

- Taking responsibility for making and maintaining relationships with research participants, members of the research team, and staff for partnership organizations
- Solving personal problems between and among research team members, research participants, members of the research team and partnership organizations, and community institutions whose activities impinge upon the research project
- Identifying and avoiding, or extricating themselves and members of the research team from, risky or dangerous situations
- Figuring out how to give feedback—and how much to give—to various players in such a way as to maintain both candor and civil relationships
- Determining what kinds of feedback will be most helpful in furthering the objectives of partnership institutions and research participants
- Developing ways to say goodbye or for attenuating the relationships, if researchers are leaving the study setting, as well as changing/reducing interdependencies created in the field once the project is over (LeCompte, 2008b)
- Maintaining necessary contacts at a distance if and when the researcher has left the field
- Serving as a spokesperson for or commentator on the events that transpired in the field once reports have been finished and the researchers' contractual obligations have ended and bringing partners into the process as appropriate
- Bringing members of the study community into dialogue with others in the dissemination and discussion of study results and their use

In the pages that follow, we discuss

- The role of the learner
- Creating a field identity and/or role(s)
- Handling power asymmetries between roles

- Addressing conflicts of values and perceptions between researcher roles and actions and those expected in the research community
- Determining how the multiple roles of the researcher can facilitate the conduct of ethnographic research
- Addressing issues involved in sponsorships, associations, affiliations, and friendship

BEING A LEARNER

The first and wisest role choice for ethnographers to take, once having established a relationship with people in the population under study, is that of a learner or student. This role is important regardless of the start point of the research; that is, whether it involves exploratory observation, ongoing ethnography, or a planned intervention. The role of learner can be enhanced if the researcher is perceived to be a good collaborator, colleague, and coresearcher genuinely concerned about how things work in the study community. Such a stance permits the ethnographer to practice a kind of naïveté about the practices and beliefs of the study population, and it also legitimates why the ethnographer might be engaging in so much observation or asking so many questions. *Ethnographers must be learners, and as such, they must position themselves so that people in the community feel comfortable teaching them.* In order to be viewed as "in need of being taught," ethnographers find ways to engage legitimately in the primary strategies humans use for learning: watching, listening to people, and asking questions of those who are practiced in what is to be learned. The anthropologist Jacquetta Burnett (1974) advised novice ethnographers to learn about a community the way children learn: with careful observation, endless curiosity, lots of questions, and an open mind. While ethnographers clearly aren't children and should avoid resembling ignoramuses or dolts, they also should avoid seeming to know too much about the topic about which they are asking questions. "Know-it-alls" can't learn and certainly aren't in need of being taught! That said, it often is the case that community members or organizational partners want to know *why* the ethnographer wants to learn. It is at this

 **Key point**

point that ethnographers must have an approach that convinces study participants that learning leads to some form of benefit, not only for the researcher but for the community or study setting as well.

A well-known anthropologist, James Spradley (1979), argued that key informants or local experts will not tell much to ethnographers who already seem quite familiar with the life, activities, beliefs, or tasks of the community under study because these experts do not want to embarrass themselves by telling ethnographers something they already know. However, Spradley also notes that it is particularly difficult to maintain such a stance in cases where ethnographers are, in fact, studying what they already know. Such cases are fairly typical for applied ethnographers, who can be called upon to study the institutions or programs for which they work or in which they have previous similar experience. It is quite easy to forget to ask detailed questions about or take copious notes on activities whose routines or history one already knows. Doing so, however, ignores the fact that what one person does routinely may be done, explained, or conceptualized differently by others or in other settings.

EXAMPLE 4.1

HOW BEING PERCEIVED AS SOMEONE "IN THE KNOW" IMPEDES DATA COLLECTION

A graduate student in a university's business school was interested in studying innovative software uses among several telecommunications companies. He began by interviewing the directors of research and development for each of the companies, but he found that it was difficult to get them to spell out in detail the different stages in their product development and training programs. "I don't need to tell you about *this!*" was a common statement made by the interviewees. "You've been studying this in your classes for years!" However, the student's investigations demonstrated to him that the practices of most companies differed considerably from what had been taught as best practices in the business school; they also differed considerably among themselves. The novice researcher had to develop techniques that reassured interviewees that though he had, in fact, studied *something* about such practices, he really was interested in the particular way *they* defined problems or carried out their work which might be different from textbook examples or principles.

Leaving out important bits of description because researchers and informants both know that each knows about the issues under consideration can create gaps in reporting, gaps that need to be filled because people who read the reports of a study or who use the data may have considerably less shared knowledge of such practices, beliefs, or history than the original informants and ethnographers. Failure to document fully all aspects of the research site and population may result in significant and dangerous lapses in the investigative record which could be misleading to users. By the same token, hearing again and again the same story or one that differs only slightly, and by using mixed methods approaches to observe and measure how it manifests in different forms, ethnographers can be confident that they actually have collected an authentic, or valid, story, complete with all its nuances of difference. Thus, the ethnographer's task in any situation is to reassure informants continually that researchers really *are* learners, interested in minute details of history, behavior, and belief, and that they really have *not* already heard what is being recounted, or even if they have, repetition is important in convincing others of patterns and processes. Further, it is important for ethnographers to explain that variations in what people believe or say may exist, and that understanding these differences is part of understanding the larger community story.

Being perceived as a learner or student is not always easy. Adding to the difficulty is the way in which research participants perceive ethnographers. It is especially difficult when significant status differentials exist between researcher and informants.

EXAMPLE 4.2

BRIDGING CLASS DIFFERENCES IN THE FIELD

Ethnographic field researcher Nitza Diaz was a young, middle-class Puerto Rican woman from a family of educators and activists who was trained as an ethnographer. She was involved in a study designed to collect data on Puerto Rican children's activity expenditures. Part of her work required her to visit the homes of over seventy children at least twice. The first time involved describing to mothers the study and record-keeping requirements; the second visit involved an in-depth,

semistructured interview on perceptions of chronic health problems (cardiovascular disease, cancer, diabetes, and arthritis) and steps that could be taken to prevent these diseases. She was able to obtain access to caregivers and to establish excellent field relationships. The refusal rate for the study was very low. She was very successful at convincing caregivers and children to record data on energy outputs measured with electronic instruments for measuring energy unit and caloric outputs. But when she questioned her respondents about the etiology, prevention, and management of chronic health problems such as diabetes, they argued that she already should know the answers since she was more educated than they. Recognizing the class difference between themselves and Diaz—evidenced by educational disparities—the respondents felt uncomfortable telling her how to care for problems about which they felt she knew more than they did.

Regardless of obstacles and social distance that might be created by differences between researchers and research participants in status, gender, ethnicity, or education, it is important for ethnographers to work toward roles or identities that permit them to be good listeners and appropriate questioners, and acceptable inquirers in the community setting. These roles and identities make it possible to observe and interview widely and to record their observations. Good listeners are good learners; good learners must be able to record their observations and carry out other data collection strategies fully and competently in order to perform their duties as social scientists. Even where researcher characteristics and ascribed roles make being a learner or a student difficult, the ethnographers' roles must facilitate these activities.

SUGGESTIONS FOR BEING A GOOD ETHNOGRAPHIC LEARNER

- Learn and adopt the cultural cues that denote "attentive listening" within the cultural context of your research site.
- Ask lots of questions.
- Make sure that your informants talk more than you do.

- Focus the conversation on your informant's experiences and background rather than your own.
- Start out by counting to three—slowly—after your informant stops speaking and before you say something else, then adjust your own response time accordingly. The rate of speaking and thinking across cultures is different—sometimes slower, sometimes faster.
- Write down what your informants say. It gives people time to think and makes them feel that what they said was important.
- Always ask permission to record using digital or other devices.

We cannot emphasize sufficiently the importance of field notes. Field notes constitute the heart of the science of ethnography. While they may be bolstered by a variety of other data collection approaches, it is critical to record observations and all interviews carefully for coding later on. Otherwise, researchers may be forced to rely on their usually less than accurate memories of people, places, activities, and events. It is worth remembering that in the normal course of events, researchers forget about 50 percent of what they learn within twenty-four hours of an interview if they do not record it digitally and write notes immediately after the interview is completed.

 Cross Reference: See Books 3 and 4

Notwithstanding the above suggestions, ethnographers should remember that these suggestions will not work in every culture, because what constitutes good listening in one culture may be defined as bad manners in another. In North American and many European settings, for example, good listeners look directly into the eyes of their fellow conversationalists while they are talking. However, in many non-Western communities, direct stares are considered to be signs of aggression or hostility. Some European-Americans, and others as well also speak quickly, tend to interrupt each other, and begin speaking as soon as a pause in the conversation occurs. American Indians wait for a considerable period of time between a speaker's phrases to make sure that the speaker has finished talking. Norwegians like to signify that they are attending closely to what a speaker is saying with a sharp and audible intake of breath, accompanied by an upward jerk of the chin. By contrast, European Americans repeatedly nod their heads up and down, while saying "uh-huh." Sri Lankans typically show agreement by shaking their heads sideways, a sign that would signal disagreement to the average American. Learning the postures, gestures, and speech patterns that accompany polite listening in the research site will greatly facilitate an ethnographer's ability to be viewed as a good listener, learner, and communicator. Though we describe these "typical patterns," all experienced ethnographers know that they have to identify variations in such behaviors within a setting and learn to adapt accordingly. Acting in accordance with stereotypes about what "countries" and "cultures" expect and do only scratches the surface; it is merely the beginning of learning how to be perceived as—and to be—a good listener.

Ultimately, by asking endless questions, for which we provide guidelines in Books 2, 3, and 4 of the *Ethnographer's Toolkit*, and listening patiently and attentively, ethnographers gradually can learn from their community partners, colleagues, and key informants the story of their communities, their lives, and their cultural experiences and their history. Those questions may include the kinds of structured questions contained in ethnographic surveys and the elicitation strategies described in Book 4 of the *Ethnographer's Toolkit*, including pilesorts, mapping, and the discussion of artifacts or other approaches that researchers invent on the spot.

Cross Reference: See Book 4 on ethnographic surveys and structured observations

Ethnographers also soon learn the ethics that govern how people in the field interact appropriately with one another, how they treat strangers, and how they might feel about a stranger living among them. Ethnographers also learn how these elements change as the local people get to know and trust the researcher. Initial reactions and responses may be tempered over time as local people test the responsiveness, empathy, and responsibility of researchers to them and their welfare. As we suggest later on in this chapter and elsewhere, responding to expectations on the part of people in the study setting is one of the challenging aspects of field research. Doing it well retains relationships and ensures reciprocity. Doing it poorly restricts access to information and prevents the formation of the trusting relationships that are required for good field research and intervention.

Since an ethnographer's most powerful data collection strategy is empathic engagement with their research participants, participant observation and in-depth interviewing require that the researcher share in and empathize with the difficulties and joys of participants' lives, and show authentic curiosity about and interest in their experiences. As we have said, ethnographers do not have to agree with every aspect of participants' lives and the culture of the community setting. But empathetic responses to life experiences, however foreign they may seem, are a central part of the life of any ethnographer. Example 1.7 in chapter 1 describes how LeCompte's prior experiences in school districts facilitated conversations with the principal of a school in the Navajo Nation; it also raises ethical questions, since LeCompte was shown confidential personnel files which contained serious allegations that had not been substantiated. The specific information really was not relevant to the overall research question, and not only were the data "private and identifiable" but LeCompte also had no consent to examine them from the individuals whose files were revealed. In cases such as these, the ethnographer needs to change the subject, indicate that the information isn't really relevant to the study, or is something the researcher does not need to know. Barring that, researchers can delete the information from their notes.

CREATING A FIELD IDENTITY

The second role the researcher takes on is constructed upon entry to the field. In the early days of ethnographic research, researchers usually were foreigners or strangers to the study site—at least in the initial stages of investigation. Since experienced ethnographers were quite aware that no community would tolerate for very long a stranger who didn't seem to have any purpose for being present and who asked all kinds of questions, one of the first tasks novice ethnographers were urged to accomplish was the construction of a **field identity** or introductory script that provides an identity and tells the story of the study plan in language that is immediately understandable to people in the site.

An introductory script provides an initial position and identity for a researcher new to the research site. Early ethnographers often simply arrived at their research sites, unknown to anyone in the community. They had to find a way to explain why they were there with a story that served to legitimate their presence by providing themselves with an introductory role or social identity. Without such an identity, members of the community would define them as irrelevant tourists, nonpeople, ghosts, or worse, as spies, saboteurs, witches, or persons who might do harm to others. The identity chosen would have to be feasible—that is, based upon role niches that existed, or at least made sense within, the experience of people within the community (Davidson, 1996)—and it had to be plausible when applied to the given ethnographer. A very young ethnographer would find it difficult to be a "grandmother" in the community, for example. The field identity also had to be devoid of as many negative connotations as possible. The initial script that ethnographers used to present such an identity usually was a simplified, nontechnical, but accurate portrayal of who the researcher was and what he or she planned to do. The field identity is especially important in situations in which ethnographers are there to study and learn about another culture and community, but not to work with residents to bring about changes directly. In the latter situation, ethnographers usually will describe what they are interested in and try to find partners and collaborators who share similar interests in relation to social change efforts. We discuss entry into applied settings and building partnerships in greater detail in Book 7.

In this section, we define both initial scripts or stories and the special kinds of identities ethnographers need when working in field settings. We also make a clear distinction between field identities and accompanying scripts and "undercover" or intentionally misleading stories, which we feel are unethical. Example 4.3 describes some of the consid-

Definition:
A field identity provides an introductory position or initial identity for a researcher new to the research site

Cross Reference:
Book 7, chapter 2

erations that affected the field identity created by a Swedish researcher from a Canadian university who was studying a First Nations' community on the Canadian prairies.

EXAMPLE 4.3

CREATING A FIELD IDENTITY IN SHORT GRASS

"The problem was to gain access to behavior settings in which Short Grass [Canadian] Indians would communicate things about themselves that were not ordinarily accessible to Whites. I had to be defined as a 'safe' person, one who could be trusted not to shatter the delicate balance of Indian-White relationships, and before whom the usual presentation of Indian self-image to White could be dropped . . . the immediate suspicion that I was a spy from the Indian Affairs Branch was dispelled when it became clear that I was not a Canadian citizen [the writer, in fact, is from Sweden] . . . When it became apparent that my car was as liable to be stopped and searched by Mounties [police] as were those of Indians, the possibility that I was an agent of the government was similarly discounted . . . [as were suspicions] that I was a spy for American oil companies . . . a communist spy . . . a White man in search of the sexual favors of [Indian] women . . . [or] an American draft dodger" (Braroe, 1971, 20–21).

EXAMPLE 4.4

CREATING A FIELD IDENTITY THAT AVOIDED BEING VIEWED AS A "NARC"

A young male drug researcher exploring the interface between the formal and informal economy in a neighborhood of Hartford, Connecticut, had to explain that he was a researcher rather than a "narc"—an undercover narcotics policeman or informant. This was difficult for several reasons. First, though he actually was Puerto Rican, he looked "white" to neighborhood residents. He was light skinned, he wore a ponytail, he was a student at a local university, and he carried a backpack. Because he didn't fit any neighborhood stereotype, local businesses and independent drug sellers thought he was in the community to spy on their activities. Though he explained his study, no one believed him at first. However, over time, he came to know some of the drug users and business owners in the area. He also carried a badge indicating that he was a researcher for the Institute for Community Research, and a letter explaining what he was interested in. After six or seven months, he was accepted as a legitimate member of the local Puerto Rican community, was no longer under suspicion, and was given access to information about formal/informal economic exchanges between drug sellers, drug users, and local businesses.

Important to both of the stories above is that developing the trust needed to do good fieldwork often takes quite a bit of time.

Cover stories or initial scripts should simply serve as an introduction or initial identity for the ethnographer. Therefore, they should share the following characteristics:

RULES OF THUMB FOR CONSTRUCTION OF INITIAL SCRIPTS AND COVER STORIES

- Not be too specific lest they limit the researchers' options for role taking or the information that community members offer
- Be safe; that is, they should not present the researcher as someone with whom association could be risky
- Be true stories, though they don't have to tell all the details about a researcher's role because local people often don't understand the technicalities of researchers' work at first
- Try to avoid partisan affiliation or being identified with one or another faction in the community
- Avoid close identification with anyone known to be an authority figure or person with special interests or biases
- Be created with knowledge of the community in mind
- Be directly connected with the research to be done, so that they will reflect what people actually see the ethnographer doing and people will know what the researcher is looking for
- Make reference to organizations that the ethnographer is part of or works with
- If possible, have meaning for future developments in the community or community benefits, without overpromising results

EXAMPLE 4.5

CREATING A FIELD IDENTITY THAT USES PEOPLE'S PARTIAL UNDERSTANDINGS ABOUT RESEARCHERS

Rosalie Wax was the first social scientist to study life in the internment camps where Japanese residents of the United States forcibly were confined during World War II. Initially she found it impossible to do (or to explain to residents) the participant observation her project required, given the suspicion that the Japanese residents had of anybody they thought might be associated with the camps' officials. Deciding that it was her job to convince the camp residents that she was the kind of person they could trust, Wax began "to behave more like a formal interviewer than a participant and observer. I undertook studies that had little connection with the kind of data I was supposed to be getting. I invented questionnaires and interviewed women on how they thought evacuation had altered their way of life. I interviewed parents on what they thought evacuation had done to their children. I interviewed anyone at all for information and attitudes on social stratification in Japan and the United States. I talked to [community leaders about] what they thought about juvenile delinquency" (1971, 75–76).

Residents of the camps were familiar with this more formal kind of research. Wax got to know people by doing these studies; they "gave respondents a reasonable story to tell to curious neighbors" who might have wondered what camp members were talking with her about. They also helped to clarify what Wax's ultimate role was to be: to observe and ask questions. Sometimes, however, initial field identities backfire and need to be modified.

EXAMPLE 4.6

WHEN PARTICIPANTS MISUNDERSTAND THE RESEARCHER'S TOPIC AND ACT ABNORMALLY BECAUSE THE INITIAL SCRIPT IS POORLY RELATED TO THE RESEARCH QUESTION

A teacher participating in LeCompte's (1974) study of fourth-grade classrooms told her students that the researcher was observing their class in order to "write a book" about life in fourth grade. The students decided to give LeCompte better material to write about by clowning around, wisecracking in response to teacher questions, and generally making instruction impossible and life miserable for the teacher. In response to the teacher's pleas to help her get the students to settle down, LeCompte had to redefine her role as "author" (and the students' roles as "actors") by explaining that her book was about every day and *serious* work in classrooms.

LeCompte's cover story fulfilled some of the criteria listed above; it *was* simple, safe, and true. However, it thoroughly confused the children because it wasn't clearly enough linked to the real task that LeCompte was trying to accomplish: describe an ordinary classroom and teacher behavior. And it was conveyed by a teacher who may have been somewhat unclear about how to describe ethnographic research in classrooms. In modifying how she described her research, LeCompte did not have to change how she acted. However, changes in identity can sometimes alter how people feel they can interact with the researcher, and can raise ethical concerns. In Example 2.4 in Book 2, Schensul describes how a fieldworker known to the community who began his research while still an ordained priest found that people interacted with him quite differently when he left the order and had to communicate with them as an ordinary person, not as a person religious. When he was a priest, people entrusted him with many kinds of confidences. However, when he became a layperson, they no longer felt as free to disclose private matters. Without the patina of priesthood, he had to work hard to reestablish trust based on other factors.

It is equally important for cover stories to avoid creating preconceptions about how persons in the community should act toward the ethnographer. Thus, though it may seem quite tempting to enter a community as the "adopted" member of a respected family or under the sponsorship of authority figures, doing so can be risky. If ethnographers are, for example, identified with a high-status family, lower-status persons in the community may find it difficult to approach them, may feel they need to approach them with deference, or may distrust them. Similarly, if the ethnographer is identified with authority figures such as social workers, administrators, evaluators, government agents, or someone from a specific community interest group or constituency, persons with whom the researcher may wish to have candid interactions are likely to censor what they say and do in accordance with their customary behavior vis-à-vis such individuals. However, sometimes these identities are unavoidable because some kind of sponsorship or allegiance usually is necessary before a researcher can even get in the door. Therefore, ethnographers should simply try to create a plausible entry story and expand upon its details as interaction ensues in the field. At the same time, they should strive to associate themselves with multiple sectors of the community simultaneously so as not to appear too closely affiliated with any one group. Most important is for researchers to realize that any form of identification that leads research participants to act differently from their ordinary demeanor (as in Example 4.6 above) or conform to what they think the researcher expects or wants is problematic.

One significant exception to these rules of thumb is when ethnographers enter a community with a specific change agenda, such as school improvement, the introduction of new service programs, or the training of new forms of community professionals. In such cases, ethnographers will try to communicate with multiple sectors of the community bearing on the problem, but they will also seek to identify and ally themselves specifically with others in the setting who aspire to the same goal.

A problem is that adhering to all these suggestions requires more knowledge of the community than ethnographers usually have in the initial fieldwork stages. Thus, it is imperative for ethnographers at least to learn something about the community that he or she plans to enter prior to beginning work. Ethnographers can talk to former residents, teachers, public figures, politicians, or relatives of residents to find out how people "line up" and how to avoid—to the extent possible—becoming too early affiliated with various contentious groups. They also need to discover what roles are possible and feasible. Sometimes, as Example 4.7 describes, researchers can be almost overwhelmed by the multiple demands of roles they have had to acquire in order to conduct their work.

EXAMPLE 4.7

JUGGLING FIELDWORK REQUIREMENTS WITH REQUIREMENTS OF ROLES ACQUIRED IN THE FIELD SITE

A Senegalese male medical anthropologist was working in two urban areas of Senegal. Both areas included members of two groups important to his study: the Dimba, a traditional self-help society of women and men who have had twins

or who have lost a child, who engage in reproductive health education; and the Laobe, an ethnic group in which women traders sell reproductive health goods. He was told that he could learn more about the Dimba if he agreed to be inducted formally into the society as an assistant to the Dimba "father," a senior male counselor. In that role, he was able to do the ethnographic work necessary to introduce an AIDS prevention program. However, at the same time, in his role as an assistant to a senior counselor, he regularly was "on call" for consultation on problems men encountered with reproductive health and fatherhood—even from his birth city three hundred miles away. He had to do both counseling and fieldwork while at the same time worrying about the degree to which his counselor role influenced behavior of his research subjects in the field.

As mentioned above, ethnographers may enter communities with a specific research assignment or problems to solve. In such cases, the problem itself determines some of the associations they must make. Ethnographers interested in health care problems may find themselves of necessity seeking the help of highly educated health care professionals who may or may not be perceived positively by the community. The same health care professionals may, in turn, believe community recipients of health services to be unreliable or poor informants. In such cases, ethnographers will need to make it clear to all constituents that their responsibility is to respond to and record the viewpoints of all community members.

EXAMPLE 4.8

CONDUCTING RESEARCH ON COMMUNITY UNDERSTANDING OF ALZHEIMER'S DISEASE

The Institute for Community Research (ICR) joined forces with several other institutions to conduct a formative study of community knowledge of Alzheimer's disease (AD) and to assess a way of disseminating information about it in the Puerto Rican community. Members of the research staff decided to interview families, service providers, and community institutions—*botanicas* selling herbs and religious icons, pharmacies, and community-based organizations—to identify differences in the meaning of Alzheimer's disease and potential distribution channels for accurate information on diagnosis and management of the disease.

ICR researchers discussed the project and determined that they could identify themselves as investigating perspectives on AD to service providers and community

institutions, but not to families. The researchers felt that families would be upset if researchers used the term *Alzheimer's disease* because it was associated with loss of control and mental health problems, both of which family members feared. This might result in their reluctance to participate in the study. Thus, the researchers decided to identify themselves to families as persons investigating health problems associated with aging. They planned to ask about symptom identification first, and only later about dementias—including Alzheimer's disease.

Despite precautions such as these, the issue of affiliation with a particular constituency, the wrong constituency, or with multiple constituencies is always relevant. The roles ethnographers necessarily adopt and those that become ascribed to them do affect how they will act in the field, the kind of data to which they will have access, how they will interact with people inside and out of the study site, and the kinds of duties and responsibilities they will be defined as having.

Often, people in the field do not understand just what a collaborative relationship with an ethnographer means. They can confuse ethnographic work with the traditional stereotype of researchers that we discussed in chapter 1. Initially they may not view the researcher as a partner, and they also may be reluctant to discuss needs, issues, or problems that they would like to address. While we discuss collaborative and team research more fully in chapter 6 of this book and Book 7, here we simply note that ethnographers generally will need to construct three kinds of field identities:

- In relationship to staff of the organizations or members of the community who permitted or invited them to do a study
- In relation to the persons and situations about and with whom information is sought
- In relation to the scientific community that may have funded them, and would benefit from the results of their work

These three categories sometimes, but not always, overlap. As the *Ethnographer's Toolkit* makes clear, ethnography does require very complex and multilayered sets of relationships!

Going Undercover

Initial scripts should not be confused with going undercover. As indicated earlier, we believe the construction of undercover stories to be unethical. In most cases, such stories will not survive scrutiny by review panels whose task is to assure that people are not deceived or tricked into being research participants. *Whereas field identities and initial scripts—or cover stories—provide an initial identity, undercover stories are intended to deceive, as, for example, when researchers pretend to be drug users in order to study addicts or homosexuals in order to study the behavior of that population (Bolton, 1995).* Undercover identities also can involve avoiding identifying oneself as a researcher in order to study stigmatized or illegal behavior, as Humphreys (1970a, 1970b) did when he secretly observed and recorded homosexual behavior in public toilets. Some methodologists *do* advocate the adoption of false identities, especially in cases where the behavior of interest is secret or illegal, or where letting community members know that one is a researcher would preclude access to the site. *However, we do not advocate "going undercover" for several reasons.* First, it is difficult to maintain a false identity among the intimate relationships and long periods of residence in the field customarily required in ethnography. Getting caught is always a danger, and being unmasked can destroy the trust between researcher and informants upon which good ethnographic data collection is predicated. It also can endanger the ethnographer. Second, except under special circumstances, most **Institutional Review Boards** (IRBs) forbid the use of undercover positions because they make it impossible for people to give truly informed consent to their participation. Third, because they are designed to deceive, undercover stories can be unethical. Finally, the very nature of collaborative ethnography described throughout in the *Ethnographer's Toolkit* precludes working undercover, since the process of problem identification, understanding, and solution requires collaboration with and full disclosure to most, if not all, participants in the community.

In the next section, we first discuss how the characteristics ethnographers bring to the field "with their bodies"

Key point

Key point

Definition: Institutional Review Boards are committees mandated by the US government that oversee the ethical treatment of human subjects in research

(Metz, 1978) affect their relationships in the field. Then we describe the roles ethnographers acquire by virtue of their friendships and professional relationships, the tasks they perform, the institutional affiliations they possess, and the purposes for and outcomes of their research. We also address ways to ameliorate differences in status between researchers and those whom they study and with whom they work.

COPING WITH RELATIONSHIPS IN THE FIELD: PERSONAL CHARACTERISTICS, ASYMMETRICAL RELATIONSHIPS, AND POSITIONALITY

Here we are concerned with the bodily or physical, personality, ascribed, and background characteristics of the researcher. Some researchers have advocated being as unobtrusive as a "fly on the wall"; others have asserted that they wished they could be invisible when in the field doing research. These desires arise in part from the discomfort researchers feel when interacting with people while simultaneously observing them, listening in on conversations, recording interactions, attempting to build relationships and at the same time, engaging in other data elicitation strategies. Further, constant interaction with people, especially new people, can be exhausting. Much of the discomfort, however, derives from the fact that if researchers *were* invisible, they wouldn't have to worry about the conclusions people might make based on their appearance or the meanings associated with their perceived or actual backgrounds. Researchers could stop worrying about what diverse adolescent youth from the city thought about a middle-aged, well-dressed, gray-haired, female researcher, how those thoughts might censor what the adolescents were willing to talk about in the researcher's presence, and what the researcher might have to do to reduce the social distance between them. Neither would the researcher need to worry about what those teenagers thought about being seen by their friends while in her company. However, being invisible also raises questions of ethics: people who do not know they are being observed cannot legitimately be fully informed about the nature of a study, and cannot freely consent to participation.

EXAMPLE 4.9

WHY NAVAJOS ONLY VISITED THE ETHNOGRAPHER AT NIGHT

An ethnographer studying the implementation of a Navajo/English bilingual program at a school district in the Navajo Nation in the southwestern United States found that Navajo parents and community members would never visit her home during the day. She learned that although her informants trusted her as an individual, they didn't want their neighbors and friends to know that they were socializing in the home of a *bilagaana*—the Navajo name for "white people." By coming and going under cover of darkness, they could visit without creating gossip within specific factions in the Navajo community.

The aforementioned Senegalese anthropologist, when conducting research with male sex workers, met with them behind shaded windows in the dark, in his university office after 11 p.m. The young men were very fearful of arrest at a time when sex between same sex partners was illegal and subject to imprisonment and other punishments. At night, in the dark of a faculty office, they could speak freely without fear of stigma or arrest.

EXAMPLE 4.10

WHEN TEEN ACTION RESEARCHERS WOULDN'T TAKE RESEARCHERS TO VISIT THEIR NEIGHBORHOOD

A team of ethnographers under the guidance of Jean Schensul were conducting a study of young drug users between the ages of sixteen and twenty-four. Incorporated into the study was the opportunity for young people who might be former or even current drug users to act as consultants to the study. Two young adult men, nineteen and twenty, volunteered to participate as advisors in return for an internship stipend and class credits. Both had experienced life on the streets, and one had strong leadership skills, visibility, and a reputation for being invincible within the community. Both claimed they knew many people, and one said that everyone respected him. These young men were quite comfortable talking to the slightly older male ethnographers from the local community in the offices of the Institute for Community Research or in a neutral restaurant downtown, but even after several months they were still reluctant to take these researchers into their neighborhoods or introduce them to their peers.

Experienced fieldworkers know quite well that ethnographers cannot be invisible or work only at night or in their offices, and therefore, who they are in real life affects profoundly how they can behave, with whom they can interact, and how they interact in the field. Below we discuss some of the most important characteristics that ethnographers bring to the field with them and how these characteristics might affect their research activities. We discuss the impact of these characteristics not because we believe that researchers should try to eliminate them—which is an impossibility—but because we believe that before they become skilled and competent fieldworkers, ethnographers must develop an understanding of how their own personal characteristics—gender, age, physical features, clothing and style, culture, class, and educational level—are likely to affect the process and outcome of their research efforts, and the kinds of conflicts and ethical dilemmas to which their own "selves" might lead.

Sex and Gender

One of the most obvious characteristics that researchers bring to the field with them is their biological sex and their culturally expressed gender. No culture is without its norms regarding proper sex and gender-role behavior. These constrain how men and women should dress, talk, and handle their bodies, the places where men and women are allowed to be, with whom they are allowed to speak and interact, the kinds of information deemed appropriate for them to have, and the kinds of activities in which they are permitted to participate.

EXAMPLE 4.11

SOCIAL DISTANCE BETWEEN MALE RESEARCHERS AND FEMALE RESIDENTS IN SHORT GRASS

Anthropologist Nils Braroe writes of his fieldwork in a community on the Canadian prairies: "During my first summer in Short Grass, I [a white male researcher] had insurmountable difficulties in talking with women. If there were no men home when I visited an Indian house, women would not answer my knocks at the door and pretended no-one was there. In mixed company, women hardly ever contributed to the conversation and would avoid even eye contact on streets in town" (Braroe, 1971, 22).

Ethnographers sometimes can transcend these constraints; male researchers can learn something of the life of women by asking men about them, and they often can talk to women under special circumstances or about less intimate issues. Braroe initially had encountered social practices that made it difficult for women in general to speak to men, but he managed to overcome many of them by demonstrating over time that he was not a threat. He indicates that when his wife joined him during his second summer in the Short Grass community, it became easier for him to communicate with women; some even came to tea at his house. And by the end of his several years of fieldwork, women talked to him as freely as men did, even when men were not present. However, some topics are especially difficult to discuss in cross-gender groups. It is often difficult for women to talk about many issues of intimate concern—for example, childbirth, nursing, sexual practices, relationships with spouses, domestic or sexual abuse—to a researcher who differs from them in gender or social status.

EXAMPLE 4.12

REDUCING STATUS DIFFERENCES TO IMPROVE COMMUNICATION ABOUT BEHAVIOR TOO INTIMATE TO DESCRIBE TO MALE RESEARCHERS

Male Latino physicians were unable to engage Mexican American women in conversations about their prebirth, labor, and postbirth experiences and about their own health and that of their children because of gender and status differences between the doctors and the women. However, when *female* anthropologists trained groups of community leaders to conduct in-depth interviews and surveys with the same women, they were able to elicit detailed stories about the same issues.

EXAMPLE 4.13

USING SAME-SEX RESEARCHERS TO RUN FOCUS GROUPS ON SEXUAL BEHAVIOR IN SRI LANKA

A mixed gender research team of Americans and Sri Lankans was conducting a study of sexual behavior and sex risk in an urban area of Sri Lanka. Knowing that cross-gender discussions of sexuality are considered to be taboo in Sri Lanka, the team decided to hold separate interviews and focus groups for young men and women, with young female ethnographers collecting data on early and current experiences with partners from the same and opposite sex from young women, and young male ethnographers collecting similar data from young men. The interviews,

which went very well, also entailed the collection of detailed data on twenty-three explicit sexual behaviors. Respondents were eager to talk with their same-sex interviewers about their concerns and about issues of reproductive health. Then, once both groups—and the interviewers themselves—were prepared for cross-gender discussions, it became possible to hold successful mixed-gender conversations to discuss ways of negotiating intimacy together (Nastasi et al., 1998–1999).

Sexual mores also exacerbate cross-gender relationships. In most societies, women still are viewed by men as potential sexual objects, regardless of their status. This factor complicates the life of fieldworkers, since the attentive listening and the studied—and *scholarly*—interest in informants' lives and stories that are the stock in trade of the competent ethnographer can be interpreted by informants as *personal* interest and an invitation to intimacy. It is made doubly difficult since interviewing often requires taking an informant aside and interviewing them in a quiet place, isolated from other people—a kind of intimacy that can be misinterpreted, at best, and at worst, tabooed in many cultures.

EXAMPLE 4.14

CONFUSING ATTENTIVE ETHNOGRAPHIC LISTENING WITH SEXUAL INTEREST

A young female ethnographer, a novice member of an evaluation team, attended a three-day retreat for researchers, teachers, community members, and administrators involved in a community-based school restructuring project. Part of her job was to conduct ongoing interviews with teachers in the project to assess their understanding of and commitment to the project. At the end of the second day of meetings, one of her informants, a young male social studies teacher, told her he had time to finish their interview and invited her to his room where it was quiet enough for her to tape record his remarks. After setting up her recorder, the ethnographer was dismayed to find her informant taking off his coat and shirt, telling her that it was time to go beyond all the "nice talk" they had been engaged in and "get serious."

Situations such as the one above can be avoided if fieldworkers take care never to become so isolated from other people that extrication from awkward or dangerous situations is difficult or impossible. They also can have conversations or hold interviews in teams. *It is also very important for women working alone in the field to learn from key informants and others familiar with the sexual norms of the culture which specific cues attract sexual attention.* In most cultures, women should avoid living alone if possible, not have male friends from home visit when they are alone, avoid low-cut blouses and short skirts, not walk alone after a specific time in the evening, avoid going out alone with a male friend, or have a "boyfriend" or romantic interest in the field setting. Living alone in the field can also be viewed as a message that a female researcher is available for sexual liaisons, or could be vulnerable to them.

Key point

EXAMPLE 4.15

AVOIDING UNWANTED SEXUAL ATTENTION

When Jean Schensul was completing her fieldwork in Mexico, she lived alone in a small house in an industrial town. One day, she found signs behind the house that someone had been standing on a ladder, trying to observe her through the window of her bedroom. Such a thing had never happened earlier when she was living in a family household in a nearby community. After her discovery, she made sure that the curtains were always closed even during the day, and she never invited males, even other male anthropology students, to the house alone.

While it is good practice for women to avoid such behaviors, men also must learn the cues that make them targets for accusations of rape or sexual abuse, such as talking with a woman alone in a private spot. In addition, females are not the only targets for possible unwanted sexual attention. Male researchers can be approached in the field by women for sexual intimacy or transactional sex as well. They also can be targets for sexual rapprochement or harassment by other men anywhere, but especially if they are doing research in settings involving sexuality among men.

In general, we believe that sex and fieldwork do not mix very well, regardless of whether it is heterosexual or same-sex sex. While some methodologists argue that since ethnographers are human beings, they are subject to the same romantic and human inclinations in the field as out of it (see Bernard, 1995), we believe that even without romantic attachments, it is difficult enough to manage the ambiguities of friendship with the key informants and colleagues upon whom ethnographers depend in the field. These special kinds of ethnographic friendships do, after all, have as their initial and fundamental basis the ethnographer's desire to elicit information, rather than ordinary friendship. That "need to know" often strains relationships under normal conditions of acquaintanceship. When friends and colleagues who are informants also become lovers, additional strains are created. Furthermore, stresses in or the breakup of a romantic relationship can seriously jeopardize access to crucial information. In Example 4.14 described above, the ethnographer was trying to do a good job and believed that her informant would talk more freely in private. She ended up unable to complete the interview and in a compromising situation. Few pieces of data are so valuable that they warrant ethnographers risking their physical, emotional, or mental health, their well-being, or their life. Using same-sex interviewers or teams of interviewers can alleviate sexual mishaps to some degree, but this is not always possible, nor is it always a safeguard. A more secure safeguard is the savvy and vigilance of an experienced fieldworker; this should be supported by a vigilant project director lest entire research programs be jeopardized by the behavior of a team member.

EXAMPLE 4.16

HOW A TEAM MEMBER'S ROMANCE DESTROYED A RESEARCH PROJECT

A professor of education and his team of graduate students had been studying the process of innovation in an alternative school. The members of the research team were viewed by the administration as having the same status as teachers or administrators—and certainly higher than student teacher interns. One of the female graduate students previously had taught classes in the school of education; there she had met and began to date an undergraduate student who was doing his student teaching internship at the school. The couple often was seen together around the school premises. Because the school district had strong policies forbidding intimate relationships between subordinates and superiors, and because the relationship between

the research team member and the student intern was viewed as flagrant, the professor was told to leave the school and to close down his two-year-long study.

In a contrasting case, a novice female researcher in another project avoided potential difficulty by first contacting the project director to learn what school district and project policies governed such situations when a young male teacher asked her for a date.

Up to now, we have been discussing the impact of sexual or romantic relationships between researchers and research participants. However, an ongoing problem is the possibility that researchers may engage in sexual predation of other team members, especially those who are students or junior members of the team. Such relationships can be encouraged by the close quarters in which team members often live, by the long duration of much fieldwork, and the mutual excitement generated in the process of doing intellectual work together. Predatory behavior is never acceptable and should be reported immediately regardless of the consequences. Other romantic relationships and entanglements within the research team also can be disruptive of an effective collaborative effort and lead to emotional pain and difficult social relationships. It is well for such relationships to be minimized to the extent possible.

Age

Age is another characteristic that, like biological sex, is impossible to alter. However, it affects the kinds of people and information to which ethnographers have access. Depending upon the population of interest, the ethnographer's age may either facilitate or impede data collection. Age also influences the kinds of people who will feel comfortable associating with the researcher. Some female anthropologists have argued that older women have fewer difficulties in the field; intimacies in the field are less problematic because older women are less often seen as sex objects. In many cultures, older people are granted a degree of status and respect that younger researchers could not enjoy. On the other hand, closeness in age—or the appearance of closeness—between research participants and ethnographers sometimes can be helpful. Donna Deyhle (1986) was able to win the confidence of Native American students she wished to study because, as a young woman who herself possessed a pair of the parachute pants that all the young people coveted, she could talk with them about common interests in clothing, hang out around the school as a student might without being too noticeably adult, and actually participate in adolescent break-dancing activities. Similarly, in her study of teenage punks, Leslie Roman (1988) was able to "go native" to some degree because she appeared to be about the age of the punks and, when attending rock concerts, she could dress in the kinds of clothing they favored. Even being older does not preclude "passing" to some degree; age did not stop Jean Schensul from attending electronic dance events by dressing in black, going with younger dancers, and staying in the shadows. On the other hand, a young Puerto Rican male researcher on an ICR team doing research on HIV exposure among older adults was very uncomfortable interviewing older men about their sex lives. He perceived it as a culturally inappropriate behavior, even though the respondents were quite open with him. He eventually left the project.

 Key point *It should be kept in mind that in some cases, it is impossible for the ethnographer to blend in, so different strategies for building rapport must be developed.* Had Deyhle and Roman looked much older than their young research participants, they could have hired as research assistants "junior ethnographers" (Heath, 1996) or other individuals who were closer in age to the teenagers in the study and who could, therefore, interact more easily and communicate more freely with them. Shirley Brice Heath's use of junior ethnographers to study adolescent artists resembles the concept of the ethnographic team—a group of researchers who vary in gender, age, ethnicity, and level of training. Team research can permit ethnographic research to be much more unobtrusive, as members go about in pairs, or as researchers are selected, insofar as is possible, to match with the respondents or informants from whom they seek information. While trying to blend in or to use surrogate researchers is effective in some situations, in others, it is not possible. In most societies, certain information is not deemed appropriate for young people to possess, as Margaret Mead later discovered in her study of Samoan young girls (1928). As a young woman herself, she simply was not told of many things about which Samoan elders thought she was too young to know. Gender and age often create conflated problems; young females may be privy to information available to women but not to men of any age. While young male and female ethnographers are more likely to have social problems with informants of the opposite sex, age and gender alone do not preclude ethnographers from being considered attractive social or sexual partners by members of the participant community. In fact, though in many societies older women cease to be viewed as sexual objects, they may, nonetheless, be sought out as counselors to younger persons who seek access to various forms of cultural knowledge or initiation into specific social or sexual behaviors (Silva et al., 1997).

Physical Features

Characteristics such as body size, hair color and texture, eye and skin color, and facial features can be the source of all kinds of nicknames in the field, both flattering and insulting. More important, they cause informants and research participants to make judgments about an ethnographer's competence, attractiveness, and energy levels. These judgments, in turn, determine what informants are willing to divulge and the extent to which they will interact with ethnographers—at least in the initial stages of research. Judgments are context-specific, so it is necessary to determine the possible influence of appearance in each cultural setting the ethnographer enters. Furthermore, judgments may influence initial reactions to the researcher, requiring the ethnographer to work harder to gain acceptance. Eventually, however, with perseverance and good intentions, such prejudices usually can be overcome, and researchers will come to be perceived as "real people" and as friends and associates in the field setting. On the more positive side, some ethnographer characteristics may be viewed as valued or "endearing"; for example, the ability to play basketball well, an interest in gardening, a good "native" linguistic accent, naivete or innocence, or the willingness to be helpful. These are characteristics that can help ethnographers gain access to and become part of the study community.

One exception may be in cases where a country or a community has passed laws that discriminate against or criminalize specific characteristics of an ethnographer, such as his or her religion or sexual orientation. In several African countries, for example, homosexuality currently has been declared criminal, even a felony. Simply associating with people who are gay, lesbian, or in some manner gender nonconforming can put individuals at risk of being beaten, arrested, and jailed; individuals themselves—including ethnographers—who are openly gender nonconforming may wish to safeguard themselves by choosing other sites in which to do their research, or prepare to spend their fieldwork time deeply in the closet. At the risk of seeming to stereotype, we list a few physical characteristics and how they affect perception in Western European society; perceptions may be quite different in other cultures. Not recognizing these differences—and biases—could cause ethnographers to violate the rules of good taste and manners within the community.

STEREOTYPICAL PREJUDICES LINKED TO PERSONAL APPEARANCE IN WESTERN CULTURES

- Obesity is a sign of laziness and lack of intelligence.
- Slim people are attractive, energetic, and intelligent.
- Very thin people—especially if they are females—are likely to be wealthy.
- Tall people have leadership qualities; however, extremely tall people are clumsy and unathletic.
- Short people are aggressive.
- A soft voice denotes weakness or indecisiveness.
- People who are very beautiful or handsome are not extremely intelligent or competent. The common

stereotype of the "beautiful dumb blonde" applies to both men and women.

- People who wear glasses are intelligent.
- People with red hair lose their tempers easily.
- Good athletes (especially those in football) are poor students.
- Male ballet dancers probably are gay. Female athletic coaches probably are lesbians.
- Very good students, especially if they are girls, aren't attractive or athletic.

Though these statements reflect stereotypes, their applicability or other similar criteria related to judgments about difference need to be assessed in any environment and on an ongoing basis.

EXAMPLE 4.17

EQUATING PHYSICAL CHARACTERISTICS WITH MORAL CHARACTERISTICS OR COMPETENCE

A project director received a number of complaints about one member of her research team—a man who was extremely overweight. Despite the man's extensive prior research experience, his excellence in all other assignments, and the confidence expressed in him by the project director, her counterparts in the community organization continued to argue that her assistant could not carry out his assigned tasks. "There must be something wrong with him. Why doesn't he take better care of himself? Can't he go on a diet?" they asked. Preoccupied by their association of great weight with an undesirable personality or incompetence, and not wanting to interact with the staff member, the community organization staff never invited the assistant to informal gatherings at which much project business was transacted. Not until the man left the project for another job and the project director was able to assign another assistant—one who was less experienced but who was thin and attractive—did the complaints cease and more fruitful interaction between staff and researcher begin.

Standards of attractiveness or physical acceptability vary by culture, however. A contrasting list of common assumptions about physical features from Sri Lanka might look quite different.

- Thin people are poor and uneducated.
- Men who wear the national dress (white shirt and sarong) on the street are rural farmers.
- Professionals do not wear a sarong in public.
- Women who wear pants/trousers are upper class, have traveled internationally, and are likely to be somewhat arrogant.

A similar list from the eastern United States might look something like this:

- Women who wear pearls work in insurance companies.
- Black community advocates come from specific urban neighborhoods.
- All residents in upper income parts of town are white.
- Men who wear ties are in business.

However, in Boulder, Colorado, men in ties probably are Mormon missionaries, undercover narcotics police, or lawyers on their way to court. Virtually no other males are dressed that way!

EXAMPLE 4.18

WHERE IS FAT CONSIDERED TO BE ATTRACTIVE? DIFFERENCES IN BEAUTY BETWEEN THE UNITED STATES AND SOMALIA

Margaret LeCompte, who at five feet six inches weighed more than 160 pounds by the end of her Peace Corps service, was considered to be considerably overweight by the US doctor who cared for volunteers. The Somali teachers with whom she worked, however, kept urging her to eat more heartily. "Don't they pay you enough to eat?" they asked. By Somali standards, LeCompte was underfed and couldn't possibly have the energy needed both to teach the children in her charge and to provide adult classes in the evenings. Her thin ankles (a lingering source of pride for LeCompte) were a particular source of concern to her Somali women friends, because Somali men considered thick female ankles to be a sign of attractiveness.

Physical characteristics associated with ethnicity—such as skin color—are special cases. Some survey research methodologists advocate matching the ethnicity of interviewers with the ethnicity of potential interviewees, on the grounds that people will feel more comfortable talking with someone who resembles them. There is some evidence to substantiate that matching interviewers and interviewees improves data quality. There is equally good evidence, however, that difference can be an advantage in interviewing because respondents may be more likely to confide in someone less like themselves, or whom they perceive to be more trustworthy because they are disconnected from anyone they know. ***When choice is possible,*** **Key point** ***we recommend asking participants whether they prefer to talk with someone who resembles them by gender and/or ethnicity or someone who is different from them in these or other aspects.***

Some communities may be openly hostile to researchers whose ethnicity is different from their own.

 **EXAMPLE 4.19**

PROTECTING A FIELDWORKER FROM RACISM

The project director for a team of Midwestern educational researchers decided not to send a highly skilled, female African American fieldworker to collect data in a rural community in the southern United States because the school district administrators, teachers, and most of the children were white, and historical patterns of racism and discrimination in the area almost guaranteed the fieldworker would encounter a lack of cooperation. The project director, a white woman, did the fieldwork in that site herself, and she dispatched her assistant to a different site in a community in the Pacific Northwest, where racial prejudice was not so prevalent.

On the other hand, as we said earlier, confidential or intimate behavior may be more readily revealed to interviewers perceived to be sympathetic outsiders.

EXAMPLE 4.20

INTERVIEWING YOUNG WOMEN IN MAURITIUS: WHETHER TO MATCH INTERVIEWERS
TO RESPONDENTS OR NOT

In 1992 and 1993 a joint American-Mauritius ethnographic research team was conducting a study of AIDS risk among young, unmarried women in the workforce. Mauritius is culturally and linguistically diverse. The major ethnic/linguistic groups are Christian Creoles (people of French and African origin), Hindu Indo-Mauritians and Indo-Mauritian Muslims originally from India, and Chinese people from southern China. All groups speak Creole, Mauritius's lingua franca, and most groups speak some French and a third language (Hindi, Urdu, Cantonese, etc.), depending on their country of origin.

Approximately ninety young women in the industrial sector were interviewed about their family and work background, their relationships with their peers, their sexual experience, and their knowledge of HIV/AIDS and sexually transmitted diseases (STDs). Interview topics were considered to be sensitive, especially since Mauritian families still place high value on female virginity. In addition, the multiethnic interview team consisted of both males and females ranging in age from twenty-six to fifty-two, and part of the interview focused on participants' sexual behaviors, partners, conflicts, and problems. Team members and project directors gave considerable thought to what the match between interviewers and respondents should be. For the most part, interviewers and respondents were matched first by gender and language, and second by ethnicity. In some cases, foreigners—the project's lead researchers—interviewed female workers as well as managers. Foreign interviewers seemed able to elicit extensive responses despite occasional language and clear cultural differences. Occasionally, young women asked the non-Mauritian interviewers questions about their physiology, pregnancy, menstruation, and other reproductive health issues that they might not have asked a Mauritian interviewer. One of the field team members was a young American male who, despite his gender, had good results when interviewing several young unmarried women about their sexual behavior, including loss of virginity. Team members concluded that foreign males as well as females could in fact successfully carry out interviews too sensitive for nonforeign interviewers of the same sex to conduct.

Because "insiders" may be viewed as already knowledgeable, it may be difficult for an interviewer who is from the same group or background as the informants to obtain detailed information the informant feels the ethnographer already knows (see Example 4.1 in this book). Furthermore,

informants may be unwilling to divulge sensitive information to an insider who might identify which members of the community have revealed community secrets.

EXAMPLE 4.21

ALTERING DATA COLLECTION STRATEGIES IN A YOUTH-LED PARTICIPATORY ACTION RESEARCH PROJECT TO BETTER ELICIT SENSITIVE INFORMATION

Each summer, youth in the National Teen Action Research Center of the Institute for Community Research conduct a team research project of their choice. Two of the topics chosen one summer by the summer research team of thirty youth were "sex at an early age" and "factors accounting for dropping out of school." During a six-week period, youth learned basic ethnographic field research methods, two of which involved in-depth interviewing and ethnographic surveying. As they learned each method, they had the opportunity to apply it to the collection of data related to their topic. In both groups, youth were reluctant to interview their peers in face-to-face interviews on the topics chosen that year because they feared that their peers would not share accurate information about their own behavior in these areas with them. Consequently, they conducted their face-to-face, in-depth interviews with adults, and used an anonymous survey with their peers.

Cross Reference: See Book 3, chapter 9, and Book 5, chapter 9, on the definition and description of the concept of the ethnographic survey

Patterns of deference, prejudice, and discrimination affect the access that researchers from subordinated groups within a society have to certain kinds of data. The reverse also can be true, when researchers perceived to be from privileged cultural or ethnic backgrounds are discouraged or even prevented from accessing important information about subordinated or minority populations. The United States Bureau of the Census, for example, often has been prevented from enumerating specific groups in the population—or from defining them in specific ways—because such groups argue that doing so either underrepresents their numbers or could single them out for racial discrimination. In some societies, rigid formal and informal social practices can make contact between researchers and community members difficult.

EXAMPLE 4.22

RACE AS AN IMPEDIMENT TO RESEARCHER ACCESS

Hortense Powdermaker (1966), a white female anthropologist, found that racist patterns of social distance and avoidance made it difficult for her to carry out observations or interviews in the African American neighborhoods of the small southern community she studied in the United States in the 1940s. Blacks came to white residences only as servants or laborers. White men were not supposed to be in the African American community unless they were collecting bills, arresting inhabitants, or on other business. A white woman had no legitimate reason for visiting blacks at all. In fact, doing so risked endangering any black male individual whom she encountered, because he might be accused of molesting or even raping her if anything went awry.

EXAMPLE 4.23

HOW ETHNIC PREJUDICE CREATES SOCIAL DISTANCE

Getting to her research site in the Navajo Nation required that LeCompte fly in to the nearest airport, rent a car, and then drive for three hours across an isolated, rural landscape. On her first trip to the Pinnacle community, LeCompte's flight arrived late, necessitating a three-hour drive on a cold, dark, winter night. Stopping at a small restaurant near the airport, LeCompte asked for coffee and directions to make sure that she was on the correct road. "Whatever are you going *there* for, little lady?" asked the waiter. "All you're going to find is a bunch of drunken Indians." When she persisted in asking for directions, the waiter threw a map at her, poured her coffee, and left without charging her. "You're going to need that coffee to survive, lady, if you insist on driving to *that* place!" he retorted over his shoulder.

Cosmetics, Clothing, and Bodily Decoration: The Researcher's Visual Identity Kit

Human beings never go naked into any social situation. Even in societies where little actual clothing is used, various forms of decoration, body or face paint, jewelry, and regalia are put on to enhance beauty, establish one's status, or maintain norms of propriety. In addition to physical props, people adopt styles of speaking, moving, and interacting with others that conform to established ideas about behavior appropriate for the kind of people they are and establish or reinforce their identity and position within the limits of social and cultural expectations. The well-known sociologist, Erving Goffman (1960), called the adornments, props, trappings, and styles of behavior that people use to establish or reinforce who they are an *identity kit*. ***Ethnographers need to be aware of those aspects of their customary identity kit that might offend people in the field or that might lead them to make assumptions detrimental to the relationships that ethnographers need to establish in the field.*** The anthropologist Shirley Heath (1996, personal communication), who worked with low-income and minority urban adolescents, asserts that she tries to be as "neutral" in her appearance as possible; she doesn't wear jewelry or clothes that make a statement, and she even limits the color of the clothing she wears to white, beige, black, and gray. She feels that doing so avoids to some extent the assumptions that people make about who a person is based on what they look like; it interferes less with the natural behavior and expression of members of the group she is studying. While it isn't necessary to adopt such a practice, it is important to know what local norms and expectations for appearance are.

Key point

EXAMPLE 4.24

WHEN TO AVOID LOOKING LIKE A "HIPPIE"

LeCompte was assembling a team of interviewers for a study that explored why American Indian students in one high school in the Navajo Nation had begun to experience significantly higher rates of failure in their classes than in previous years. The interviewers were recruited from among LeCompte's graduate students, and the work required a stay of several days in the Navajo Nation. When she asked staff members at the Navajo school what specific advice she should give to the interviewers before they came, the high school librarian said, "I know that you all come from Boulder, Colorado, and that Boulder is the land of hippies. But Indian people down here don't like hippies. They are tired of all these blue-eyed blondes coming down in their cut-off jeans and Birkenstocks,[1] trying to live in teepees and acting like Indians when they don't know what they are doing. They are just trespassing. And they trash up sacred sites. So tell them: No long hair, no nose rings, and no Birkenstocks."

---

1. Birkenstocks are a kind of sandal, made in Germany and popular among young people in the United States. In the 1970s, Birkenstocks were a symbol of countercultural, or hippie, lifestyles, and they still carry that connotation.

As important as adopting behavior that conforms to the standards of the host community can be, ethnographers also must be aware that trying to "act like Indians"—as in Example 4.24 above—can be as offensive as outright defiance of cultural norms.

EXAMPLE 4.25

THE IMPROPRIETY OF "GOING NATIVE": WHEN TO AVOID IMITATING RESEARCH PARTICIPANTS

A politically committed white female ethnographer was hired to coordinate an AIDS research project conducted among injection drug users in an urban area in the northeastern United States. Many of the staff members were African American or Latino. Anxious to learn more about the African American community, the coordinator began to spend long—but appropriate—periods of time in households and community organizations and at public events in the black community, learning more and more about black culture. Soon she began to use language and body movements that imitated those of her new friends and associates. At a staff meeting, the issue of cultural differences surfaced. Some black staff members strongly objected to what they perceived to be the coordinator's attempt to gain intimacy with black people by appropriating elements of a cultural experience that was not hers. Fortunately, the staff members were able to resolve the conflict in an open discussion of the behaviors and what they meant to all members of the group and adapt their behaviors accordingly.

Culture, Class, and Education

Among the most important components of what ethnographers bring with them to the field are the patterns of behavior, beliefs about how the world does and should operate, and the preferences, skills, and ways of looking at the world that are shaped by their own cultural heritage, social class and consequent sense of entitlement, and educational levels. These aspects of identity profoundly affect one's presentation of self, and, more importantly, expectations about how others should behave. Unfortunately, these components of identity often are those of which people are least aware. They are taken for granted and believed to have little effect on oneself and those with whom interactions take place, because they are not considered to be aspects of the power asymmetry between researchers and people in

the field. And yet, these unconscious identity traits are of critical importance.

Class in particular is problematic. Persons from the middle and upper classes, who constitute many, if not most, of the persons who direct research projects, have developed attitudes about work and responsibility, comfortable living, use of leisure time, and commitment to jobs that correspond to the kinds of middle- and upper-middle-class lives and careers they pursue. They also have beliefs about standards of personal hygiene, punctuality, and appropriate dress that serve them well in their homes, social interactions, and on the job. In some cases, these attitudes derive from the relatively greater privilege that middle- and upper-class people enjoy in society. Such attitudes also are facilitated by the more stable, predictable, and hygienic conditions in which the more affluent live. When researchers expect the people they study also to hold similar attitudes and beliefs, they may well be surprised at best; at worst, they risk offending research participants by appearing to be elitists, snobbish, or simply ignorant of the realities of local living conditions.

EXAMPLE 4.26

CLASS DIFFERENCES IN APPROACHES TO DENTAL CARE

Access to the lower-income community on the south side of Chicago where J. Schensul's educational intervention was located depended upon her relationship with the project's parent coordinator, an African American woman from the community in her early forties. While the relationship generally was positive, there were uneasy moments, primarily because of class and educational differences between Schensul, a young, middle-class, married professional with a PhD and no children, and the coordinator, an older woman with some college education, three children, and a limited family income. These differences came into clear focus when the coordinator decided to have all her teeth pulled and replaced with dentures. Shocked, Schensul tried to convince her to repair—and save—her own teeth. The coordinator informed Schensul that dentures were a far preferable solution, not only because they were cheaper but also because they were permanent. Further, she did not, in fact, have the insurance or the cash to pay for regular dental care and maintenance. This decision, which illustrated the class and resource difference between them, was the subject of discussion over a long period of time. Recognizing these differences made it possible to discuss them openly, which increased trust between them and improved their working relationship.

EXAMPLE 4.27

CLASS AND ETHNIC DIFFERENCES IN WAYS TO "RELAX"

The director of an enrichment program for American Indian children often tried to have lunch with her Indian staff members so that they could, as the director said, "just be relaxed." She hoped that such events would build more closeness among the staff members. For the director, whose husband had a well-paying job and who came from an upper-class community in the Eastern United States, a "relaxing place" was a restaurant with tables, cloth napkins, and waiters. For the Indian staff—most of whom were single parents struggling to meet expenses—such places were anything but relaxing. "Nice" restaurants were too expensive and reminded the Indian teachers of past patterns of discrimination, which had precluded them from even buying meals they could carry out to eat at home from such restaurants. The Indian staff members also had short official lunch breaks, so taking longer breaks to "relax" with the director meant falling behind in their daily duties. The director never understood why her staff members kept suggesting picnics in the park as an alternative, and neither the lunches nor the team building that the director wanted to organize ever occurred.

Incidents such as these illustrate how people in the study community may prevent the ethnographer from accessing important information because they believe either that ethnographers will demonstrate too little sensitivity to the needs and lives of people in the community or that the conditions under which the information must be acquired violate standards for treatment to which they expect ethnographers to adhere.

PERSONAL FRIENDSHIPS IN THE FIELD

Ethnographers should not move quickly to establish close relationships in the field, even though doing so is tempting, since fieldwork can be a lonely enterprise. It is common for ethnographers to be befriended or "adopted" by atypical or eccentric individuals in the community who, lacking indigenous friends or support structures, seek legitimation or status in the company of the ethnographer. This can be a problem, because such persons often are marginalized or outcasts and certainly have idiosyncratic perspectives on the community. Further, being known as a friend of such people may prevent developing contacts with other, more socially cen-

tral, members of the community. Ethnographers also should avoid fully believing everything that initial informants tell them about the community, since the marginalized people who initially befriend them may have idiosyncratic ideas about the community or have sets of friends and enemies whose perspectives do not typify the community.

 **EXAMPLE 4.28**

THE DANGER OF BEING ASSOCIATED WITH MARGINAL GROUPS IN A COMMUNITY

A young, white anthropologist in a large Midwestern city in the United States joined a community research team whose mission was to establish relationships with a broad spectrum of community leaders and organizations. He was sought out, and then befriended, by two socially marginal left-wing community activists who were interested in building an interethnic political organization; he became personally and politically involved with these two individuals. As a consequence, his capacity to enter the wider Latino community with which the research team wished to work was compromised to some degree, and he was unable to fulfill his responsibilities as a member of the research team. In subsequent years he still was perceived to be associated with this small faction in the community, even when he had moved on to other work.

Careful ethnographers take pains to befriend as many different kinds of persons in the community as possible, thereby preserving the opportunity to create new contacts. They try both to avoid creating enemies or being identified with specific factions.

 **EXAMPLE 4.29**

AVOIDING NEGATIVE ROLES AND MAINTAINING OPEN COMMUNICATION

Niels Braroe, a Swedish anthropologist studying an Indian community in Canada, said, "My wife and I [n]ever became identified as 'Indian' (although I did become the adopted son of one couple and sibling to their children). Instead, since we could not be placed in any of the White roles familiar to Indians [and since we were not Indians, either], we were given a special place in the community" (Braroe, 1971, 22).

Braroe's strategy permitted him to be situated as neither Indian nor white, but as sympathetic to the Indian point of view and uncritical of Indian behavior. He did not conform to beliefs among whites that Indians were dirty, lazy, and irresponsible. To be so positioned permitted Braroe to move to what is called the "back regions" (Goffman, 1959)—those behavior settings or parts of the social scene that normally would be inaccessible to outsiders. Such a location, while desirable, is sometimes impossible for applied ethnographers to achieve because of affiliations and allegiances—real or imagined, as in the example of LeCompte's experience in Pinnacle—that the researcher brings to the field.

In the best cases, of course, the researcher's prior affiliations are viewed positively and serve to legitimate the presence of the ethnographer in the research site. Further, it is the case that close friendships eventually do emerge among researchers and participants, and they evolve in the field. Many researchers maintain close contact with their friends from fieldwork over long periods of time. Stephen and Jean Schensul regularly visit and stay in touch with close friends and co-workers in Chicago's southwest side Mexican community where they worked from 1968 to 1974 and close friends with whom they worked in the Puerto Rican community of Hartford over many years. And a number of anthropologists marry people they have met in the field.

SUMMARY

In this chapter, we have examined how the researcher's roles and personal characteristics affect his or her capacity for conforming to the informal ethics of everyday interaction in the field. In particular, we call attention to the necessity of learning as much as possible as quickly as possible about how people are expected to behave in the field site. Much of that learning is directed at figuring out appropriate behavior for the ethnographer to adopt; it also makes possible mapping out the informal ethical rules and etiquette that govern the community under study. In the next chapter, we discuss the kinds of informal or everyday ethical responsibilities that evolve as researchers spend more and more time in the field and find that their relationships with people deepen. We also note how researchers can, to some extent, manipulate their everyday identity kit and behavior so as to appear less intimidating or strange to research participants.

5 ━●━●━

Introduction:
Feasible and
Possible
Responsibilities

Coping with
Associations
in the Field:
Affiliations and
Sponsorships

Maintaining
Good
Relationships

Coresearchers
and Research
Partners

Negotiating an
Exit and Leaving
the Field

Reciprocity and
Feedback

Dissemination
and Disposition
of Data

Assuring Program
Continuation

Summary

INFORMAL ETHICS: LONG-TERM RELATIONSHIPS AND REASONABLE RESPONSIBILITIES

INTRODUCTION: FEASIBLE AND POSSIBLE RESPONSIBILITIES

The *Anthropology Newsletter*, published by the American Anthropology Association, has regularly published columns on the everyday ethical dilemmas ethnographers face in the field. These columns have covered a variety of topics ranging from the ethics involved in exchanges of goods and services, such as, "Would providing an antibiotic ointment to parents in the field site whose child suffered from trachoma violate the tenet that a certain distance be maintained between participant and researcher?" to questions about relationships. For example, how deep should a researcher's friendship with participants go without compromising the authenticity of behavior observed or the validity of the researcher's interpretation of that behavior? Could researchers date, fall in love, or have sex with research participants without compromising their work? Would their close relationships affect how objective their interpretations and observations were? Could they become public advocates for or with the community they studied? What about helping to send an informant's child to school? Or organizing friends in the United States to purchase handicrafts from the researcher's participants? Or providing taxi money to a mother to enable her to take her severely wounded child to the hospital? These are relatively ordinary requests that occur in everyday life. They develop especially in the course of long-term fieldwork, when ethnographers form deep friendships, long-term associations, sets of mutual expectations, and deep understandings of community dynamics and the implications of refusal. Such situations call for a profound consideration of ethical implications when they involve requests that ethnographers cannot honor, disturb existing relationships, involve the disclosure of information that participants wish to keep private or to be presented in a different light, are felt to be defamatory, or involve ending relationships, associations, and even exchanges of resources in the field that participants value highly.

EXAMPLE 5.1

ESTABLISHING BOUNDARIES BETWEEN "REASONABLE" AND "IMPOSSIBLE" INFORMANT REQUESTS

Ariana Mangual, a doctoral student, spent several years studying a community of migrant workers living near her university. One family in particular became the focus of her study. The more time she spent in the community, the more she became integrated into the family's daily life, and the more she began to hear people talk about the difficulties of living in a country without legal papers. Most particularly, parents worried about the need to find someone who would sign a *carta de responsabilidad*, a letter guaranteeing the care of their children—most of whom were born in the United States and hence, legal residents—in case the parents were deported. As pressures from the Immigration and Customs Enforcement agency of the US government intensified to deport people who were not legal residents in the United States, Ariana came to understand the full import of a *carta de responsabilidad*: the guarantor had to be a legal resident, preferably a US citizen, and it had to be someone who knew and loved the children, was trustworthy, and was financially able to take the place of the parents. As the weeks passed, though the parents did not mention specifics, Ariana began to dread the time when the family would ask her to become the potential guardian of the family's three children. It wasn't that she did not love the family and the children, but her fiancé and she planned to leave at the end of the school year, when Ariana finished her research and graduated; they had already accepted jobs across the country, in California. More important, she did not feel ready for a family, especially an adopted one. At the same time, she felt torn. There were few people in the community capable of taking on a *carta de responsabilidad*, and Ariana knew that she was one of those few. She owed her dissertation research and her new career to the family's patience and willingness to have her study them. All spring, she agonized over the matter. As she was beginning to say her good-byes on one of her last days in the community, the father and mother finally approached her gently and obliquely asked if she felt she could think about signing a *carta*. Taking a deep breath, she explained that she could not (Mangual Figueroa, 2013).

This example shows that the current framing of issues of informal ethics centers on the management of everyday reciprocities of life in the field. It was completely reasonable for the family to have made such a request to Ariana, given the relationship they had developed and her status in the community. But the relationships established in the field are somewhat unique: they are friendships, but special kinds of friendships (Agar, 1982), and they are time bounded, insofar as unlike local residents, investigators usually do not plan to remain in the field and to make their lives there. The special relationships established in the field complicate the daily "doing good" in interactions with research participants, audiences for research, and fellow researchers. However, such ordinary or "everyday" (Lambek, 2010) ethics nonetheless do fall into the general area of good manners and respectful and caring treatment of others. Thus, Ariana found it impossible to comply with her study family's "reasonable" request, given her life circumstances. It may have been that despite her intimacy with the family, Ariana had not been fully forthcoming about her own life and plans. If she had been, they might not have asked. However, like Ariana, most researchers, particularly those engaged in participatory or ethnographic investigations, struggle with the effort to translate "normal," everyday good behavior, including revealing personal aspects of their lives and decision making, into informal ethics governing the somewhat artificial relationships obtaining.

COPING WITH ASSOCIATIONS IN THE FIELD: AFFILIATIONS AND SPONSORSHIPS

Experienced ethnographers are aware that they are known by the company they keep. They know that they will bring personal and professional relationships into the field with them and acquire more of them once they have arrived. They also know that the existence of these relationships will affect how research participants interpret their behavior and motivations. They are aware that they will be affected by past history; in many cases, they will be expected to behave similarly to the last researcher who visited the site, whether that researcher was viewed with favor or disfavor.

Initiation of any research project requires that the ethnographer find people in the research site to grant them access and help them to make initial contacts. We already have indicated that this necessary step in a research project can create problems for ethnographers, who cannot avoid being identified in some way with those who preceded them or who first introduced them to the community. Those identifications can color how researchers are perceived by the community. In this chapter, we first discuss the impact such identifications have on interaction with research participants before ethnographers enter the field and how they can act to reduce any negative impact of such prior impressions. For example, ethnographers can organize their "presentation of self" (Goffman, 1959) so as to allay the fears that research participants have about what they might be like.

Cross Reference:
See Book 2 for a discussion preparing for entry into the field, and Book 3 for the way gatekeepers can affect a researcher's reception

EXAMPLE 5.2   ━●━◆━●◆━

WHEN PERCEPTIONS INFLUENCE HIRING DECISIONS

A new program of the Institute for Community Research involved training women from the community to carry out mixed methods research on women in Hartford. The purpose of the project was to fill a significant information gap on women's needs, interests, challenges, and educational mobility in the city and to expand the model to other cities in the state. The women of Hartford, Connecticut, are diverse, including African Americans, African Diaspora women, those from various countries in Latin America, those from Puerto Rico, the West Indies, and Brazil, from various European countries, and even those born in New England. The program was guided by a steering committee composed of an equally diverse group of women. The goal was to hire someone as the director who could relate to *all* the women of Hartford. Several candidates were interviewed, and one in particular stood out. She was an African American woman from New York who had recently arrived in the city. Her husband was a physician hired to work in a large community health center. Stylishly dressed, she had a background in marketing research and a strong commitment to women's issues. She also was light skinned with freckles and wore a blond, short afro, thereby not fitting any local stereotypes of professional African American women. While several members of the committee were uncomfortable with her business background (it was not social science), her appearance (not "black enough"), and her orientation (not progressive enough), she ultimately was hired, and her many experiences and somewhat nonstereotypical presentation of self enabled her to maintain a "neutral" positionality, relate to all the women well, and to guide the program successfully for several years.

EXAMPLE 5.3

DRESSING TO CONTRADICT NEGATIVE STEREOTYPES

Medical anthropologist Stephen Schensul's first assignment from the medical school he represented was to build community placements for medical students by creating collaborative projects that linked the university medical school with agencies in the Hartford, Connecticut, area. Because the medical school had just moved away from the city of Hartford to the suburbs, Hartford community residents felt betrayed, believing that its physicians and faculty had abandoned them. When Schensul first approached the heads of community agencies, they were reluctant to meet with him . . . until they saw his cowboy boots, blue jeans, and leather vest. Dubbing him the "cowboy anthropologist," they set aside their stereotypes of the health center (known as the "white elephant") and its personnel and were able to more easily establish the collaborative research relationships the community placements required.

While Dr. Schensul was able to set aside negative medical stereotypes, the negative impact of other kinds of affiliations and initial impressions are not so easily set aside, even when ethnographers spend extensive time in the community and make strenuous efforts to limit their effects.

EXAMPLE 5.4

WHEN THE WOUNDS OF HISTORY WON'T HEAL: WORKING WITH AN INTRACTABLE STEREOTYPE

LeCompte's work with a school district in "Pinnacle," an American Indian community, had been preceded by a parade of consultants and researchers who had provided advice and counsel to teachers and administrators alike. Each had charged substantial fees for their efforts, and few were described as very helpful by teachers and staff. By contrast, LeCompte, an expert on current school reform initiatives, received no fee or honoraria, even though she served as a consultant and evaluator for some of the district's projects and taught a miniclass for teachers on evaluation. Her own interest in the district was to investigate what educational needs such a community had and the kinds of innovations that might be possible there. The primary purpose of the grant she had written was to hire local people for several innovative programs designed to increase the number of Native Americans who were certified to teach in the local schools. The grant also provided scholarship money for several Indian teacher aides to complete their university training; however, it provided only travel and living expenses for LeCompte's monthly trips to the community. Notwithstanding that LeCompte was not paid for her services, she still was viewed by many in the community as "one of those high-priced consultants" who came to the community "like used car salesmen. They all talk very loudly, don't tell us much that we could use, and then leave with their fees." This point of view, which had been established before she arrived in Pinnacle, colored the reception that LeCompte received and made some school staff unwilling to work with her. Even before LeCompte arrived in Pinnacle, she was identified as a university-based researcher—like many of the previous consultants. Thus, she walked into a set of preconceptions about consultants that her predecessors had established.

All these roles—consultant, educational reformer, evaluator—were real ones that LeCompte brought with her to the field. They were among the reasons the superintendent had invited her to the start of the year in-service. She subsequently came to the district on funds she herself had procured, for a program the superintendent wanted to implement. LeCompte had a number of ideas about how she could help in the district and what her roles could be. However, the fact that she was imposed from the top, by the superintendent's invitation, meant that she was associated with the superintendent's ideas about innovation in the district. Further, her role definitions became conflated with the way some district staff defined previous occupants of those roles—as shysters, con artists, or hired guns. Even people who didn't hold these stereotypes tended to view her as a person whose ideas would increase the work overload teachers already experienced. Differences between the roles as LeCompte defined them and roles as they were defined by significant community members made it difficult for LeCompte to play the other roles she found more desirable: collaborator, researcher, and colleague.

Like LeCompte, ethnographers commonly balance— and carry out—all these roles simultaneously, with and without "baggage," even though doing so is never easy and is always fraught with tensions and ambivalence. Sometimes, however, ethnographers get lucky; the affiliations with which researchers are associated turn out to be especially welcomed by the community.

EXAMPLE 5.5

WHEN INFORMANTS THINK RESEARCHERS' PRIOR AFFILIATIONS ARE BENEFICIAL

When LeCompte presented her proposal for a collaborative evaluation of the Arts Focus Enrichment Program to Centerville Middle School's faculty and staff, she met with unexpected enthusiasm from the principal of the school. "We are the only enrichment program in the district that will have its own researcher," he said. "We really are lucky to have Dr. LeCompte work with us, because she's a link to the University and its resources." Within several weeks, the principal and his assistant had found several ways to assist with LeCompte's data collection. In return, he solicited LeCompte's advice in locating consultants, securing financial support from foundations for the Arts Enrichment and other programs, and gaining access to the University's Art Gallery for student field trips. Similarly, Jean Schensul found that doors opened to her readily in the diverse communities of the greater Hartford area when she took over the directorship of the Institute for Community Research, because she had been known for a decade of applied research and development at the Hispanic Health Council, another community research organization.

MAINTAINING GOOD RELATIONSHIPS

Just as friendships and colleagueships outside the research site often require diplomacy and judicious fostering, so also must ethnographers "work" at their relationships in the field during their fieldwork, and even after their fieldwork ends, regardless of whether or not they take up or continue residence in the field setting. Sometimes that "work" can land an ethnographer in serious difficulty if participants establish "tests" that the ethnographer must pass in order to appear trustworthy. Such tests can be relatively benign, such as eating food that the ethnographer finds to be virtually inedible or disgusting, or attending concerts of music that the ethnographer either dislikes or finds to be deafening. Other tests can be unhealthy—such as being asked to drink alcohol in competition with others or to eat food that the ethnographer knows to be contaminated with microbes. More dangerous tests exist when ethnographers studying drug cultures, gangs, people without homes, underground political groups, or cults find that they are invited to places where violence or illegal activities could occur, or to participate in activities that could cause arrest and prosecution if revealed.

EXAMPLE 5.6

PROVING ONE'S CHOPS IN TRADITIONAL DRINKING COMPETITIONS

Undiagnosed pneumonia in infants and small children was a significant health problem in parts of rural China. A WHO project was funded to create and test materials designed to help country doctors and mothers identify and differentiate pneumonia (acute respiratory infections) from other more benign and typical respiratory problems. Jean Schensul was asked to consult on the project, and in the process, to accompany a team of WHO staff and pediatricians to various locations in China. One of the goals of the trips was to involve county and provincial officials in endorsing the project and public health staff in delivering the intervention materials to rural doctors. Local officials prized good food, and banquets at each stop sponsored by the project were part of the "marketing" program. At the final banquet, the study team was honored by the presence of the provincial governor, a woman. In traditional practice, the senior official invites the honored guest to a drinking duel in which both parties drink small glasses of Chinese white local wine, and toast until one can drink no more. The provincial governor was known as a woman who could drink more than anyone else and had won many such drinking duels. Schensul was the honored guest and, in the interest of the Chinese research team, could not refuse to participate in the competition. Both parties drank a very large amount of alcohol. Even worse, Schensul drank more

than the governor, thereby jeopardizing relationships between the governor and the research team. In turn, however, the governor arranged for a Chinese/Russian language musical competition in which she, as a noted performer, fluent in both languages, sang. Schensul could do nothing but hum. The governor thereby managed to embarrass Schensul in an equitable tit for tat. Relationships were maintained between the project team and the governor, and the price for Schensul was momentary embarrassment and a fortunately short-lived hangover.

EXAMPLE 5.7

"TESTS" THAT PLACE RESEARCHERS IN PHYSICAL AND LEGAL DANGER

In a study of young adults and drug use in an eastern American city, female members of the research team were involved in participant observation at downtown bars and clubs. One evening, several study participants invited the researchers to attend a known hangout downtown, a place where spontaneous or planned fights between individuals or groups of young people might occur. The invitation was designed to test researchers' willingness to enter into a more risky component of study participants' lives. Study participants had shared the information that if they wanted to "chill out," they used the drug ecstasy, and if they wanted some exposure to excitement and potential fights, they used "dust" (PCP), a drug that numbed feelings of fear and enhanced feelings of bravery. Usually prior to going to this club, "dust" was the drug of choice. One evening, a planned fight between two opposing gangs erupted at the bar. One of the young men had a gun, and shot it, seriously wounding another. The bar was crowded, and people pushed their way out of the bar through the single exit, trying to avoid danger and the arrival of the police. Though the "test" did substantiate that the researchers were, indeed, willing to enter more deeply into the young people's lives, and while no one else was hurt, this event exposed all attendees to physical danger both from the rush to exit and from the presence and use of guns.

Often, dilemmas arise when the time comes for the dissemination or publishing of research results. If participants disagree with, or do not like the results of, a study, how should publication be negotiated? In chapter 6, we describe how Margaret Gibson faced such a dilemma; faced with a disagreement over the research results and their meaning, Gibson and her dissenting coprincipal investigator created two reports. Sometimes, however, researchers are unaware of a conflict until they are right in the middle of it. LeCompte faced just such a situation after completing a number of years of fieldwork investigating attempts at school reform in a school district serving an American Indian reservation.

EXAMPLE 5.8

DECIDING NOT TO PUBLISH A STORY SO AS TO PRESERVE GOOD RELATIONSHIPS

LeCompte's research had begun to focus on why many tribal communities that had developed their own teaching methods and curricula that were responsive to their particular language and culture so easily abandoned their own efforts when confronted by mainstream and European-American demands for dominant culture comprehensive school reform (Aguilera, 2003). LeCompte planned to argue that tribal communities were so accustomed to having their own efforts deprecated by whites that they lacked the self-confidence—and funding—to withstand pressure to abandon their native language instruction and instructional content in favor of a Eurocentric, English-only approach. The school district LeCompte was studying had spent five years working on a language and culture approach, but then dropped it overnight for an approach called "The Modern Red School House." Developed by E. D. Hirsch and promoted by the Hudson Institute, a conservative think tank, the Modern Red School House is a Comprehensive School Reform Model that emphasizes high achievement and a core curriculum focusing on European-American content (www.mrsh.org). LeCompte had prepared a paper for presentation at a professional conference about the problems of implementing indigenously created curricula, in which she had intended to point out that the disparity of self-esteem between whites and Native Americans contributed to causing the latter to abandon their indigenous programs in favor of those from outside. In the middle of her presentation, she was confronted by two Native Americans who were visitors at the conference. They felt that LeCompte's conclusions were racist because they implied that all Native Americans suffered from low self-esteem. They particularly objected to LeCompte's use of the metaphor "circling the wagons"—a term that she used to describe how mainstream educators resisted implementing indigenous efforts to create curricula and instructional programs that supported Native American culture. While neither of the two individuals came from the community LeCompte had studied (they were, in fact, school bus drivers who worked in an adjacent community and were pursuing college degrees near the conference venue), they saw a paper on Navajos in the program and decided to attend. LeCompte realized that her work might be taken as highly critical of Native Americans (exactly the opposite of her intent) and that other indigenous people might conclude similarly. She dropped the metaphor and ultimately abandoned the idea of publishing her findings because the topic was too controversial. Moreover, it was likely to be viewed as a negative

critique of individuals who still worked in the school district under investigation—people who did not deserve such treatment (LeCompte, 1993a, 1993b).

CORESEARCHERS AND RESEARCH PARTNERS

When researchers work as a team, they generally "cover each other's backs," both in the field and in the "research office," while writing up notes, having meetings, and engaging with research participants. In chapter 6, we will discuss ethical issues in team and other forms of collaborative research. Here we point out three types of situations that can occur among co-workers and partners that are important to address in maintaining the integrity of the research and the integrity of the research team. The first is when a member of the research team takes admirable action to protect the interests of the study and the study team; the second is when a study team member "blows the whistle" for research misconduct or ethical violations carried out by another team member who may also be a friend; and the third is when a team member takes a controversial action in the field that could affect other team members and the team's ability to continue future research in a setting.

 **EXAMPLE 5.9**

WHEN A TEAM MEMBER SHOWS GOOD JUDGMENT IN TAKING PROTECTIVE ACTION

In a study of pathways to hard drug use, research team members went out in pairs to investigate club and party venues in the city of Hartford, Connecticut. One evening, the team leader and another researcher decided to visit a club on the outskirts of the city that was known as a place where underage drinking and drug use took place under the surveillance of the police. The police were there primarily to address any fights or other eruptions of conflict as people left the club, and they occasionally conducted surveillance with drug-sniffing dogs in the club, but they never arrested anyone. The team leader had some concerns about the presence of the police, but overall the site was considered to be safe for observation. On arrival, the team found that the club was private. Luckily, one member of the team knew someone near the door who invited them in. Once in the club, the team discovered that it was a weekend party venue for LGTBQ youth, and that the primary drug used there was marijuana. The air was filled with marijuana

fumes, seriously affecting the team leader, who had asthma. Though the setting was welcoming, and the researchers had just begun to explore the different groups of attendees who were there and whether substances such as ecstasy were being used in the club, the team leader was having severe breathing difficulties. The team leader was comfortable with waiting outside alone in her car, especially given the protective presence of the police. Also, the second researcher had friends in the site and was comfortable remaining there by herself. Despite the promise of the site for yielding good information on the study, however, both researchers left together to protect each other and to avoid any potential problems that could arise for a lone researcher in a first-time visit to such a site.

The second situation, in which a team member blows the whistle, can be especially painful for those immediately affected (the whistleblower and the person committing the unethical or even illegal act), for the rest of the team, and even for the project.

EXAMPLE 5.10

WHEN A TEAM MEMBER BLOWS THE WHISTLE

The first year of a long-term action research project involving a diverse group of urban women residents and activists involved in advocacy research for women's rights was focused on training Hartford, Connecticut, women to develop a survey and collect information about other women in the city. The data were to be used by the city's Permanent Commission on the Status of Women to advocate for better attention to women's needs, with support from the advocacy group represented by the women in the program. Since there were no data other than census data on women in the city, the survey was quite long. One white woman on the team, a well-known and well-liked advocate for women's welfare, was suspected to be "faking the data." A team member reported this privately and in confidence to one of the staff. The team member was very uncomfortable because she knew it would affect her co-worker's reputation as an advocate and as a researcher, and that it also would affect the quality of the data collected legitimately by the rest of the group from other women in the city. The team member recognized that if the rest of the team knew about this situation, it would seriously affect their morale in this highly experimental program and jeopardize the status of the program as a statewide model for urban women's participatory action research and advocacy. The staff talked the situation over and decided to confront the woman with

the possibility that she had been filling in responses herself. She confessed that she had. Rather than terminating her, which would have been disastrous, she was asked to redeem herself by recollecting data from "real" women, which she did. None of the women on the Participatory Action Research team knew about the transgression, and her reputation and that of the program remained intact.

The third type of situation can occur in the field when a serious event occurs in a setting and a debate among research team members ensues over how to address it. For example, what should researchers do if they witness, for example, a woman who is in labor and about to give birth, a child hit by a car or mauled by a tiger, or a drunken man who falls and injures himself? Differences of opinion about how to handle such situations can affect the integrity of a team. The following vignettes illustrate how such problems were solved to everyone's satisfaction, protecting the team and the research as well as a participant in the study.

EXAMPLE 5.11

TAKING ACTION IN A CRISIS

Researcher Christina Huebner was a member of a team doing participant observations for a study on club drugs including ecstasy, GHB, rohypnol, and other substances that could result in the loss of consciousness to young people in dance and party situations, especially if mixed with alcohol. Some mixes of such drugs and alcohol were known to be lethal. While doing participant observation with another team member in a Connecticut club, Huebner saw a young woman drop to the dance floor, obviously unconscious. No one was paying any attention to the young woman. Christina did not want to identify herself as anything other than an attendee in order to continue her participant observation activities and to avoid drawing attention to herself and her co-worker. Her co-worker was of the opinion that their role was to observe but not to act. At the same time, Christina's personal ethical stance did not permit her to leave the young woman to suffer and possibly even to die without doing something about it. After consulting with the team member and the team leader and some rapid soul searching, she finally decided to use her cell phone to call 911 and report the situation. In this way she could protect her status as an observer, and that of her co-worker, while still making sure that the young woman was taken quickly to the hospital.

EXAMPLE 5.12

TAKING A DRUNKEN MAN HOME

Researchers Steve and Jean Schensul, librarian Levine, and all their children were traveling together with anthropologist Amarisiri de Silva back to their residence in Kandy, Sri Lanka, after a long drive from the southern coast. To return to Kandy they had to pass through the capital city of Colombo, and then up into the hills. It was getting dark, and villagers were out enjoying the fresh air, shopping and socializing. About halfway up to the hills, they passed through a large market town that was very crowded; along the main street through which they were traveling, people were so densely packed that they were touching the truck, causing the driver to slow down nearly to a stop. At a critical moment, a man hit the front of the truck and fell down right in front of the left front wheel. The driver stopped immediately. Dr. De Silva knew that in this part of the country, villagers were easily angered if they thought a stranger had harmed one of them. In this case, it appeared as if the car had knocked the man down, even though to those in the vehicle it was apparent that the man was very drunk. Dr. De Silva quickly came to the decision that if the group was to avoid being beaten, it was necessary to place the man in the car and drive quickly out of the setting, hoping to avoid other pedestrians. The man was thrown, vomit and all, into the back seat of the car, and was able to provide his address. He was returned home, whereupon his wife expressed anger and requested that the driver take her husband to the hospital. He had apparently used this strategy in the past to obtain treatment for his drinking or to obtain a ride home when he could no longer walk. The driver refused, and the travelers went quickly on their way. Dr. De Silva remarked later that despite the risks associated with picking the man up, the decision had been a good one.

NEGOTIATING AN EXIT AND LEAVING THE FIELD

In certain ways, ethnographers really never leave the field. Fieldwork is a life-altering experience, to which ethnographers refer and about which they write throughout their lives. They may maintain lifelong friendships and collegial relationships with people encountered in the field. Field participants also retain their memories of life with the ethnographer, who may even decide to reside in the field. More and more often, "the field" actually is the researcher's home community or even their own "back yard." Regardless, when a study or a project is over, saying good-bye is challenging. Thus, the delicacy of negotiating an exit from a research site resembles gaining initial access, which involves:

- Handling relationships
- Deciding how, when, and if to return to the field
- Deciding how to remain 'in the field" while not continuing the project or study
- Balancing requests for reciprocity
- Identifying and responding to information needs of various stakeholders
- Arranging the disposition of data
- Assuring the program's continuation once the researcher support disappears

Relationships, Friendships, and Dependencies

Qualitative researchers create friendships, dependencies, and sometimes hostilities with field participants. Because researchers cannot simply pack up and slip away at midnight, negotiating how to say good-bye, and how to maintain desired relationships while ending those that cannot be maintained, is a crucial part of the exit process. Of first concern are key informants and good friends. Strategies for the difficult process of maintaining long-distance relationships with these intimate friends and colleagues must be negotiated. Once researchers return home to their "normal" lives, contacts become problematic. Friends in the field can become upset and alienated if they do not know if or when the researcher will return to the field and for what reasons, and how often they will write, email, or call. They also may want to visit the researcher, especially if both live in the same general area or the same city or town.

Other contact may be needed beyond that of friendships. Researchers or their students and colleagues may want to return to the field site because they need further data collection or new projects; they may discover that they have neglected to collect some critical data or need to check on the validity of their interpretations of data. Or they may require additional data to answer questions raised during data analysis that were unanticipated in the field. They also may want to return to start a new project with colleagues and partners in the study setting. If researchers cannot return because of cost, distance, and other demands on their time such as family obligations, clear lines of communication, goodwill, and firm relationships in the field make it possible to ask key informants to collect additional information or to answer questions that arise during data analysis, to check initial and subsequent formulation of results with participants, or to validate interpretations. When they are able to make return visits, preexisting field contacts can facilitate the process of reentering established networks. We should note here that increasingly researchers are required to provide feedback to the communities in which they did their research. As we mention in Book 2, they should consider building return visits for results dissemination into their research funding as a practical and ethical necessity.

Leaving the field can be more problematic for the casual field acquaintances researchers develop, given the expectations such individuals can develop of researchers. Researchers often are linked to a more cosmopolitan and sometimes wealthier community than that of participants, and therefore can be sources of information, intellectual stimulation, outside contacts, and many other resources. Participants whose slight marginalization from the community makes them a perfect inside-outsider informant also can have expectations of the researcher as a source of companionship, status, and even finances. While such people are important to the researcher for their ability to provide information, casual acquaintances may value their contact with the researcher highly for other reasons. The nature and depth of such expectations may be difficult for researchers to ascertain until later. Some participants simply mourn the loss of social and emotional ties and status. Others will miss the economic resources researchers provide when they obtain scarce foreign pharmaceuticals for participants, link local craftspeople to buyers in the United States, buy school supplies for students and teachers in a local school, rent from local landlords, or pay for language classes. Researchers represent career development for local professionals who obtain from them new ideas or techniques that enhance their performance and reputations in ways unattainable to other local residents. Since attenuating or ending these benefits can cause loss or hardship, researchers must explain what resources they are able to continue providing, or help participants develop alternative sources of supplies. Once they have left the field, researchers also must decide how to handle ongoing requests from people in the field site for a variety of different needs, including furthering their children's education, accessing much-needed health care, or as we described earlier, facilitating immigration to the United States or the researcher's country of origin.

In summary, it is undesirable, unethical, and unwise to burn bridges with field-based colleagues and participants. Ignoring formalities of farewell for uncooperative or hostile participants is tempting; so is avoidance of strategies for managing expectations held by casual acquaintances. These individuals may be exactly those who, if alienated or insulted, could bar access to needed data or prevent researchers—including new researchers—from returning.

RECIPROCITY AND FEEDBACK

Too often, researchers fail to pay participants back for allowing them to investigate their worksites and lives. Until recently, most researchers simply disappeared once their research project was finished, leaving participants totally unaware of what had been learned or written about them. Both disappearance and lack of reciprocity are poor research etiquette and unethical. Ethnographic researchers usually do not provide financial incentives for participation in studies— and even if they do, the incentives are small, as is required by their IRBs and to avoid the appearance of coercion. Thus, reciprocity involves exchanges of intangibles—friendship, information, services, and contacts. Much research has procedures for reciprocity built in; participatory or collaborative action research, for example, is designed to benefit directly the community or group participating in the study. However, too often only the researcher derives benefits from the study in the form of publications and fame. Ill will is generated when participants believe researchers have become famous at their expense. Simple acknowledgment of their contribution in publications is necessary but rarely sufficient. Some researchers share visibility with participants or key informants by inviting them to coauthor articles and papers and join them as conference presenters. Others donate publication royalties to communities they studied. In projects involving successful interventions, researchers can give control or comparison groups the same training and information that the intervention group received after the project is complete so that all participants benefit equally. Any researchers can make themselves available to answer questions, provide ongoing in-service, or give workshops.

Feedback and dissemination procedures are needed both in the field and after the project is completed. Researchers must decide what to tell participants when they are asked for information during a project, or how to explain when participants simply want to know what the researcher is finding out. Participants always are entitled to know the results of studies done about them; failure to provide such information at least causes hurt feelings and often "poisons the well" for future researchers, precluding useful continuing investigations in the same community. However, providing feedback is problematic. Participants may not want to hear what researchers actually found if it contradicts their views; researchers may be reluctant to disclose negative information provided by one group of participants about another, and researchers never are able to represent participants or their programs as favorably as participants might wish. Researchers must negotiate how to accomplish such disclosures while minimizing hurt feelings. We address this question more comprehensively in Book 7.

Researchers can consult with participant groups to find out exactly what kinds of information they need, and give them only that information. However, it usually is impossible both to anticipate future information needs and to withhold negative data. Researchers should make it quite clear from the outset that feedback may be neither positive nor in line with participant expectations. Researchers also can embed negative information in context, so that participants understand all the factors leading to specific outcomes. For example, while an educational innovation may have produced negative results, data showing that teachers received insufficient training, that the students enrolled differed from the desired target population, or that materials were delivered late, tell the "whole story" in ways that remove the onus of failure from practitioners. To minimize the conveyance of irrelevant or undesirable information, researchers can work with project advisory boards, groups of key informants, or others to determine what information can or should be shared, and in what forms they are likely to be well received. In this way, they avoid the problems that arise when the researcher's best guess about what should be disseminated and what should be avoided is a flop.

DISSEMINATION AND DISPOSITION OF DATA

Once researchers leave the field, dissemination begins. Different participant groups need different kinds of information; researchers should identify the multiple audiences in the field site first, and then negotiate in advance how and what kinds of information will be provided. Researchers can prepare several kinds of reports and use multiple dissemination modalities—oral presentations, written reports of varying lengths and complexity, workshops and in-services, artistic performances, and publications in media ranging from websites, flyers, and the popular press to scholarly publications. For example, teachers in schools will need different kinds of information from those needed by parents, school administrators, and funding agencies. Agencies in Lusaka's largest slum community need one type of reporting to assist them in becoming more efficient HIV service providers, and women in the study community who are exposed to the risk of HIV need another. Since much of the world now has access to websites, Internet technology may provide a more useful, faster, and more reliable means of communication than paper, telephone, and postal services. However, researchers never should rely on online communication alone, even in the United States.

Participants and other stakeholders have a right to know what will be done with information collected about them once a study is complete. Researchers have an ethical responsibility to maintain a clear chain of custody over data, and to vet the individuals who might have access to them. This assures that the data will not be used for purposes participants have not approved or by other researchers for purposes not originally intended—unless the data are completely blinded so that participants cannot be iden-

Cross Reference: See Example 10.2 in Book 1, "Genetic piracy: Unauthorized use of biological data from a Native American tribe"

tified. Such a clear chain of custody was not maintained in the case of the Havasupai Indians, whose DNA data were released by a laboratory entrusted by the researcher to analyze them. Researchers protect the privacy of research participants by disposing of data in special ways; this is why IRBs require that researchers describe how data will be disposed of once a study is completed. Disposition procedures should be decided upon and negotiated with stakeholders before the study begins as part of the informed consent process. These procedures may vary, depending on whether the data are in the form of audio files, videotapes, or hard copy or digital field notes.

ASSURING PROGRAM CONTINUATION

Intervention researchers collaborate with the study site to develop and set up programs or innovations aimed at solving human problems, usually with the help of funds obtained to establish both the program and the research attendant to it. As the most visible connection to the source of funding, and often as the writers who developed the funded proposal, researchers should help participants figure out how to perpetuate the program, if desired, once the funding ends and the researcher leaves. Researchers can teach participants how to write proposals and access new sources of funding and help participants "institutionalize" or "naturalize" a program so that it is adopted by the organization or community and paid for as regular practice. We discuss this approach in greater detail in Book 7.

SUMMARY

In this chapter, we have discussed the way that the characteristics that researchers bring to the field with them affect how researchers are viewed in the field, and in turn, how researchers view those participants in the field themselves. We also note the informal ethical considerations that both field researchers and participants should attend to in their work. In chapter 6, we address how the issues we have discussed earlier in this book apply to collaborative and team research.

6 ━━◆━•━◆━•━◆━

Introduction

Ethical Considerations in Intrateam Interactions

Ethical Considerations in Team Interaction with Study Communities/ Sites and Participants

Protecting the Study Community

Summary

ETHICAL ISSUES IN ETHNOGRAPHIC TEAMWORK AND COMMUNITY-BASED RESEARCH

INTRODUCTION

In this chapter we discuss topics that are rarely referred to in texts on ethnographic and mixed methods research, mainly because most ethnographers, even if they do conduct mixed methods research, seldom discuss how they work in team settings with those of the same or different disciplinary backgrounds, or together with local communities in different forms of collaborative research. Over the past several decades, however, social science and other researchers increasingly find themselves crossing disciplinary lines to forge collaborations and work in teams with other social scientists in **interdisciplinary** or **transdisciplinary** teams. These collaborative arrangements may involve research in communities, or institutions such as school districts, museums, or hospitals that have close connections with communities. The interactions that take place between individual researchers, members of the research team, and their community partners generate ethical issues and constraints that are different from those

Definition: ✺
Interdisciplinary refers to collaborations in which researchers from different disciplines combine their approaches and methods to address a particular problem; transdisciplinary refers to the fusion of these different approaches and methods to arrive at an integrated new approach to a research question or problem

179

faced by researchers working alone. These ethical issues and constraints can arise in the relationships among team members, the associations among team members with their study community, and in concerns over the protection of the study community itself from the possible effects of the study. In this chapter we discuss these three domains of challenge and how they can be addressed.

ETHICAL CONSIDERATIONS IN INTRATEAM INTERACTIONS

Team research is very different from the form of "lone wolf" ethnography that Sally Campbell Galman represents so well in her entertaining and seminal graphic methodology text, *Shane: The Lone Ethnographer* (Galman, 2007). In this work, Campbell describes the difficulties that "Shane," an ethnographer working alone, faces as she resolves each field problem and ethical dilemma by herself. However, if the challenge of attending to all matters of formal and informal etiquette and ethics is difficult for a lone ethnographer, it is made infinitely more challenging by having to be addressed consistently and uniformly by an entire team of researchers and its partners! Here we refer to a "team" as consisting of "two or more individuals who interact interdependently and adaptively toward a common goal or objective" (Cannon-Bowers and Salas, 1998, 83). The term *team research*, then, refers to groups of researchers working together on one or more research projects (funded or unfunded) and who self-identify as a research team or group. While an array of terms (e.g., *collaborative research, team ethnography*) can be found in the literature to refer to such activities, all of them describe "a group of researchers who pool their energy, time, ideas, and expertise in the service of solving a particular research issue, and all imply that all team members take at least some degree of joint responsibility for the completion of the project" (Sumsion, 2014, 150).

In community-based/ethnographic studies, team research requires two distinctly different but interacting sets of skills. The first consists of substantive and/or technical skills that include knowledge of the study topic, mixed methods and data analysis skills, and technological skills; for example, the ability to use specific computer software or cameras and editing equipment. The second consists of relational skills, including the ability to listen carefully to other team members, share information in competent written, visual, and oral forms, discuss issues openly, jointly solve problems that arise in the field, and communicate effectively with the study population. These skills are often spelled out as responsibilities to a project, specified in form of formal contractual obligations.

Formal Contractual Obligations

It is of critical importance that all members of the research team understand and have the skills to carry out what is required in the research design. Compliance with a research design is essential, especially if the research is funded by a grant or a contract. Contracts for services have very specific requirements, often requested by the funder. Grants, awarded competitively by branches of governments (such as the National Institutes of Health), are submitted independently or "from the field." Depending on the nature of the funding, researchers have some flexibility in the implementation of the study. Regardless, researchers hoping to secure such funds must submit proposals that specify what they will do to fulfill the objectives of the funder, how they will do it, how they will protect human subjects, and what products they will generate at the end. Research teams who do not conform to the expectations of a funder will be asked to explain why they have chosen an alternative route toward achieving the same scientific ends. Good ethical behavior in team research requires that team members do their best to fulfill both their contractual and informal responsibilities to make sure that the research goals are accomplished and that if there are changes in the study design or data collection approaches, everyone is in agreement with them.

Human Subjects Training

The first form of training required to fulfill contractual obligations is human subjects certification. All team members who will be collecting and handling data must take training to assure that human subjects of research are properly protected. Training is offered by all universities, often through centralized websites such as the Collaborative Institutional Training Initiative (CITI), which "provides research ethics education to the research community . . . offering both basic (initial) and refresher courses covering human subjects research and HIPAA requirements" (http://irb.northwestern .edu/training/citi), and the National Institutes of Health (NIH) Office of Extramural Research training site (https:// phrp.nihtraining.com/users/login.php). The NIH site focuses on health-related research of all types, while the CITI training is longer, more comprehensive, and relevant to research in many different fields. Most grant and contractual agreements require that all research personnel on a study complete training and present their certificates to the grantee institutions, their IRB, and even their funders. Even in student projects, if students hire or recruit others to work with them, each team member must undergo human subjects training. It should be noted that national funding sources do not always accept certification awarded by local trainers.

Beyond acceptability, a significant advantage of training for research team members through national sources is that it is standardized. Every member of the research team receives the same human subjects training and knows he or she is subject to the same regulations and constraints. However, these training programs do not cover every experience in the field, especially in cases where qualitative work is extensive or a study is complex, or when new challenges emerge from the field. In such cases, procedures must be in place to enable members of the research team to bring an ethical issue to the lead investigators or others in the sponsoring organization for discussion, negotiation, and resolution. If these situations require changes in the study, the changes will have to undergo another round of IRB review.

Assuring Compliance with Research Protocols and Procedures: Technical Training on the Study Goals, Design, and Methods

The second form of formal training has to do with ensuring that all members of the research team understand what the study is about, and what their respective roles and responsibilities are within it. Clinical trials require a manual of operations as the basis for training and external surveillance may check to make sure that all research staff and technicians understand what they are supposed to do and why. In mixed methods research and intervention studies, training on a study's purpose, aims, goals and objectives that are not specifically defined as clinical trials and study design may be somewhat less formal, and a printed operations manual may not be called for. When manuals are not required, research team leaders should develop training sessions that make sure that all initial and entering research and administrative staff are informed about the study's purposes and objectives and told what their roles and responsibilities will be. All members of the team also should receive hard copy binders and digital versions of surveys, interview guides, guidelines for protection of data in the field, and other materials for later reference. These binders should be updated when changes occur. Moreover, formal training should be ongoing. Each time a new data collection procedure is initiated, all team members should be trained in its administration, and monitored to make sure they are implementing it properly. This applies to observation procedures or protocols, interview guides, surveys, mapping exercises, elicitation techniques such as pilesorts, and any of the methods described in Books 3 and 4. Formal training avoids technical mistakes, improves the quality of the research, and helps to avoid misinformation passed from one team member to another.

Taking Care of the Research Team Itself

While human subjects and technical training provide common ground for relating to human subjects, neither focuses on the interactions among members of the research team. Ethical considerations within a research team follow the same guidelines as those relevant to the subjects of research: acquiring needed knowledge, skills, and practice, protecting the safety and health/mental health of the research team members, maintaining confidentiality, protecting the quality of the research, and avoiding personal risk. Both team leaders and team members themselves are responsible for making sure that the team is taken care of and intrateam miscommunications and conflicts or tensions are reduced. Team leaders are responsible for:

- Ensuring that team members have appropriate knowledge and skills and opportunities to practice them prior to using them in the field
- Protecting team members' safety and health/mental health
- Maintaining confidentiality with regard to information team members might disclose
- Protecting the quality of the research
- Making sure that no team members incur undue personal risk

Ensuring team knowledge, skills and practice. As mentioned earlier, some studies require training protocols to be established before the studies begin. Though these usually are clinical trials that may involve the use of new medications or technical devices, mixed methods and ethnographic studies benefit from such training as well, especially with new field staff.

EXAMPLE 6.1

TEAM RESEARCH ON ALCOHOL USE AND SEXUAL RISK IN INDIA

A joint US-Indo field study of alcohol use and sexual risk in India had two phases. In the first or pilot phase, the study team consisted of advanced master's students and PhD students who had been well trained in survey research methods but not in community-based ethnographic methods. The study team leaders (Jean Schensul, Kamla Gupta, and S. K. Singh) trained the students and supervised their exploratory field experience. As innovative data collectors, they became strong contributors to the development of methodology for a second, larger study in three communities. For this study, the field research team was hired, and though during the prior pilot study, most members of the field team had been MPhil students, in the second phase this was not the case. Most of the instruments and observational schedules were already designed, but the qualitative data component of the study was new to the new staff members. They had to be extensively trained in the study design, the observational, interview, and survey methodology, and in the use of protocols in the field. The training involved introduction and

practice both in the classroom and in the field, as well as close monitoring and feedback, especially for the qualitative data component of the study.

Best practice suggests that the research team itself should be involved in the actual design and implementation of a study. It is easier to create this possibility in a team ethnographic study in which the initial research design/approach has been specified but the details of the instruments or strategies for data collection have not. Team ethnography also makes it possible to gain from the many insights that arise in the field and that research field staff bring to the study team. In this way, all team members can participate actively in new decisions that further the life of the research.

Involvement of field personnel in the development of pilot studies also is ideal. For example, in an ICR/University of Connecticut intervention study funded by the National Institute of Dental and Cranial Research/NIH to improve the oral health of older adults, the key members of the study field team, Kim Radda, Colleen Foster-Bey, and Zahira Medina, had been involved in two earlier preparatory studies to build infrastructure for research in public housing, and to develop the measures and the intervention content and evaluation. When the full scaled-up study was funded, they already were familiar with the protocols and instruments because they had helped to design and adapt and modify them and could train the other team members they supervised.

Sometimes, training does not occur on an ongoing basis or even at all. At times busy principal investigators and project directors do not make enough time available to deliver ongoing training to research staff. When this happens, research team members, nonetheless, have an ethical obligation to request and to obtain training and supervision so that they can do their jobs adequately. Unfortunately, sometimes research staff may not recognize that they need training, or that they can request it.

EXAMPLE 6.2

WHEN STAFF MEMBERS DO NOT REALIZE THAT THEY LACK KNOWLEDGE AND TRAINING
OR WHEN THEY ARE IN NEED OF SUPERVISION

In an ongoing study of alcohol and AIDS medication in India, it became apparent that some of the study team members on the India side did not have the needed expertise for one important aspect of the study, alcohol consumption among men. However, they nonetheless perceived that they did. When an Indian physician from the United States, a member of the study team, visited the project, she noted that this was an area that needed attention, and she called for immediate training on alcohol, alcohol measures, and the language appropriate for describing alcohol use in India. In another study conducted in a southern state of the United States, the investigators did not have the time to provide supervision to the field staff doing participant outreach. They left more experienced staff in charge of providing guidance to the rest of the staff, even though they had created no formal hierarchy among the field staff. Since the more experienced staff did not have any recognized formal authority over junior staff members, both groups complained to the investigators, asking them to modify the structure of the field team and provide more ongoing and even-handed supervision and appropriate training.

Protecting health/mental health and safety of the team. Field research can be stressful. It often means long periods of interaction with many people and very little down time for team members. The stories that people tell to the empathetic researcher may be filled with personal pain and suffering, which can have an adverse effect on listeners, and cause feelings of burnout, frustration, grief, or even anger. Situations such as observed abuse, or accidents that require action on the part of the research team, can arise in the field; these, too, generate stress and emotional responses. Research team members themselves may feel pressure to perform adequately, especially if they need their jobs badly. Or they may have had bad experiences in previous jobs and consequently are especially anxious to perform well in their current positions. Managing a good field team requires sensitivity and attention to all of these possibilities.

 **EXAMPLE 6.3**

RESPONDING TO THE DISCLOSURE OF WORK-RELATED STRESS IN A TEAM MEMBER

In the course of an ICR study of depression in older adults, the then-ICR director (Jean Schensul) sponsored a workshop on research ethics. One important reason for holding the workshop was to bring to the fore issues that were not emerging in other administrative settings. During the workshop, one of the field staff mentioned for the first time that he felt under great pressure to complete his quota of interviews for the week. To cope with the pressure, he felt compelled to exert what he considered to be undue influence which he himself felt was coercive, on potential participants in order to complete his quota and preserve his job. He acknowledged that it was only because of the workshop that he felt confident enough to mention his concern with doing well on his job, at the possible expense of participants. After this, Schensul reviewed his workload and targets for survey completion with his supervisor on a regular basis to make sure that his work performance was consistent with project expectations and that he received positive feedback for his excellent work.

Some research activities are especially stressful. For example, in the same study of depression, one member of the research staff was charged with interviewing people with chronic illnesses who were experiencing symptoms of depression. The researcher was very affected by these interviews since she herself was coping with depression over her husband's chronic illness. The study team helped her deal with her emotions, and eventually she sought independent counseling in order to be able to continue her work in the study. Similarly, in studies in which field researchers are recruited because they have had the same experiences as those they are studying—for example, mental illness, or habituation to drugs or alcohol use—the work can be particularly emotionally draining. One solution to dealing with such job stress is to hold regular meetings of the research and outreach staff involved in risky, sensitive, or demanding work to enable them to share their experiences, derive emotional and social support from each other, and to obtain group counseling if required. It is also beneficial for team members to report to supervisors if and when one of their co-workers is experiencing emotional strain.

Fieldwork also can be physically stressful. It can mean walking for long periods of time in hot or rainy or cold weather, visiting unfamiliar neighborhoods, knocking on doors without knowing who is behind them, entering potentially unsafe sites or buildings, and encountering people who may be ill with infectious diseases.

EXAMPLE 6.4

STAYING SAFE IN HIGH-RISK RESEARCH SITES

In an Institute for Community Research study that involved observing injection drug behavior that placed drug users at risk of HIV transmission, field researchers had to visit "high-risk sites" that included abandoned buildings, shooting galleries (apartments or known private locations where groups of drug users were injecting together), or hidden spaces under bridges or in parks. The field researchers always went out in pairs, usually a male and a female and with a "guide," an active drug user who was participating as a peer educator in the study. They established safety principles in the field. For example, they tried to go to known sites with the assistance of a peer educator who was familiar with it. When they entered the site, one of the team stayed back to facilitate a speedy exit if necessary. They identified the exits and tried to make sure there were a minimum of two possible ways out to the street. They always carried cell phones or walkie talkies and did not lose sight of each other. They were on the alert for fires, especially in abandoned buildings in the winter. And they never approached people while they were shooting up unless they knew them personally. Even then, they took care to avoid surprising such people because their reaction at that moment could be unpredictable. Their guides also protected them by helping them to recognize when a situation had the potential for danger, such as a police raid in which they could be arrested and which could put even their guide at risk. Fortunately, these safety precautions paid off, and the study did not incur a single negative instance.

EXAMPLE 6.5

KEEPING FEMALE FIELDWORKERS SAFE IN INDIA

In another Indo-US study of smokeless tobacco among women, the field team was composed entirely of women. They always went out in pairs—one Hindi and one Marathi speaker, in part to manage the complexities of language use in the community. The other reason for pairing researchers was that some distant reaches of the community, and in particular, one area devoted to recycling (the "scrap" area), were said to be places where drug sellers and men resided who did not work and drank during the day. The researchers tried to avoid these areas, especially late in

the day, and they always remained connected when interviewing women about their tobacco use. The field team made good use of cell phones and texting. When they interviewed women alone in their homes, they made sure that other team members knew their whereabouts. If husbands arrived, they left. They called in to their supervisors regularly to ensure her of their safety. They always interviewed male tobacco sellers outside their shops and in pairs. On festival days, especially Holi, where men were known to drink and harass women, they avoided the field. Again, fortunately, no negative instances marred this three-year field study.

The following example illustrates a situation in which the short-term outcome was less positive.

EXAMPLE 6.6

REPORTING ON ACTIVITIES THAT PLACED A TEAM MEMBER AT RISK

A study of sites and situations where drug users might be at risk for HIV exposure through sharing "works" (syringes and needles) required that field researchers find out about and visit these sites. Finding out about the sites was difficult. Doing so meant hiring field team members who were not using drugs but who were familiar with drug users and the places they went to "shoot up." Some of these places were hidden—people's apartments, under bridges, and in abandoned buildings. Ethical hiring practices, in conjunction with drug treatment programs, required ruling out those candidates who were using drugs, and hiring only those former drug users who had been "clean" or free of drugs for at minimum the past six months. AIDS researcher Margaret Weeks hired a woman to work in the project who fit these criteria—she was a streetwise former drug user who had not used drugs in more than two years. At first the woman's work was excellent; later another team member spotted her at a house that was known as a drug sales site but not a "high-risk use" site. Her work started to slip. Finally, Jean Schensul, then ICR director, received a letter from the woman's son, in prison at the time, begging her to terminate his mother because her job was leading her back to her former life as a drug user. Schensul visited her son and was convinced that he had his mother's best interests at heart. The woman was released from work immediately, after she confessed that she had returned to drug use. She sought treatment and became well, but with everyone's agreement, she did not return to her job at ICR.

Infectious diseases can be a risk in fieldwork as well. Tuberculosis is not very easily transmitted, but it can be encountered in clinical settings when working with drug users or people with HIV infection, or in very crowded urban areas. In one instance, a field researcher on the Mumbai Alcohol and HIV risk study entered a household seeking to complete a survey with a male respondent who was known to have been drinking alcohol. The researcher found that the man was suffering from chikungunya, a highly infectious and very painful viral infection. He reported this, and thereafter team members were instructed to avoid situations in which they might encounter such infections.

When Good Manners and Good Sense Collide, Endangering Researchers

As we have said many times in this book and elsewhere, ethnography calls for good relationships with local people. Usually this means visiting their homes, eating food that is offered as a routine element in making visitors comfortable, drinking local drinks, and using bathroom facilities. Managing to remain healthy while enjoying and appreciating local hospitality and demonstrating appreciation for people's efforts to make researchers feel at home, requires researchers' careful consideration and is different in every setting. Sometimes ethnographers need to set their own boundaries. The well-known medical anthropologist Pertti Pelto took a risk in rural Mexico when visiting a local village by drinking "pulque," a local drink made of the fermented juice of the agave plant, prepared in large uncovered cowhide vats covered with flies. He contracted typhoid fever, from which he recovered after losing several weeks of fieldwork training. One of his field school members, cautioned about good health practices in the field, ate nothing but fried potatoes and steak. Nonetheless, he also contracted typhoid. When on his first visit to India with Jean Schensul, Raul Pino, a physician and researcher, purchased antibiotics at a local pharmacy and used them prophylactically—an ill-advised practice—to protect himself from possible infections. He did not get sick, but that might have been because he also ate on university campuses and at known restaurants, and drank bottled water as recom-

mended by the team. We suggest avoiding unnecessary risks as well as unnecessary precautions or prophylaxis, following team health practices and assuming that no situations are completely risk free.

EXAMPLE 6.7

DECIDING WHERE TO EAT AND SLEEP

While doing fieldwork in a Guatemalan village, Sheryl Ludwig was repeatedly invited to take meals with and spend the night at her research participants' home. Since she worked with her family of informants daily, her initial repeated refusals began to distress the family. Ludwig finally compromised. She felt that spending the night would be too risky to her health and safety, given the lack of sanitation and the need to take "chicken buses" to and from the village at odd hours. Chicken buses were known venues for robbery. She did, however, decide to take most of her midday meals and snacks with the family. She helped in the food preparation (and learned the local recipes), and she could see how the food was prepared and cooked. Nonetheless, she did contract a number of food-related illnesses. Ludwig was working alone, however. Had she been part of a team, she might have obtained advice and counsel regarding how to handle the requests. Her team leader also might have encouraged her to err more on the side of caution with regard to what she ate, or she might have decided to eat it anyway.

Typical rules that most researchers, whether working alone or in a team, would follow in any setting include:

- Washing hands regularly before and after eating (and/or carrying disinfectant liquid)
- Drinking only bottled water or bottled beer and making sure that the seal is unbroken
- Avoiding eating "street food" (food prepared in unsupervised situations)
- Making sure foods are properly cooked
- Peeling fruits and vegetables (and cooking them if possible) before eating them
- Learning traffic rules and ways of using local transportation systems to avoid accidents and robbery or violence
- Avoiding walking alone in places where there are few people

ETHICAL CONSIDERATIONS IN TEAM INTERACTION WITH STUDY COMMUNITIES/SITES AND PARTICIPANTS

Good intragroup relationships require that all members of the study team understand the study, communicate with each other, share references and information with each other, complete and share their field notes, and otherwise comply as a group with the requirements of the study.

Ethical considerations with respect to relationships *beyond the team itself*, that is, between team members and the community of study, fall into several discrete categories. The first category involves the start point, the initial relationship established between the research investigators (project directors, principal investigators) and members of the study community. These relationships may involve various degrees and complexity of collaboration, or be no more than a simple agreement that the research be conducted in the site and that information from the study be available to residents and organizations. Regardless of the degree or intensity of collaboration, researchers are ethically bound to be open and transparent with the community and research partners about the purpose, goals, objectives, and methods of the study, funding sources, longer-range efforts, and especially, what the study can and cannot do. All members of the research team must be fully informed about these points and consistent in their delivery of information about the project to people outside of it. It is both ethical and good professional behavior for all members of the study to provide the same information to community members so that they are not confused about the study or distrustful of the investigators.

Researchers who take a more participatory stance (e.g., those who do participatory action research or community-based participatory research) must follow an additional set of guidelines. They are required to engage communities in the design and implementation of the study, and they must focus the study around mutual interests, or at times, exclusively around the interests of the community itself. This means that preliminary work must be done to learn what those interests are and to help community members learn how to design and implement a study—processes with which they may be unfamiliar. The ethical guidelines of the

American Anthropological Association state that "consultation with groups or communities affected by . . . any . . . type of research should be an important element of the design of . . . projects and [consultation] should continue as work progresses or circumstances change. It is explicitly understood that defining what constitutes an affected community is a dynamic and necessary process" (http://www.aaanet.org/issues/policy-advocacy/code-of-ethics.cfm). This statement highlights that collaboration of any kind calls for constant negotiation as study designs, personnel, communities, and the nature of the fieldwork shift.

There are a variety of guidelines for conducting Participatory Action Research (PAR)/Community Based Participatory Research (CBPR). One such set of guidelines was published in 2008 by the Clinical Translation Science Award (CTSA) Consortium's Community Engagement Steering Committee's workshop planning members and operations committee members. These guidelines include:

- Being aware of the community's perspective on research. Clear and transparent explanations go a long way toward dispelling distrust of researchers.
- Asking the community what it wants at the individual, family/household, *and* community level, even if none of the researchers involved can offer partnership opportunities at the time. Partners can always be found when needed.
- Offering technical assistance and evaluation methodology to support service enhancement while negotiating research topics, thus ensuring equitable interaction and mutual benefit
- Hosting community events where residents and organizations can dialogue with researchers and find common ground
- Finding long-term partners who may be able to use the results of the research and partner on new studies so the research is community embedded and can persist, rather than simply be researcher driven
- Using multiple media outlets, artists, and other creative efforts to recruit people into shared events

- Identifying barriers to communication between researchers and community residents and other stakeholders and addressing them together
- Acknowledging (and informing the community about) past mistakes and unethical science practices by others. In this way, residents can articulate any misconceptions or worries they might have about the research and obtain information about the legitimate root causes of their concern about research and its effects on them and their families.
- Finding creative ways of rewarding research participants *and* community members so they feel valued and appreciated and include their advice and comments

Another set of guidelines for collaborative or participatory community-based research was originally published by Israel, Eng, Schulz, and Parker (2005). These researchers, who are well known for their seminal work in CBPR for health, list the following obligations for researchers:

1. *Respect and Recognize the Community as a Unit of Identity*: The Community is a group of individuals who share some common interests, values, goals, politics, and characteristics.
2. *Build on Strengths and Resources in the Community*: Researchers use the resources that are internal to the Community when possible, including facilitating the use of resources that may require some additional support or development.
3. *Facilitate Collaborative, Equitable Involvement of All Partners in All Phases of Research*: This means that all members of the team will be informed about, and included and involved, in all aspects of the research process.
4. *Integrate Knowledge and Intervention for the Mutual Benefit of All Members*: Knowledge is informational research findings: the data. Inter-

vention is a plan of action for effecting change in the world based on that data. Information desired by the community will be considered integrated with the community's needs for intervention to create positive change for the community.

5. *Share Information and Learning Equally among All Members*: Everyone shares their ideas, perspective, and expertise with each other. All parties learn equally from each other.

6. *Involve Project Members in a Cyclical and Iterative Process*: The process of doing science itself is iterative, as is the process of doing CBPR. As project members learn from each other, the work itself is refined. All phases of the research process may be gone over more than once before being implemented, as the community adds its insights.

7. *Address Research Topics from Both Positive and Ecological Perspectives*: Positive means an emphasis on outcomes that are beneficial to the health, happiness, and success of the community. Ecological means that whole systems and whole people are looked at, rather than isolated events or single causes.

8. *Disseminate Findings and Knowledge Gained to All Partners*: Research findings will be communicated back into the academic and research context, and into the other Communities, in ways that are most useful for each. For example, findings may be disseminated both as published research papers in scientific journals and as interventions for the direct benefit of the Community.

9. *Ensure a Long-Term Commitment by All Partners*: This means that "the big picture," or future impact, of work done should be considered by all parties. This does not mean that the same people must be involved in the project over the long term, just that the goals of the project should take the future welfare of all parties into consideration (Israel et al., 2005).

These guidelines and others like them are living documents, to be kept in mind in both formal negotiations and informal ongoing relationships with study communities. Ethical collaboration calls for reviewing and operationalizing as many of these principles as are feasible in the study setting. It is important to recognize, however, that not all of these principles are likely to be implemented at the same level in every situation. They will be tailored to the specifics of each study and each study community.

The principal reason that we so heavily stress the need for shared understandings about the research, its purposes, implementation, and consequences is that different members or member organizations within a collaboration or alliance may understand roles and responsibilities quite differently. Those differences can be the genesis of serious misunderstandings and conflict. The ethical guidelines of the American Anthropological Association note: "Collaborations may be defined and understood quite differently by the various participants. The scope of collaboration, rights and responsibilities of the various parties, and issues of data access and representation, credit, and acknowledgment should be openly and fairly established at the outset" (http://www.aaanet.org/issues/policy-advocacy/code-of-ethics.cfm). A primary role of the lead study investigator(s) is to work with collaborators to articulate these issues and translate them into memoranda of agreement and/or subcontractual arrangements.

Collaborations call for constant monitoring and surveillance because members change, organizational goals and missions shift, and financial support and staffing security may unravel. As these conditions change, the nature of the collaborative relationship also must change to reflect new realities. Failure to attend to the new situation can cause misunderstandings and friction within the study team. Attending to these issues as they arise can go a long way to furthering ethical relationships between the research team and the study community.

PROTECTING THE STUDY COMMUNITY

Research teams can be threatening to a study community. Research teams usually operate with more funding and more visibility than individual researchers. The presence of multiple researchers in a community can signal that something is awry, something that requires attention by outsiders. This can cause anxiety or concern among community participants or could even be seen as stigmatizing a community. For this reason it is very important for members of the research team to think about the potential effects and outcomes of their study on the study community—including the impact of their own presence. As we have already discussed, introducing a study properly and garnering support for it in a community is one way to address this dilemma. Another more commonly used strategy is to find ways of collaborating with the study community. Beyond working with existing community alliances and coalitions, there are a variety of ways to accomplish this purpose, many of which both individual researchers and research teams can use. Below we discuss some of these strategies.

Establishing a Community Advisory Board

Many public health researchers and their teams begin their study by identifying key people in the study community and inviting them to participate in a community advisory board (CAB) (Newman et al., 2011). Community advisory boards can be helpful in several ways. They can:

- Provide useful preliminary or orienting information about the study community, including identifying local experts, providing community history, assisting with local jargon and technical terms, and describing key events related to the study
- Link the research team to others who might have useful information or can lead the investigators to important resources
- Endorse the study in the community
- Prevent occurrences that might cause harm to the community or to sectors of it. For example, avoid situations in which some community persons or sectors are more likely to experience risks or benefits from the research than others.
- Ameliorate the impact of instances such as breaches of confidentiality, should they occur during the research

- Advise on the contents and wording of interview guides and surveys and assist in translations if required
- Assist in the dissemination of study results
- Use the results in the community to take action on the health, education, or other problems addressed, thereby introducing the possibility of sustained change

Community Advisory Board (CAB) members can be chosen based on principles that include balance among groups with regard to race/ethnicity, gender, social class, religion, and other forms of diversity, as well as inclusion of various sectors in the community, and differing levels of experience, expertise, interest, and willingness to be vocal participants in study development, critique, and use. The following list of groups adapted from Cargo and Mercer (2008) provides some suggestions as to who might be included on a CAB:

- Beneficiaries of the project
- Community advocates and activists
- Potential interventionists and policymakers
- Cultural advocates
- Gatekeepers controlling access to resources important for the study
- Voluntary associations whose members might provide helpful linkages to other organizations in the community, or as a source of volunteers to help with the current project

Participation on voluntary boards takes time from CAB members' often very busy schedules. Community advisory board members must have an incentive for participating in an advisory capacity. Incentives can include opportunities for research training, or to engage in ongoing decision making, a chance to discuss ways the research can contribute to desired change, recognition through compensation, opportunities for social interaction, and various forms of public recognition (Newman et al., 2011, 6).

There are other ways of ensuring the protection of communities from research harm (Marshall and Rotimi, 2001). For example, IRBs, especially those that are university based, may be insufficiently aware of, and thus ignore, community needs and concerns (cf. Quinn, 2004). One strategy for improving this situation is to train and place experienced community representatives on IRBs in sufficient numbers that they have a voice on the IRB. Community advisory board members may be prime candidates for membership on local university, hospital, or research center IRBs, thereby protecting communities from unethical practices and ensuring that research teams are able to exert proper measures to protect their relationships with study communities and make sure the communities themselves are protected.

Maintaining Confidentiality

One of the advantages of team research is the opportunity for multiple team members to share in data collection, discussion, ongoing analysis, and interpretation. Individual researchers always must take care to avoid sharing private information with others in the community setting. Team researchers must take care to avoid sharing or acting on information obtained about community events and persons from other team members. For example, under mandatory reporting requirements for abuse or suicide, a researcher trying to fulfill reporting responsibilities might decide to report on an abusive situation based on information obtained from a team member. A researcher might hear from the young teen-age daughter of a key informant that her mother was abusing her. If the researcher did not know the family very well, she might not recognize that there was ongoing disagreement between them about whether or not the daughter could go out alone with her boyfriend. She might not know that the savvy daughter was trying to punish her mother for not allowing her to have her way by trying to report her to the authorities without really knowing what she was doing. Thus, such secondhand information could be wrong or incomplete. Inaccurate reporting—which generally produces an invasive response from authorities—could damage both the community and the research team as a whole.

Team members are more likely to discuss the meaning of observations or interviews in the field among themselves. Often these discussions take place in the privacy of their office setting. However, when researchers travel in teams, these conversations could take place on the street, in a restaurant, or even on the bus. In these public settings anyone might overhear a conversation that might even be about someone they know. In a bus, the conversation might be about a neighbor or friend of people sitting close enough to overhear it. In one such case, two researchers working on an HIV prevention project were sharing information on a bus about a participant who was HIV positive. This information was only known to members of the research team. Someone sitting directly behind the researchers overheard the information, thereby learning that a friend of theirs, who had not disclosed her HIV status, was infected. This constituted a significant breach of confidentiality with serious consequences for the individual whose infection was now public, including her job status and her relationship with intimate others. It also had the potential to affect in significant ways the community's trust of the research team. Finally, it had to be reported to funders as an adverse event, thus affecting the overall project status.

Communities are often divided along lines of class, race, religion, ethnicity, political clout, and other factors. These divisions have deep historical roots. For purposes of the research it always is best to have a good understanding of these splits, frictions, and fractures so as to avoid them. Many applied or public health researchers prefer to work with communities of "identity." While this can mean "communities experiencing a specific health problem" such as asthma, it also can mean "communities characterized by specific racial/ethnic or national identity." The problem is that the simple act of selecting the latter can act to reinforce the divisions just mentioned. This is not to imply that researchers should not work with communities of "identity" (that is, groups that have already self-identified). But researchers may find themselves working with communities that are very diverse, in which case part of their responsibility is to help "construct" a sense of cross-group identity around a research problem or issue. In general, it is important for the research team to avoid enhancing divisive elements, either inadvertently or through selective attention. They should work with all groups in the community and if possible, use the research to bring about dialogue across groups (Schensul, 2009). To confront this challenge with adequate preparation, research teams should consist of members that represent all sectors in the study community. They should engage in frequent reflective exercises to ensure that any unintended or deeply held biases or prejudices are addressed and do not play out in public as team members interact with diverse communities on sensitive issues.

Finally, community sensibility can run high with respect to certain topics or ways of presenting information. If there are religious divides, presenting research results on drinking or sexual risk behavior by religious groups may not be well received, even if there are significant differences either across or within groups (for example, fundamentalist Christians versus secular Catholics). The same problem could apply in settings where there are strong prejudices held about racialized groups or ethnic/national groups. In disseminating data in India, especially on topics such as HIV, substance use, gender-based violence, or other topics that may be sensitive or stigmatizing, presenting differences by caste and religious group is avoided. In Mauritius, a country that prides itself on its multilingual, multicultural orientation, comparisons by ethnic/national group are avoided. Usually advisory board members, key informants, or research partners can help researchers avoid inflaming such differences by guiding public dissemination of data to focus on other important differences. We deal more specifically with the dissemination of study results in Book 7.

SUMMARY

In this chapter we have tried to address some of the ethics-related challenges that occur in team research in community settings. While all research in communities is to some degree collaborative, much research is driven by researcher interest. Nevertheless, researchers must find ways of protecting themselves, the team's relationship with the community of study, and the community itself. Intrateam protection includes being fully trained in study goals, objectives, and field procedures, providing good monitoring and supervision, developing a team ethos, and practicing good communication and information sharing. We also discussed team orientations in regard to protecting health and taking safety measures in the field. Protecting the team's relationship with the community involves good partnerships and relationships between senior members of the team and community leaders, and among team researchers and organizations and study participants. Finally, the last section of the chapter addresses the need to protect the study community from harms, including the loss of confidentiality and stigma through public discussions of research findings that reveal confidential information through the inappropriate reporting of study results.

In the following chapter we move "beyond Belmont" to discuss how the research landscape and environment has changed since the initial formulation and codification of principles and procedures for protecting human research subjects were devised.

7 ⬤▬●▬◆▬●▬⬤

GOING BEYOND BELMONT: NEW ISSUES AND CHALLENGES

Intro_____

Challenges to IRB
"Surveillance"
and Control

Contesting
Western
Epistemological
and Ontological
Hegemony

Redefining Key
Terms in the
Twenty-First
Century

Obtaining
Consent

Exposure to Risks
and New Forms
of Vulnerability

Technology and
Retrievability of
Information

Ethics and the
Consequences of
Interpretation

Summary

INTRODUCTION

Throughout this book we have been tracing the evolution of concerns over the way researchers treat human beings during their investigations. From the late 1800s when scientists were bound by few, if any, formal ethical considerations, to the rising concern in international arenas over sadistic experiments carried out by the Nazis, to the subsequent broadening of concern for the treatment of human beings in research in both the physical and social sciences, and followed by the codification of research principles and the establishment of enforcement mechanisms in the Belmont Report, researchers increasingly are required to seek approval for the procedures they plan to use from Institutional Review Boards. As we have noted, these bodies create and enforce the formal procedures used to govern the ethical treatment of human participants in research. They have the power to halt research projects they deem to be unethical and punish the individuals who conduct them and the institutions that sponsor them.

Over time, several critiques of IRB procedures have emerged. One accuses IRBs of "mission creep" as their surveillance becomes increasingly detailed and expands into a variety of research modalities. A second argues that the

203

composition of IRBs tends to reflect the hard sciences and experimental researchers whose understanding of alternative forms of research is limited, and whose narrow perspective often makes it difficult for ethnographers, mixed methods researchers, and those attempting complex social interventions to get their studies approved (Parker, 2007). Another criticism has its origin in the emergence of alternative epistemologies governing how researchers view themselves vis-à-vis their research participants. These epistemologies govern whose view has primacy in interpreting research: participants or researchers, and whether interpretations should be a combination of both perspectives. Embedded in an analysis of power relationships, these critiques argue that researchers' power over their participants has moral and ethical valence and must be seen and addressed in that light. This critique has emerged not so much because the ethical imperatives have changed, but because the world of research has changed, and the ethical principles and the procedures in which they are embedded are being applied to types of research and research sites that were not envisioned by the Belmont Commission. Further, research participants and medical patients in health research are being accorded more and more power with regard to how research is done, its purposes, and the degree to which its objectives should be directed toward improving the quality of the environment in which participants live and the quality of services they receive.

In the beginning of Book 1 of the *Ethnographer's Toolkit*, we described the major epistemological frameworks that provide the concepts and theoretical frameworks that orient research questions, inform subsequent research designs, establish the stance of researchers with respect to power relationships in the field, and determine the degree to which researcher interpretations achieve primacy in the final results. We also made clear that the shift from positivism through interpretivism to critical and postmodern perspectives has deeply influenced how researchers approach the field, how they relate to their research subjects, and in turn, the kind of research they want to undertake and hope IRBs will approve. In addition, network, ecological, and participatory perspectives make isolating a single site, individual, problem, or community for study far more problematic than they once were. In the pages that follow, we elaborate on discussions initiated earlier in this book about the mismatch between epistemological perspectives that informed the actions of members of the Belmont Commission and those governing current research, especially ethnographic, qualitative, and community-based research. We also address how the procedural definitions outlined in the Belmont Report have had to be modified in order to conform to new realities in the field. Finally, we move to the future, addressing the issue of ethics in interpretation, rather than in the conduct, of research. Such a move expands concerns about ethics from ones that only affect the *conduct* of research to an examination of how ethics are involved in the way *interpretations* of research are represented. These can have a profound impact on both research participants and other stakeholders.

CHALLENGES TO IRB "SURVEILLANCE" AND CONTROL

Mission "Creep"

IRBs have considerable power over whether researchers receive, and continue to enjoy, approval to carry out their research in the field. IRBs try to assure that their oversight is sufficiently rigorous to avoid audits of their institutions and campuses by federal government monitors. Over time, however, the workloads of IRBs have expanded to such an extent that they have difficulty paying sufficient attention to research that actually is risky and does warrant scrutiny of its protection of human participants, given the volume of proposals they must consider. Some of the workload increase is a consequence of the ballooning responsibilities that IRBs face, some is a consequence of subjecting all proposals to a higher degree of scrutiny than is really necessary, and some is a function of vague regulations and procedures that invite ever-broadening and variable interpretations by IRBs. IRBs are also increasingly wary of being audited by the Office of Human Research

Protection. **Auditing** occurs when a team of monitors examine everything from the composition and qualifications of IRB members to the degree to which researchers have established paper trails confirming that they have implemented their research as promised, including accurate reporting of adverse events. The Common Rule defines **adverse events** as "unanticipated problems" involving risks to study participants or others. Specific adverse events are defined in accordance with the type and topic of the study; most studies that generate adverse events involve an intervention involving medication, technology, or some other treatment that might involve specific risks. Though audits can occur any time, they often occur when too many adverse events in studies are reported to federal funders, raising questions about how stringent security procedures are for studies at that institution.

Federal monitors are particularly concerned about the conformity to procedures protecting the three primary principles of respect, social justice, and beneficence; they look for evidence that confirms or denies that researchers actually are following the prescribed guidelines. They also look for reasons for adverse effects that are reported, especially if they occur more than once. To protect themselves, IRBs have embedded their regulations in an enormous number of rules, record-keeping procedures, and standards to which researchers must adhere. They also have created detailed templates and checklists of required items to guide researchers in the construction of proposals and consent forms—which, as a consequence, have become ever longer, less intelligible, and more intimidating to research participants. IRBs also have outlined Standard Operating Procedures documents (SOPs) as well as a welter of forms to cover every conceivable eventuality that might transpire—even ones that are not relevant to the research design being vetted and which researchers, in turn, often view as noisome and unnecessary obstacles to their research. For example, some IRBs may ask ethnographers doing exploratory work to describe exactly how many "subjects" they plan to recruit; deviations from that number may require an explanation—on the appropriate change request form. Fortunately, most IRBs are not as picky with exploratory studies, and in any case, change forms usually receive an expedited or rapid turnaround review and do not require full board approval. Further, experienced researchers *are* able to approximate how many observations of what kinds in what settings will be needed, or how many key informant, group, or in-depth interviews are required. Qualitative researchers have to do this all the time in order to design meaningful budgets and receive approval from review committees, and novices are advised to practice such estimates. Studies designed to map out a previously undescribed population may pose particular problems. However, while these studies probably cannot come up with a highly specific and precise description of the populations to be described, they can devise a list of the characteristics that they think might be relevant to look for, as well as factors that would affect such a population. IRBs then can have some idea of the type of respondents that investigators are seeking. Researchers often are asked to include all protocols and instruments to be administered, but to practitioners of exploratory research which does not use such standardized instruments, or to those who are simply proposing to gather initial cultural data *prior* to creating survey instruments and observational protocols, such requirements can be irritating. However, IRBs usually can be induced to understand such study objectives, especially when they are described as pilot studies, and when the categories of knowledge to be assessed are described.

More problematic, however, is that the lists created to *guide* researchers can be viewed as imposing a "one size fits all" *template* on an activity—human research—which is far too varied to be so regimented, and which would be better governed by principled and informed decisions about which activities should be monitored, how, and to what degree. It is also problematic when the IRB requires that all bilingual non-English materials be translated and back-translated to ensure equivalence, using certified translators, especially when there are no qualified speakers of those languages on the IRB to check the results. Researchers who do not want to take the time to undergo full review of all bilingual materials sometimes prefer to conduct their research with dominant language speakers only, a practice which may be contradictory to funder policies and study site needs. The result is a system that does not always function as intended, can be burdensome to researchers, and often does not make for better outcomes for research participants.

The Missing Social Scientist

Social scientists were not included in the original drafting of the regulations and procedures contained in Title 45, section 46, of the Code of Federal Regulations. In fact, since the 1970s, social scientists have complained that the procedures outlined in the Common Rule reflect a biomedical and behavioral science model that is inappropriate for much social science research. That model assumes that the research under question usually always focuses on clearly defined research problems and populations, involves an experimental treatment, a pretest, and a posttest to measure impact, exercises researcher controls over all aspects of the research, uses well-established and normed instrumentation or data collection protocols, and poses known risks to participants. Unfortunately, qualitative, ethnographic, exploratory, or descriptive research, including studies in education and the health sciences, seldom follow these assumptions. In addition, much of what qualitative researchers must do prior to establishing a well-thought-out research project may look like research to IRBs but actually is not research. For example, initial discussions with potential community research partners, informal discussions to gain familiarity with realities in the field, informal mapping in open and public places, and collecting artifacts and secondary data are necessary as *preliminary fieldwork* but are not considered to be formal research. Researchers should carefully distinguish between what research really is—systematic studies designed to advance scientific knowledge and intended for dissemination to wider publics—and how it differs from necessary preliminary fieldwork, and should make clear to local IRBs what these distinctions are. Fortunately, more and more IRBs now are set up especially or partially to review social science applications. Moreover, IRB members increasingly are beginning to realize that experimental studies are not the only ones done by scientists; they also do observational studies, epidemiologic studies, clinical case studies, and even qualitative "basic social science studies."

The US Code of Federal Regulations does require that IRBs include members of, or advocates for, the most vulnerable communities involved in research—including prisoners, teachers, people with disabilities, children, and immigrants—but the same diverse representation has not been required for people with expertise in a variety of research modalities. As a consequence, often missing is any representation from fields such as sociology, anthropology, education, community studies, public health, and a variety of applied fields that conduct both research and interventions based on that research in communities and organizations. Since many IRB members have little understanding of diverse and more interpretive forms of research such as ethnography, they do not always understand what sociobehavioral, qualitative, ethnographic, or action researchers do. Therefore, qualitative researchers and ethnographers cannot assume that their shorthand terminology will be understood by IRB members, or that IRB members will be able to visualize what will happen to research participants.

A number of undesirable consequences have emerged from this situation. One is that some researchers simply choose not to seek IRB approval. While they may, in fact, adhere personally to the highest of ethical standards in the implementation of their work, side-stepping IRB approval because they feel it to be inappropriate or an unnecessary obstacle to their own research can have serious negative consequences for everyone else in their institution if, as is usually the case, they are caught. We have pointed out how audits of IRB oversight, as well as citation searches for IRB approval of published research, can fairly easily identify people who are by-passing approvals, as can examining whether or not departments such as anthropology, sociology, and communications, whose faculty and student research obviously would involve human beings, are submitting proposals to IRBs.

Another negative consequence can be that researchers may avoid carrying out studies that, while important, are deemed to be too much of a hassle to attempt because of the challenges of convincing an IRB that the procedures required by the study are appropriate and ethical. More problematic from an ethical standpoint are researchers who attempt to carry out risky or controversial research in settings that they feel are outside the purview of IRBs. This is most common not with publically funded research, but among private companies that do clinical trials and other studies in developing nations. Increasingly, for example, clinical trials for commercial medical research by private companies—which do not need to undergo IRB scrutiny—are being implemented in rural areas of Eastern Europe, Asia, and Africa, with low-income and poorly educated populations whose capacity to understand the procedures they are undergoing, or especially, their risks and consequences, is limited (Khan, 2008; Lurie and Wolfe, 1997; Macklin, 2004; Petryna, 2007). The compensation that the companies offer in exchange for participation often could be considered coercive, as they are proposed in regions where people may be very needy. Under such conditions, the principles of informed consent and volunteerism are honored in the breach rather than practice. While organizations such as the American Anthropological Association, the American Sociological Association, the American Psychological Association, and other professional associations have codes of ethics that attempt to address these complaints, and the American Folklore Association officially has been able to obtain clearance for folklore as "not research" (Dobrin and Lederman, 2010), these organizations have little power over IRBs, the OHRP, or commercial enterprises not receiving federal dollars for support. The following example illustrates what can happen when there is lack of oversight of clinical trials in other countries.

EXAMPLE 7.1

PROBLEMS ARISING WHEN OVERSIGHT FOR CLINICAL TRIALS IS LACKING

Recognizing the need for concern over the safety of human subjects and appropriate protections in the India context, India's social scientists convened more than fifteen years ago to develop a code of ethics based on the Belmont Report (1978). The resulting code of ethics was endorsed by many prominent Indian social scientists. At

the same time, the Indian equivalent of the US National Institutes of Health (NIH), the Indian Council of Medical Research (ICMR), created a carefully crafted structure and processes for reviewing government-funded clinical trials. All US clinical trials funded by the US government now must undergo ICMR procedures, in addition to those required by the institutions with which they are collaborating.

However, and separate from this rigorous set of requirements, India has become a fertile ground for clinical trials privately conducted by commercial enterprises. Private organizations were established to manage these international trials, but they do not subject the companies to the same stringent reviews and constraints as domestic and internally funded trials are. Commercial enterprises thus have the capacity to engage in unethical practices such as recruiting people with limited education who could not understand the procedures or offering money that poor rural people could not easily turn down.

In 2013, an Indian newspaper reported that over four thousand deaths had occurred during these privately run clinical trials. Though it was not clear whether the participants would have died anyway or whether they died as a result of the medication received or procedures in which they had participated, public opinion called for action on the part of the government. The response of the government was to suspend all clinical trials, including those that had undergone government review, until each one could be reviewed, and a decision made as to whether it could be restarted. This left researchers and participants in a difficult position since medications could no longer be dispensed, recruitment was halted, and any nonmedical interventions also were suspended under this edict. At the same time, the Indian government held all funders, including NIH institutions, responsible for any adverse reaction that occurred to any participant during that person's lifetime, making it difficult to authorize a continuation of a trial. Eventually, the clinical trials were reviewed, NIH agencies decided individually whether to renew funding for trials, and some behavioral trials were deemed nonclinical trials and thus were deemed eligible to continue without constraint (http://www.ipsnews.net/2013/11/over -2500-deaths-during-indian-clinical-trials/).

Such actions were possible because of the advocacy efforts of Indian NGOs (nongovernmental organizations) who identified these adverse events and because of the competence and power of the Indian government agencies charged with protecting human subjects of research. Other countries, however, do not have such a well-established regulatory system, and may not protect research participants as carefully.

Helping IRB Members Understand What Social Science Research Involves

As a matter of course, social science researchers often explore or try to identify and operationalize variables that may be "unmeasurable" or "unquantifiable" and whose measurement may be defined as "subjective." The problems to be investigated also may be unclear—especially when the research is, in fact, designed to clarify what those relevant problems might be. Populations or vectors may be hidden or unknown, and what instrumentation exists may be in the most rudimentary of states. It certainly is not likely to be normed or standardized. In addition, the risks of the research may be unclear or unknown. Fieldworkers—ethnographers, qualitative sociologists, clinical workers, public health researchers, and participatory or collaborative researchers—are not distressed by these conditions; they follow "fuzzy" canons involving "messing around" (Dewey, 2004) and mapping (Cromley, 2013) to size up a site, and then rely on attentive and careful observation, listening, interviewing, photographing, and taking notes to create formative or working hypotheses. These are focused and elaborated in recursive processes of analysis, problem posing, and question answering, and iterative collection of new data—including survey data—to answer ongoing questions and hypotheses. Further, and perhaps most baffling to more traditional researchers, social scientists sometimes define *new* populations, sites, data collection techniques, and even research questions in the early stages of their study or in mixed methods studies, as well as in purely qualitative work. Thus, the research environment and practice that ethnographers take for granted—and that are both the stock in trade of exploratory or descriptive research and the foundational processes for all scientific research—can look like a very scary, profoundly unsystematic Martian terrain to experimental and quantitative researchers.

As a remedy, we suggest that it has become an ethical imperative for researchers to begin a concerted campaign to educate IRB members about the nature and purposes of their research. In the first place, they should include in their proposals explanations of methods that are far more detailed than that to which they have become accustomed. Earlier in this book and in Books 2, 3, and 4, we have suggested a number of strategies that ethnographers can use to enlighten IRB members. Simply stating that "ethnographic methods will be used" is insufficient. Researchers should describe where, how, and when they will meet with and recruit members of the potential research population, and how they will elicit consent and for what purposes from at least approximate numbers of people. They should describe how, where, and with whom participant observation will be carried out, to the best of their ability. A proposal to carry out a school ethnography, for example, should indicate that "nonparticipant observation will be conducted in classrooms, libraries, parent teacher conferences, and assemblies, and other instructional settings; participant observation will be conducted in the teachers' lounge, hallways, lunchrooms, restrooms, on the playground and field trips, and other noninstructional activities." They also should define and distinguish between nonparticipant and participant observation, and the approximate number of times they plan to be involved in each of these types of activities; for example, from daily to several times a week or even several times a day. Researchers should include in their consent forms and proposals descriptions of research designs, methods, recruitment strategies, and plans for safeguarding the privacy of personal information that are excruciatingly clear. We have provided examples of consent forms in the appendices to this book. If waivers of signed consent are requested, as in cases where signed consent could identify participants or pose a historical threat to them, a brief history of why the waiver is necessary should be added. Special attention should be paid to issues of risk, since these more often involve "informational risks" or disclosure of private information and consequential social and cultural opprobrium than they do actual physical harm. We discuss new areas of risk later in this chapter.

Cross Reference: See Book 6, chapter 3, and Book 2, chapter 3, on modeling, as well as Books 3 and 4 on details of mixed methods data collection; these materials can serve as a guide not only for one's own research but also for educating IRBs

Getting Involved with IRBs and Other Researchers

However, simply reading revamped and more explicit ethnographic proposals is not likely to accomplish the task of enlightening hard scientists on IRBs. Rather, face-to-face and ongoing dialogue is required. IRB members and others with little experience with exploratory research need to understand that many crucial questions have not and cannot be answered with experimental means, and that real questions that people have about human life and processes need to be unpacked and explored with more descriptive, inductive, abductive, and exploratory approaches. This sort of investigation needs to be explained exhaustively and patiently, over time, and in the presence of knowledgeable experts in qualitative and ethnographic research. The task of educating IRB members and researchers from more empirical or experimental paradigms, including standardized survey research and other types of investigation that do not involve engaging with research site communities, constitutes a kind of "**cultural brokering.**" Such culture brokering across the multiple cultures of scientific disciplines to explain complex social research methodologies and their ethical implications contributes to the overall scientific purpose of understanding the human world and its context, and at the same time can be personally and professionally rewarding.

> **Definition:** Cultural brokering refers to the cross translation and interpretation of cultural practices across groups

EXAMPLE 7.2

MAKING LEMONADE OUT OF A SOUR REQUIREMENT TO PERFORM PROFESSIONAL SERVICE TO THE UNIVERSITY

All university faculty members are required to participate in committee work as part of their service to the university. As a newly arrived associate professor, LeCompte was no exception. When asked by her dean to assume a position on the Institutional Review Board that recently had been vacated by the death of another member of the education faculty, LeCompte assumed that the position would last only until a more suitable replacement could be found. Little did she know that twenty years later, she would be reluctant to give up her place because it was the best service position she could imagine. She remained excited, puzzled, and intrigued by the variety of dilemmas and complications that would arise during the consideration of, and deliberation over, the myriad research proposals from all fields submitted to the IRB. The IRB posting provided opportunities to meet researchers from all over the campus, as well as community members interested in research. Reading the multiple proposals was a way to become familiar with new lines of research and alternative methods, and it permitted LeCompte to slowly but

surely persuade several cohorts of IRB members that ethnography was legitimate. In addition, her consultation with researchers themselves facilitated the construction of proposals that the IRB would find more appealing.

LeCompte's experience could be replicated by any university or research institution-based researcher, and as well, by external ethnographers or ethnography-familiar community representatives who would like to volunteer to serve on IRBs of nonprofits, research institutes, or universities.

EXAMPLE 7.3

ESTABLISHING A NEW IRB AT THE UNIVERSITY OF CONNECTICUT HEALTH CENTER

To ensure consistencies among participating IRBs from associated hospitals and campuses, the decentralized University of Connecticut Health Center (UCHC) agreed that a single IRB could act as the coordinating center for all partner IRBs. This was a remarkable breakthrough, since it required negotiating different processes, decisions, and policies across multiple IRBs. The UCHC Connecticut Institute for Clinical and Translational Science (CICATS) IRB now reviews most of the clinical and social research studies across campuses, clinics, hospitals, and participating organizations in the Central Connecticut area. The CICATS IRB is charged with reviewing many different types of studies, including qualitative and mixed methods basic and intervention research investigations with individuals and larger groups, and in communities as well as in clinical and hospital settings. The IRB and its director, a social scientist, have gone to considerable lengths to include on the CICATS IRB people who understand community-based and mixed methods research. While this does not completely obviate the requirement of complying with methodological descriptions, research interview schedules, and informed consent protocols, it does mean that this specific IRB has a better working knowledge of "ethnographic" or community-based mixed methods research and can offer good suggestions for the improvement of individual and community protections.

CONTESTING WESTERN EPISTEMOLOGICAL AND ONTOLOGICAL HEGEMONY

Epistemologies are ways of knowing or of finding out and inquiring about the world. Ontologies are ways of being in the world and defining what constitutes a sense of self. For many generations, Western observers have assumed that their epistemological and ontological leanings matched those of the people they plan to study, as well as those of the agencies that grant approval to researchers attempting to bring an investigation. Both researchers and the IRBs who approve their research have been governed by assumptions about the world that pertain mostly to the Western, modernized urban world. Their primary allegiance is to science and to disciplinary notions of rigor and validity, and also to ideas of individual rights and the assumed equality between researchers and participants (D'Andrade, 1995). As we have discussed, such a position is congruent with Western notions of the primacy of the individual and the "self-centering" of the researcher's perspective on the field. Unfortunately, it becomes increasingly dysfunctional as more and more researchers study, and give credence to, the needs of local communities and the worldviews and practices of non-Western and indigenous cultures. Further, researchers themselves increasingly come from the once-exotic cultures studied by social scientists. Maintaining a wholly Eurocentric perspective is more and more at variance not only with the interests and wishes of local people but also with the approaches of interpretive, critical, and collaborative researchers, who tend to owe greater allegiance to solidarity with the community under study, issues of justice, and responsibility for improving the conditions in which research participants live (Minkler and Wallerstein, 2010; Scheper-Hughes, 1995; S. Schensul et al., 2014). The issue of voice is involved as well; interpretive, critical, and participatory approaches recognize the power that having knowledge of other people gives to researchers; the issue of power suggests that researchers have a primary ethical responsibility to those "others" in all aspects of their investigation, including how and with whom they write the story to be told in the research results.

REDEFINING KEY TERMS IN THE TWENTY-FIRST CENTURY

The Belmont Report was published in 1978. Since that time, much in the sociopolitical, economic, and cultural world has changed. In the pages that follow, we attempt to problematize the issues of consent, vulnerability, confidentiality and privacy, risk and exposure to risk so as to point to ways in which they need to be modified and broadened to conform to current realities. We pointed out in chapter 1 that free, prior, and informed consent (FPIC) is critical to good research with communities that have been marginalized. The doctrine of free, prior, and informed consent was first applied not so much in terms of consenting to participate in research projects, but rather, to protect indigenous communities from despoliation and expropriation of their land and resources by mining and energy companies and plantation agriculture. Researchers certainly are more likely to be comfortable with the idea of FPIC than mining and energy companies, as it parallels the Belmont principles of consent and voluntarism. They also are more likely to understand that obtaining free, prior, and informed consent from potential participants mandates that researchers do sufficient advance fieldwork in an unfamiliar site to establish a trusted presence and begin to learn just what areas of consent are problematic, how vulnerabilities might be defined, what might constitute threats to confidentiality and privacy, and perhaps most important, what hitherto unknown risks might exist. ***We argue that there are no known shortcuts to achieving this level of understanding and trust.***

Key point

OBTAINING CONSENT

Research participants customarily have become part of research projects first by being identified by a researcher as having characteristics of relevance to a research question, and then by being invited to participate in a study. In the past few decades, the straightforward assumption in the foregoing—that anybody invited would be inclined to participate—has been challenged, and researchers have begun to realize that participation involves inconveniences and costs as well as potential benefits for the invitees. They have, therefore, begun to describe their efforts to garner an appropriate population to study as strategies to *recruit* participants, often with the promise of some tangible or intangible reward, or to describe their efforts as *negotiating* consent. The shift, then, has been one from a rather arrogant belief that people should participate in research simply because it's a good thing to help advance the cause of science, to one in which research not only is viewed as a possible imposition with risks and annoyances, but also a relationship in which potential research participants can and should hold equal power over what they will and won't do in a research setting with the researcher. In this section, we raise questions about the whole process of obtaining consent, as well as asking who or what in current life can consent, for whom, and under what conditions. As well, we ask how researchers can address consent issues when groups are divided over whether or not to participate, and when the consenting entity is not a conventional human being.

Determining Who Can Give Consent for a Community

When the Belmont Report was published in 1978, it was informed by the Western cultural notion of individuals as autonomous beings who are, under most circumstances, free agents who can consent for themselves—except for persons legally unable to consent, impaired in their ability to understand the research, or who might feel coerced to participate. The Belmont Report reflected as well the culture of Western science, which is highly focused on the life and activities of individuals. Even research on groups starts with single individuals as units of analysis; data are then aggregated and reported for the whole, notwithstanding that social scientists believe that an individual's behavior cannot be understood without understanding his or her social and cultural context—and hence, the people within that context.

One problem is that the IRB requirement for individual consent privileges individualistic cultures over communal or collective cultures. In the latter, it often is the case that no one individual can speak or consent for the group. In other cases, the person or persons who are empowered to give consent may do so without consulting significant components of the community. For example, in patriarchal communities where men are predominant, men may not only feel entitled to give consent for women, but also to *speak for* them. In most societies, researchers will find that trying to interview women in the presence of their husbands can be difficult, because the husbands talk for or over them. The same may be true with respect to male relatives other than husbands; fathers, brothers, uncles, and even more distant relatives who may hold significant power over their female relatives and can make eliciting their perspectives difficult. Researchers need to take into account the power dynamics in communities, not only within the community as a whole, but also culturally determined interpersonal social class, cultural, gender, and power dynamics that affect what individuals can or will say as well. Researchers will have to take into consideration not just individuals, but the patterns of deference and control in his or her family, group, social network, community, and even nation.

In addition, as we indicated in chapter 1, studies may include beings that are nonhuman, but which nevertheless must be accorded the same respect and be treated with the same degree of justice and beneficence as are accorded to human beings. In these cases, the collective or tribal group or its designated representative(s) must speak and act for the nonhuman entity. All of these issues make problematic the question of who can consent, under what conditions, and for whom.

Many indigenous communities have made finding answers to such questions simpler by establishing IRBs or their equivalent of their own. Indigenous communities use their own regulatory agencies not only to control the flow of researchers into their community but also to make clear the formal procedures required so that researchers conform to the community's ethical standards. Obtaining approval resembles procedures followed for gaining access to school districts and other organizations that require permission in addition to the researcher's own IRB approval. Researchers simply need to identify what the IRB-like body is, to whom and how a proposal should be submitted, and what it should contain. While researchers still need to establish initial trust with the community and learn its culture in order to craft a meaningful proposal, the procedures followed usually resemble the customary: submitting a proposal; answering questions; providing information about research methods, risks, and research purposes similar to those that might arise when confronting an ordinary IRB; and then waiting for a determination. Key informants, research conducted by prior researchers, and others knowledgeable about the specific populations or others similar to it can be helpful in determining risks, vulnerabilities, sensitive and forbidden topics, and as well, specific areas of interest that the group itself may wish to investigate, and around which a collaborative project might be developed.

What happens, however, when no such clearly identifiable body exists? How can a researcher determine who or what is empowered to give consent for that group? Prior fieldwork is required to answer a long list of questions that may produce an answer to this question. Who leads the group? Are there different types of leaders who may have jurisdiction over different aspects of life? Who or which one can consent on behalf of the group? What contributes to the capacity to give consent? Gender? Age? A special role? In many groups, different leaders are designated to be in charge of such things as war and conflict, religious expression, medical care, agriculture and hunting, and the education and training of youth. Which of these might be in charge of granting access to the population for research purposes? Can that person or entity decide on behalf of the group? Does the majority rule? Or is a consensus required? If so, how is it achieved?

If the group to be studied is divided over whether or not a study should be allowed, how should a researcher proceed? Can the sources of conflict be identified, so that any potential risks accruing to the individuals in the group, subgroups, and the group itself can be isolated? Each case obviously is different, so that checklists and protocols guiding researcher behavior realistically cannot be created. However, researchers who guide their actions by the principles of beneficence, respect, and social justice, especially when working closely with members of the study setting, will be able to identify how those principles are expressed in the society in question, and then act in culturally appropriate ways.

EXAMPLE 7.4

IMPLEMENTING AND EVALUATING A NEEDLE EXCHANGE PROGRAM IN HARTFORD, CONNECTICUT

In the late 1990s, it had become increasingly clear that HIV transmission among drug users could be significantly reduced if users could obtain clean needles and syringes (or "works") for use each time they injected their drugs. Without clean needles, they were sharing, or borrowing their works, and in the process the virus was passing from one person already infected to another through the virus-laden blood in their equipment. The provision of needle exchange opportunities, where drug users could take in their used works and exchange them for an equal number of new works for their personal use, could cut down infection transmission by close to 100 percent. Many communities, however, were reluctant to allow needle exchange programs to operate within their boundaries. They were concerned that this public health approach, though potentially effective, actually was endorsing and encouraging the continued drug use that they considered to be a scourge in their communities. They were also concerned that such programs could attract more drug users into their communities or stigmatize the community by public recognition that HIV was a problem there. In one neighborhood of Hartford, both the HIV rate and the resistance to a needle exchange program were very high. Many public discussions and protests demonstrated on both sides of the argument. In the end, the city and HIV prevention programs were able to win over the protesters and to get agreement for the program to travel throughout that area. One element in convincing reluctant residents was the promise of an evaluation that could show that HIV rates were declining, a significant concern. At the same time the evaluation might show that the program could convince drug users to go into drug treatment. Over time, the evaluation was able to demonstrate both of these outcomes, and until recently, the program was a well-established and popular fixture in that neighborhood (Singer, 1997; Singer et al., 1997).

EXAMPLE 7.5

OBTAINING INFORMED CONSENT FROM INDIAN WOMEN IN A STUDY ABOUT GENDER INEQUALITY AND MARITAL INTIMACY

Formative research on women's exposure to HIV risk in a low-income area of Mumbai required in-depth interviews with women who might be at risk. Earlier research had demonstrated that a risk factor for HIV was the husband's involvement with other women who might be infected, such as girlfriends, women working in bars, and commercial sex workers. While obtaining informed consent from adult married men was not a problem, some of the investigators on the study team argued that women might be exposed to risk if they were asked to consent to an interview without the permission of their husbands. India is a patriarchal society where gender norms favor men's maintenance of power and control over women and reward women's subordinate behavior. Independent decision making such as consenting to participation in a research study, especially when it involved the discussion of intimate aspects of a woman's marital relationship, might expose the woman to verbal or even serious physical abuse. The study itself posed an inherent contradiction since the anticipated intervention was to focus on building more equitable gender norms. This goal argued in favor of the woman's own ability to consent to an interview about herself. In the end, the Indian feminists on the team argued that it was acceptable to ask women to consent as independent agents. However, it was agreed that if a woman felt she needed to discuss the interview with her husband or her mother-in-law first, and then consent, she would have the opportunity to do so. Thus, a way was found to enable women comfortably and safely to consent by themselves, and researchers made sure to conduct the interview in a private setting in the absence of both the husband and the mother-in-law.

Is Consent Really Negotiable?

Anthropologists speak about "negotiating" consent with informants and communities. However, the notion of negotiation is not without problems (Barrett and Parker, 2003; Boulton and Parker, 2007). Negotiation requires a more or less equitable and respectful relationship between researchers and those whose consent is sought, or at least that the potential research participants have a degree of trust in the motives and actions of the researcher. Further, negotiating involves reciprocity, or give-and-take, such that both parties gain something from the process. Negotiation can be facilitated if, as is described in the previous chapter, researchers seek to establish research partnerships with the community and to work on issues of interest not only to the researcher, but to the community itself. This is why collaborative or participatory researchers may have fewer problems in obtaining consent; their relationship with communities and individuals already has been negotiated and already has established a pattern of reciprocity.

Consent Issues with Secondary Subjects

One issue that commonly arises in social science research involves defining who the objects of study are.

The population of interest in social science research may grow because it is somewhat difficult to study specific individuals in natural settings, or to engage in wide-ranging interviews with them, without also getting quite a bit of information about other people who have not consented to be research participants. This generates some ethical issues because if these people are identified by name, they can become **secondary subjects**. These secondary subjects are persons who are not in the study but about whom information is gathered—intentionally or accidently—from individuals who *are* in the study, information that may lead to their identification.

Asking children or any family member general questions about other family members' behavior and characteristics does not make either the children or the parents secondary subjects, if the information gathered cannot be traced to the person from whom it was elicited. Thus, asking about their parents' churchgoing activities, preference in television shows, or if they know how to swim, or even if their parents like to read or sleep late, is not particularly private and it is not identifiable, unless both the name and identity of the child are known and can be linked to the parents. However, knowing the family member's identity makes it possible to identify other members of the family, and in cases where, for example, churchgoing behavior or specific leisure activities (such as kite-flying, watching television, or dancing in strict Islamic societies) may be proscribed, that information might, if disclosed, put secondary subjects at risk. Similarly, asking one member of a group whether or not other members of the group engage in illegal activities can reveal information that the group members might prefer to remain private.

Some common research methods automatically generate secondary subjects. Researchers who use "reputational case," "network," "snowball," or "chain referral" sampling, in which a known individual identifies for researchers other individuals who share the same characteristics as the initial respondent—HIV positive people, shoplifters, undocumented families—also creates secondary subjects since knowing a person's identity and as well, the group to which he or she belongs, reveals information

Definition: Secondary subjects are individuals who have not consented to be part of a research study but about whom "private identifiable" information is obtained from another person who has been recruited into the study and given consent

that the individual may wish to keep private. Field notes kept by ethnographers can record information about others in the field without their consent; this creates secondary subjects as well. Reference to these subjects must be done with anonymous acronyms and alteration of the biography or physical descriptions of such people so as to preserve their anonymity.

IRBs generally have not created specific regulations for handling the problem of secondary subjects, and much social science research does, in fact, ask the kinds of questions that elicit information about people from others. Because they may not know the complete characteristics of the populations they wish to study, ethnographers in particular may find that as their study population grows, it includes people who did not originally "consent." This is an ethical gray area, in which researchers must decide whether or not the information they are gathering on nonparticipants in their research is general and nonspecific, and therefore will not need consent, or whether it could pose a risk to those individuals should it become known. If questions can be asked in such a way as to avoid the identification of sources, then consent may not be needed. In other cases, however, obtaining consent can be required; it should be obtained in the same way that it was requested of regular participants, and those "secondary" participants should be treated in the same way as those initially contacted.

EXPOSURE TO RISKS AND NEW FORMS OF VULNERABILITY

According to human subjects guidelines, vulnerable participants include people who are unable to consent because they are unable to understand what the research entails. This includes people who cannot speak the language of the researcher, who are poorly educated, or who are so unfamiliar with research procedures that they cannot envision what participation might entail. Ethnographers may or may not have an idea about what constitutes a vulnerable population in a different culture. However, working in new settings that are unfamiliar to researchers can reveal new vulnerabilities, even when researchers are working hard to avoid them. Often these are "situational vulnerabilities" in which under most conditions, the individuals in question would not be by definition vulnerable. However, given their own life situation at the time, or given what the researchers want them to do, or given how they are situated within larger institutional or sociopolitical conditions, they are rendered at risk. One example of such situational vulnerability might be the situation of young men of color living in an urban environment, for whom being contacted by researchers of any background who are strangers to the neighborhood could be viewed with suspicion by neighborhood residents. As a student from Puerto Rico, Jose Garcia experienced such suspicion when he approached neighborhood merchants and men chatting on the street in the initial stages of his study of the informal economy in the Puerto Rican neighborhood of Hartford, Connecticut. Both groups were concerned that he was working for the "government" as a narcotics agent.

EXAMPLE 7.6

CREATING VULNERABILITY BY USING A PARTICULAR DATA COLLECTION TECHNIQUE

Research methods also could cause risks, and thereby create vulnerabilities. A team of researchers seeking to understand the impact of war and conflict on the economic and social life of women in Afghanistan knew that they could not expect to talk with women in any public space, or even to visit them in their homes, given the religious and social prohibitions against contact by women with men who were not members of their family, and especially foreigners. They proposed instead to provide women who were interested in the study with cell phones, with which they could communicate with researchers from the privacy of their homes and without visible face-to-face interaction. What the researchers did not know was that cell phones were a widely used—and illicit—means for young men and women to contact one another for romantic purposes. Even possessing a cell phone raised suspicions among parents and extended family members that a young person was trying to circumvent parental surveillance and control. In a country where such actions could lead to so-called honor killings, the data collection technique proposed constituted a considerable risk to any participant.

Another form of situational vulnerability can arise when participation in research offers benefits that are so

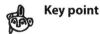

Definition: Situational risks involve investigations of the context in which a person finds themselves, if that context involves elicitation of proscribed information, research about stigmatized characteristics, or studies of illegal activities, or if it requires participants to engage in proscribed or dangerous activities

Key point

Definition: Informational risks are those that involve disclosure of sensitive or private information, knowledge of which by others could cause harm to participants

great as to be coercive. These rewards can be intangible, including friendship, access to information and social contact, intellectual partnership, or needed medication, but they can induce potential participants to join research projects that could render them vulnerable, despite their understanding of the potential costs. Again, researchers must fully understand the impact of their activities on the community and its members in order to identify such conditions.

The kinds of vulnerability-by-definition discussed in chapters 2 and 3 of this book are relatively straightforward, as are the kinds of risks that accrue to those conditions. However, social scientists more often deal with the vaguer categories of what have been called **situational and informational risks**, in which vulnerability and risk are linked because of the research topic or context. We should be clear about the distinction between vulnerability and risk. *Situational risk inheres in the research topic addressed, the act or activities in which potential participants are asked to engage, or the type of information participants are asked to divulge. Situational vulnerability inheres in the person who engages in those activities, discusses specific topics, or reveals sensitive information.* Most often, the risks involved in situationality are *informational.* A person who normally would not be considered to be vulnerable might become quite vulnerable, depending on whether the topic of research, the information requested, or the activities asked of them were risky.

EXAMPLE 7.7

SITUATIONAL AND INFORMATIONAL RISKS

A person involved in aiding and sheltering illegal migrants in the United States could participate without risk in a neighborhood study eliciting information about the kinds of recreational facilities the community desires, and a serious gardener could participate in a study of how to grow native and drought-resistant plants in the state of Colorado. However, participating in a study about immigration could be dangerous, because harboring undocumented migrants is illegal in the United States, and the individual's sheltering activities could be revealed. And if the study of gardening included how to grow marijuana, participation could be risky if it took place in a state where marijuana is classified as a controlled substance—because known growers could be subject to arrest—but not in Colorado, where growing marijuana is legal. Asking people in the United States to identify their political party affiliation generally is unproblematic—unless the questions include whether or not the individual is a member of the Communist Party, the Aryan Nation, or the American Nazi Party. But in countries that suppress political dissent and render opposition parties illegal, answering such questions could be life threatening should the answers be disclosed. Further, in virtually any country, disclosure of stigmatized characteristics such as infection with HIV or leprosy, or being a homosexual or transgendered person, can be very dangerous indeed.

A problem is that while most IRB members understand and are oriented toward the mitigation of physical risks, they may need to be convinced that nonphysical risks can be as serious and life threatening as medical risks. Researchers have an obligation to explain these risks fully to IRBs, and also, to the best of their ability, to participants. However, all of the social, emotional, and financial risks of a study may not be fully known to sociobehavioral researchers, especially when the researcher is working in a culture different from his or her own, including with people who are poor, powerless, or who do not have the linguistic, cultural, or intellectual ability to understand the research. As a means to alert researchers to unfamiliar kinds of risk, we outline in the section that follows a variety of potential nonphysical risks, especially those arising in cultures that are unfamiliar to researchers.

- *Social Risks.* Social risks are those that could lead to loss of friendships and jeopardize family relationships, cause embarrassment or lead to stigmatization, result in social isolation, and lead to shunning and banishment. For example, in religious communities such as the Amish, failing to follow religious dictates, violating standards of dress, or being "worldly" by moving away, seeking further education, or engaging in nonagricultural employment can lead to shunning or banishment. A shunned person is no longer welcome in the church, at weddings or funerals and other ceremonies and holidays, and cannot share meals with family members. As far as the community is concerned, they no longer exist. Seeking to marry outside one's own group can have similar consequences, as does engaging in sexual behavior that is stigmatized—including homosexuality. Researchers who seek to study these kinds of activities must be aware that even discussing them with outsiders could be risky to participants.

- *Financial Risks.* Disclosure of many kinds of behavior—including possession of a criminal record, affliction with a chronic or stigmatized illness, or belonging to proscribed organizations—can lead to loss of employment or investments or denial of insurance coverage. So-called whistleblowers who reveal such things as sexual predation in graduate schools, sources of contamination in a community food or water supply, or illegal activities in an organization also can find themselves without support, out of a job, or at the end of their educational career, simply for revealing what they know to outside sources.

- *Emotional Risks.* In chapters 1 and 2, we discussed several famous experimental studies that made clear the degree to which participation in social science research could cause severe emotional upset (Milgram, 1963; Zimbardo, 2007), and which led to the recognition that social science research also should be monitored to assure that it did not harm participants who had not been fully informed of the potential risks of the study. However, other kinds of research also can prove harmful if they involve asking participants to reveal embarrassing or traumatic events such as witnessing violent events, experiencing rape or domestic abuse, or having survived a disaster. Telling such stories can stimulate flashbacks or feelings of guilt, shame, anger, and depression, severe emotional distress, and mental breakdown. Asking people about historical trauma, or negative events that were not directly experienced by participants but which constitute part of their cultural history, also can generate distress, such as asking Native Americans about how entire villages died from introduced diseases or were killed in massacres by European Americans. These risks are usually addressed by offering relief from interviewing, emotional support, or referral to counseling services. Care should be taken, however; trauma or distress may not be manifested immediately in the interview session but show up later. Further, the kinds of counseling services offered must be culturally appropriate and offered by individuals who have a deep understanding of and experience with the kinds of trauma the participants suffered. Historical trauma, in particular, may be difficult for counselors with little knowledge of its impact to understand.

- *Legal Risks.* Many kinds of activities and status of interest to researchers could, if revealed to police or governmental authorities, lead to legal difficulties for participants. These include such issues as a lack of documentation among immigrants; illegal drug use or alcohol distribution among senior citizens or teenagers; and engaging in proscribed activities such as pot hunting and grave robbing, selling or making illegal drugs, or accessing and disseminating child pornography.

- *Political Risks.* Possessing unpopular perspectives or belonging to unpopular or banned organizations could lead to imprisonment, torture, or death, as many dissidents, artists, and journalists have discovered. Studying such beliefs and the organizations that support them can be dangerous not only to participants but also to the researchers who study them. Studying social movements can also lead to political risks as movement activities may be banned or monitored by police, and resulting clashes with authorities may lead to physical violence.

   **EXAMPLE 7.8**

THE DANGERS POSED BY INEXPERIENCED RESEARCHERS IN REVOLUTIONARY SOCIETIES

A number of years ago, a young and inexperienced undergraduate student researcher submitted to her IRB a proposal to study the role of religion in stimulating revolutionary activities in Central America. She wanted to begin by identifying dissident lay and religious persons in the Chiapas region of Mexico to interview them about the trajectory of their beliefs and actions. Aside from some rather romantic notions about masked revolutionaries and dissident priests, the researcher had little real experience with or knowledge of the level of conflict currently in the area, and she did not speak Spanish well. Further, the project was to last only for part of a summer. On the grounds that her inexperience, lack of a research language, and the short period of time she had to devote to the study posed a risk not only to the potential participants but also to the researcher herself, the IRB denied approval. However, not wishing to completely destroy her enthusiasm or to prevent her from writing her honors thesis, members of the IRB worked with her and her advisor to recraft the project so that the student could use the summer to attend a language institute in Mexico where she could improve her Spanish and become more familiar with politics and culture in Central America, and where she could interview people who had already publicly acknowledged their sympathy with dissident leaders. These were primarily priests, who already were identified and not in danger of arrest, as would have been the lay people whom the researcher originally hoped to sleuth out.

Situational risks can be particularly salient for ethnographers whose research questions are exploratory if they are doing research in politically volatile or war-torn areas, or other regions that are dangerous. They can be viewed as spies and as sympathizers with proscribed views, and the people with whom they associate can be viewed similarly. Researchers in such areas are well advised to learn as much as possible about all the political cleavages, allegiances, and conflicts in the area—and which sides people are on—prior to beginning fieldwork so that they can avoid unnecessarily endangering potential participants—and themselves.

■ *Cultural Risks.* Cultural risks involve violating cultural taboos. Some common everyday activities and questions, such as photographing people, asking for people's names or first names, and collecting genealogies that display all familial associations and names can be dangerous to participants in cultures where providing such information is taboo. Associating with or touching persons of the opposite sex; talking about sex, stigmas, and taboos; engaging in behavior that could disturb ancestors, offend spiritual beings, violate taboos, or disclose sacred or secret cultural knowledge to outsiders who do not have the right to possess it—all can lead to the same kinds of harm associated with social risks, described above. However, in addition to the risk of social isolation, running cultural risks can bring about sickness and death to individuals and destruction of aspects of the culture as well. For example, taking researchers to sacred sites, or going with them to places associated with the dead or to places such as burial grounds or houses in which people have died—as is a common practice among archeologists—can make native participants accompanying researchers sick or lead to their being visited by evil beings or spirits. Similarly, removal of critical sacred objects by one individual without consent of the group can make it impossible for the group to carry out important ceremonies and can trigger punishment for the individual who stole the object.

■ *Collective Risk or Harm.* Actions taken by one or a few members can affect the entire group, and information about one or a few members of a community can be applied to all members of a group. We have described earlier how early ethnographic studies of indigenous people "froze" their characterization so that they are forever seen through that often dated lens. An analogous problem occurs when a whole group suffers harm or stigmatization by the results of a study, even if it was conducted with only a few members of the group. We already have discussed the case of the Havasupai Indians in the American state of Arizona, in which DNA data were correlated with a variety of other health, psychological, and sociodemographic information, and then sold publicly by a laboratory that, though it had been contracted by researchers to conduct the DNA analysis, had no right to disseminate the information.

Cross Reference: See Example 10.2 in Book 1

Below we provide other examples of collective risk.

EXAMPLE 7.9

RISK INCURRED BY A GROUP BECAUSE STUDIES REVEALED CHARACTERISTICS POSSESSED OR EXPERIENCES HAD BY SOME MEMBERS OF THE GROUP

In the southwestern United States, some of the children of descendants of very early Spanish settlers were born with a mysterious form of retardation and birth defects, and experienced an early death. Careful historical, genealogical, and ethnographic research combined with medical studies revealed that these children had a chromosomal abnormality called Recombinant Eight (Rec8) that could be traced back to a single male ancestor centuries ago. People in that lineage carried the trait, and if two carriers married, the chances of producing Rec8 children were high. Once the research was completed, people who knew they were part of the lineage worried about who they could safely marry, and even wondered if they should marry at all. Others living in the area worried whether they themselves might be unknown carriers. All were worried about what might become of them if their Rec8 status were known to others. Rec8 children were stigmatized by the medical community, which counseled Rec8 carriers not to have children; most members of the local community, however, embraced Rec8 children, including them fully in community life, their handicaps notwithstanding. In the end, the community view prevailed (Blake, 2001).

In such studies, it is exceedingly important to make sure that appropriate education and counseling programs are in place, should the research results indicate their need; the Rec8 study also makes clear that what one group of counselors advocates may not be the same as others. Reconciling differences in trauma treatment can be problematic, as can determining which approaches are most appropriate for each individual.

EXAMPLE 7.10

CULTURAL AND PHYSICAL RISKS ASSOCIATED WITH THE ENVIRONMENT

Environmental factors also can create both physical and sociocultural risks. In Bangladesh, efforts to create clean sources of water led to the sinking of tube wells deep into unpolluted aquifers. Unfortunately, those aquifers also were in arsenic-bearing rock, and the resulting well water was contaminated with arsenic. Many people became chronically ill with arsenic poisoning. Not understanding the source of the illness, villagers came to believe that the families suffering from the poisoning actually were sick from some contagion or genetic cause, and shunned them. Girls from the families were considered unmarriageable. Researchers trying to identify the location of the contaminated wells did so by identifying families with arsenic poisoning; to the extent that this information was revealed, the stigma attached to the affected families was increased. A similar situation existed in Japan, in the fishing community around Minamata Bay, where industry had left the bay and its bottom heavily contaminated with mercury. Many fishermen and their families suffered from mercury poisoning, and children developed mental retardation; people from the Minamata Bay area also were stigmatized and shunned because the cause was believed to be a genetic or moral failing and not an environmental contaminant.

■ *Confidentiality and Privacy.* For social scientists, assuring confidentiality of data and concealing the identity of informants and participants may be the most knotty problem they face. Individuals or teams of ethnographers cannot avoid knowing a great deal about a great many people. Sometimes, as in LeCompte's conversations with staff members at the school district in Pinnacle, private information is disclosed accidently by others. Sometimes ethnographers may discover that information they possess is, in fact, dangerous, though that wasn't known initially. Knowledge of sexual liaisons between members of the community, for example, may be taken for granted until one learns that these relationships are forbidden by taboos and punishable by banishment and other sanctions. Similarly, it may be dangerous for community members if research is disclosed that shows that they are involved in selling marijuana or purchasing female condoms. To the extent that researchers acquire sensitive information and then discuss or publish it without fully understanding how sensitive it might be, they can cause informants and participants to become vulnerable. A serious threat to privacy is that research participants often know each other, or know who is participating in various studies. If they also know that they both

Cross Reference: See Example 6.6 in Book 6

are participants in a particular study, they will likely know that they each possess characteristics relevant to the study that may be undesirable or stigmatized and that they are trying to keep private.

Some fairly normal research activities also can jeopardize the privacy of information provided by research participants. In long-term fieldwork, participants can forget the researcher is a researcher and reveal information that may be sensitive and not relevant to the research in question. Group interviews or focus groups also can jeopardize privacy, when participants fail to adhere to the requirement that no information revealed in the interview should be discussed outside of that specific group event and that they themselves as participants should not reveal private information about themselves. The more people who have access to sensitive data, the more likely it is for leaks to occur, especially if some of those people are not well versed in the risks attendant to violations of privacy. Thus it is particularly important, as we noted in chapter 6, for researchers involved in partnerships and collaborative projects to provide rigorous training to their colleagues in the ethical responsibilities of research, especially prevention of harm.

TECHNOLOGY AND RETRIEVABILITY OF INFORMATION

Having noted all these issues of risk, and particularly of disclosure risks, we now move to an important and daunting question: How does a researcher protect the privacy and identity of potential research participants when technology has turned into public information nearly every possible factoid about them? People in the twenty-first century face data gathering and retrievability capacities unimaginable in the very recent past. Just an Internet connection and a simple computer can generate sufficient access to data sources to produce doctoral dissertations. While the Internet is an immense boon to researchers, marketers, and intelligence agencies, it also creates serious violations of one's right to privacy. In the first place, the scope and location of data gathering and storage is poorly understood. What *is* known is that beyond the level of individual data mining, national intelligence gathering agencies monitor and collect information on all phone calls and emails sent by every single human being in many countries, and include information about the people whom those monitored have contacted. Most commercial enterprises, including cosmetic companies, automobile vendors, purveyors of clothing and electronics, and book sellers maintain databases on their customers' characteristics and preferences. Records of library circulation are collected to determine what kinds of literature people are reading—and if they are reading materials about terrorist activities. Cell phones collect and store internally or in "the cloud" personal information, photographs, maps of places visited, records of purchases, conversations, favored contacts, texts, emails, Internet searches, entertainment preferences, and games played—even where individuals purchase gas for their cars. Google and other search engines have records of materials produced by individuals and newspaper and media articles about them. Social media sites such as Facebook, Twitter, Pinterest, ResearchGate, and LinkedIn store volumes of information, much of it volunteered by individual participants, including photographs and addresses, and therefore identifiable, but probably never intended by those individuals for use in research projects or governmental sleuthing. Social media also can be used to map and follow networks of friends, family, associates, and professional contacts. Dating sites show who people prefer as partners. And in addition, the research that investigators present, publish, and disseminate is stored and can be monitored.

The mere existence of this technology and its ever deeper penetration into every aspect of human life raises serious questions about privacy and confidentiality. Even if an individual researcher promises confidentiality to potential informants, it is likely that whatever the researcher is interested in can be accessed—and then revealed without the individuals' permission—by means other than direct contact. Further, the archives technology creates cannot be edited; one's information cannot be deleted. This situation has created an unfinished international debate over whether or not people have a "right to be forgotten," to excise information that they do not want remembered or

publically available from all Internet sources, and even to
drop out of sight and surveillance by electronic monitors
and data collectors. The extent to which this is even possible
is debatable, but it pits the rights of individuals to privacy
against the demands for freedom of access to all information and makes increasingly difficult the task of researchers wishing fully to protect their informants. One way that
researchers still can preserve information confidentiality is
by avoiding sending data via email or in nonsecure cloud or
information sharing arrangements. They also can use safe
and encoded means for sharing and storing large amounts
of data from multiple sites. While learning about and using
these technologies can seem like an onerous task, it only
takes one serious security breach and loss of information to
make researchers understand just how necessary they are.

ETHICS AND THE CONSEQUENCES OF INTERPRETATION

Interpretation is the final stage of the actual research process. It means going beyond "just the facts" of the data,
whether quantitative or qualitative. By themselves, unana-
lyzed data, or results, have very little meaning. Data that
have been analyzed, but are left uninterpreted are mere
results. The simple fact that a particular community was
divided in how it explained a series of disasters occurring
in its school district is not very meaningful. Neither is the
fact that different stakeholders' experience of and perspectives regarding "what happened" during particular educational reforms vary widely. This would be expected, given
stakeholders' different points of view, ways of articulating
with the reforms, and particular vested interests. In a sense,
such results often only explicate the obvious. To go beyond
the obvious, researchers must respond to the questions, "So
what?" and "Why is this important?" and "What do these
findings mean for future actions?"

Researchers "go beyond" results by explaining them
to a variety of readers using various levels of theory. The
process begins with the conceptual framework that initially informed the study and its research questions; it may
include additional concepts and theories that were not
anticipated at the beginning of the study but emerged as

crucial as data collection and analysis proceeded. It then links findings to existing literature and paradigmatic understandings. The first level of interpretation consists of local theory, or concrete explanations of specific events given by local people and participants. Higher-level, middle-range, or substantive theories step away from the local scene and explain events in terms of the wider community and the discipline informing the study. The third, or paradigmatic, level examines the findings in terms of what the social sciences generally say when comparing studies in similar situations that generated similar results. This requires an examination of prior literature as well as theory. As the explanations they generate go from the local and concrete to more abstract and generalizable, studies become more and more capable of altering or modifying existing understandings and even generating new theoretical explanations. In this way, knowledge is advanced.

"Good" Interpretation

It is at this point that interpretation enters the realm of ethics. Since all kinds of policy decisions can be made on the basis of their interpretations, researchers have an ethical imperative to make sure that their interpretations are as fair and humanely put as possible. Different interpretations can lead to different courses of action, which in turn have different consequences for different groups. Only the integrity of the researcher in exposing his or her own biases and those of the data sources can protect research from bias, and hence, from running the risk of being unethical because it is of poor quality.

What, then, makes an interpretation "good"? As we have pointed out, in the not-too-distant past, researchers could posit that good interpretation served to uncover some single foundational and fixed meaning explaining the data or textual evidence. Often, as in Example 7.11 below, such a single and fixed meaning cannot be identified. As is increasingly the case, particularly in the social sciences, interpretation resides in more pragmatic, temporally bounded, polyvocal, and dynamic presentations. What *is* now is conceived of as dynamic, often contextual, and even more frequently,

multiple. Meaning making is the province of all stakeholders in an investigation, from researchers to participants to
users of findings. More common than the search for a single interpretation is the question whether an interpretation
is "good." But that question raises others: "Good for whom
or good for what?" For funding agencies? For the discipline?
For the applied field in question—education, for example?
For the people studied? For which sectors among the people
studied? For the individual researcher's career? The criteria
for determining the answers to such questions, naturally,
are themselves subject to different understandings.

Criteria for Goodness

Among the criteria for good interpretations are:

- being true to the data
- providing a coherent interpretation
- remaining true to, or respecting, the subjects' views
  of things, at least insofar as member checks are done
  to assure the validity of the researcher's interpretation
- articulating the views of the multiple voices in the
  field setting and being fair in representing emic, etic,
  and other versions of what happened
- in action or collaborative research, negotiating
  among participants and researchers until a shared
  view of reality emerges that can be represented to
  the public

Thus, regardless of the researcher's epistemological stance, at one level, criteria for assessing the quality of
interpretation rest with definitions of good research in general. Good interpretation is linked closely to and supported
by evidence, and it is based on clear and plausible argumen-
tation. It is supported by theoretical understandings from
the disciplines, or grounded logically in data from the field,
or both. It considers all points of view. It advances understanding of the specific phenomenon under study, and
in some cases, it "does good" by promoting or improving
educational processes, service agencies, and human institutions. It also takes into consideration the different cultural

conditions and contexts in which the study was embedded. Good interpretations also make sense at the local level and to external constituencies. We use Example 7.11 below to illustrate many of these issues. LeCompte compiled the description in Example 7.11 while she was studying and working with communities in the Navajo Nation in the southwestern United States.

EXAMPLE 7.11

MULTIPLE REALITIES IN SEARCH OF A SINGLE STORY

The Pinnacle school district had experienced a number of disasters: the roof on the brand-new gym leaked and ruined the very expensive basketball floor—a key issue in a community in which basketball was a very important sport. A teacher had tried to commit suicide by jumping off the roof of one of the school buildings. A well-respected and very popular student had died in a car accident. Half the senior class had compiled sufficient numbers of unexcused absences to be counted as failing key classes needed for graduation. And rumors swirled about pedophilia and drug use among teachers. Why these misfortunes occurred was explained differently by two constituencies in the communities. Most of the Anglo administrators and staff members in the school district felt that the explanations—and hence, the solutions to the problems—were issues of contractor incompetence, mental instability on the part of the teachers, inexperience on the part of the teenaged driver, bus drivers who failed to report when students missed school because the roads were washed out on the reservation and the buses could not complete their routes, and a group of disaffected and very traditional parents initiating rumors. These explanations were based on rational, scientific, and technical insights that constituted an *etic* understanding; they made sense to the researchers. By contrast, the Navajo teachers, staff members, and key components in the community felt that all of the seemingly unconnected adverse events could be attributed to an underlying factor: a lack of harmony, or *hozho*, in the community. Balance in the universe had been deranged because taboos had been violated and important cultural norms transgressed—an *emic* explanation rooted in local cultural understandings. Though the community did not need to know which taboos had been violated, they did know that only a traditional Blessing Way ceremony could restore the balance of harmony in the community and end the string of disasters. The two communities resolved the conflict in cultural explanations by implementing two sets of solutions. The technical rational response from the administration included instituting better screening for contractor competence and a program of more closely scrutinizing potential teachers for mental health problems and potential instability. The bus drivers were drilled in how and to whom to report problems with the bus routes and which children rode problem buses.

Antidrinking campaigns for students also were initiated, and discussions were held with parents to better understand what some of their concerns about relationships between teachers and students were. By contrast, the more traditional Navajos in the community organized a week-long Blessing Way ceremony, and the superintendent of schools, a Navajo, represented the district by volunteering to be the "patient" whose disconnection with the universe needed to be restored in the ceremony.

The researchers ended up by telling both stories (LeCompte and McLaughlin, 1994) as an illustration of the complexities involved in figuring out "what's going on" during fieldwork. However, as mere researchers, they were not called upon to come up with a single solution to the problems, as often is the case in policy-oriented and evaluative studies.

Epistemological Considerations: Emic and Etic Approaches

Good interpretation makes sense at the indigenous or local level (the emic level) and to external constituencies (the etic level, or the one imposed by scientists). Anthropology long has addressed some parts of these questions—as the community in Pinnacle did—by recognizing the legitimacy of insider/outsider, or emic/etic, positions. Emic, or insider perspectives, are those embedded in the culture and experiences of the people studied; they constitute what "makes sense" in their local setting. Etic, or outsider, perspectives are those applied to the community being studied by researchers or others external to the community. Insider/outsider, or emic/etic, positions affect what story is told, to whom, and for which purposes. Given the heterogeneity of groups and communities and the contested nature of many phenomena in which interpretive researchers are interested, issues of validity arise regarding the fit between what researchers find and understand (the etic) and the research participants' own experiences and understandings (the emic). Interpretations based on the cultural frames and understandings of the participants only (the emic perspective) can be internally consistent and perfectly logical, but in direct contradiction to the cultural frames and understandings of wider cultural, political, or legal communities (the etic perspective) in which the "little community" (Redfield, 1956) is embedded—and which therefore is externally invalid.

Thus, interpretation has come to involve more than simply finding or generating a theory that seems to fit with or explain what happened in the site from the researcher's perspective; rather, questions now focus on whose story should be foregrounded and how. These problems are particularly acute when the language and/or culture of the researcher differ substantially from that of the researched. This lack of congruity can morph into ethical issues when the political, legal, economic, or cultural consequences of the story or stories told for the participants are considered. Polygamy among Mormons, homeschooling among evangelical Christians, initiation rituals involving scarification and circumcision among African tribes, migration across national boundaries in search of better economic circumstances, wearing of headscarves by Muslim female students, the limited schooling permitted by Amish communities for their children, and the granting of "personhood" to rivers and mountains by indigenous groups (or, for that matter, the granting of personhood to corporations in the United States, as has happened through a series of Supreme Court decisions [see *Citizens United, Appellant v. Federal Elections Commission*, 558 US 310, Docket No. 08-205, 2010])—all can be explained in terms of their practical and survival value for a specific people, a culture, or its beliefs. Most have been declared illegal at times by the "larger community" for reasons of conflict with the culture, economics, religion, or politics of dominant groups in society. Thus, interpretations always have consequences for the people being studied; the political economics and power asymmetries within a community affect which set of reasons or interpretations should prevail. If communities are isolated, these practices may be able to survive without interference. However, to the extent that they overlap with more powerful communities, such practices can be outlawed in the interests of the "greater good" of the mainstream—as is the case when bodies of water held sacred by indigenous groups are polluted and destroyed by mining corporations because they contain gold. Clearly, those interpretations with the greatest power behind them are more likely to be accepted. However, other interpretations that represent emerging constituencies or power groups can pose a threat to existing power relationships, especially insofar as they threaten the values and structure of privilege in the larger community. In these cases, dominant regimes can make adherents to such nonmainstream beliefs and practices into scapegoats to deflect criticism—as is the case when religious or cultural minorities are held responsible for social unrest. Looking at the differences in these interpretations often can help to identify serious cleavages in the society, and, as well, areas in which researchers could identify the greatest weakness in the prevailing regime.

Whose Story Prevails?

Telling an "incorrect" or incomplete story can be unfortunate or poor research; at worst, it can be unethical, particularly if researchers do not consider the consequences that could emanate from turning faulty or partial interpretations into policies and applying them in practice. Unfortunately, what the "story" to be told *is* is not always straightforward or obvious. Ethnographers often struggle with how best to portray a combination of their own or disciplinary understandings—an *etic* perspective—and the stories told and understandings held by informants—an *emic* perspective—when the two sets of understandings and explanations are in conflict.

The problem that the example above highlights is, "Which story should be foregrounded?" Such a question poses considerable difficulty for positivists, who long held that some kind of underlying truth is present in all phenomena; the task of researchers simply was to uncover that truth and to get the story "right." This meant transforming the "other" into something that is the "same" as, or at least familiar to, the "self" of the researcher—erasing differences, in a sense. The problem is that interpretive research often involves studying groups, and groups rarely are homog-

enous with regard to opinions, values, or perspectives, as Example 7.11 above demonstrates. Interpretive researchers more and more frequently find that what the field "says" to them consists of a cacophony of stories that disagree with and contest each other, depending upon the vantage points, experiences, and positionality of both participants and researchers. No collective and uniform story from the field exists; thus no one story really is "right." The task of interpretation is greatly complicated by the fact that all communities subsume multiple truths and multiple realities, including that of the researcher. Which one should be reported? Whose sense of reality is privileged over another?

EXAMPLE 7.12

TWO STORIES, SAME DATA

In a collaborative study with the Mauritius Family Planning Association, the field research team collected information on specific intimate and explicitly sexual behaviors of young, unmarried women working in industries throughout the island in order to understand better their exposure to sexually transmitted diseases and HIV. In Mauritius, virginity was a widely valued virtue, and women were expected to be virgins at marriage. Much attention was paid to the intact nature of the hymen, and both women and their boyfriends were very concerned about "hymen health." Thus they avoided sexual behaviors that risked injury to the hymen (those that resulted in blood and pain), but all other forms of intimate sexual behavior were acceptable. Intimate relationships were kept secret from family members.

It was widely believed by older adults that young working women were dangerously involved in sex. Though their economic contributions to the household through their work were considered very important, their sexual safety was even more so. Discovery of illicit sexual intimacy could result in a young woman being prevented from leaving the house to go to work.

The data collected by the research team produced a "Guttman scale of risky sexual behavior." The Guttman scale, as a type of cultural consensus tool, ranked the sex behaviors in order of their accrual across all the women with percentages of young women who participated in from one to all of the behaviors, starting with holding hands and ending with anal sex. At least four of the behaviors involved some form of penetrative sex. These results, it was decided, would not be revealed to the public, at least in that form, because doing so could risk harming the reputation of the collective of young women in the industrial sector. Further, the number of women involved in penetrative sex behaviors was relatively small. Most of the behaviors involved nonpenetrative forms of intimacy, and most of the women were involved in these "safer" (at least from an HIV-related perspective) forms of sex. Thus, one study story was that women were indeed meeting and seeing men, but that for the most part, they were taking precautions to protect themselves. They just needed more support and education about penetrative forms of sex.

One day, a member of the research team was riding the bus to work when she overheard two Mauritian professionals speaking in English directly in front of her. In looking at them, she observed that they were reading a newspaper article written in English in a local newspaper. The newspaper article included the Guttman scale and a story about women's sexual risk in the industrial sector—just the story the team had decided *not* to make available to the public. When the study team asked how this article and the Guttman scale could have reached a newspaper reporter, they were told that the story was meant for the very small audience of professional and international readers of the English newspaper and would never reach the eyes and ears of Creole speakers: two different stories for different audiences.

In the Pinnacle community, the conflict in explanations troubled the researcher more than the community, which implemented two solutions, thus according equal importance to both traditional and bureaucratic rational explanations. Such an approach is increasingly realistic in a world where multiple, powerful, and competing realities require more delicate treatment than a simple declaration of winners and losers. Further, as chapter 6 made clear, working in collaborative ways with communities can help forge understandings and agreements-to-disagree that render the inability to come up with a single "truth" unnecessary or at least less dire.

Handling the Task of Recounting Multiple Realities

Whether they liked it or not, and regardless of the ethics involved in arrogating the voice of others, researchers used to find that they always stood in a position of asymmetrical power vis-à-vis the community they studied. *They* were the ones who told the story. And in so doing, they created a reality for the participants vis-à-vis the outside world that spoke more powerfully and for longer periods than anything participants could articulate. However, to the extent that ethnography has become collaborative as a consequence of criticisms over arrogance, a remedy has been created. Ethnographers have learned that Weber's suggestion that researchers "bracket" their own persona and moral concerns, separating them from an objective consideration of and portrayal of events, is insufficient. It also is insufficient to simply "step in" and then "step out" of participants' lives and perspectives, as Weber's notion of *verstehen* (1949, 1968) suggests doing. Ethnographers now must be careful to consider and integrate the views of participants, even if they are "studying up" to elite groups or people with more structural power than their own. The stories now should be created with the advice and consent of the participants, even if the researcher still creates the documents. And herein lies a problem: no matter how much research participants contribute to a story, *what* researchers study and the data they collect always are filtered in such a way as to create at least an implicit narrative, and their recounting of that narrative creates the final portrayal of the community—at least until contradicted or modified by subsequent research.

The Researcher, the Self, and the "Other"

In earlier eras, that the researcher created the story to be told was not problematic; it was, in fact, the researcher's primary task. However, critical and postmodern theories now ask researchers to take sides. They posit that it is unethical and arrogant to speak for a community that is not one's own, and that doing so silences the voices of true community participants (Said, 1978, 1994; Spivak, 1988). This raises the problem of the "self" and the "other," and what Sandoval (2000) calls the essentially colonizing force that is constituted by defining a research site as a field for study and then imposing on the site and its inhabitants a new structure or a set of definitions deriving from the researchers' disciplinary concepts and logics. Clearly this is a direct assault on the "etic" approach itself. Rather than taking the site as it is named by and exists in the minds and lives of participants, the colonizing aspects of fieldwork remap a territory that ethnographers in large part already have drawn up, based on the frameworks of their discipline (Abu-Lughod, 1991, 37). It is this redefinition of participant reality that critical researchers find to be an arrogation of control over participants' voices. Further complicating the issue of story is that the "other," something defined as "outside of [normal] being," often is so singular, so apart from mainstream experience that it cannot be synthesized, summarized, and made equivalent to the understandings or worldviews of outsiders (Benson and Lewis O'Neill, 2007). So how do researchers portray the outside-of-normal (that is, outside the Western researchers') experience? How do they explain what appears to be unintelligible, and seemingly irrational? These questions frame the struggles that researchers have over "story" and "legitimacy" in a postmodern intellectual world that remains uneasy with the use of raw power and force to resolve differences in perspective, behavior, belief, and status. These questions require that researchers struggle to engage in an ethical redress of balance in the field by doing more than simply developing intersubjective understanding (Ryle, 1949; Weber, 1949, 1968) with participants, writing up their results, and then leaving.

Whose Story to Foreground

One tactic researchers have used to resolve at least part of the power asymmetry has been to eliminate the researcher's own story altogether in the write-up. By refusing to provide an interpretation, investigators try to let the data "speak for themselves." The problem is that no data speak for themselves, if only because they have been collected in selective ways that reflect, however unconsciously, the researchers' own filters. Further, as simple "results," even analyzed data mean very little. They are simply the raw materials with which researchers work, using filters from their discipline, experience, feedback from their field, and cultural notions of common sense (Geertz, 1973) to determine what is important and what sense can be made of the data. All researchers base what they produce on what they believe audiences will understand and be able to use; these beliefs are, at their heart, simply interpretations of particular perspectives, presented in and for specific contexts.

Further, eschewing interpretation not only is virtually impossible to achieve in any kind of study—some would even say that it represents an abdication of responsibility (Geertz, 1989–1990); it also abandons readers to determine the meaning of the story by themselves, deprives them of insights the researcher might have contributed, and makes it impossible to interrogate researcher biases and omissions that might have influenced the story. While not exactly arguing for the primacy of the researcher's story, Geertz (1989–1990) holds that omitting a carefully argued interpretation by the investigator simply creates poor scholarship.

Other postmodern investigators have tried to establish parity among the "voices" in the field (Lather and Smithies, 1997; Bloom, 1990; Foley, 1994, 1995; LeCompte and McLaughlin, 1994) by creating co-constructed or "bivocal" and "multivocal" texts that present everybody's story. These efforts can be effective in presenting all multiple versions or interpretations of a story, and they have resulted in creative, dialogical texts, but they do not always tell a coherent story, or, and perhaps more important, provide guidance for problem solving, policy formation, or advances in theoretical understanding.

When the Field Talks Back

Ethnographers once could be fairly confident that whatever they wrote about a community would remain primarily within the scholarly community. Most of the people whom they studied never would read what they wrote. However, the individuals and communities ethnographers study increasingly are literate, well connected, and educated. Sometimes, they even write and publish their own accounts of a project, one that contradicts that of the researcher (Medicine, 2001; Gibson, 1985). Often, as we describe in chapter 6, they have become coinvestigators and partners in the research enterprise.

Community leaders, educational administrators, and target populations—all participants in research ventures—also are increasingly politicized (Brosted et al., 1985; Whyte, 1991; Greaves, 1994; Manderson et al., 1998;

LeCompte, Schensul, Weeks, and Singer, 1999; LeCompte and Schensul, 2013; Schensul and LeCompte, 2013). The Internet offers to communities from one end of the globe to the other the power of instant communication and access to information never before available; communities have learned that they have the right to question, and that research, if conducted properly, can work to their advantage. They also have something to say about how best to carry out aspects of the research since they know their constituents better than the researchers do. They also tend to be aware of the adverse consequences that might ensue from participating in a research project. This history not only might make participants reluctant to become part of a research study, but it also might make the researcher wary of trying to "speak for" or "as if they were members of" a community being studied.

Consequences of Interpretation

Interpretations of research can have good consequences for some and not for others. In these cases, one must return to philosophy—does one adhere to the principle of the greatest good for the greatest number? Or to compensatory logics that argue for the greatest good going to those who have suffered most? Or those most capable of wresting the good from others? Is there some notion of "fairness" or equity that should apply? Should local notions of how good should be apportioned be paramount? Or do mainstream notions of the good even prevail in other cultures? With the Belmont Principle of beneficence in mind, we call for a great deal of cultural-historical sensitivity and a certain degree of clairvoyance among researchers with regard to future impacts of their work on the people they study.

Further, while qualitative researchers might originally have more difficulty working through ethical issues in everyday interaction with participants simply because they *do* interact with them daily and over long periods of time, no researchers, no matter what their particular epistemological bent is, are exempt from considering the ethical consequences of their interpretations. Because all research is a human enterprise, all research effectively is interpretive. We hold, therefore, that ethical considerations regarding interpretation apply equally to every research modality and any purpose for which research is put. Every step of any research project is informed by the interpretations that researchers make about what is worth studying, how studies should be carried out, and how their results should be understood and applied. Although qualitative or interpretive, and quantitative or positivistic researchers may approach the resolution of ethical problems differently, the fundamental issues faced are similar, regardless of the approach taken. All researchers formulate guiding questions or hypotheses, collect data, and transform it into evidence in support, or for the development, of propositions. Further, all researchers must first generate sets of meaning for their data at the local level, then seek to explain what consequences the propositions might have for midrange or substantive theory within a discipline, and finally integrate these understandings and consequences into existing paradigmatic and theoretical understandings within science as a whole. All of these steps involve the interpretation of what is important to study, how it might best be studied, what theories are most meaningfully applied, and what significance the results actually have. All of these questions can be answered only through the value system and sets of cultural and personal meanings informing the researcher's work, whether that work is considered to be "qualitative" and "interpretive" or "quantitative" and "logico-deductive" (Sherman and Webb, 1988).

Researchers must be cognizant that their research results can both positively and adversely affect the entire people being studied, far beyond the consequences of a study for any given individual. These consequences require that researchers take special care with regard to which story is being told, about whom, to whom, and why. We have noted that important concepts to be considered include researcher positionality, conflicts between insider/outsider perspectives, levels of power within a community and between it and the outside world, and questions about the agendas extant in agencies that support and fund research. Fundamentally, the ethical imperative of all interpretation returns to the Belmont Principle of beneficence. This requires researchers to consider the consequences of their research for all levels of human organization and human beings. As we have argued in this chapter, interpretation of research results is an integral part of the research process, and as such, what the research results *mean*, or their interpretation, is not exempt from the ethical test of consequence.

SUMMARY

In this chapter, we have identified contemporary and ongoing problems with the current system of oversight for research on human beings, and we have attempted to demonstrate areas in which the procedures implementing basic principles for ethical treatment of human subjects need to be modified to conform to the realities of contemporary cultural and global diversity. We have, as well, raised the issue of threats to basic principles such as confidentiality and privacy, given exploding and hitherto unknown technologies for data storage, preservation, and recovery. In addition, we note that ethics must govern not only the conduct of research but also its consequences, in that differing interpretations that researchers give to their data can have differential ethical impact on the studied communities.

In the final chapter of this book, we argue that research is not simply a mechanical or technical matter of applying formulae to procedures and problems and coming up with brilliant ideas. Rather, some of the most difficult work that investigators do is that of *reflection*—on their own actions, and on what meaning those activities have in the context both of the communities they study and the wider disciplinary arenas in which that work is embedded. It is through reflection that problems are identified, parsed, and investigated, and it is through reflection that the results of investigations are modified, clarified, and used. We close this book by examining how and why researchers must engage in reflection.

8 ━◆━◆━◆━

THE ROLE OF REFLECTION IN ETHNOGRAPHIC RESEARCH

Identifying
Subjectivities

Positionality and
Power

The Risks of the
"Other"

Taking Stock

Summary

INTRODUCTION: WHAT IS REFLECTION?

Reflection involves holding a mirror and a microscope to one's own work, and at the same time, using a crystal ball to anticipate its consequences. The mirror, the microscope, and the crystal ball all are used to assess the quality of the work; they also provide metaphorical tools to assure that researchers adhere to the best canons of both formal and informal ethical practice. Reflection is linked to the issue of ethics in research because it plays a large role in keeping researchers honest and investigations rigorous.

Reflection is used in every stage of ethnography: in identifying research questions, assembling a formative theory upon which to base the study and research teams and infrastructures to implement investigation, collecting data and conducting analysis, adhering to ethical principles, and constructing an interpretation of results.

Like all other aspects of the ethnographic research process, *the process of reflection is both recursive and reflexive.*

Definition:
Reflection is the process of looking back on and critiquing what has occurred in the past for its quality, righteousness, and rigor. It also is used in anticipating what might happen in the future by interrogating a variety of alternative paths

Key point

251

Key point

Key point

Recursivity is a cyclical process of examining what has been done so far, developing next steps, anticipating results from those steps, and then beginning again on the basis of those results. As we have indicated previously, ethnographic research is inherently recursive, and so is the process of reflection that is a crucial component to the investigation. *Reflexivity involves holding a mirror to one's own self and work, then looking back on and evaluating what is reflected.*

Researchers generally are familiar with formal ethical requirements, but actually adhering to them requires systematic and disciplined reflection. Some requirements are quite straightforward: responsible researchers do not falsify data, plagiarize, or avoid conclusions that they did not anticipate or are contrary to their expectations and hopes. They must avoid doing harm to subjects, either unanticipated or anticipated, and refrain from actions to which participants have not consented. They must attend to the social justice aspects of recruitment and its impact on participants, and remember to respect the privacy and confidentiality of participants. Less formally, researchers must not claim as valid any interpretations that participants have not first vetted through "member checks," feedback from representative participants, and/or comments from a community advisory board, key informants, community coauthors, or others representing the study community. More conventionally, and in the realm of everyday or informal interaction with participants, researchers are ethically bound to interact fairly and decently with other human beings, including their own co-workers, in accordance with their own values and with the norms and practices of the community under study. Less conventional are postmodern concerns that require researchers to assemble valid and authentic interpretations. If it is impossible to get the interpretations "right" or to obtain consensus from members of the study community, researchers must respect and represent the range of interpretations extant in the field site. Most important in our view is that researchers have an ethical responsibility to be aware of the effects of the research process and the uses to which research might be used both with respect to and within the cultural setting or community where the study was carried out. Awareness in all of these areas requires self-reflection, so that researchers constantly audit their work, examine their actions, question their procedures and hunches, and assess their own involvement in the process.

Reflection and Self-Reflection

Systematic reflection examines past activities and uses that information to plan for the future. It also is the process by which researchers interrogate their own past actions within a research site. Reflection is not mere meditation or navel-gazing. It is informed by the researcher's own cultural values, experiences and sensitivities, and emotional responses, by the tenets of his or her discipline, and by feedback and reactions from the researched community.

Key point

One of the most important attributes an ethnographer can bring to his or her project is a keen ability to engage in *self-reflection.* *Self-reflection is that same systematic process applied to one's own behavior and the reactions of others to it. It is the means by which researchers examine the quality of their own work, the integrity with which results have been assembled and interpreted, and the degree to which they have treated all participants—partners, colleagues, informants, and members of the community—according to their own ethics, those of their discipline, and those of the study community.* Without self-reflection, ethnographers are unlikely to be able to take stock of how they are perceived by or interact with others in the field. They also are unlikely to recognize potential gaps, errors, or biases in the data they collect because of how research participants felt about them; those feelings can lead participants to censor access to information and to limit discussions in order to obviate disclosing information that they feel researchers should not possess, or that they feel uncomfortable disclosing. The unreflective ethnographer—a term that is nearly oxymoronic unless applied to someone who does bad ethnography— seldom is able to learn from the inevitable mistakes made in the field or to identify potential misunderstandings or dangerous situations before they become very serious or even—in rare cases—life threatening. In

Key point

addition, self-reflection also facilitates exploration of the profound consequences of research interpretations for the people in whose histories, values, norms, and behaviors they are embedded. Self-reflection permits ethnographers to examine their mistakes, successes, wrong turns, and new directions; it relies on strict and honest interrogation of the researcher's own motives, values, actions, and intentions.

We have suggested that researchers who have greater sensitivity to cultural issues (as, for example, ethnographers do) are more likely to be attuned to certain ethical issues, and to be more able to come to valid conclusions about what actually happened. Further, they are more likely to suggest ways in which the multiplicity of descriptions and explanations can serve not to obfuscate a problem by embedding it in a polyphony of voices, but to aid in a more nuanced presentation of the reality in which participants live. We also suggest that researchers in other fields who make use of ethnographic understandings of the people with whom they are working can find their relationships with those people more harmonious and productive as a result.

EXAMPLE 8.1

SACRED MOUNTAINS VERSUS ENORMOUS TELESCOPES

Astronomers have always prized the clear, cold, dark sky atop remote high mountains because it provides optimal conditions for exploring the universe. Those mountaintops are prime real estate for building observatories. The Atacama Desert that runs north and south almost the length of Chile is one such place, and currently, nearly a half-dozen mountains are being remodeled to accommodate very large and extra-large optical, radio, and linked telescopes. The mountaintops are being blasted away to provide flat surfaces, and roads are being built right up to the sites, which include large buildings and considerable technological infrastructure. But those same mountaintops also often are sacred sites to indigenous people; they are the sites of ceremonies, indigenous sky-watching practices, and burial grounds for important people. Little evidence of concern for indigenous practices is evidenced in Chile, though ancient burials have been found in those mountains, including the presence of mummified human remains. However, it also is the case that most of Chile's indigenous people are gone, replaced by the descendants of colonists from Europe and elsewhere, whose knowledge of the history and culture of indigenous peoples is limited.

In the Hawaiian Islands, however, native Hawaiians have maintained a robust culture, and Mauna Kea, the largest volcano in the islands, holds a special and sacred place in their culture. Mauna Kea also is home to one of the biggest telescopes in the world, and astronomers now are constructing additions to the existing array. Despite ongoing conflicts, the astronomers have worked hard with local people to assure that the additional construction atop Mauna Kea does not encroach on burial sites or ceremonial grounds, and that roads and buildings remain peripheral to the ceremonial purposes. In this way, the two cultures exhibit respect for one another and minimize—despite not eliminating—friction.

Example 8.1 highlights a range of cultural considerations that ought to be of concern to all kinds of researchers—even those who do not think they actually are studying "culture." What also is clear is that none of the considerations above can be addressed if researchers view the process of their investigation as merely a mechanical or technical matter of applying formulae to known problems. By contrast, we hold that reflection is key to good research, intervention, program planning, and evaluation.

Reflection is no simple process; it requires preparation, practice, and professionalism. Before entering the field, ethnographers should first learn as much as possible about the research setting. In this way, they will be more able to identify cultural practices and values in the field that could be discomforting to them or which might challenge their values and ways of viewing the world. They then should apply the same learning processes to themselves, exploring their own cultural practices and values, ways of viewing the world, and their deeply held and often unconscious biases and prejudices.

IDENTIFYING SUBJECTIVITIES

Good researchers need to identify their own biases, prejudices, and patterns of thought which, though taken for granted, actually constitute their culturally specific ways of viewing the world and the beliefs and behaviors of others. These perspectives derive from the ethnographer's socio-economic status, educational levels, sense of entitlement, ethnicity, religion, and a whole host of likes and dislikes generated in the course of life experiences. Taken together, these perspectives constitute what feminist scholars Sandra Harding (2002; 2004), Nancy Hartsock (1983), and Joyce Nielsen (1990) call a *standpoint*, a set of unconscious preferences and ideas about how the world should be—and one's place in it—that create a lens of biases and subjectivities through which the world is seen. Notwithstanding that subjectivities are socially constructed and contextual, they still are acted on as if they were real, and can jeopardize a researcher's ability to "see clearly" in the field.

In Example 8.2, we borrow Alan Peshkin's (1988) terminology and define subjectivities as "hot" spots and "cold" spots—or issues and behaviors that, given the researcher's background and past experiences, either attract or repel researchers.

EXAMPLE 8.2

DISCOVERING A "COLD SPOT"

LeCompte found the director of Special Programs in one district where she was a consultant to be rather unlikable and very difficult to work with. Many of the tasks needed for the implementation of the programs LeCompte was to set up required the cooperation of the director. However, though the director always was affable and seemed amenable to their joint project, her staff never seemed to accomplish the tasks that the director and LeCompte agreed to share among their respective teams. The director's passive resistance to the innovative projects LeCompte was initiating was described by one of LeCompte's research team members as "trying to batter down a wall of feathers"; arrangements were set up fell through, materials to be ordered never came, and rooms that that were to be available were already booked when the research team arrived. Further, the director seemed to resent the entire project that LeCompte had been asked by the district to implement. Although LeCompte was exhorted by the superintendent just to keep working with the director, she began to avoid the informal meetings and conversations with the director that she held regularly with all the other staff members in the district. It seemed too uncomfortable to continue trying to collaborate when all she could think of were the many times that cooperation had failed. Fortunately, LeCompte conducted an audit of her observations, and after enumerating her contacts with important participants in the field, she discovered that she really lacked sufficient data on the director and her activities to adequately describe her programs and

impact. As a remedy, LeCompte doubled down on the time she spent with the director to fill holes in the record and better understand her behavior.

Learning, or reflecting, about one's own self can help ethnographers identify their subjectivities, and as well, their commitments to specific research topics and outcomes, as well as the potential that such behaviors might have for biasing or negatively influencing research results. For example, researchers can ask themselves what they think is most important to *them* about their research, what they hope (rather than hypothesize) to find, and what they believe is "wrong with" or "needs fixing" in the setting or in the behavior of the people who occupy it. From these questions ethnographers can begin to identify those personal viewpoints that could cause them to privilege a particular perspective or interpretation, prevent them from obtaining a well-rounded set of data for analysis, or lead them *not* to ask questions or pursue lines of investigation that counter their prejudices or expand their database. They also may be able to identify issues and problems of interest to members of the community, and therefore find rapport among people who might serve as research partners or collaborators.

Disciplining Subjectivity

Engaging in such reflection systematically turns the ethnographer into what one could call a "self-interrogator," or someone who constantly holds his or her own opinions, conclusions, and beliefs about what has happened in the field site up to the bright light of inspection and critique to assure that they are valid. Self-reflection, or systematic self-interrogation, however, requires "taming" or controlling one's subjectivities. Theorists call this activity **disciplined subjectivity** (Erickson, 1985/1986), or the practice of rigorous self-reflection about one's own impact on the field, as well as one's preferences, prejudices, hopes, and concerns and how they affect the course and outcomes of a research project. Disciplined subjectivity is a critical check on

Definition: Disciplined subjectivity is the practice of rigorous self-reflection about one's own impact on the field, as well as how one's preferences, prejudices, biases, hopes, and concerns affect the course and outcomes of research

misinterpretations as well as a necessary practice for all careful ethnographers. We encourage this kind of systematic self-reflection before, during, and after the field experience.

Auditing and Inventorying One's Subjectivities

Before beginning research, researchers may have some idea of how their statuses and personal characteristics could be viewed by participants. However, things can get far more complex once fieldwork has begun and interaction between the research team or investigator and real people in the field begins. Once in the field, ethnographers should continue to engage in a scrupulous review of all their personal characteristics and foibles, seen through the eyes of real people in the field. They will need to reimagine how they presented themselves in the community, and ask how that might affect their interactions with research participants. One way to approach this is, having taken an inventory of his or her personal appearance and behavior, an ethnographer can ask, "If I were *they* [people in the research site], what would I think of *me*? What would I think of my intentions, my social status, and whatever it is that I plan to do here?" "What about me appears to be attractive, if anything? What makes me stick out like a sore thumb or look ridiculous? Does what I am trying to accomplish make any sense to anyone in the community? Should I even try to fit in, or is that possible?" Clearly, a blonde, blue-eyed, middle-aged female North American ethnographer in a rural Guatemalan village will always *look* different from nearly everyone else in the village. The issue remains, what could she do to reduce discomfort levels between herself and the villagers? Putting one's self into the shoes of people in the field provides a starting point. Careful observation of one's self and others also is useful, as is taking careful notes on people's reactions. It also is helpful to solicit the direct input of key informants and to observe carefully their responses to one's behavior. Further practices for maintaining disciplined subjectivity throughout a study include the strategies listed below.

Cross Reference: See chapters 4 and 5 to review a discussion of how characteristics such as age, status position, gender, educational levels, religion, physical size, body hair, and dress can affect interactions in the field

STRATEGIES FOR PRACTICING DISCIPLINED SUBJECTIVITY

- Create a checklist of all of one's prior hunches and theoretical biases and examine them regularly to see if they are "leading" the data collection and analysis in ways not warranted by what actually occurs in the field
- Maintain personal logs and observations
- Keep diaries and journals
- Write letters "home" that may or may not actually be sent, but which, since they are written ostensibly for an outside reader, can summarize the field experience from a personal point of view
- Create "reflexive accounts" describing the field-worker's thoughts and reactions in an account that parallel the descriptions of what he or she has observed in the field. Reflexive accounts are not really field notes; they record the researchers' emotions and feelings, and are written from an affective, or subjective and emotional, perspective, rather than simply seeking to record dispassionately "what happens."
- Review one's own theoretical underpinnings as well as one's personal preferences. These are the "hot" and "cold" spots (Peshkin, 1988) that become clear as one is drawn to—and therefore spends more time exploring—the "hot" spots—and those that one tends to dislike or feel uncomfortable with and therefore spends less time exploring and learning about—the "cold" spots.
- Solicit the help of mentors or other professionals who are not connected to the research project to review data, examine analysis strategies and interpretations, and provide feedback on areas that might need more attention, those that are overemphasized to the exclusion of other important topics, and conclusions that the researcher has missed, inflated, or arrived at prematurely.

- Create a formal review panel of outside consultants, funded by the project budget, whose tasks
  are to audit data, examine analysis strategies and
  interpretations, and provide feedback in ways
  resembling those of the volunteer mentors and colleagues described above.
- Solicit the help of key informants and other community advisors in the field to review data, data
  collection strategies, analysis procedures, and interpretations to identify similar omissions and commissions not intended by the researcher or deleteri-
  ous to an authentic portrayal of the cultural scene
  under study. Researchers will need to take care
  that their attempts to achieve authenticity will not
  reveal the identities of individuals who have been
  promised confidentiality.

Reflection on Formal Ethical Principles and IRB Requirements

Reflecting on one's personal subjectivities applies not
only to ongoing life in the field and relationships with key
informants, local families, community organizations, and
other institutions, but also to the formal requirements of
the ethical codes to which researchers are bound. These
include the Belmont Report and discipline-based codes
of ethics. As we have said, these involve doing no harm,
describing the study so that it is understood by all important constituencies, ensuring that consent to participate is
voluntary and informed, providing accurate information
about known risks and benefits of participation, making
sure that risks and benefits are equally allocated—that is,
that their distribution follows the principle of distributive justice—and so on. We have described these principles
in detail in prior chapters of this book and elsewhere in
Books 1 and 2. These formal considerations are spelled out
for each study in the human subjects sections of grants,
in IRB applications submitted for approval, and in formal
and informal consent procedures for individuals. However,

concern about their implementation does not stop there. At every step of the way there may be crossroads moments when researchers are confronted with decisions regarding, for example, how to "do no harm," when specifics about implementation are not spelled out in any of these formal documents. The researcher in the situation described in chapter 5, Example 5.9 did not have a rule that guided her as to whether to assist someone at potential risk of death in a dance club. Instead she reflected on her own values, biases, altruistic impulses, and the formal constraints and requirements of her IRB training, and determined a way in which she could "do good" while doing no harm to herself, others in the setting, or her study.

Team research makes the process of ethical decision making easier. Ethnographers working alone have to monitor themselves and struggle, but ethnographers working in teams have the benefit of both other researchers and community partners to help them think through dilemmas and problems. The researchers who mulled over data from the Centers for Disease Control suggesting that high levels of HIV were being reported among Latino injection drug users might have decided to focus on this vulnerable group only, except that as a group, they also considered the principles of distributive justice—that is, "Do the harms and benefits apply equally to the entire population?" Once recognizing that HIV resides elsewhere as well, and that focusing on Latino injectors only would stigmatize both a group of people and a geographic area of the city where they reside, they realized that a better decision would be to conduct a citywide study of people injecting drugs that included all potential groups, not just one. The researcher faced with a respondent who had earlier been a friend, and with whose health risk behavior he was familiar through personal experience, might try to persuade the respondent to report his behavior in a survey; indeed, he might even use indirectly coercive strategies for doing so. However, remembering the importance of voluntary consent, that researcher also would have to avoid coercion regarding entry into the research study, and would avoid reporting what he/she had observed elsewhere if the former friend refused to join the study. Despite great reluctance, that researcher also would have to leave the most important part of the survey empty. Many researchers can come to these decisions on their own in the field. It always is a good idea, however, to discuss such decisions with colleagues, friends, and teammates. To assist reflection on the formal principles protecting human subjects and communities, repeat training and group human subjects training is helpful as it gives both individual researchers and research teams a chance to deepen their thinking through discussion about the ways in which their personal circumstances, biases, needs, and values interact with formal principles in complex field settings. Further, an adherence to the reflexive and recursive nature of regular reflection helps to manage and maintain good relationships in the field, and to balance the sometimes competing pressures of multiple stakeholders with different and principled ideas about what is good, valued, necessary, and beneficial.

POSITIONALITY AND POWER

Definition: Positionality refers to the power and status that individuals hold over and vis-à-vis others as a consequence of the roles they occupy

In Book 1, we raised the issue of researcher **positionality** and how it affects both interaction between researchers and participants, and as well, the kinds of information to which researchers have access. Ethnographers enter the field with a set of roles and statuses that confer power on them over participants. Some may derive from their level of education relative to participants, or from their economic and cultural capital, given that they often are university professors or staff members of organizations. They are usually at least employed, and often have more income and social capital than community participants as well. If they are involved with organizations that provide services to the community, they may be perceived as gatekeepers who could control the flow of those services, and their age, sex, ethnicity, and other characteristics could well affect the degree of status they are accorded in the community. Female ethnographers, for example, may not be held in the same level of esteem as male researchers. Throughout these books, we have provided examples in which the roles and status researchers held, which they acquired, or which were ascribed to them both limited and facilitated their access to information during fieldwork and data collection. However, one very special category of power that researchers always hold with respect to the people they study is that it is the researchers' story that ultimately is disseminated and published, even if coresearchers and community individuals participate in the write-up. Since the written or published word survives long after the projects are done, they form a lasting portrait of a community that colors all subsequent portrayals and influences how that community is viewed by others. This inescapable fact means that researchers must act ethically in writing up their final reports so as not to damage the people who have been studied.

THE RISKS OF THE "OTHER"

According to critical and interpretive theorists, adopting a stance of neutrality or so-called objectivity with respect to one's research, the people involved in it, and toward the results and consequences of that research—as once was required—is to separate oneself off as sovereign, oblivious to what matters to others. Being closed off to the "other," in turn, brings death of the imagination and of the ability to care.

Contemporary postmodern researchers call at least for disciplined and critical self-reflection. However, they also require incurring a new kind of risk—that of letting the "other" touch them in ways that changes them. Rather than mere intersubjective understanding, what is required is engagement, care, and openness to being marked, and deeply influenced, by the knowledge and experience of others. Scheper-Hughes (1995) suggests that such a stance makes the researcher accountable, responsible for, and answerable to the "other" in ways that are prior to any other allegiance.

Perhaps most unsettling to many researchers is the fact that being "marked by the other" involves more than a commitment to help communities solve overwhelming social problems. It also requires including participants in the research process in ways that render incomplete researchers' control over the direction and conclusions of the research. This can be both irritating and emotionally risky, since it forces researchers into critical reflection on the cultural, moral, ideological, and even methodological assumptions guiding their work and on the consequences of its findings. However, actively maintaining openness to being touched by the "other" can lead to better research, because it permits researchers to entertain competing explanations and models, to take seriously what others might consider to be "folk theories," and to explore alternative epistemologies.

TAKING STOCK

Cross Reference: See Book 5 for a discussion of ways researchers control for their own biases when interpreting data

Once the researcher has left the field, it is especially important to continually implement strategies that will serve as a check on the researcher's own theoretical or conceptual leanings. Some of the same strategies used in the field can be put to good use during the data analysis and interpretation phases of the study. These include soliciting feedback on preliminary conclusions and interpretations from key informants and knowledgeable outsiders—including one's mentors and other professionals in the field. However the reflection process is initiated, its systematic use assures not only that the final reports will be more authentic representations of the cultural scene the study was intended to portray but also that the entire study will have the sheen of rigorous implementation.

SUMMARY

This chapter concludes our review of ethics in ethnographic mixed methods research with a discussion of a key process in ensuring the ethical conduct of research in complex field situations—reflection. We define reflection as the process of looking back on and critiquing what has occurred in the past for its quality, righteousness, and rigor, and anticipating what might happen in the future by interrogating a variety of alternative paths. Reflection involves a deep understanding of the study site and constant examination of the interaction between researchers and the people, places, and activities that constitute their chosen study environment. Reflection helps ethnographers to assess whether they are behaving in culturally acceptable ways, whether people like and trust them, and whether or not they are therefore likely to provide good information over time. The scientific rigor of ethnography depends on the degree to which ethnographers can assess and modify their behavior properly. We also have noted that good reflection requires that researchers recognize their own interests, needs, and biases and the ways in which their appearance, demographic characteristics, academic base, and other aspects of their persona affect or even interfere with their relationships. Reflection before, during, and after the field experience provides the basis for guidance in taking action in difficult situations, for self-correction, for improved analysis, and for personal and professional growth. Finally, we argue that reflection helps keep researchers connected to the formal requirements of ethical practice in relation to individuals and communities.

The seven volumes of the complete *Ethnographer's Toolkit: A Mixed Methods Approach to Research*, are offered to the research community, the wide range of social service organizations, and any individuals wishing to have an impact on the human condition. We believe that it is a guide to a particularly rewarding and useful approach to investigating real problems in the human environment and how they are embedded in a physical context. Whether investigators are novices or experts, we believe that they will acquire considerable useful knowledge and gain skills in research strategies by following the approaches in these texts. We wish you fruitful work with our materials.

Margaret D. LeCompte, PhD
Jean J. Schensul, PhD

APPENDIX A: IRB PROPOSALS

EXAMPLE ONE

The first proposal is from Sheryl Ludwig, and involved the research for her doctoral dissertation in a Guatemalan village. The high level of detail included in the proposal and especially the matrices that included exactly what she wanted to study, how, when, where, and why helped the IRB, largely unfamiliar with how ethnographic research was conducted, understand her study. The extensive lists of questions that she included for each group she planned to interview and observe were quite acceptable to the IRB in lieu of formal interview and observational instruments.

REQUEST FOR REVIEW SUBMITTED SEPTEMBER 23, 2002

Sheryl A. Ludwig, dissertation study titled "Making Fast the Thread: How Guatemalan Women Maintain and Construct Cultural Identity in Changing Times."

Purpose and Significance of Project

In today's rapidly changing world, with its global flows of knowledge and media and increasingly large migrant streams, traditional focal points for identity construction become attenuated as structuring social and institutional relationships and practices from outside the home culture mediate (modify) the home culture and as large numbers of people move far away from sites where their original identities were constructed. In order to make sense of the worlds in which they live, people work within what Bourdieu (1993) calls "fields of practice"—of everyday behavior and belief—to enact, learn, and practice how to be effective participants in changing communities. Thus, identity constructed within cultural fields of practice is a timely and significant subject (Appadurai, 1996; Giddens, 1991; McCarthy, 1998, 2002). Most specifically, it is critical to identify the factors, if any, that help to anchor people to a stable and positive sense of self and their culture, as well as to facilitate their adaptation to changed contexts. I feel that it is also timely and significant to focus on the constructions of meaning and self-identification of mothers of school-attending children, for the mother is a primary force in the shaping of children's habitus, that original and relatively stable sense of what is right, how things are supposed to be, and what one's place in the world should be (Bourdieu and Passeron, 1977). For this reason, one lens of this study will involve how the mother, a primary source of cultural transmission (Greenfield and Cocking, 1994), teaches children, defines the world, and constructs her own reality and identity. Another focus of the study will be one of the most important agencies for inducing change in traditional cultures, the public school. This will enable me to examine the teaching/learning practices and cultural transmissions within a formal learning setting and an informal learning setting in Guatemala. In the informal learning setting, a Mayan woman's weaving cooperativa located in the village of San Sebastien, analysis of material culture and cultural activity will focus on Mayan weavers' teaching/learning practices and interactions as well as the creation of a learning environment that sets up supportive conditions for teaching and learning. In the formal learning setting, a local primary school, analysis of material culture and cultural activity will focus on curriculum content, teaching resources, teaching strategies, and the school's (as well as teachers') expressed philosophical mission. The study will further evaluate the impact of weaving and children's school attendance on Mayan weavers' maintenance of cultural self-identification in changing times. Specifically, I will look at the possible discontinuities created by two potentially incongruous cultural practices embodied in two potentially differing communities of participation, the formal learning community of the public school and the informal learning community of the weaving cooperativa.

In the summer of 2000 I had an opportunity to talk with Mayan mothers whose school-attending children were being encouraged to attend afternoon tutorials sponsored by Project Common Hope, a Minnesota-based, not-for-profit agency dedicated to assisting indigenous peoples in the development of economic self-sufficiency. Much as Project Head Start operates in US school districts, the purpose of the tutorials is to enrich Mayan children's readiness for and developmental skills with schoolwork, so that children might ultimately experience greater achievement in the schooled curriculum. As I sat in the meetings between project personnel, teachers, and parents, and as I talked with mothers on the walk back to Antigua, I was struck by mothers' complaints that children were needed at home to help with child care, food preparation, selling goods in the marketplace, and producing the little clay figures, wooden objects, and weavings that were sold there. I wondered about the instrumentality of countless hours spent drilling students on their multiplication tables when they already exchanged dollars for quetzals and made change in two currencies in Antigua's marketplaces. I wondered how children's formal learning in schools would provide value in an economy where unemployment hovers well over 50 percent and work opportunities for the indigenous usually involve harvesting coffee or bananas on distant fincas (plantations). I wondered about the thoughts and feelings that the mothers, who were already sacrificing to give their children the opportunity to attend school, might be experiencing in this tug of war between the exigencies of home reality and the opportunities education may hold. Also, I wondered about my own students back at Angevine Middle School in Boulder Valley, the many children of Mexican, Hmong, and Russian immigrants, among others, who struggle to make sense of the formal curriculum with its implicitly inscribed hegemonic messages of value and ideology. Many of these students develop oppositional behaviors or merely quit coming, perhaps personally unable to navigate the difficult terrain that characterizes the gulf between two cultures. Such discontinuities mandate new ways of thinking strategically about broadening conceptions of education so that they include topics such as identity and its formation, the characteristics of legitimating practices for learning, and learning in settings outside the traditional walls of the school. Such new ways of thinking could make a difference to the experiences of minority and third world children in US schools and elsewhere—as well as to the teachers who provide the conditions for and guidance of that learning.

Background to the Study

Formal Communities of Participation: Public Schools

In the summers of 1999 and 2000, while I studied Spanish in Guatemala, I also volunteered my time in local schools. In the capacity of volunteer, I drilled students in multiplication tables, helped them practice their printing, and quizzed them on their rote memorization of vocabulary. When I had the opportunity to observe, I saw teachers using transmission modes of teaching, prescribing material to children who often appeared to be disengaged and/or confused. All instruction was conducted in Spanish, which is the second language of most indigenous Mayan students. Given my background in teaching, I was struck by the "symbolic violence" (Bourdieu, 1993) being done to the Mayan children in the form of privileging and teaching in a language, curriculum, and teaching style that is possibly incompatible with that of their birth and habitus.

Informal Communities of Participation: Learning to Weave in a Mayan Women's Cooperative

In November 2001 I spent a week weaving in the San Sebastien cooperativa. As I learned to set up the loom, use its tools, and weave the patterns I was taught to weave, I became aware of the fact that, although feeling inept and incompetent beside the deft weaving of the Mayan women, I felt very comfortable—indeed, I loved—being a learner of a strange, new activity in a cultural setting that was also new to me. In reflecting upon the experience, I realized that my feeling of comfort in the status of "other" and novice was a probable product of the noncompetitive, observational style of teaching and learning I experienced. I wish to explore this traditional form of teaching that seems to be different from our Western orientation to teaching and learning as documented by numerous studies of how indigenous communities socialize their children (Breningstall, 1996; Deyhle and LeCompte, 1999; Rival, 2000).

While the learning I had experienced in the women's cooperativa had seemed inclusive of me, a novice and a foreigner, the schooling Mayan students experienced in traditional Western paradigms of practice did not seem compatible with their habitus. Similarly, it also felt foreign to migrant newcomers whom I taught in our US schools. While the teaching I had experienced in the cooperativa in San Sebastien seemed to link seamlessly to the "funds of cultural knowledge" (Velez-Ibanez and Greenberg, 1992) and life ways of the Mayan people, I have also often wondered whether the curriculum we teach in mainstream schools can serve as a valued fund of knowledge for the life ways of all of our students.

I view these two differing sites of education—the informal site of the cooperativa and formal site of the school—as separate "fields of practice" that generate practice and perceptions (Bourdieu, 1993). As fields of cultural production, each setting can be interpreted as a community of participation in which situated tools and signs are used as mediators (modifiers) of meaning and reality (Vygotsky, 1978). I would like to explore each setting, examining its community of practice, its use of cultural tools and signs, its pedagogies and its instructional procedures, and its differing modes of participation, teaching, and learning. I would also like to assess the potential impact of each field on its members' self-identifications.

Situating Myself within This Study

Construction of Meaning and Identity

I am a mother of three children, and I have been a public school teacher for thirty-five years. My interest in understanding how Mayan women seemingly maintain a strong sense of ethnic identity—if they do—stems from my experiences as both a parent and a teacher. When messages encountered by my children within the culture of the school conflicted with the cultural messages of home, I experienced a strong sense of dissonance and unrest. I wonder if such discontinuity occurs among the Mayan women who sacrifice to send their children to the Ladino-run schools that teach their children in Spanish, the language of the ruling elite in Guatemala. As a teacher in the United States, I have often wondered how to engage students from diverse backgrounds in the hegemonic curriculum and learning activities of our schools. As a volunteer in Guatemalan schools, I have also wondered if discontinuities are manifested in the divide between the cultural transmissions of the home (as possibly experienced through learning to weave) and the cultural transmissions of the school (as possibly experienced through the study of Ladino curriculum taught in the Spanish language).

That schools make and mold the identity of students (Davidson, 1996) is not new information (see Flores-Gonzalez, 2002). My specific interest in this study is the potential of learning sites as fields of cultural production in which mothers' identities are also made and molded as their children's schooled experiences become a possible location of cultural conflict.

For these reasons, my research proposal foregrounds the following questions:

Stage One:

1. What teaching/learning processes are involved in learning to weave?
2. How do women in the cooperativa set up a learning environment that creates supportive conditions for teaching and learning?
3. In changing times, how does weaving help Mayan women maintain a sense of who they are and what is important about their culture?
4. If an enduring sense of identity does not derive from weaving, then where might it come from?

Stage Two:

1. What teaching/learning processes occur in the public school?
2. What kind of learning environment exists in the public schools, and what do the teachers and other school personnel do to support teaching and learning?
3. In changing times, what do public schools do to help children of the Maya maintain a sense of who they are and what is important about their culture?
4. If the schools do not promote an enduring sense of Mayan identity, then what kind of identity do they promote?

Central to the study is the notion that traditional weaving on backstrap looms serves as a metaphor for traditional forms of teaching and learning. More specifically, I want to explore whether or not the act of weaving in this way is one of the factors central to the identity construction of women weavers and their children. If it is not, I hope to explore other factors that are relevant.

Methodology of the Project

General Description of the Structure of the Project

This ethnographic study is designed to investigate the teaching/learning practices of highland Guatemalan women weavers and their everyday activities as weavers in cooperatives and as parents of school-attending children. In Phase One of this study, the role of the researcher will entail learning to weave in a Mayan women's cooperative located in a village near the Guatemalan tourist center of Antigua. In this phase of the study, I will focus on the roles of teaching/learning within the weaving community of participation (Lave and Wenger, 1991; Rogoff et al., 1993, Rogoff, 1994, 1995). In Phase Two I will engage in observation and informal interviews in the local schools (where I will participate as a volunteer) and among women who weave but not in a cooperativa. In the interest of assessing the potential of sources contributing to an enduring sense of identity other than weaving, I will also assess the range of crafts engaged in by both men and women in the villages. This will provide me with a fuller picture of what local Mayan people do to survive and make do in changing times.

Specifically, in Phase One, this study will explore:

- the weavers' constructions of reality and identity
- the potential of weaving as a creative and generative activity on the development of identity
- whether learning to weave in communities of participation affects identity and agency
- the impact of women's weaving (and potentially other influences) on their children and consequent implications for maintenance of culture and identity in the context of globalization and children's attendance in formal and informal learning settings

In Phase Two, this study will explore:

- the educational philosophy of the schools and its teachers
- the potential linkages of formal schooling to the cultural transmissions of the home
- the potential impact of children's school attendance in a formal learning setting on their mothers' and their own maintenance of culture and identity in the context of changing times

The data collection matrix in the table presents the research questions, design, timeline, and details of access.

Description of the Subject Population Including Recruitment Methods, Age, Type, and Number of Subjects

The subject populations for this study will consist of the five groups of participants listed below. With respect to convenience sampling, I will talk informally with people who are conveniently in the research environment and willing to talk with me. In that case, consent forms will be presented, read, and signed—or, in the case of Mayan indigenous who do not read and/or write— consent forms will be read and marked with a sign to indicate understanding in the presence of witnesses who will sign for the person if the participant is unable to do so for himself or herself.

Group One: All of the women in the cooperativa (potentially four to ten)

- Contact in San Antonio Aguas Calientes: via Lilian Santizo, Escuela A.P.P.E. (appe@infovia.com.gt)

Group Two: All of the children of the cooperativa members (potentially four to ten)

- Especially a convenience sample of female children who are learning to weave
- Range of ages from infant to adult

Group Three: Various members of each village, including:

- Convenience sample of villagers and village women who weave but are not members of the cooperativa (not to exceed ten in total)
- Convenience sample of other Mayan villagers in the local area who participate in a practice of art (craft) other than weaving (not to exceed ten in total)

Group Four: Convenience sample of children in each of the village schools (if informal interviews are conducted, not to exceed twenty)

Group Five: Convenience sample of teachers and other school personnel in the village schools (as many as are willing to talk)

What do I need to know?	Why do I need to know this?	What kind of data will answer this question?	What data collection methods will be used?	Where can I find the data?	Whom do I contact for access?	Timeline for acquisition
What teaching/ learning processes are involved in learning to weave?	In order to document the qualities and types of teaching pedagogies and instructional procedures. In order to describe the cultural activity of weaving and the use of cultural tools and signs.	Participant Observation Observation Informal interviews with weavers, children of weavers, other village residents who weave, village children, village school personnel.	Videotaping myself learning to weave Audiotaping Photography Handwritten field notes Personal Journal Local newspapers, periodicals, and news broadcasts (ongoing) Artifact Collection (ongoing) Historical research on Mayan weaving, Museo Ixchel del Traje Indigena	Cooperativa Women weavers who are not members of a cooperativa	Gloria (teacher of weaving) through Lilian Santizo, director of APPE at appe@infovia. com.gt (Language School in Antigua, Guatemala) Director of Primaria and/or Director of Education, Project Common Hope Project Colibri (4 Calle Oriente, 3B, Antigua) Casa del Tejido (@casadeltejido. com) Museo Ixchel del Traje Indigena (Guatemala Cuidad)	October/ November 2002 and January–July 2003 Follow-up research and member checking: December/ January 2003/2004

(continued)

What do I need to know?	Why do I need to know this?	What kind of data will answer this question?	What data collection methods will be used?	Where can I find the data?	Whom do I contact for access?	Timeline for acquisition
How do Mayan women set up a learning environment that creates supportive conditions for teaching and learning?	I want to name and understand the qualities that create supportive conditions for teaching and learning in the cooperativa.	Participant Observation Observation Informal interviews with weavers, children of weavers, and other village weavers.	Videotaping Audiotaping Photography Artifact Collection Handwritten field notes Personal Journal	Cooperativas Noncooperativa weavers in village	In San Antonio Aguas Calientes: Gloria (teacher of weaving) through Lilian Santizo, director of APPE at appe@infovia.com.gt	October/ November 2002 and January–July 2003 Follow-up research and member checking: December/ January 2003/2004
In changing times, how does weaving help Mayan women maintain a sense of who they are and what is important about their culture?	I want to know if weaving on the ancient backstrap looms of the cultural antiquity—as well as the persistent reproduction of historical patterns and designs— provides conscious linkage to cultural past. If so, I would like to explore the extent to which this linkage and this action provide a voice and source for agency.	Participant Observation Observation Informal interviews with weavers, children of weavers, and other village weavers. Possible semiformal interviews with weavers.	Videotaping Audiotaping Photography Artifact Collection Handwritten field notes Personal Journal	Cooperativas Noncooperativa weavers in village	In San Antonio Aguas Calientes: Gloria (teacher of weaving) through Lilian Santizo, director of APPE at appe@infovia.com.gt In rural northeast highland village, to be selected once in the field.	October/ November 2002 and January–July 2003 Follow-up research and member checking: December/ January 2003/2004

Research question	Purpose	Methods	Data collection	Setting	Contacts	Timeline
If enduring sense of identity does not derive from weaving, then where does it come from?	I want to know how Mayan women seemingly keep an enduring sense of identity alive even in times of political and economic oppression and social change.	Participant Observation Observation Informal interviews with weavers, children of weavers, other village residents, village children, village school personnel.	Videotaping Audiotaping Photography Artifact Collection Handwritten field notes Personal Journal	Cooperativas of both villages Among the women weavers who are not members of a cooperativa Village Schools of both villages (after 1/03)	Gloria (teacher of weaving) through Lilian Santizo, director of APPE at appe@infovia.com.gt (Language School in Antigua, Guatemala) Director of Primaria and/or Director of Education, Project Common Hope Project Colibri (4 Calle Oriente, 3B, Antigua)	November 2002 and January–July 2003 Follow-up research and member checking: December/January 2003/2004
What teaching/learning processes occur in the public school?	I want to document the kinds and qualities of teaching/learning experiences, pedagogies, tools, and signs available in the public schools and classrooms so that I might have a comparison to the teaching/learning experiences of the informal setting of the cooperativa.	Observation in village schools while volunteering Informal interviews with school personnel including teachers and school-attending children	Handwritten field notes Possible photography Possible audiotaping	In the village school	TBA in October/November with the assistance of Lilian Santizo, director of APPE at appe@infovia.com.gt (Language School in Antigua, Guatemala)	To begin in January 2003 if HRC approval has been granted

(continued)

What do I need to know?	Why do I need to know this?	What kind of data will answer this question?	What data collection methods will be used?	Where can I find the data?	Whom do I contact for access?	Timeline for acquisition
What kind of learning environment exists in the public school, and what do the teachers and other school personnel do to support teaching and learning?	I want to name and describe the kinds and qualities that support (or do not support) creative and supportive conditions for teaching and learning within the schools.	Observation in village schools while volunteering Informal interviews with school personnel including teachers and school-attending children Examination of artifacts, including national and local curriculum, mission statements, teachers' planning and teaching	Handwritten field notes Possible photography Possible audiotaping Textual analysis	In the village school	TBA in October/ November with the assistance of Lilian Santizo, director of APPE at appe@infovia. com.gt (Language School in Antigua, Guatemala)	To begin in January 2003 if HRC approval has been granted

In changing times, what do public schools do to help Mayan children maintain a sense of who they are and what is important about their culture?	I want to document the various ways in which the materials, organization, and processes of schooling do (and/or do not) affect the possible development of an enduring sense of cultural identity.	Observation in village schools while volunteering Informal interviews with school personnel including teachers and school-attending children Examination of artifacts, including national and local curriculum, mission statements, teachers' planning, and teaching materials	Handwritten field notes Possible photography Possible audiotaping Textual analysis	In the village school	TBA in October/November with the assistance of Lilian Santizo, director of APPE at appe@infovia.com.gt (Language School in Antigua, Guatemala)	To begin in January 2003 if HRC approval has been granted
If the schools do not promote an enduring sense of Mayan identity, then what kind of identity do they promote?	I want to know the possible effects (negative or positive) of school attendance on learners' sense of enduring, cultural identity.	Observation in village schools while volunteering Informal interviews with school personnel including teachers and school-attending children	Handwritten field notes Possible photography Possible audiotaping	In the village school	TBA in October/November with the assistance of Lilian Santizo, director of APPE at appe@infovia.com.gt (Language School in Antigua, Guatemala)	To begin in January 2003 if HRC approval has been granted

Recruitment of Participants

In the summers of 1999 and 2000 and in November 2001, I studied Spanish at Escuela A.P.P.E. in Antigua, Guatemala. Through a local project (Project Common Hope), I volunteered my time tutoring indigenous children in five *aldea* (village) schools. In November 2001 I met the women in the cooperativa when I began a week-long pilot study for this dissertation research. These previously established contacts will assist me in recruiting and securing access to the participants of this study.

The recruitment of participants in schools will be secured through volunteering my time to tutor and/or teach English in the local village schools. Based upon previous experience gained while volunteering my time in village schools in the summers of 1999 and 2000, I anticipate that teachers will welcome my presence and assign me to work with small groups of students. This small group interaction will allow the kind of natural conversation that I seek for informal interviews.

Description of the Procedures involving Human Subjects (including procedures that may be deceptive, embarrassing, or discomforting to participants)

For the duration of this study, October–November 2002, January–July 2003, and December–January 2002/2003, my "presenting story" will be that I am a student learning to weave on the backstrap loom traditionally and historically used by Mayan women, and a researcher studying how the Mayan women teach weaving to each other, their children, and others. I also will make clear that, as an experienced teacher from the United States, I am interested in how children learn in the local schools. In the course of learning to weave in Mayan women's cooperatives, observations and informal interviews will be conducted as a natural course of daily events. Based upon the experience of a one-week pilot study conducted in November 2001, I anticipate that most questions I have about designs, colors, materials, and purposes for weaving; children and schools; and constructions of meaning/identity will arise spontaneously in the normal flow of conversation. If more structured interviews need to be conducted in order to elicit desired data, the questions asked (see interview protocols in Appendix A) will not be deceptive, embarrassing, or discomfiting (to my knowledge) to participants, nor will participants be pushed to answer questions with which they are uncomfortable. In the case that I have mis-assessed the potential of my questions to be compromising to participants, I will verbally emphasize that participants need not answer any questions they do not wish to. This admonition to not answer any questions participants do not wish to answer will be reinforced through the language of the consent forms read to and/or discussed with participants prior to initiating the study. Informed Consent Forms will be available in the participants' primary language.

Additional observations will occur in the village schools where I will volunteer to teach English and help with tutoring students, something I have done already in the summers of 1999 and 2000 when I was studying Spanish in the language school A.P.P.E. Once again, those who are willing to talk with me will be asked to indicate their willingness by signing (or marking) an Informed Consent Form (in the case of children, an assent form) and will not be asked to answer any questions to which there is sensitivity. Please see attached Interview Guides in Appendix A.

Type of Participant	Data Collection Strategy	Where	How Long
Group One: Members of the cooperativa	• Observation (field notes) • Informal Interviews (field notes) • If used, audiotaped interviews (transcriptions) • Videotaped instructions while weaving (transcriptions) • Photographs of weavers • Photographs of weavings	Cooperativa	• Observation and videotaping while weaving: two hours each day, Monday–Friday • Informal interviews ongoing during observations • Audiotaped interviews (if used) will be approximately two hours long
Group Two: Children of cooperativa members	• Observation (field notes) • Informal interviews (field notes) • If used, audiotaped interviews (transcriptions) • Videotapes of weaving (transcriptions) • Photographs of weavers • Photographs of weavings	Cooperativa	• Observation and videotaping while weaving: possible one to two hours some days, Monday–Friday • Informal interviews ongoing during observations • Audiotaped interviews (if used) will be approximately two hours long
Group Three: Other members of each village	• Informal interviews (field notes) • Possible photographs of weavers • Possible photographs of weavings	Within the two villages, where and when participants are comfortable talking to me	• Not to exceed one hour • To begin in January 2003 pending HRC approval
Group Four: Convenience sample of children attending village schools	• Informal interviews (field notes) • Possible photographs	In the village schools	• Not to exceed thirty minutes • To begin in January 2003 pending HRC approval
Group Five: Convenience sample of teachers and other school personnel	• Informal interviews (field notes) • Possible photographs	In the village schools	• Not to exceed thirty minutes • To begin in January 2003 pending HRC approval

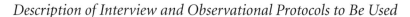

Description of Interview and Observational Protocols to Be Used

For informal/semistructured Interview Protocols for all five categories of participants, please see Appendix A. For Observational Protocols to be used for the two fields of cultural productions, please see Appendix B.

Description of the Risks and Benefits to Participants

Guatemala is a politically and economically volatile country, especially for the traditionally oppressed Mayan majority. There could be risks to my research participants because of their association with me, a foreigner, as well as because the Ladino authorities might interpret my actions as efforts to foment dissent among the Mayan people. For that reason, I will deliberately not engage in conversations and activities that would knowingly compromise the safety of my participants or myself. To do this will entail being cognizant of and responsive to potentially sensitive political and economic events and interpretations through reading newspapers, watching news broadcasts, and talking with informed associates. I realize that it will be impossible to make myself, my research, and my association with participants inconspicuous. My activities and I will be an anomaly that others immediately notice and gossip about in the small villages of Guatemala. Therefore, the following precautions will be adhered to:

1. Videotapes and audiotapes will be immediately transcribed in the field. Identities (including names and distinguishing features) will be disguised in the transcriptions. Videotapes and audiotapes will be erased and reused. Digital photographs will be downloaded, printed, and the memory card erased. Each week the originals of transcriptions and photographs will be mailed home through the Amerispan courier service, a common and accessible safe mail route for North Americans living in Antigua. No copies of these data will be maintained in the field to assure that they cannot be seized by persons wishing to have access to information about my research participants.
2. I will refrain from extending my data collection into controversial directions and topics such as birth control, women's rights, or civil rights.
3. I will personally refrain from engaging in controversial actions and from discussing politically volatile subjects.
4. I will be prepared to halt the project and leave the country if it becomes clear that my presence or participation in my study endangers my participants or myself.

Although the actual benefits to participants in this study are few, except for the women who will be paid for teaching me in the cooperativa, other potential benefits to participants are the genuine interest that I have in learning how to weave and in giving voice to the women who continue to weave, so that their cultures and constructions of reality may be shared with others. I think that such interest and expression places value upon and affirms peoples' experiences. In addition, volunteering to teach English and to tutor students in the village schools is a gift to severely underfunded public educational programs. In a country where Ladino children invariably attend private schools, the presence of a well-qualified and experienced teacher wanting to be involved over time with the indigenous and with poor Ladino students served by the local primaria is a way for me to give back to a people who are willing to share their lives and their cultures with me. For the women who teach me to weave, I will pay a weekly salary of $150 quetzals (approximately $25) for instruction. It is the standard rate paid by the many people who come to Guatemala to learn to weave. In a country where families of four too often survive on $800 per year, this salary will be very helpful to the families involved.

Description of Means for Ensuring Privacy to Subjects

1. In presenting and writing about the data, pseudonyms will be used to protect the confidentiality of participants. To the extent possible, the villages and/or other sites will be referred by pseudonyms as well. Care will be taken to eliminate or alter significant biographical and identifying data regarding persons and place.
2. In the case of photographs and videotaping, if photographs are taken, permission will be received first. If photographs are used as part of the presentation of data, participants will be asked for permission to use their likenesses and/or photographs of weavings publicly. If photographs are reproduced in reports and/or presentations, the facial features of the participants will be blurred or blocked out if participants request that I do so. Members of the cooperativa and the teacher of weaving will agree to all videotaping and/or audiotaping prior to its use. The principal use of videotaping will be to document how the women teach me to weave. While videotaping myself learning to weave, the camera will be narrowly focused on me. It is unlikely that my teacher of weaving will be pictured other than hands and arms. Other members of the cooperativa will not be filmed. The videotape will be used not only to help me understand the nuances of the weaving process, but also to assist me in learning the Spanish needed to comprehend the acts of weaving. An exception could be the filming of a cooperativa mother teaching her daughter to weave. In that case, permission would be asked and consent given prior to videotaping. Additionally, participants will be given the choice of whether or not they wish to have facial features blocked or blurred in the case of photographs and/or videos being used in written publications and/or presentations of data.
3. For all who agree to be interviewed and/or photographed (village school children, teachers and other school personnel, and villagers), pseudonyms will be used and attention will be paid to keeping identifying information out of the presentation of data. If photographs are taken, permission to photograph will be requested, permission to use visual data in written publications and/or presentations of data will be requested, and, if granted, facial features will be blocked or blurred per participant's request.
4. Following the write-up of the data, all videotapes and audiotapes will be erased and reused. Transcribed field notes will be sent to Dr. Margaret LeCompte for storage on a regular basis. No rough notes or scratch notes will remain in the field for long periods of time.

5. In the case of field notes, transcriptions, and journals, because I hope to draw from this data for longitudinal studies, transcriptions, field notes, photographs, artifacts, and journals will be stored in a locked file for approximately fifteen years. Only pseudonyms will be kept on this stored data. The log identifying participants' actual identity will be stored in a separate and locked site.

Limitations to the Study

Because my knowledge and use of Spanish is less than fully fluent at this time, I have taken the following steps to assist me in collecting the data I seek:

1. My Spanish language teacher from A.P.P.E. will accompany me to the weaving lessons. She will provide Spanish interpretation as needed. In November 2001 I found that the women of the cooperativa all speak Spanish well. It was the lingua franca for the duration of time that I was learning to weave in the cooperativa each day. Thus, I do not anticipate the need of translation services for the indigenous language, Kaqchikel, during my work in the cooperativa.
2. I am prepared to hire a Kaqchikel-speaking interpreter for semiformal interviews and transcriptions. In fact, if it is possible to afford a Kaqchikel-speaking (if possible, English-speaking as well) research assistant, I would like to do that. Not only would the experience be a valuable one for a Mayan student who might be considering a career involving ethnographic research, but having an "insider" perspective would be invaluable to me in collecting data. In consideration of hiring an interpreter, I will try to find a Kaqchikel woman who weaves. Possible sources for locating an interpreter would be one of the universities in Guatemala City, Universidad de Francisco Marroquin in Antigua, and through the director of the Museo del Tejido in Antigua.

Investigator's Qualifications to Conduct the Study

Please see the attached CV of this proposal.

Provision for Informed Consent

Prior to observation and/or informal interviews, participants will be asked to read and sign the appropriate Informed Consent form. Any interviews that must be conducted in languages other than English or Spanish will begin with the translator reading the informed consent to the participant in the language of use. In the case of participants who cannot read, the consent form will be read to them in the presence of witnesses. If possible, a literate witness will sign for the participant. If no witnesses are able to sign, a mark will be used by the participant. In the case of minor children, informed consent will be sought from the child's parents, and informed assent will be sought from the child.

Attached Consent Forms

For Consent Forms for all five categories of participants, please see Appendix B.

Bibliography

Appadurai, A. 1996. *Modernity at large.* Minneapolis: University of Minnesota Press.

Bourdieu, P. 1993. *The field of cultural production.* New York: Columbia University Press.

Bourdieu, P., and C. Passeron. 1977. *Reproduction.* London: Sage.

Breningstall, O. 1996. *Matching education and school: Cultural compatibility at Long View Middle School.* Unpublished doctoral dissertation, University of Colorado at Boulder.

Davidson, A. L. 1996. *Making and molding identity in schools.* Albany, NY: SUNY Press.

Dehyle, D., and M. D. LeCompte. 1999. Cultural differences in child development: Navajo adolescents in middle schools. In R. H. Sheets and E. R. Hollis (eds.), *Racial and ethnic identity in school practices: Aspects of human development.* Mahwah, NJ: Lawrence Erlbaum Associates.

Flores-Gonzalez, N. 2002. *School kids/street kids: Identity development in Latino students.* Albany, NY: SUNY Press.

Giddens, A. 1991. *Modernity and self-identity: Self and society in the late modern age.* Stanford, CA: Stanford University Press.

Greenfield, P. M., and R. R. Cocking. 1994. *Cross cultural roots of minority child development.* Hillsdale, NJ: Lawrence Erlbaum Associates.

Lave, J., and E. Wenger. 1991. *Situated learning: Legitimate peripheral participation.* Cambridge, UK: Cambridge University Press.

McCarthy, C. 1998. *The uses of culture.* New York: Routledge.

McCarthy, C. 2002. *Understanding the work of aesthetics in modern life: Thinking about the cultural studies of education in a time of recession.* AERA address.

Rival, L. 2000. Formal schooling and the production of modern citizens in the Ecuadorial Amazon. In B. U. Levinson (ed.), *Schooling the symbolic animal: Social and cultural dimensions of education.* Lanham, MD: Rowman & Littlefield.

Rogoff, B. 1994. Developing understanding of the idea of communities of learners. In *Mind, Culture and Activity* 1:209–29.

Rogoff, B. 1995. Observing sociocultural activity on three planes: Participatory appropriation, guided participation, and apprenticeship. In J. V. Wertsch, P. del Rio, and A. Alvarez (eds.), *Sociocultural studies of mind,* 139–64. Cambridge, UK: Cambridge University Press.

Rogoff, B., J. Mistry, A. Goncu, and C. Mosier. 1993. *Guided participation in cultural activity by toddlers and caregivers.* Chicago: The University of Chicago Press.

Velez-Ibanez, C. G., and J. B. Greenberg. 1992. Formation and transformation of funds of knowledge among U.S.-Mexican households. In *Anthropology & Education Quarterly* 23 (4): 313–35.

Vygtosky, L. 1978. *Mind in society.* Cambridge, MA: Harvard University Press.

Informal Interview Protocol for Group One: Women of the Cooperative

1. Questions about the weaver's biography
   a. Where were you born? (If different, probe re: move)
   b. How long have you lived in San Antonio?
   c. How have things remained the same here in San Antonio? (If not the same, probe re: background of difference)

    d.   What language(s) do you speak? Prefer to speak? Why?

    e.   Have you had the opportunity to go to school? (If so, probe re: How long? Where? What was studied)

    f.   Do you read and write? (If so, probe re: How use/where learned/how happened to learn)

2. Questions about the cultural/historical background of weaving

    a.   When (how long ago) did women begin to weave?

    b.   How is weaving today different from many, many years ago?

    c.   What makes it easier to weave today? More difficult?

    d.   Do you know any stories about weaving (goddess Ixcel/Popul Vuh)

    e.   What makes it easier to weave today? More difficult?

    f.   How are women's lives different today than they were many, many years ago?

    g.   How are women's lives today like they were many, many years ago?

3. Questions about learning to weave/persistence of weaving

    a.   Why did you learn to weave? Was it required that you learn to weave?

    b.   When did you learn to weave?

    c.   Who taught you to weave? How did you learn?

    d.   Why do you choose to weave on a backstrap loom?

    e.   Why do you still weave today?

    f.   What do you think about when you are weaving? Preparing to weave? Finishing your weaving?

    g.   Do you teach your daughters to weave? (probe re: why/why not)

    h.   Have you ever stopped weaving? (If so, probe re: why)

    i.   How do you feel when you are weaving? (Does it make you feel good? What parts of it do you like/not like?)

4. Questions about teaching weaving

    a.   What makes a good student of weaving? (Do you have to grow up here to weave like the Mayan women do?)

    b.   Do you teach weaving in the same way you were taught? In what ways?

    c.   How do you decide to teach someone to weave?

    d.   If someone does not understand how to do something on the loom, how do you decide to teach them?

    e.   Have you taught many people to weave? (Probe re: duration of time, student achievement)

    f.   What does it take for a person to become a good weaver?

    g.   How do you evaluate good progress in learning to weave?

5. Questions about the tools/signs/activities of weaving

    a.   Has weaving changed since you learned to weave? (Probe for differences in patterns, colors, materials, types of things that are woven/tool use and/or design)

    b.   Tell me about the loom. (How it is made, the tools, how it came to be in history)

    c.   Has the loom always been like this? (Probe for meanings about the past)

    d.   Why have you chosen to use this design? These colors? These materials?

    e.   Is this an old design? What does it mean to you? Does it have a name? Why have you chosen to use it here?

    f.   Is this a new design? What does it mean to you? Does it have a name? Why have you chosen to use it here?

    g.   How are designs created? By whom? Why?

    h.   How are the materials you weave with prepared? Is there a certain way to do so? Why? Are other materials ever used?

    i.   Do you weave at certain times? In certain places?

    j.   What makes a weaving a good one?

6. Questions about the use of handwoven weavings

    a.   Why do you wear traje?

    b.   Do you always wear it?

    c.   How does wearing traje make you feel?

    d.   Do you ever wear Western clothing?

    e.   (If so) How does wearing Western clothing make you feel?

    f.   (If not) Why not?

    g.   Other than clothing, how do you use what you weave in your home? In your daily activities?

    h.   Do you make other kinds of handicrafts? If so, what is made and why?

    i.   Do you prefer to wear the huipiles you have woven for yourself? (Probe re: why/why not)

    j.   What kinds of things do you weave?

    k.   How do you decide what new things you will weave?

    l.   Are there some things that you weave only for yourself? Why?

    m. Are there some things that you weave only to sell? Why?

7. Questions about the commercial value of weaving/weavings

    a.   Do you sell your weavings? Where? When? To whom? Why?

    b.   Do you like to sell your weavings?

    c.   How do you sell your weavings?

    d.   Have you ever tried to change something about your weaving in order to make them sell better? (Probe re: how decisions were made/what works and what doesn't)

    e.   Do you make things other than weavings? (If yes, probe re: what/ when/where/why)

    f.   How do you decide to teach someone to weave?

    g.   Do you ever demonstrate weaving in order to make money?

    h.   Have you ever traveled to other parts of the world to talk about/demonstrate your weaving?

8. Questions about children

    a.   How many children do you have? (Number of boys/girls/ages?)

    b.   What are your children doing?

    c.   Do any of your children weave? (Probe re: why they do or do not)

    d.   (If daughters learn to weave) What things do boys learn to do? Who teachers them? How?

    e.   What are your aspirations for yourself?

    f.   What are your aspirations for your children? What do you want them to be when they grow up?

    g.   How are you working to make these dreams come true?

9. Questions about children's school attendance
   a. Do your children attend school?
   b. (If so) Who? What grades? Why? Is that difficult for you? Why?
   c. (If no) Why not? Would you like for them to attend school (if appropriate)?
   d. Do you talk to your children's teachers?
   e. Do your children do well in school? If so, how do you know? What does a child have to do to be a good student at school?
   f. (If so) What do you talk to your children's teachers about?
   g. (If children attend school) Do your children like school? Why/why not? Is it difficult for you to have your children attending school? Why do you want them to attend? How long would you like them to go to school?
   h. (If children do not attend school) Would you like to have your children attend school? Why/why not? (If yes) Why are they not attending school? How could you change those conditions?
10. Questions about the cooperative
   a. How does belonging to the cooperativa help you sell your weavings?
   b. How was the cooperativa organized? When? Why?
   c. Why have you chosen to join this cooperativa?
   d. How does weaving in this cooperativa help you? Does it hurt you?
   e. What is the best part of being a member? Worst part?
   f. What are the benefits of cooperativa membership other than making and selling your weavings?
   g. Have there been other cooperatives in the village? (Probe re: are they still operating? Why/why not?)
   h. Do you belong to other organizations in this community? What do you do with these organizations? (Probe re: churches, etc.)

Informal Interview Protocol for Group Two: Children of Cooperativa Members

1. Questions about child's biography
   a. What is your name?
   b. How old are you?
   c. Where were you born? (If not in San Antonio, then probe for location and why moved)
   d. What language(s) do you speak?
   e. In what language do you speak most often? In what language do you prefer to speak? Are there certain places and times in which you choose to use one language over another?
2. Questions about school attendance
   a. Do you attend school?
   b. How long have you attended this school? Other schools?
   c. How well do you do in school? How do you know?
   d. What do you have to do to be a good student here?

    e.   What grade are you in?

    f.   What is your favorite thing to study?

    g.   What is your favorite thing to do when you are not in school?

    h.   Do you like school? (Probe re: what is liked about school)

    i.   How do you spend your time when you are not in school? (Probe re: what is favorite/least favorite uses of time)

    j.   Are there things that you are not learning in school that you would like to learn?

    k.   Does your mother (and/or father) visit the school? Talk with your teachers?

    l.   (If so) Why do they visit school? What do they talk with your teachers about? (If no, why not?)

    m.   Do you talk with your parents about what you are learning in school? How do your parents know that school is helpful to you?

    n.   How do your parents help you with school?

    o.   Is it difficult for your parents to have you in school?

    p.   How many years will you attend school?

    q.   How do you think school will help your life?

    r.   Do you wear traje to school? Why/why not?

    s.   Do you think attending school could be helpful to you in your life? (follow up with probes into possibilities (as imagination) of attending school)

    t.   Do you think that learning to weave is like learning in school in any way? (probe for similarities and differences)

    u.   Do you ever sell things to tourists? (Probe re: what/when/where/why as well as for stories about their experiences)

    v.   Do you wear traje? When/where/ why?

    w.   What do you hope to be doing five/ten years from now? (getting at aspirations)

    x.   How do you think your mother feels about your attendance (or nonattendance) in school?

    y.   Is that difficult for her? Why/ why not? (probe for child's conception of mother's rationale/hardships for school or not)

    z.   What would you like to be doing when you are eighteen years old? Twenty-five years old?

    aa.   (For those who do not attend school) Would you like to attend school? Why/why not? (probe answer)

    ab.   How do you spend your time?

3. Questions about weaving

    a.   Do you weave? (Probe: why do you choose to weave vs. is it required)

    b.   (If yes) Who teaches you? How?

        i.   What do you learn about weaving?

        ii.   Do you like learning to weave? Why/why not?

        iii.   (If weave) What kinds of things do you weave? (Probe re: making things for self and/or to sell. Use of colors, patterns, and materials and why these choices are made/what they may represent to the weaver)

        iv.   How do you feel about yourself when you are weaving?

        v.   Has learning to weave helped you in school? How/how not?

      vi.   How is learning to weave like (unlike) learning in school?

      vii. How do you use the time that you are not attending school?

      viii. What do you want to do when you leave school? What would your parents like you to do when you leave school?

   c. Have women always been weavers? (Probe for knowledge of sociohistorical knowledge of weaving)

   d. (If no, do not weave) Why not? Would you like to know how to weave? (probe those reasons)

   e. Do you make things other than weavings?

   f. Do you sell things to tourists? (Probe for experiences and perspectives)

Informal Interview Protocol for Group Three: Women of the Village Who Weave but Who Are Not Members of the Cooperative

1. Questions about the weaver's biography
   a. Where were you born? (If different, probe re: move)
   b. How long have you lived in San Antonio?
   c. How have things remained the same here in San Antonio? (If not the same, probe re: background of difference)
   d. What language(s) do you speak? Prefer to speak? Why?
   e. Have you had the opportunity to go to school? (If so, probe re: How long? Where? What was studied)
   f. Do you read and write? (If so, probe re: How use/where learned/how happened to learn)

2. Questions about the cultural/historical background of weaving
   a. When (how long ago) did women begin to weave?
   b. How is weaving today different from many, many years ago?
   c. What makes it easier to weave today? More difficult?
   d. Do you know any stories about weaving (goddess Ixcel/Popul Vuh)
   e. What makes it easier to weave today? More difficult?
   f. How are women's lives different today than they were many, many years ago?
   g. How are women's lives today like they were many, many years ago?

3. Questions about learning to weave/persistence of weaving
   a. Why did you learn to weave?
   b. When did you learn to weave?
   c. Who taught you to weave? How did you learn?
   d. Why do you choose to weave on a backstrap loom?
   e. Why do you still weave today?
   f. What do you think about when you are weaving? Preparing to weave? Finishing your weaving?
   g. Do you teach your daughters to weave? (Probe re: why/why not)
   h. Have you ever stopped weaving? (If so, probe re: why)
   i. How do you feel when you are weaving? (Does it make you feel good? What parts of it do you like/not like?)

4. Questions about teaching weaving
   a. What makes a good student of weaving? (Do you have to grow up here to weave like the Mayan women do?)
   b. Do you teach weaving in the same way you were taught?
   c. How do you decide to teach someone to weave?
   d. If someone does not understand how to do something on the loom, how do you decide to teach them?
   e. How many people have you taught to weave? (Probe re: duration of time, student achievement)
   f. How do you evaluate good progress in learning to weave?
5. Questions about the tools/signs/activities of weaving
   a. Has weaving changed since you learned to weave? (Probe for differences in patterns, colors, materials, types of things that are woven/tool use and/or design)
   b. Tell me about the loom. (How it is made, the tools, how it came to be in history)
   c. Has the loom always been like this? (Probe for meanings about the past)
   d. Why have you chosen to use this design? These colors? These materials?
   e. Is this an old design? What does it mean to you? Does it have a name? Why have you chosen to use it here?
   f. Is this a new design? What does it mean to you? Does it have a name? Why have you chosen to use it here?
   g. How are designs created? By whom? Why?
   h. How are the materials you weave with prepared? Is there a certain way to do so? Why? Are other materials ever used?
   i. Do you weave at certain times? In certain places?
   j. What makes a weaving a good one?
6. Questions about the use of handwoven weavings
   a. Why do you wear traje?
   b. Do you always wear it?
   c. How does wearing traje make you feel?
   d. Do you ever wear Western clothing?
   e. (If so) How does wearing Western clothing make you feel?
   f. (If not) Why not?
   g. Other than clothing, how do you use what you weave in your home? In your daily activities?
   h. Do you make other kinds of handicrafts? If so, what is made and why?
   i. Do you prefer to wear the huipiles you have woven for yourself? (Probe re: why/why not)
   j. What kinds of things do you weave?
   k. How do you decide what new things you will weave?
   l. Are there some things that you weave only for yourself? Why?
   m. Are there some things that you weave only to sell? Why?
7. Questions about the commercial value of weaving/weavings
   a. Do you sell your weavings? Where? When? To whom? Why?
   b. Do you like to sell your weavings?

    c.   How do you sell your weavings?

    d.   Have you ever tried to change something about your weaving in order to make them sell better? (Probe re: how decisions were made/what works and what doesn't)

    e.   How do you decide to teach someone to weave?

    f.   Do you ever demonstrate weaving in order to make money?

    g.   Have you ever traveled to other parts of the world to talk about/demonstrate your weaving?

8. Questions about children

    a.   How many children do you have? (Number of boys/girls/ages?)

    b.   What are your children doing?

    c.   Do any of your children weave? (Probe re: why they do or do not)

    d.   (If daughters learn to weave) What things do boys learn to do? Who teachers them? How?

    e.   What are your aspirations for yourself?

    f.   What are your aspirations for your children?

    g.   How are you working to make these dreams come true?

9. Questions about children's school attendance

    a.   Do your children attend school?

    b.   (If so) Who? What grades? Why? Is that difficult for you? Why?

    c.   (If no) Why not? Would you like for them to attend school? (if appropriate)

    d.   Do you talk to your children's teachers?

    e.   (If so) What do you talk to your children's teachers about?

    f.   (If children attend school) Do your children like school? Why/why not? Is it difficult for you to have your children attending school? Why do you want them to attend? How long would you like them to go to school?

    g.   (If children do not attend school) Would you like to have your children attend school? Why/why not? (If yes) Why are they not attending school? How could you change those conditions?

10. Questions about the cooperative

    a.   Are you a member of a cooperativa? (Probe re: why/why not)

    b.   Have you ever been a member of a cooperativa? (Probe re: choice to stop being a member)

    c.   How might belonging to a cooperativa help you sell your weavings? Help you in other ways?

    d.   How might belonging to a cooperativa harm you?

    e.   Are there many cooperatives in the village? In other villages? Have there been cooperatives in the past? (Probe re: are they still operating? Why/why not)

Group Three Continued: Villagers (M/F) Who Do Not Weave

1. Questions about participant's biography

    a.   How old are you?

    b.   Where were you born?

    c. Have you always lived in San Antonio? (If not, probe re: where born/why moved/when)

    d. How is life in San Antonio different now than it was before?

    e. What languages do you speak? Prefer to speak? Why?

    f. Do you have children? (Probe re: how many)

    g. Have you attended school? (Probe re: extent/what learned)

    h. How has attending (or not attending) school been helpful to you? Harmful to you?

    i. How is your life different today than it was five/ten years ago?

    j. Can you walk me through a typical day? (How do you use time?)

    k. What work do you do? Where do you work? (Home or not/how use of space is conceived)

2. Questions about children's school attendance

    a. Do your children attend school? (Probe re: why or why not children attend school)

    b. What kinds of things do your children learn in the school?

    c. Are there things you wish your children could be learning in school?

    d. Do you talk with the teachers of your children?

    e. (If so) What kinds of things do you talk about with the teachers?

    f. (If no) Why not?

    g. How will your children use the knowledge they are learning in school?

    h. What aspirations do you have for your children who attend school?

    i. (If applicable) What aspirations do you have for your children who do not attend school?

    j. How do your children use the time they are not in school?

3. Questions about children's weaving

    a. Do your children weave? (Probe re: why or why not)

    b. If children weave, who teaches them? Where? How? How many hours per day/week is spent weaving?

    c. Do your children make things other than weaving? (Probe re: why or why not)

    d. Do your children sell things to tourists?

4. Questions about participant's weaving participation

    a. Do you weave? Have you ever woven? (Probe re: why choices were made)

    b. Do you make thing other than weavings? (Probe re: what/why/when/where)

    c. Do you sell things to tourists?

    d. (If so, probe re: what is sold. Who makes it and how)

    e. (If no, probe re: why not. How time is used instead)

    f. Do you encourage your children to learn and practice skills such as weaving? (Probe re: parents'/villagers' perceptions of value/connections to Mayan past)

    g. What do you know of the cooperativa? (Probe re: positive/negative attributes of cooperativa membership)

    h. Have you ever been a member of a cooperativa? (If yes, probe for why joined/what happened) (If no, probe for why not) (What happened to the cooperativa?)

    i. Have you ever thought about joining a cooperativa? (probe for reasons pro/con)

    j. What other organizations are you a member of?

    k. Do you sell things to tourists? (Probe for experiences and perspectives)

Informal Interview Protocol for Group 4: Children in Village School

1. Questions about child's biography
   a. What is your name?
   b. How old are you?
   c. Where were you born? (If not in San Antonio, then probe for location and why moved)
   d. What language(s) do you speak?
   e. In what language do you speak most often? In what language do you prefer to speak? Are there certain places and times in which you choose to use one language over another?
   f. Does your mother (father) weave? (probe re: why or why not)
2. Questions about school attendance
   a. Do you attend school?
   b. What grade are you in?
   c. How well do you do in school?
   d. What do you have to do to be a good student here?
   e. What is your favorite thing to study?
   f. What is your favorite thing to do when you are not in school?
   g. Do you like school? (Probe re: what is liked about school)
   h. What is your favorite subject to study?
   i. What is your favorite thing to do in school?
   j. How would you change school if you could?
   k. How do you spend your time when you are not in school? (Probe re: what is favorite/least favorite uses of time)
   l. Are there things that you are not learning in school that you would like to learn?
   m. Does your mother (and/or father) visit the school? Talk with your teachers?
   n. (If so) Why do they visit school? What do they talk with your teachers about? (If no, why not?)
   o. Do you talk with your parents about what you are learning in school?
   p. How do your parents know that school is helpful to you?
   q. How do your parents help you with school?
   r. Is it difficult for your parents to have you in school?
   s. How many years will you attend school?
   t. How do you think school will help your life?
   u. Do you wear traje to school? Why/why not?
   v. Do you think attending school could be helpful to you in your life? (follow up with probes into possibilities (as imagination) of attending school)
   w. Do you think that learning to weave is like learning in school in any way? (probe for similarities and differences)
   x. Do you ever sell things to tourists? (Probe re: what/when/where/why as well as for stories about their experiences)
   y. Do you wear traje? When/where/why?
   z. What do you hope to be doing five/ten years from now? (getting at aspirations)

    aa. How do you think your mother feels about your attendance (or nonattendance) in school?

    ab. Is that difficult for her? Why/why not? (probe for child's conception of mother's rationale/hardships for school or not)

    ac. What would you like to be doing when you are eighteen years old? Twenty-five years old?

    ad. (For those who do not attend school) Would you like to attend school? Why/why not? (probe answer)

    ae. How do you spend your time?

3. Questions about weaving

    a. Do you weave? (Probe: why do you choose to weave vs. is it required)

    b. (If yes) Who teaches you? How?

        i. What do you learn from learning to weave?

        ii. Do you like learning to weave? Why/why not?

        iii. (If weave) What kinds of things do you weave? (Probe re: making things for self and/or to sell. Use of colors, patterns, and materials and why these choices are made/what they may represent to the weaver)

        iv. How do you feel about yourself when you are weaving?

        v. Has learning to weave helped you in school? How/how not?

        vi. How is learning to weave like (unlike) learning in school?

        vii. How do you use the time that you are not attending school?

        viii. What do you want to do when you leave school? What would your parents like you to do when you leave school?

    c. Have women always been weavers? (Probe for knowledge of sociohistorical knowledge of weaving)

    d. (If no, do not weave) Why not? Would you like to know how to weave? (probe those reasons)

    e. Do you make things other than weavings?

    f. Do you sell things to tourists? (probe for experiences and perspectives)

Informal Interview Protocol for Group Five: Teachers and Other School Personnel

1. Questions about participants' biography

    a. How old are you?

    b. Where were you born? (If not in San Antonio, probe re: where born/why moved)

    c. How are things different in San Antonio now than they have been in the past?

    d. How many years have you taught school? (Where have you taught?)

    e. What grades do you teach?

    f. How is the school different now than it has been in the past?

    g. What languages(s) do you speak?

    h. What language do you prefer to speak? Do you choose to speak a certain language in certain places and at certain times?

    i. Why did you decide to become a teacher? (Probe re: reasons)

    j.   What kind (and how much) training did you receive to become a teacher? (probe re: where/when/perspectives about how well prepared)

    k.   Do you weave? Why/why not?

    l.   Do you make things other than weavings?

    m. (If yes) Who taught you? How?

    n.   Does your mother weave?

2. Questions about material resources of schooling

    a.   Do you use books in your teaching? (Probe re: what teaching resources are used/how they are obtained/teacher's perception of their usefulness as a teaching tool)

    b.   How do you organize the teaching day? (Probe re: teacher's use of time/social interactions/creation of the conditions of community of participation)

    c.   What do you teach to students? (Probe re: curriculum/how it is imposed or not/teachers' responses to a standardized curriculum/what is included/possible links to Mayan culture)

    d.   Do you have to teach certain subjects? (Probe re: national and/or local standards and system of accountability)

    e.   If so, who tells you and how do you know what to teach and at what level?

3. Questions about teachers' philosophy of education/teaching

    a.   What do you think is important to teach to students? (Probe re: personal teaching philosophy)

    b.   How do you know if a student is doing well or learning what you are teaching?

    c.   How does a student show you that s/he is a good student—one who is interested in learning?

    d.   Do you like teaching? (Probe re: Why/why not?)

    e.   What is difficult about teaching? What is easy about teaching here?

    f.   What do you like most about teaching (here)? What do you like least?

    g.   Do you know the parents of your students?

    h.   Do you talk with the parents about their children?

    i.   (If so) What kinds of things do you talk about?

    j.   How do the parents help their children learn at home?

    k.   How do parents make it difficult for the children to learn?

    l.   Do you notice a difference in the behavior and achievement between the children with mothers who weave and those who don't?

    m. What do your students wear to school? (Probe re: differences in dress)

    n.   Does attire make a difference in student behavior? Achievement? Confidence? Willingness to learn?

    o.   Can you please describe your students/what are they like?

    p.   How (in what conditions?) do they seem to learn best?

    q.   What are your hopes (goals) for your students?

    r.   Do any of your students weave? (Probe effects of weaving vs. not weaving)

    s.   Do any of your students make things other than weaving?

    t.   Do any of your students sell things to tourists? (If so, probe for teacher's perception of impact on studies)

Observational Protocol: In the Cooperativa

1. What are the objects in the cooperativa (home)?
   - How are things used and why?
   - When are they used and why?
   - Where are they placed and why?
   - Who uses them and why?
   - What is used most often and why?
2. What are the interactions between the objects and the actors?
   - What are the actions associated with use of the objects?
   - In what activities are they used?
   - Who participates in those interactions?
   - What facial expressions/body language is exhibited and why?
3. Who are the actors in the cooperativa?
   - What are their roles?
   - How do they represent themselves?
   - What time/space is used and how?
   - What are their acts and activities?
4. What are the interactions between the actors in the cooperativa?
   - Where do they occur?
   - When do they occur?
   - Who is involved?
   - What is the purpose of the interaction?
5. What are the acts, activities, and events within the cooperativa?
   - What things occur frequently? Less frequently?
   - How are those activities incited? Why?
   - What objects are involved?
   - Who is involved? Why?
   - Where/when do they occur?
6. How is time organized and enacted within the cooperativa?
   - Keep time chart.
   - How is time used?
7. How is space used within the cooperativa?
   - Make a map of the cooperativa.
   - What activities occur in what spaces? Why?
8. What is talked about in the cooperativa?
   - What are the subjects?
   - Who initiates the various subjects?
   - How do the topics begin to be discussed? How do they end?
   - Where and when do discussions occur?
9. What are the feelings expressed in the cooperativa?
   - What feelings are expressed?
   - How are feelings expressed?
   - When/where?

- What activities and what objects are involved with the expression of feelings?
- Who is involved in these expressive interactions?

10. How is weaving taught?
    - Who teaches it?
    - When and where is it taught?
    - How is it taught?
      1. Verbal methods of teaching
      2. Nonverbal methods of teaching
      3. Observational methods of teaching
      4. Other methods of teaching
    - What are the activities of teaching?
    - What are the interactions of teaching?
    - What is taught?
    - How does the learner express task accomplishment?
    - How is discipline and approval transmitted?
    - What tools and materials are used?
    - What are the goals of teaching weaving?

11. What are the acts and activities of weaving within the cooperativa?
    - What are the materials: loom, tools, thread?
    - What are the patterns, colors, and objects?
    - How are the patterns, colors, and objects of weaving selected?
    - What are the physical activities of weaving?
    - What are the goals of weaving?
    - How do women weave quickly?
    - Are any objects woven slowly? Why?
    - How are the goals of weaving related to time periods?
    - What are the ways weaving objects are used by weavers while weaving?

Observational Protocol: In the Village School

1. What are the objects in the school/classrooms?
   - Where are these objects located?
   - How are they used?
   - When are they used?
   - Who uses them? Why?
   - How are the objects used in activities?
   - How do the objects affect use of space?
   - How are objects used for the attainment of goals?

2. How is time organized within the school/classroom?
   - Make a time chart.
   - What activities take place at what times?
   - What activities take place at what time periods?
   - How do acts fall into time periods?
   - How are goals related to time periods?
   - What actors are involved in what time periods?

3. How is space organized within the school/classroom?
   - Make maps of the space in the school and in the classrooms.
   - What are the ways in which space is organized by objects in the classrooms?
   - What are ways in which space is organized by activities in the classrooms?
   - What changes in space occur over time?
   - How is space used by students? The teacher?
   - How is the use of space related to goals?
   - What spaces are associated with feelings?
4. What are the acts and activities within the school/classroom?
   - Who is involved with what acts? Activities?
   - What acts/activities occur within the school? The classroom?
   - When and where do these acts/activities occur?
   - What objects are involved with acts/activities in the school? Classroom?
   - What are the ways in which acts and activities are related to stated school and learning goals?
   - How are acts and activities related to feelings?
5. Who are the actors within the school/classroom?
   - What kinds of actors are there?
   - What are the actors' goals?
   - Where and when do actors participate?
   - How do actors participate?
   - What are the acts and activities in which they participate?
6. What are the goals of the school/classroom?
   - What are the ways in which goals involve acts and activities?
   - How are objects used in seeking goals?
   - What are the ways in which acts and activities are related to goals?
   - How are goals related to the uses of space and time periods?
7. What are the feelings exhibited in the school/classroom?
   - What places and time periods are associated with feelings?
   - What objects are associated with feelings?
   - In what ways are acts and activities related to feelings?
   - What are the feelings experienced by students? Teachers?
   - In what ways are feelings expressed?
8. What are the participation possibilities in the school/classroom? (participation refers to movements in trajectory from novice to expert)
   - In what ways are objects used in participatory acts and activities?
   - Who acts and in what ways?
   - What feelings are associated with acts of participation?
   - What kinds of participation opportunities are possible for students? Teachers?
   - What are the spaces and time periods in which participation may change?
9. What are the relationships exhibited between actors in the school/classroom?
   - What are the kinds of relationships between students and students? Students and teachers? Teachers and other school personnel?
   - In what spaces and time periods do these relationships occur? How related?

- How do varying relationships relate to goals?
- In what ways are relationships affected by objects?
- Who are the actors in these relationships?

Ludwig attached her curriculum vitae at the end of the proposal to confirm her qualifications to conduct the work.

EXAMPLE TWO

The second example is drawn from a proposal to study the move of an innovative middle school arts program from its original home to a new campus. LeCompte had already spent five years studying the original school, so the teachers, children, and staff were familiar with her and her work.

REQUEST FOR REVIEW: MERGING CULTURES: THE INTERSECTION OF ARTS AND ACADEMICS, SUBMITTED FALL 2003

The proposed research conducted by Margaret LeCompte, professor in the CU School of Education and a team of graduate student researchers, involves an ethnographic study of the newly constituted Manhattan School of the Arts, in the Boulder Valley School District. Manhattan School, located on Manhattan Drive, is the site of the former Burbank Middle School. It will house students from both the former Burbank Middle and Base Line Middle School and Boulder School of the Arts, which was closed because of budget cuts, and students who transfer to the school from out of the attendance zone. About 95 percent of the teachers from Base Line are moving to the Burbank campus, and the school will become the Arts Focus School for Boulder Valley School District, supplanting the program at Burbank. A number of the teachers from Burbank also remain at the school, including the visual arts teacher. The principal from Base Line will become the principal of the newly constituted school, replacing Burbank's principal.

I began research at Base Line in 1996, when I was asked to evaluate the newly initiated Arts Focus program. I continued those evaluations for three years, until funding ran out. I then continued contact with the school sporadically, acting as a consultant and serving as the instructor of record for a class in arts integration for three semesters. For this reason, teachers and staff at the school have become quite familiar with my own, and the presence of my research assistants, at the school. Last spring, the principal, who is assuming the leadership of the newly constituted Manhattan School of the Arts, asked me to consider studying how the new school evolves and its impact on students and staff (letter of invitation attached as soon as school staff return to campus). Such research would be a logical continuation of research questions I pursued in papers written about the Base Line experience (see Holloway et al., 1998; LeCompte, 1999; Holloway and LeCompte, 2001; LeCompte, 2004), where I and a research team examined the impact of the arts program on students' career and self-identity, and the conflict between the culture of the arts and the bureaucratized culture of public schools—in the context of school reform.

The principal asked that I do a study of the new school with these objectives:

1. To monitor and describe how the two very different cultures now in place at the school integrate
2. To describe the new school culture that evolves
3. To assess the impact of the arts program on student achievement schoolwide
4. To assess the impact of the arts program on teachers in both the arts and the academic program

For various reasons, the previous research project at Base Line never was able to assess the impact of the program on the achievement of students, either in the Arts Program itself or in the school more widely. Because all of the students in the school were affected by the program, regardless of whether or not they were actually enrolled in it, this seemed important. The proposed study would remedy that gap. However, at this time, I am only requesting approval to begin participant observation and interviewing among adults at the school, specifically, the teachers and school staff. I wish to attend faculty and staff development meetings, "community building" meetings organized by the principal, and to interview teachers about their approaches to teaching and attitudes toward the school merger, as well as their perceptions of the current environment at the new school (see attached interview and observational guides).

Data to be collected for this phase of the study are as follows:

1. Notes taken during faculty meetings, staff development meetings, school performances, and other activities in the school. While taking these notes, I'll be noting not only what's happening but also what people say, what they plan, the concerns they have, and how they react to events.
2. Interviews with teachers and staff. I'd like to interview all of the current professional and para-professional staff at the school this year. Questions will request information about teacher background and teaching style prior to coming to Manhattan School, what led them to decide to come to this school, their opinions about their students and what their plan for them during the coming year are, their opinions about integrating the arts with regular instruction, and how they feel about the process unfolding at Manhattan. If they were a teacher at either Base Line or Burbank last year, I'll also ask them to tell me about the history leading up to the decision to close Base Line and move to Burbank.
3. Documents, including minutes of meetings, announcements distributed throughout the school, grant applications, and any other materials that might elucidate what's happening and being planned at the school.
4. Notes taken during visitations in classrooms. In these visits, I will simply be interested in seeing what instruction looks like and in viewing any lessons teachers think I might find interesting.

Observations by me and the other members of the research team in meetings, at events, and in classrooms will not take any teacher time and will not disrupt meetings or classroom activities. We will not be audio or videotaping any of these activities. Interviews, which *will* be audiotaped so we can remember what is said, will last from forty minutes to an hour, and will be scheduled at a place and time convenient to participants. We may wish to do a brief follow-up interview for clarifications at a later time.

A subsequent proposal will request approval to collect data on students and from their parents.

History and Description of the Site and Populations

The Base Line program was conceived of in academic year 1995 to 1996 by the then-principal, a veteran of some twenty years at the school, as a way to stem enrollment loss from the school. It was enthusiastically endorsed by most of the teachers, and began in fall 1996. Despite four principal and many staff changes (especially in the Arts Focus program), policy vicissitudes at the district level, budget cuts and other obstacles, the Arts Focus program flourished, was institutionalized, accepted by all the faculty, and integrated throughout most of the academic program. The school's enrollment soared; the school was at building capacity as of spring 2003, when BVSD closed it. As described by both the current principal and teachers, as well as students we interviewed, Base Line always had been a school with strong teachers and a good academic reputation—especially for the arts. Strong efforts were made to maintain the strength of the academic program. Notwithstanding, Base Line strongly subscribed to a "middle school concept" that strove to give young students a wide variety of experiences in a noncompetitive atmosphere. The "school culture" at Base Line was collaborative, collective, multidisciplinary, and integrated; as part of the "middle school concept" informing the school, it provided emotional and social support for middle schoolers in homerooms scheduled daily. The school already had instituted integrated blocks for social studies and language arts as well as a multidisciplinary "Explo" class for sixth-graders (where they explored everything from computer technology to environmental studies; the new ninety-minute blocks for the Literary, Visual, and Theater Arts, as well as Instrumental Music, did not come as a major shock. Further, a critical mass of content-area teachers—though not the majority—were very receptive to learning how to integrate all of the arts into their regular classroom teaching).

By contrast, Burbank sought to resolve its enrollment problems in the mid-1990s by stressing a traditional and rigorous academic program, with strong subject-matter distinctions. While the Base Line program admitted students to any of the arts programs on a space available program controlled by a lottery, Burbank required competitive auditions. Conversations with former teachers and researchers who worked in the school describe the culture at the school as competitive, individualistic, and discipline focused. The school also had lost enrollment so that by spring 2003, the building was seriously underenrolled.

The differences between the schools led to pejorative characterizations of each by the other; Burbank staff and students described the Base Line program as "soft and mushy" academically, while Base Line's staff and students felt that Burbank's program was "dog eat dog." These differences became especially marked during spring 2003, as the battle over which building would be closed and its program supplanted by the other raged. To some extent, despite the departure of some teachers from both schools, tensions over philosophical differences remain as the school year begins in fall 2003 at the new school; hence the principal's request for the study.

Risks and Benefits

The anticipated risks of this research are minimal. I will supply feedback on my general assessment of the school climate and program progress with both the faculty and the principal, as has been my practice in past collaborative research of this nature in public schools (in schools in Texas, Tennessee, Arizona, on the Navajo Reservation, and in the Denver Metro area). Risks will be limited to the discomfort that teachers, students, parents, and staff may feel in describing (and reliving) the recent conflicts over the school merger, as well as emerging conflicts during the coming school year over resources, philosophical differences, and personality conflicts. They may also feel some discomfort in having an observer present during discussions of heated conflicts. I will abide by the counsel of the principal and individual teachers' wishes as to whether or not my presence is an obstacle, and absent myself when such action seems necessary. My research assistants, all advanced doctoral students, will abide by the same policy.

Benefits include the corrective actions that school faculty and staff can take as a consequence of formative assessments and feedback deriving from the research project, as well as more focused evaluation of the impact of the program on students, staff, and teachers. Such data may help the school seek funding and to fine-tune its program offerings. Benefits will not generally accrue directly to individual participants.

Research Participants and Recruitment Procedures

The population for this study is all the teachers, nonteaching, and administrative staff at Manhattan School for the Arts, as well as the students enrolled at the school and their parents, for whom approvals will be requested at a later date. All participants for whom approval is sought in Phase One of this study are adults, and professional or paraprofessional staff at the school. Recruitment will be voluntary; interview participants will be solicited from among all the faculty, staff, and administrators at a faculty meeting and in notes placed in their mailboxes. Persons not wishing to be interviewed will inform me via email, telephone, or via a note in my mailbox at the school (see attached Interview Invitation Note). The principal will introduce me, and I will explain the purpose of and procedures involved in the study at an initial faculty meeting; the principal already has explained the possibility of this study to the Base Line faculty and staff, who will constitute the majority of the faculty at the new school. At that initial faculty meeting time, I will tell people who wish for me not to record anything they say or do at the meetings I attend to let me know, and I will comply with their wishes. At the faculty meeting when I am introduced, and also at the time of the interviews, I will ask for permission to visit and observe the teachers' instruction in their classrooms. I will not visit the classroom of any teacher who does not give me permission to do so.

Protecting the Privacy of Participants

I will adhere to a policy of confidentiality. Pseudonyms will be assigned to or chosen by all participants. Data will be recorded only with those pseudonyms. Field notes and interview transcripts (whether taped or handwritten) will be coded with the pseudonyms, and information from them will not be shared with others in ways that individuals can be identified. The key to the pseudonyms will be retained in a locked data cabinet in my home. Because this is an ethnographic study, and because many of the individuals in the school occupy unique positions (there is only one voice teacher, for example), it will be impossible to disguise their identity completely to individuals within the school community and the wider Boulder educational arena. Every effort will be made, however, to negotiate disclosure with individuals; my past practice has been to show initial drafts of my writings about individuals to them for feedback and corrections; in cases where the individual and I disagree, both sides are presented, and I always negotiate the language used in accord with the wishes of the participant. I also share any report to all interested parties before it is disseminated beyond the school. Further, in any published documents, pseudonyms for the school, district, and state will be used.

Disposition and Storage of Data

All data, whether field notes, interview transcripts, or documents, will be maintained in a locked cabinet in my office on campus, accessible only by members of the research team. The tapes will be erased after transcription; raw transcripts and field data will be kept for seven years and then destroyed.

Principal Investigator's Qualifications

I am a full professor of education and research methodology at the School of Education at CU Boulder. Please see attached resume.

References

Holloway, D. L., and M. D. LeCompte. 2001. Becoming somebody!: How arts programs support positive identity for middle school girls. In "The Arts, Urban Education, and Social Change," edited by B. Krensky and D. L. Holloway. Theme issue of *Education and Urban Society* 33, no. 4 (August 2001): 354–66.

Holloway, D. L., M. D. LeCompte, and W. Maybin. 1998. Two bloats and a gloat: Constructing identity in Arts Focus. Paper presented at the annual meetings of the American Educational Studies Association, Philadelphia, Pennsylvania, November 5.

LeCompte, M. D. 1999. Subverting reform, subversive reforms: Transforming education through integrated arts programming. Paper presented as part of Invited Professorship lectures at

Monash University, Melbourne, Australia, Clayton campus, May 13; Peninsula campus, May 25; and Melbourne University, Melbourne, Australia, June 1, 1999.

LeCompte, M. D. 2004. Using the arts in research. Plenary session presentation at the Conference on Networks and Participatory Action Research, Institute for Community Research Hartford, Connecticut, June 11.

EXAMPLE THREE

Request for Review, "Project VIP: A Peer Education and Intervention Study to Increase Influenza Vaccination Rates Among Residents of Senior Housing"

Below is the human subjects section of a large grant proposal from the Institute for Community Research to conduct an intervention with older adults to improve flu vaccination uptake. Because it is an intervention, it has a section called "DSMP," which is a plan for monitoring research safety and adverse events in the intervention specifically. Procedures for when and how to report and monitor adverse events also are included.

E. Human Subjects

E.1 Risks to the Subjects

E.1.a. Human Subjects Involvement and Characteristics. A minimum of approximately 650 people aged fifty years and above, living in publicly subsidized senior housing or attending senior centers in Hartford, Connecticut, will be interviewed directly in this study. Participation will involve a survey, focus group, resident VIP committees, peer-to-peer vaccine health counseling, and voluntary on-site influenza immunization offered independently by the VNA Health Care Inc. Anticipated gender and ethnic/racial breakdowns are as follows:

Gender: 60 percent female, 40 percent male
Ethnicity: 40 percent African American
            45 percent Latino (primarily Puerto Rican)
            5 percent West Indian/Caribbean
            10 percent White/other

The criterion for inclusion of individuals participating in surveys, VIP committees, and peer-to-peer education is official residence in study buildings. Exclusion criteria are:

1. Not living in one of the sample buildings
2. Considered by research staff to be cognitively unable to give informed consent
3. Under legal protection of conservator who has not given permission
4. Exhibition of continued disruptive behavior while participating in the project

Both male and female building residents, and minorities and nonminorities who meet the above criteria, will be recruited into the study.

E.1.b. Sources of Materials. Data to be collected in this project include:

- Personal demographics
- Health history and current health status, including influenza immunization experience and decision making
- Self-reported information regarding knowledge, beliefs, and attitudes about influenza infection, vaccine, and immunization; self-report information on access to influenza vaccination

These data will enable us to answer questions with respect to influenza knowledge, access to immunization, and vaccine decision making. The data will be aggregated at the ICR and made available without unique identifiers to our research partners.

Data will be collected for research purposes. The purposes of the research are to obtain qualitative and survey data on influenza and vaccine decision making among older, low-income, and minority adults residing in senior housing; to identify barriers to influenza vaccination; and describe and test the efficacy and sustainability of a peer-led, empowerment-based building-level education intervention to improve influenza vaccine acceptance in the target population.

E.1.c. Potential Risks. Risks to respondents from participation in this study are limited. These might include: a) adverse reactions to the influenza vaccine, b) negative responses to VIP committee members from other residents; or c) possible loss of confidentiality if peer educators reveal communications between themselves and residents related to opinions about the vaccine.

E.2. Adequacy of Protection against Risks

E.2.a. Survey Recruitment and Informed Consent. Residents from sample buildings will be recruited via random sampling of apartment units at four time points for participation in survey data collection. Candidates eligible to participate in the project will be fully informed about the study, their right to refuse or to withdraw, and existing procedures for ensuring confidentiality of interviews and focus groups. We have found the following procedure, used in one of our previous studies, to be effective with this population. Using this procedure, the consent form is read to each prospective participant, after which the researcher reviews the main points regarding the nature of the study and the risks and benefits involved in participating. The researcher then asks the respondent three key questions on these topics. If the respondent cannot answer these questions correctly after two attempts, he/she is deemed ineligible to participate. Eligible respondents then will be asked to sign a written project consent form prior to conducting the interview. If they cannot write (approximately 10 percent of respondents cannot write at all), they will mark their form with an X. Separate consent forms will be completed for participation in surveys, resident VIP committees, and vaccination clinics.

On-site influenza vaccination will be offered as a service through the study as well as part of the intervention. Onsite flu vaccination clinics will be offered by VNA Health Care,

Inc., twice in every treatment and control building. We will obtain informed consent, separate from the research informed consent, from all residents who choose to be vaccinated. Vaccination will be administered by VNA Health Care, Inc. Consequently, we will use the VNA protocol for informed consent that involves screening for contraindications of vaccination, the review of vaccination fact sheet, and the signing of consent form.

E.2.b. Protection Against Risks. The following procedures have been developed to address the areas of potential risk outlined above (Section E.1.c). To avoid loss of confidentiality, participants' names will not appear on any document associated with the project. All project staff will be trained and monitored to maintain confidentiality under the supervision of the Institute for Community Research, the University of Connecticut Health Center, and VNA Health Care, Inc., of Greater Hartford. Unique ID numbers, *not* participants' names, will appear on all interview records used for computer data entry. Records will be kept in locked files and used only for research purposes. No records will be kept at building sites at any time. Names and apartment numbers, which will be used for creating unique identifier lists for each building, will be kept under lock and key at the ICR project office, and used by project tracking staff only (project director and field interviewers). A hard copy of transcribed focus group narratives will be kept in locked file cabinets, coded by participant identifier, location, and date, transcribed and erased at the end of the project. Electronic versions of interviews will be password protected. Numbers will introduce each interview. All narrative and other forms of data will be maintained in locked computerized data files to which only project staff will have access.

To minimize risks from negative responses to VIP committee members, when recruiting for flu campaign activities, we will include approaches to when and how to interact with residents, and how to handle such responses in the VIP committee training program.

Prior to administering influenza (or pneumococcal) vaccinations, VNA nurses who are licensed and trained in medication administration will screen all participants who request vaccination at the building-based influenza clinics. Furthermore, participants will be monitored immediately after receiving their vaccination for possible adverse reactions.

IRB Approval

The "Project VIP: A Peer Education and Intervention Study to Increase Influenza Vaccination Rates Among Residents of Senior Housing" study will be reviewed and approved by the Institute for Community Research's Institutional Review Board (IRB) before contacting prospective participants.

Training in the Protection of Human Subjects in Research

All research personnel working with study participants or study data on the "Project VIP: A Peer Education and Intervention Study to Increase Influenza Vaccination Rates Among Residents of Senior Housing" project will have completed training in the protection of human subjects per the guidelines issued by the US Department of Health and Human Services, Office of Human Research Protections, before contacting prospective participants or working with study data.

E.2.b.1. Data Safety Monitoring Plan

Maintenance of Data: Confidentiality

Access to Data

A subject's participation in this project will be kept confidential within the "Project VIP: A Peer Education and Intervention Study to Increase Influenza Vaccination Rates Among Residents of Senior Housing" study team.

Data Security

To ward against loss of confidentiality, all participants will be assigned a personal identification number that will be used for identification on all documents except consent forms. Names and other personal identifying information, such as addresses, phone numbers, photographs, contact persons, and names of social network members, which are collected for the purposes of intervention and network tracking of project survey respondents, will be maintained in separate, locked file cabinets (both computerized and hard copy) under the protection of the PI, project director/coordinator, and data analysts. Such records will be kept in locked files and will not be used for any reason other than research purposes. No information a participant gives project staff about their personal contacts or people they are close to will be shared with said contacts without the participant's permission. Contact names and information about them will also be kept in separate, locked file cabinets (both computerized and hard copy) under the protection of the PI, project director/coordinator, and data analysts.

Computerized data will be located in hidden files and will be password protected.

Any audiotaped records of group meetings will be stored in locked cabinets and once transcribed, the audiotapes will be destroyed.

Outside Requests for Access to Data

Data requested from researchers from organizations not collaborating on this research project with ICR will only be shared in aggregate form.

Protections for Confidentiality

Researcher Statement of Confidentiality

All project staff working with study participants or study data will review and sign a Statement of Confidentiality before contacting study participants (see attached). When the study ends or project staff terminate their involvement in the study, they will meet with the research ethics monitor for a debriefing/exit interview in which the Researcher Statement of Confidentiality will be reviewed and signed once again, indicating their understanding that they are bound by the Statement even though their involvement in the study has ended.

Handling Breaches in Confidentiality

Despite ICR's commitment to ensuring participants' confidentiality, it is possible that, despite our best efforts, confidentiality might be breached. In such instances, the project staff person who identified the breach in confidentiality will immediately report the incident to the PI and/or their project director/coordinator. The PI, project staff, and the research ethics monitor will then discuss the circumstances that instigated the incident, the implications and ramifications of the breach, and any possible actions that need to be taken to address the breach of confidentiality.

Reporting Breaches in Confidentiality

The PI will report in writing each breach in confidentiality and the outcome of the discussion between the PI, project staff, and the research ethics monitor to the IRB. Upon review, the IRB may suggest an amendment to the research protocol.

Adverse Events

Definition

An adverse event is an event, occurring in the context of a research project, that causes physical or psychological harm to a participant.

Handling Adverse Events

The project staff person who identifies or observes the adverse event will immediately report the event to the PI and/or their project director/coordinator. The PI, project staff, and the research ethics monitor will then discuss the circumstances of the event, any implications and ramifications of the event, and any possible actions that need to be taken to address the adverse event.

Adverse Event Reporting

The PI will report in writing each adverse event and the outcome of the discussion between the PI, project staff, and the research ethics monitor to the IRB. Upon review, the IRB may suggest changes in the research procedures.

Monitoring Plan Review Process

Who Monitors?

The project director/coordinator and the research ethics monitor will be responsible for carrying out the monitoring plan. The project director/coordinator will monitor study progress, protections of confidentiality, and adverse events on a daily basis as he/she is responsible for supervising project staff and overseeing implementation of the study. The research ethics monitor will offer support to the project director/coordinator with regard to daily monitoring and will be responsible for initiating an annual review of the project.

Frequency of the Review

Initial review will take place three months into the collection of data from participants. Subsequent review will take place annually, unless more frequent review is necessitated by the complexity of the project design or deemed necessary as a result of a breach in confidentiality or adverse event.

Triggers for Interim Reviews

The research ethics monitor, IRB, PI, and the project director/coordinator may initiate at any time an ad hoc review in light of a breach of confidentiality, an adverse event, or any other incident in which the safety of participants and/or data is called into question.

Content of the Review

The review itself will involve an on-site visit from the research ethics monitor in which the research ethics monitor and the project director/coordinator will discuss the overall progress of the study, review data maintenance (as outline in section 2.C above) and the process for obtaining informed consent from participants, confirm that the study has current IRB approval, and ensure that all of the project staff have completed the NIH computer-based training in the protection of human subjects in research. At this time, the research ethics monitor and the project director/coordinator will also review any adverse events reported since the last review.

The DSMP Report

Content

The research ethics monitor and the project director/coordinator will coauthor the DSMP report. The project director/coordinator will be responsible for writing the following sections of the report:

1. Study Description
   a. Project Organizational Chart (personnel)
   b. Brief statement of the purpose of the study
   c. Projected timetable and schedule
2. Brief overview of study progress to date

The research ethics monitor will be responsible for writing the remaining sections of the report:

1. Confirmations
   a. Current IRB approval
   b. Project staff completion of NIH CBT in the protection of human subjects in research
   c. Signed Pledge of Confidentiality by all project staff
2. Comments on the project's compliance with plan for the maintenance of data (as outlined in section 2.C above).
3. Comments on the process used by project staff to obtain participant's informed consent.
4. Comments on the protection of confidentiality and any breaches of confidentiality that occurred in the past year.
5. Comments on the incidence of any adverse events in the past year and how they were handled.

Who Receives Copies of the Report?

The research ethics monitor, PI, and the project director/coordinator will retain copies of the DSMP report. The DSMP report will also be submitted to the IRB for review and comment.

Steps Resulting from the Review

The review may result in an amendment to the research protocol, which must be approved by the IRB and the research ethics monitor.

Independence of Review

The research ethics monitor should be separate and independent from the research staff. The research ethics monitor should not have scientific, financial, or other conflict of interest related to the research study. Current collaborators of the PI are not eligible to be the research ethics monitor.

Research Ethics Monitor's Credentials

The research ethics monitor for the "Project VIP: A Peer Education and Intervention Study to Increase Influenza Vaccination Rates Among Residents of Senior

Housing" study is Molly A. Lauck, PhD. Dr. Lauck is a medical anthropologist with experience in ethnographic, participatory action research, and intervention research methods. She facilitates the IRB review process at the Institute for Community Research, chairs the Institute's Research Ethics Committee, and oversees the Institute's program in the Responsible Conduct of Research.

E.3. Potential Benefits of the Proposed Research to the Subjects and Others

The risks for involvement in this project are limited and the benefits are significant, given the relatively large population of older low-income and minority adults who have limited access to appropriate influenza disease and vaccine information, immunization, and are at special risk for complications related to influenza infection. Participants in the project receive age- and language-appropriate influenza and pneumococcal health education materials, as well as a standard package of health and social service referral information, which includes times, locations, contacts, and phone numbers of health clinics, social service agencies, drug and alcohol treatment programs, and primary health and STD clinics. Building residents also will have the opportunity to participate as members of the resident VIP committees that will be established in each intervention building that will increase their knowledge of influenza and influenza immunization and empower them as health advocates.

E.4. Importance of the Knowledge to Be Gained

Project findings will contribute critical information to the effective reduction in gaps in influenza knowledge and communications-related barriers to vaccine acceptance among older, low-income, ethnically diverse residents in senior housing, and a successful intervention with sustaining capacity can be manualized, scaled up, translated into other similar sites, and used as a national model for public health mobilization and influenza prevention in other similar sites throughout the state and beyond.

Additionally, the project brings together a community coalition in Hartford and a national advisory team that has the potential for improving influenza education and vaccine delivery, increasing influenza immunization rates, and advocating and seeking funding for expanded, improved, and sustainable services for the target populations of this study.

EXAMPLE FOUR

REQUEST FOR REVIEW: A STUDY OF YOUTH AND DRUG RISK—ECSTASY (MDMA)

The following example is taken from a fairly sensitive, funded study of drug use done by the Institute for Community Research in 2007. It identifies the data to be collected, risks to participants, ways risks will be addressed, maintenance of participant confidentiality, staff protections, and procedures for monitoring and reporting "adverse events" that increase risk or violate principles of confidentiality. Finally, it discusses and weighs the benefits of the study in relation to the potential risks. Though most researchers try to minimize risk to study participants, communities, and research staff, there are studies in which there may be considerable participant risk. Regardless, all studies must justify the risk/benefit ratio, and if the risk is substantially greater than the benefits, reasons for conducting the study must be very convincing. "E" refers to the format lettering for the "Human Subjects" section of that particular grant.

E. Human Subjects

E.1. Risks to the Subjects

E.1.a. Human Subjects' Involvement and Characteristics. Approximately 248 young people between the ages of eighteen to twenty-five living in the Greater Hartford area, at least 120 of whom will have used MDMA two times or more in the past thirty days, will participate in this study. An additional approximately 120 participants will be interviewed in focus groups consisting of eight people each. Each focus group is expected to last approximately two-and-one-half hours. Eight participants will take part in the pilot test of our in-depth interview, which will take approximately one-and-a-half to two hours to complete. The 120 MDMA-using participants will take part in two in-depth interviews roughly one week apart. Each interview will be one-and-a-half to two hours long.

Anticipated gender and ethnic/racial breakdowns are as follows:

Gender: 50 percent female, 50 percent male
Ethnicity: 33 percent African American
            34 percent Latino (primarily Puerto Rican)
            33 percent Caucasian/White/other

*Less than 3 percent of the area's population is American Indian or from Southeast Asian countries, and American Indians or Southeast Asians may be included among index referrals but will not constitute a specific subsample within the study population.

Criteria for the *inclusion* of individuals as participants include the following:

- Between ages of eighteen and twenty-five
- Currently a resident of the greater Hartford area
- Self-reported use of ecstasy on at least two or more separate occasions in the past thirty days, with one of these occurrences involving ecstasy use within no more than approximately six to eight hours prior to having sex

Criteria for *exclusion* include:

- Under the age of eighteen or over the age of twenty-five
- Not a resident of the greater Hartford area

- Has not used ecstasy twice or more in the past thirty days
- Candidate is considered by research staff to be unable to give informed consent

E.1.b. Sources of Materials. Data to be collected in this project include:

- Constructed narratives (cultural scripts) involving the use of ecstasy and/or other substances in the context of sexual behavior collected in focus groups
- Ethnographic field notes/documentation of the focus groups
- Data from in-depth interviews with sexually active ecstasy users on the history of their ecstasy use and sexual activities, including self-reported information on demographics; background experience; party and social experiences; peer norms, behaviors, and social influence; ecstasy and other drug use; sexual behavior; sexual risks (unprotected sex with different types of sex partners); sexual aggression and violence; and STI and HIV knowledge and experience
- Data from in-depth interviews with sexually active ecstasy users about personal relationships (peers and partners), history of experience with ecstasy use, with and without other drugs, and sexual history
- Data from in-depth interviews with ecstasy users comparing their sexual experiences while using and not using ecstasy as well as other drugs
- Anonymous (non-named) information about personal relationships between participants and their partners, including details of sexual and drug exchanges and condom use or other forms of protection (or nonprotection)
- Locator information on where to find participants for their second in-depth interview, approximately one week after the first interview

Data will be collected for research purposes only.

E.1.c. Potential Risks. Risks to respondents from participation in this research project include: a) potential loss of confidentiality regarding highly sensitive information (drug use, involvement in illegal activities, STI and HIV status); and b) inadvertent exposure of illegal drug use, drug selling, or HIV status to local authorities.

E.2. Adequacy of Protection against Risks

E.2.a. Recruitment and Informed Consent. Participants will be recruited through face-to-face recruitment in locations known to be popular among poly-drug users of diverse ethnic backgrounds and by advertising the study in media popular with youth in the target area, such as fliers and community newspapers. Sites for face-to-face recruitment and the distribution of advertising media include major shopping avenues, parks with basketball courts, and commercial establishments located near college campuses that cater to young people.

Focus Groups. Youth of the target age group who reside in the study area, and who self-identify as having experience (either personally or through friends who use MDMA and other drugs) will be eligible for participation in focus groups. They will be recruited on the street, or those who respond to media advertisements or via phone will be screened for their eligibility (age, residence, and familiarity with MDMA) and will be invited to attend a focus group. LGTBQ youth who fit the same criteria will be recruited through known staff or ICR's organizational partners (such as Children of the Shadows) working with these and experimenting youth, including Children of the Shadows. Before beginning the focus group interview at the ICR, participants will be fully informed of the nature of the study, their right to refuse to answer any questions or to withdraw from the study at any time without penalty, existing procedures for ensuring confidentiality, and the risks and benefits of their participation, and then will be asked to sign a written project consent form. A second set of focus groups with approximately seventy participants representing policymakers, youth-serving educators and program personnel, entertainment media, and youth in the target age group will respond to study results and provide input into multilevel intervention approaches.

Pilot In-Depth Interviews/In-Depth Interviews. Prospective participants recruited on the street will be screened for MDMA use (two or more times in the past thirty days) and will then set an appointment for their interview at the ICR. Prospective participants who call in response to media advertisements will follow the same screening/appointment procedure. Before beginning the in-depth interview at the ICR, prospective participants will be given a brief overview of the study and then will be further screened for their eligibility to participate in the study (including age, residence, and use of ecstasy twice or more in the past thirty days, with one of these occurrences involving ecstasy use prior to having sex). This eligibility screening will be anonymous—no names or any other identifying demographic data will be collected. Prospective participants' verbal consent will be obtained before the eligibility screening is administered. All eligible participants will then be fully informed of the nature of the study, their right to refuse to answer any questions or to withdraw from the study at any time without penalty, existing procedures for ensuring confidentiality, and the risks and benefits of their participation, and then will be asked to sign a written project consent form prior to conducting the interview.

E.2.b. Protection against Risks. The following procedures have been developed to address the areas of potential risk noted above. To avoid loss of confidentiality, participants' names will not appear on any forms entered into the general databases. Personally constructed ID numbers will be used for identification on all data records. Transcribed audiotaped in-depth interviews and focus groups will be erased at the end of the project, and only ID numbers will be used to introduce the interview on tape. Electronic versions of interviews will be password protected. The master list, which matches names with unique identifier codes, will be kept in a locked filing cabinet in the office of the project director.

Participants in the focus groups will periodically be reminded during the discussion not to share personal information about themselves or others as the content of the group discussion is not confidential. For ethnographic field notes/documentation of the focus groups, special attention will be paid to protecting individuals that might identify them even in the absence of names, addresses, and other features of ethnographic data. We will also pay attention to ensuring the protection of names associated with clubs, hotels, after-hours, home parties, and other party sites to prevent unintended exposure to public officials and the press.

Names and other personal identifying information, such as addresses, phone numbers, and contact persons collected for the purposes of locating project participants for their second in-depth interview, will be maintained in separate locked files and will only be used for research purposes. Project staff will not release any information to a third party, even if that person is also in the study. However, we will obtain permission during the informed consent process to share participants' names with other ICR research outreach staff strictly for the purpose of seeking their assistance with follow-up tracking of participants. All project staff and all outreach staff of other ICR projects are highly trained and monitored to maintain confidentiality, and are under the supervision of the ICR to ensure that they strictly adhere to confidentiality protection procedures established by the ICR's Research Ethics Committee and Institutional Review Board.

To minimize discomfort in the discussion of personal drug use, HIV risk, or sexual practices, staff will be trained to provide information about appropriate supports and services available to those who wish to reduce or stop his/her use of drugs, or anyone who is at risk of HIV infection.

In addition to all consent procedures outlined above and confidentiality protections put into place, the project will apply for a Certificate of Confidentiality for the protection of all participants and contacts in the project.

E.2.b.1. Data Safety Monitoring Plan

This study will be reviewed and approved by the Institute for Community Research's Institutional Review Board (IRB) before contacting prospective participants. All research personnel working with study participants or study data on the project will have completed training in the protection of human subjects per the guidelines issued by the US Department of Health and Human Services, Office of Human Research Protections, before contacting prospective participants or working with study data.

Maintenance of Data: Confidentiality

A subject's participation in this project will be kept confidential within the study team and other related research projects at the Institute for Community Research; that is, it will be restricted to staff of the AIDS/STI and substance abuse–related research projects at ICR. This means that information from our different AIDS/STI and substance abuse research projects might be shared between projects.

To guard against loss of confidentiality, all participants will be assigned a personal ID number that will be used for identification on all documents except consent forms and follow-up locator forms. Names and other personal identifying information, such as addresses, phone numbers, and contact persons, which are collected for the purposes of follow-up, will be maintained in separate, locked file cabinets (both computerized and hard copy) under the protection of the project director. Such records will be secured in locked files and will not be used for any reason other than research purposes. No information a participant gives project staff about their personal contacts or people they are close to will be shared with said contacts without the participant's permission.

Computerized data will be located in hidden files and will be password protected. Audiotaped focus groups and in-depth interviews will be stored in locked cabinets and once transcribed, the audiotapes will be destroyed. The study will obtain a Certificate of Confidentiality, issued by the federal Department of Health and Human Services, to help protect participants' privacy. This certificate will help to protect project staff from being forced to release any data in which participants are identified, even under a court order or subpoena, without the participant's written consent.

Data requested from researchers who are from organizations that are not collaborating on this project with ICR will only be shared in aggregate form.

Protections for Confidentiality

All project staff working with study participants or study data will review and sign a Statement of Confidentiality before contacting study participants. When the study ends or project staff terminate their involvement in the study, they will meet with the research ethics monitor for a debriefing/exit interview in which the Researcher Statement of Confidentiality will be reviewed and signed once again, indicating their understanding that they are bound by the Statement even though their involvement in the study has ended.

Despite ICR's commitment to ensuring participants' confidentiality, it is possible that, even with our best efforts, confidentiality might be breached. In such instances, the project staff person who identified the breach in confidentiality will immediately report the incident to the project director of the relevant project. The PI, project staff, and the research ethics monitor will then discuss the circumstances that instigated the incident, the implications and ramifications of the breach, and any possible actions that need to be taken to address the breach of confidentiality.

The PI will report in writing each breach in confidentiality and the outcome of the discussion between the PI, project staff, and the research ethics monitor to the IRB. Upon review, the IRB may suggest an amendment to the research protocol.

Adverse Events

An adverse event is an event occurring in the context of a research project that causes physical or psychological harm to a participant. The project staff person who identifies or observes the adverse event will immediately report the event to the relevant project director/coordinator. The PI, project staff, and the research ethics monitor will then discuss the circumstances of the event, any implications and ramifications of the event, and any possible actions that need to be taken to address the adverse event. The PI will report in writing each adverse event and the outcome of the discussion between the PI, project staff, and the research ethics monitor to the IRB. Upon review, the IRB may suggest changes in the research procedures.

E.3. Potential Benefits of the Proposed Research to the Subjects and Others

While the risks resulting from participating in this project are both real and significant, they are reasonable and justified by the very real benefits to participants and the community. All participants will receive STI and HIV prevention materials; health and social service referral information, which includes information about drug treatment programs, primary health clinics, HIV and STI testing sites; and specific referral to HIV and STI testing if requested or warranted. Project findings will address and establish the validity of a potentially significant public health problem—the interaction of a drug perceived and marketed as enhancing sexual experience with youth who are developmentally at the highest risk of ecstasy and other related drug use and sexual experimentation and unprotected sex. The study will disseminate results to the study population in innovative ways that will stimulate discussion about the issues it raises.

APPENDIX B: CONSENT FORMS AND ASSENT FORMS

EXAMPLE ONE

From Sheryl Ludwig's study, "Making Fast the Thread"

Note: This example includes consent letters for all adults and assent letters for all children over the age of seven. All of these letters were translated into Spanish. For those who did not speak Spanish well, a translator read them in Kakchiquel, the native language of the community. For illiterate members of the community, a witnessed mark was used in lieu of a signature. Since it was unlikely that any person in the community could contact IRB staff back in the United States for questions, Ludwig included the name and contact information for a knowledgeable local person whom people could contact if they had questions about Ludwig or her work. This is generally required.

Letter of Informed Consent: Group One, Mayan Women in Cooperative

Dear Friend,

My name is Sherri Ludwig. I am a graduate student at the University of Colorado in Boulder, Colorado. While I am studying weaving in San Antonio Aguas Calientes I will be living at 1a Calle de Chajon, 19E, in Antigua. I can always be reached through email at sherylaludwig@hotmail.com.

I am hoping that you will agree to be part of a study I am doing about how weaving is taught in your cooperativa and what is learned as a result. I am learning to weave in your cooperativa because I want to know how you teach your children and yourselves to be such good weavers. By studying the way you create and produce your weaving, I am also studying ways to teach outside of a school classroom. I am also interested in knowing how weaving makes you feel about yourself and your culture. What I learn from you will be written into a long report called a dissertation. I will use what I learn to finish my educational studies and to help me in teaching people to be good teachers for all children, including the children of people who have emigrated from Guatemala to the United States.

While I am studying weaving with you, I will be asking you questions about weaving, such as "When did you learn to weave?" "Who taught you to weave?" "What do the patterns and colors mean to you?" "How has weaving changed since you learned to weave?" and "Why have you chosen to weave with this cooperativa?" I will also ask you about how you sell your weavings in the market, how your children go to school, and what your children do to help you. I will be watching you when you weave, and when you teach me to weave, and I will be writing down notes so that I can remember how things are done and what is said. I will also be videotaping myself as I am learning to weave, but I will not be focusing the camera on you. I need to have a way to remember all that you are teaching me as well as the words you use in teaching me. When I have watched the videotape and written down notes about what I am seeing, I will erase the videotape and send the notes to Dr. Margaret LeCompte, my professor at the University of Colorado, in the United States. Sometimes I may want to interview you and use a tape recorder to remember your words. Those tapes will also be erased and the notes from them sent to Dr. LeCompte. I will also ask if I can take photographs of you and your beautiful weavings. If I want to use those photographs in my reports or in presentations, I will ask for your permission first. If you don't want your faces shown, just tell me and I won't use your photograph or I will block out and/or blur the features of your face. When I return to Guatemala next year, I will bring you copies of all the pictures I have taken of you. When I refer to you in my writing and presentations, I will always use a different name, for I want to protect your true identity.

I do not think that there are any real risks to you for participating in my study. However, I hope that you will feel that my sincere interest in your weaving and how it is taught and learned, and how it may affect how you think about yourself and your culture, will be benefits to you in participating in this study. I want to be able to tell other people in the world about your weaving and your stories. I am very excited to be learning to weave with you in the cooperativa and to be volunteering to help the teachers work with your children in the school. I feel fortunate to be able to learn more about you and your culture through learning to weave with you—and then to be able to share with teachers all that I have learned about new ways to think about teaching people to learn.

If you do not feel comfortable when I am asking you questions, you do not have to answer them. You can also tell me to stop videotaping or audiotaping any time that you wish. You also can stop participating in this study any time you wish to. When I refer to you in my writing and presentations, I will always use a different name for you, for I want to protect your true identity. When I finish copying the information on my audio and videotapes, I will erase them, and I won't put your name on the transcripts. When my study is over, I will store the data in a very safe place in the United States. Your names will be kept in a separate place from the notes that I have made from the videotapes, audiotapes, field notes, and photographs.

If you have questions about my project, please feel free to ask Lilian Santizo at Escuela de Espanol A.P.P.E. (502-832-1795 or appe@infovia.com.gt) or my professor at the University of Colorado, Dr. Margaret LeCompte (303-492-7951 or margaret. lecompte@colorado.edu). If you have questions regarding your rights as a subject, or if you are unhappy about any part of this study, you may report your feelings—confidentially if you wish—to Ms. Sheryl Jensen, the executive secretary of the Human Research Committee at the University of Colorado. The address is Graduate School, 026 UCB, Boulder, CO 80309-0026. The telephone number is 303-492-7401.

If you give your permission for me to observe you while I am weaving, to interview you using a tape recorder and a camcorder to videotape how I learn and to use the information I learn from you in my dissertation, please read the statement of understanding below and sign on the line so that I can show my university that you have voluntarily agreed to be part of my study of your weaving and teaching practices.

Sincerely,

Sheryl A. Ludwig

I understand the purpose of Sheryl Ludwig's research project about weaving in my cooperativa and I agree to be part of her research and to let her observe me and to ask me questions in an interview. I understand that I don't have to answer any questions that I don't feel like answering, and that I can stop participating any time I wish.

Signed: _____

Date: _____

I give permission to Sherri (the researcher) to use photographs and/or videos of me in her writing and in her presentations.

Signed: _____

_____ My facial features may be shown.
_____ I would like my facial features to be blurred.
_____ I would like my facial features to be blocked.

I do not give permission to Sherri (the researcher) to use photographs and/or videos of me in her writing and in her presentations.

Signed: _____

Letter of Informed Consent: Group Two, Parent Consent and Child Assent Forms, Children of Cooperativa Members

Dear Parent,

My name is Sherri Ludwig. I am a graduate student at the University of Colorado in Boulder, Colorado. While I am studying weaving in San Antonio Aguas Calientes I will be living at 1a Calle de Chajon, 19E, in Antigua. I can always be reached through email at sherylaludwig@hotmail.com.

I am hoping that you will agree to allow your child to be part of a study I am doing about how weaving is taught in your cooperativa and what is learned as a result. I am learning to weave in your cooperativa because I want to know how you and the other members teach your children and yourselves to be such good weavers. By studying the way weavers create and produce their art, I am also studying ways to teach outside of a school classroom. I am also interested in knowing how weaving makes you and your daughters (children) feel about yourselves and your culture. What I learn from you will be written into a long report called a dissertation. I will use what I learn to finish my educational studies and to help me in teaching people to be good teachers for all children, including the children of people who have emigrated from Guatemala to the United States.

While I am studying weaving in the cooperativa, I will be asking you questions about the ways in which you are teaching your child to weave and writing down notes about your answers. For example, I may ask you "Why are you helping your child in this way?" or "Why are you teaching your child to weave?" I may ask your child questions such as "Why do you want to learn to weave?" or "How can knowing how to weave help you in your school work?" At times I will ask for permission to videotape your child while s/he is learning to weave. I need to have a way to remember all that s/he is learning and the words you use while you are teaching. If you or your child do not want me to videotape, or if you do not wish to have your faces shown, just tell me and I will stop. When I have finished watching the videotapes, I will erase the videotapes and send the notes I have made to Dr. Margaret LeCompte, my professor at the University of Colorado, in the United States. Sometimes I may want to interview you and your child and use a tape recorder to remember your words. Those tapes will also be erased after I have transcribed them, and the notes about them will be sent to Dr. LeCompte. Many times I will want to take photographs of you and your beautiful weavings but I will ask for your permission before I do so. If I want to use those photographs in my reports or in presentations, I will ask for your permission first. When I return to Guatemala next year, I will bring you copies of all the pictures I have taken of you.

I do not think that there are any real risks to your child for participating in my study. However, if you feel uncomfortable with any of my questions, you do not have to answer them. You can ask me to stop audio or videotaping at any time if you wish me to stop. You can also stop participating in this study any time you wish to. When I refer to your child in my writing and presentations, I will always use a different name for him/her, for I want to protect your child's true identity. When I am finished copying information from my audio and videotapes onto a transcript, I will erase the tapes, and I will not put your real name on the transcripts. When my study is over, I will store the data in a very safe place in the United States. Your real names will be kept in a separate place from the notes that I have made from the videotapes, audiotapes, field notes, and photographs.

I hope that you and your child will feel that my sincere interest in your weaving and how it is taught and learned, and how it may affect how you and your child think about yourselves and your culture, are benefits to you in participating in this study. I want to be able to tell other people in the world about your weaving and your stories. I am very excited to be learning to weave with you in the cooperativa and to be volunteering to help the teachers work with your children in the school. I feel fortunate to be able to learn more about you and your culture through learning to weave with you—and then to be able to share with teachers all that I have learned about new ways to think about teaching people to learn.

If you have questions about my project, please feel free to ask Lilian Santizo at Escuela de Espanol A.P.P.E. (502-832-1795 or appe@infovia.com.qt) or Dr. Margaret

LeCompte, my professor at the University of Colorado (303-492-7951 or margaret. lecompte@colorado.edu). If you have questions regarding your rights as a subject, or if you are unhappy about any part of this study, you may report your feelings—confidentially if you wish—to Ms. Sheryl Jensen, the executive secretary of the Human Research Committee at the University of Colorado. The address is Graduate School, 026 UCB, Boulder, CO 80309-0026. The telephone number is 303-492-7401.

If you give your permission for me to observe your child learning to weave, to interview your child using a video camcorder and an audiotape and to use the information I learn from you in my dissertation, please read the statement of understanding below and sign on the line so that I can show my university that you have voluntarily agreed to allow your child to be part of my study of your weaving and teaching practices.

Sincerely,

Sheryl A. Ludwig

I understand the purpose of Sheryl Ludwig's research project about weaving in my cooperativa in Guatemala and I agree to allow my child and I to be part of her research. I understand that my child and/or I do not have to answer any questions that we do not feel like answering, and that we can stop participating any time I wish.

Signed: _____

Date: _____

I give permission to Sherri (the researcher) to use photographs and/or videos of me and/ or my child in her writing and in her presentations.

Signed: _____

_____ My facial features may be shown.
_____ I would like my facial features to be blurred.
_____ I would like my facial features to be blocked.

I do not give permission to Sherri (the researcher) to use photographs and/or videos of me and/or my child in her writing and in her presentations.

Signed: _____

Child's Assent Form (Child of Cooperativa Member)

I am willing to be part of Sheryl Ludwig's study about teaching and learning weaving in a Mayan women's cooperativa. I understand that she is hoping to learn about ways to teach and learn and how I feel about myself and my culture. I understand that, while I am learning to weave in my mother's cooperativa, Sherri will be observing and asking questions about what I am doing, such as "Why are you using that color or this pattern?" or "Why do I want to learn to weave?" I understand that she will write down notes about my answers and that she will ask to videotape me being taught to weave. She will only watch and videotape when I want her to be there. If I do not want my face in the videotape, she will not film it. I know that I can ask her to stop videotaping or observing at any time. If I do not like her questions, I know that I can refuse to answer them. I know that I can stop participating in her study any time I wish to. I know that no one will know about the questions I choose to answer because Sherri will keep my real name a secret.

Name: _____

Signature: _____

Date: _____

Age: _____

I give permission to Sherri (the researcher) to observe me and my mother and to ask me questions while my mother is teaching me to weave.

Signed: _____

I give permission to Sherri (the researcher) to use photographs and/ or videos of me in her writing and in her presentations.

Signed: _____

_____ My facial features may be shown.
_____ I would like my facial features to be blurred.
_____ I would like my facial features to be blocked.

I do not give permission to Sherri (the researcher) to use photographs and/or videos of me in her writing and in her presentations.

Signed: _____

Letter of Informed Consent: Group Three, Various Village Members

Dear Friend,

My name is Sherri Ludwig. I am a graduate student at the University of Colorado in Boulder, Colorado. While I am studying weaving in San Antonio Aguas Calientes I will be living at 1a Calle de Chajon, 19E, in Antigua. I can always be reached through email at sherylaludwig@hotmail.com.

I am hoping that you will agree to be part of a study I am doing about how weaving is taught in the cooperativa and what is learned as a result. I am learning to weave because I want to know how women here teach their children and themselves to be such good weavers. By studying the way weavers create and produce their weavings, I am also studying ways to teach outside of a school classroom as well as how weaving makes women feel about themselves and their culture. What I learn from you will be written into a long report called a dissertation. I will use what I learn to finish my educational studies and to help me in teaching people to be good teachers for all children, including the children of people who have emigrated from Guatemala to the United States.

I also want to learn more about how people here who are not part of the cooperativa think of weaving and how and why you weave if you do. If you agree to let me interview you, I will be asking questions such as "Why have you chosen not to be a part of a cooperativa?" "Why do you continue to weave?" "How do you sell your weavings in the market?" "How did you learn to weave?" "Do your children attend school?" and "How do they help you at home?" While you are sharing your ideas with me, I will be writing down notes about your answers. I may want to take photographs of you and your beautiful weavings. If I do, I will ask for your permission first. If I want to use those photographs in my reports or in presentations, I will ask for your permission. When I return to Guatemala next year, I will bring you copies of all the pictures I have taken of you. Those notes and pictures will be sent to Dr. Margaret LeCompte, my professor at the University of Colorado, in the United States.

I do not think that there are any real risks to you for participating in my study. However, if you feel uncomfortable with any of my questions, you do not have to answer them. You can also stop participating any time you wish. If I refer to you in any of my writing and presentations, I will always use a different name for you, for I want to protect your true identity. Any notes that I make about our interview will be safely stored in the United States, and your real name will not be on them. When my study is over I will store the data in a very safe place in the United States. Your real name will not appear on any of the stored data.

I hope that you will feel that my sincere interest in your weaving and how it is taught and learned, and how it may affect how you think about yourself and your culture, will be benefits to you in participating in this study. I want to be able to tell other people in the world about your weaving and your stories. I am very excited to be learning to weave in San Antonio and to be volunteering to help teachers work with your children in the school. I feel fortunate to be able to learn more about you and your culture through learning to weave—and then to be able to share with teachers all that I have learned about new ways to think about teaching people to learn.

If you have questions about my project, please feel free to ask Lilian Santizo at Escuela de Espanol A.P.P.E. (502-832-1795 or appe@infovia.com.qt) or Dr. Margaret LeCompte, my professor at the University of Colorado (303-492-7951 or margaret. lecompte@colorado.edu). If you have questions regarding your rights as a subject, or if you are unhappy with any part of this study, you may report your feelings—confidentially if you wish—to Ms. Sheryl Jensen, the executive secretary of the Human Research Committee at the University of Colorado. The address is Graduate School, 026 UCB, Boulder, CO 80309-0026. The telephone number is 303-492-7401.

If you give your permission for me to interview you and use the information I learn from you in my dissertation, please read the statement of understanding below and sign on the line so that I can show my university that you have voluntarily agreed to be part of my study of your weaving and teaching practices.

Sincerely,

Sheryl A. Ludwig

I give permission to Sherri (the researcher) to use my photograph in her writing and in her presentations.

Signed: _____

　　　　_____ My facial features may be shown.

　　　　_____ I would like my facial features to be blurred.

　　　　_____ I would like my facial features to be blocked.

I do not give permission to Sherri (the researcher) to use photographs of me in her writing and in her presentations.

Signed: _____

Letter of Informed Consent: Group Four, Parents of Children In Village Schools

Dear Parent of Village School Student,

My name is Sherri Ludwig. I am a graduate student at the University of Colorado in Boulder, Colorado. While I am studying weaving in San Antonio Aguas Calientes I will be living at 1a Calle de Chajon, 19E, in Antigua. I can always be reached through email at sherylaludwig@hotmail.com.

I am hoping that you will agree to allow your child to be part of a study I am doing about how weaving is taught in the cooperativa here in San Antonio and what is learned as a result. I am learning to weave in San Antonio because I want to know how the women here teach their children and themselves to be such good weavers. By studying the way weavers create and produce their beautiful weavings, I am also studying ways to teach outside of a school classroom as well as how weaving may make weavers feel about themselves and their culture. Because I am a teacher in the United States, I am also interested in what and how children learn in the local schools and how that may be different from what is learned at home. What I learn from your child will be written into a long report called a dissertation. I will use what I learn to finish my educational studies and to help me in teaching people to be good teachers for all children, including the children of people who have emigrated from Guatemala to the United States.

I would like to visit your child's school and observe what the teachers and children do there during their classes. If possible, I would like to ask your child some questions, such as "What are you learning in school?" and, especially if s/he weaves at home, "How are you using what you know about weaving in your schoolwork?" I may want to take a picture of your child. However, I won't take a picture of your child unless you and your child say that I can. If I do, I will be sure to give you a copy of it. If I refer to your child in my writing and presentations, I will always use a different name, for I want to protect his or her true identity. If I want to show his/her picture in my writing or in presentations, I will ask you both first.

I do not think that there are any real risks to you or your child for participating in my study. However, if I ask your child questions that s/he does not want to answer, s/he does not have to answer them. S/he can stop participating in this study any time s/he wishes to. When I refer to your child in my writing and presentations, I will always use a different name for him/ her, for I want to protect his/her true identity. When my study is over, I will store the data in a very safe place in the United States. All real names will be kept in a separate place from the notes that I have made from the interview notes.

I hope that you and your child will feel that my sincere interest in the schools of San Antonio, how classes are taught and what is learned there, are benefits to you and your child for participating in this study. I want to be able to tell other people in the world about your weaving and your stories. I will also be volunteering to help your child's teachers in the school. I also want to be able to tell other people in the world about teaching and learning here in Guatemala.

I am very excited to be learning to weave here in San Antonio and to be volunteering to help teachers work with children in the school. I feel fortunate to be able to learn more about you and your culture through learning to weave—and then to be able to share with all teachers all that I have learned about new ways to think about teaching people to learn.

If you have questions about my project, please feel free to ask Lilian Santizo at Escuela de Espanol A.P.P.E. (502-832-1795 or appe@infovia.com.qt) or Dr. Margaret LeCompte, my professor at the University of Colorado (303-492-7951 or margaret. lecompte@colorado.edu). If you have questions regarding your rights as a subject, or if you are unhappy about any part of this study, you may report your feelings—confidentially if you wish—to Ms. Sheryl Jensen, the executive secretary of the Human Research Committee at the University of Colorado. The address is Graduate School, 026 UCB, Boulder, CO 80309-0026. The telephone number is 303-492-7401.

If you give your permission for me to interview your child and to use the information I learn from him/her in my dissertation, please read the statement of understanding below and sign on the line so that I can show my university that you have voluntarily agreed to allow your child to be part of my study of your weaving and teaching practices.

Sincerely,

Sheryl A. Ludwig

I understand the purpose of Sheryl Ludwig's research project about weaving and its connection to school and I agree to allow my child to be part of her research. I understand that my child doesn't have to answer any questions that s/he doesn't feel like answering, and that s/he can stop participating any time s/he wishes.

Signed: _____

Date: _____

I give permission to Sherri (the researcher) to use photographs of my child in her writing and in her presentations.

Signed: _____

_____   My child's facial features may be shown.

_____   I would like my child's facial features to be blurred.

_____   I would like my child's facial features to be blocked.

I do not give permission to Sherri (the researcher) to use photographs of my child in her writing and in her presentations.

Signed: _____

Child's Assent Form (Child Attending Village School)

I am willing to be part of Sheryl Ludwig's study about teaching and learning weaving in San Antonio. I understand that she is hoping to learn about ways to teach and learn and how learning to weave and going to school makes children feel about themselves and their culture. I understand that, once in a while, while I am at school, Sherri will be asking questions such as "What am I studying?" "What do I like to study?" "What kinds of things do I do when I am not attending school?" and "Am I learning to weave at home?" I understand that she will write down notes about my answers. I know that, if I do not wish to answer her questions, I can refuse to answer them. I know that no one will know about the questions I choose to answer because Sherri will keep my real name a secret. I know that Sherri may wish to take my photograph, and that, if I do not want her to, I can refuse to be photographed.

Name: _____

Signature: _____

Date: _____

Age: _____

I give permission to Sherri (the researcher) to use my photograph in her writing and in her presentations.

Signed: _____

_____   My facial features may be shown.

_____   I would like my facial features to be blurred.

_____   I would like my facial features to be blocked.

I do not give permission to Sherri (the researcher) to use photographs of me in her writing and in her presentations.

Signed: _____

Letter of Informed Consent: Group Five, Teachers and Other School Personnel

Dear Teacher,

My name is Sherri Ludwig. I am a graduate student at the University of Colorado in Boulder, Colorado. While I am studying weaving in San Antonio Aguas Calientes I will be living at 1a Calle de Chajon, 19E, in Antigua. I can always be reached through email at sherylaludwig@hotmail.com.

I am hoping that you will agree to be part of a study I am doing about how weaving is taught in the cooperativa San Antonio and what is learned as a result. I am learning to weave in San Antonio because I want to know how the women here teach their children and themselves to be such good weavers. By studying the way weavers create and produce their beautiful weavings, I am studying ways teaching occurs outside of a school classroom. I am also interested how weaving makes women feel about themselves and their culture. Because I am also a teacher in the United States, I am also interested in how and what children learn in your school as well as how that learning connects to what children learn at home and how they feel about themselves. What I learn from you will be written into a long report called a dissertation. I will use what I learn to finish my educational studies and to help me in teaching people to be good teachers for all children, including the children of people who have emigrated from Guatemala to the United States.

While I am studying weaving in San Antonio, I want to learn more about how students use what they learn from weaving in their studies. If possible, I would like to ask you some questions, such as "What you are teaching in school?" and "How might students be using the lessons they have learned at home in their schoolwork?" I will also be interested in knowing what you find difficult and what you find rewarding about teaching here. If I want to take a picture of you, you do not have to agree. If I do take a picture, I will be sure to give you a copy of it. I may also wish to tape record our conversation. If I do, I will erase that tape recording as soon as I have transcribed the data. Your real name will not appear on the transcription. The transcribed notes will be sent to Dr. Margaret LeCompte, my professor at the University of Colorado in the United States for safekeeping. When and if I refer to you in my writing and presentations, I will always use a different name, for I want to protect your true identity, and if I want to show your picture in my writing or in presentations, I will ask you first.

I do not think that there are any real risks to you for participating in my study. However, if I ask you questions that you do not want to answer, please do not answer them. You can stop participating in this study any time you wish to. When I refer to you in my writing and presentations, I will always use a different name for you, for I want to protect your true identity. The notes that I make about what I am seeing and/or what you are saying in the classroom will not have your real name on them, and they will be sent to the United States for safe keeping. When my study is over, I will store the data in a very safe place in the United States. Your name will be kept in a separate place from the notes that I have made from the interview.

I hope that you will feel that my sincere interest in your country and its people—as well as the women's weaving, how it is taught and learned, and how that may affect how women and girls feel about themselves and their culture—are benefits to you in participating in this study. I want to be able to tell other people in the world about weaving and its stories. I am very excited to be learning to weave in San Antonio and to be volunteering to help teachers work with children in the school. I feel fortunate to be able to learn more about you and your culture through learning to weave. I also look forward to volunteering in the schools—and then to being able to share with teachers all that I have learned about new ways to think about teaching people to learn.

If you have questions about my project, please feel free to ask Lilian Santizo at Escuela de Espanol A.P.P.E. (502-832-1795 or appe@infovia.com.qt) or Dr. Margaret LeCompte, my professor at the University of Colorado (303-492-7951 or margaret. lecompte@colorado.edu). If you have questions regarding your rights as a subject, or if you are unhappy about any part of this study, you may report them—confidentially if you wish—to Ms. Sheryl Jensen, executive secretary of the Human Research Committee at the University of Colorado. The address is Graduate School, 026 UCB, Boulder, CO 80309-0026. The telephone number is 303-492-7401.

If you give your permission for me to interview you and use the information I learn from you in my dissertation, please read the statement of understanding below and sign on the line so that I can show my university that you have voluntarily agreed to be part of my study of your weaving and teaching practices.

Sincerely,

Sheryl A. Ludwig

I understand the purpose of Sheryl Ludwig's research project about connections between weaving at home and education in the schools of San Antonio and I agree to be part of her research. I understand that Sherri will come to my class, observe my teaching, and ask me questions in an interview. I understand that I don't have to answer any questions that I don't feel like answering, and that I can stop participating any time I wish.

Signed: _____

Date: _____

I give permission to Sherri (the researcher) to use photographs of me in her writing and in her presentations.

Signed: _____

_____ My facial features may be shown.

_____ I would like my facial features to be blurred.

_____ I would like my facial features to be blocked.

I do not give permission to Sherri (the researcher) to use photographs of me in her writing and in her presentations.

Signed: _____

EXAMPLE TWO

From Margaret LeCompte's Study, "Merging Cultures: The Intersection of Arts and Academics," Submitted September 2003

LeCompte's earlier study of the arts program on its original campus had focused on both students and teachers, and most of the teachers were familiar with LeCompte and her research team and how she collected data. This particular proposal did not include students, since the new school board had forbidden any academic researchers from doing studies of children. Hence, the desired study was divided into Phase One and Two, with the hope that the second phase, which would include students, could be implemented later.

Please read the following material that explains this research study. Signing this form will indicate that you have been informed about the study and that you want to participate. We want you to understand what you are being asked to do and what risks and benefits—if any—are associated with the study. This should help you decide whether or not you want to participate in the study.

The purpose of this letter is to invite you to participate in a research project on the evolution of the newly constituted Manhattan School of the Arts in the Boulder Valley School District. The study is being conducted by Margaret (Marki) LeCompte, professor in the School of Education at the University of Colorado at Boulder. Marki's address at CU is UCB 249, Education 124, UCB, Boulder, CO 80309. She can be reached via telephone at 303-492-7951, or email at Margaret.lecompte@colorado.edu. The research assistants involved in this study are Sally Campbell and Sherri Ludwig; Sally can be reached at sally.campbell@colorado.edu or 303-XXX-XXXX, and Sherri can be reached at sherylaludwig@hotmail.com.or 720-XXX-XXXX.

Project Description

This research study will investigate and describe the process by which the two separate schools, Base Line Middle School and Boulder School of the Arts, and Burbank Middle School, combined cultures and practices into the Manhattan School of the Arts, located on the former Burbank campus. I hope to identify successes and obstacles to the development of the new program and to document just how the school year unfolds. We'd also like to begin an investigation of the impact of the program on all the children in the school. I think that the information I'm gathering will be helpful in planning and the implementation of the program, as well as in writing grant proposals to support the school, and I'll be happy to share this information with the school staff. I'm inviting you to be a part of this study because you are one of the staff members who currently are employed at the school; I hope that all teachers, administrators, and staff will agree to participate. Participation in this study is entirely your choice.

Procedures

There will be two phases of this study. One phase, beginning now, will examine how the culture and climate of the Manhattan School evolve, what kinds of instruction and collaborations take place, the school's programmatic successes, and what obstacles, if any, arise during the year. In this Phase, I and the graduate researchers working with me will be "hanging out" on campus. Phase Two will assess the impact of the school's program on students and will involve accessing student achievement data. At this time, we are requesting to begin Phase One, which involves Manhattan School teachers and staff only. During Phase One, I will be collecting the following kinds of data:

1. Notes taken during faculty meetings, staff development meetings, school performances, and other activities in the school. While taking these notes, I'll be noting not only what's happening, but also what people say, what they plan, the concerns they have, and how they react to events.
2. Interviews with teachers and staff. I'd like to interview all of the current professional and para-professional staff at the school this year. I'll be asking about your background and teaching style prior to coming to Manhattan School, what led you to decide to come to this school, your opinions about your students and what you plan for them during the coming year, your opinions about integrating the arts with regular instruction, and how you feel about the process unfolding at Manhattan. If you were a teacher at either Base Line or Burbank last year, I'll also ask you to tell me a little about the history leading up to the decision to close Base Line and move to Burbank.
3. Documents that I collect, including minutes of meetings, announcements distributed throughout the school, grant applications, and any other materials that might help me understand what you are feeling and what's happening and being planned at the school.
4. Notes taken during visitations in classrooms. In these visits, I will simply be interested in seeing what your instruction looks like and in viewing any lessons that you think I might find interesting. I won't come in to your classroom unless you specifically give me permission to do so, and I will only come in, with permission, at times you specify.

Observations by me and the other members of the research team in meetings, at events, and in classrooms will not take any of your time and will not disrupt meetings or classroom activities. We will not be audio or videotaping any of these activities. We'd like to be more or less invisible when we are in your classrooms, though we know that's hardly possible in middle schools! Interviews, which *will* be audiotaped so that we can remember what you say, will last from forty minutes to an hour, and will be scheduled at a place and time convenient to you. We may wish to do a brief follow-up interview for clarifications at a later time. That, too, will be scheduled at your convenience.

We'll be trying to talk with everyone on the campus so that we get as complete a picture as possible of the school's evolving processes and culture. We think that what the Manhattan School is doing for kids and for middle school education is critically important; for that reason, we really hope that everyone on campus will participate.

Limitations on Participation and Study Withdrawal

You don't have to participate in this study if you don't want to do so. You have the right to withdraw your consent or stop participating at any time. You have the right to refuse to answer any question(s), ask that I not record anything you say or do in meetings, or refuse to answer any questions that you don't want to answer.

Risks, Discomforts, and Benefits of Participating in this Study

Participating in this study won't benefit you directly as an individual. However, we will supply feedback about the school climate and program progress with both the faculty and the principal. We will do so without identifying specific individuals. This has been my practice in similar collaborative research in public schools (in schools in Texas, Tennessee, Arizona, on the Navajo Reservation, and in the Denver Metro area). This feedback may enable school faculty and staff to take corrective actions from the formative assessments and feedback of the research project, as well as more focused evaluation of the impact of the program on students, staff, and teachers. Such data may help the school seek funding and fine-tune its program offerings.

The anticipated risks of this research are minimal. They will be limited to the discomfort that you may feel in describing (and reliving) the recent conflicts over the school merger, as well as emerging conflicts during the coming school year over resources, philosophical differences, and personality conflicts. You may also feel some discomfort in having an observer present during discussions of heated conflicts. We will abide by the counsel of the principal, as well as your own wishes, as to whether or not my presence is an obstacle, and I will absent myself when such action seems necessary. My research assistants, all advanced doctoral students, will abide by the same policy.

Confidentiality

In this study, I will adhere to a policy of confidentiality. Pseudonyms will be assigned to all members of the school staff and faculty. Data will be recorded only with those pseudonyms. This means that field notes and interview transcripts (whether taped or handwritten) will be coded with pseudonyms, and information from them will not be shared with others in ways that you can be identified. The key to the pseudonyms will be retained in a locked data cabinet in my home. Because this is an ethnographic study, and because many of the individuals in the school occupy unique positions (for example, there is only one voice teacher), it will be impossible to disguise their identity completely from individuals within the school community and the wider Boulder educational arena. Every effort will be made, however, to protect your privacy. I will negotiate what I say about you with you. My past practice has been to show initial drafts of my writings about individuals to them for feedback and corrections; in cases where the individual and I disagree, I have presented both sides in my writing. I will follow the same policy for this study. I also will reword what I say in accord with the wishes of the participant if they find it discomforting. I also share any report to all interested parties before it is disseminated beyond the school. Further, in any published documents, I will use pseudonyms for the school, district, and state.

Other than the research team, only regulatory agencies such as the Office of Human Research Protections and the University of Colorado Human Research Committee may see your individual raw data as part of routine audits. There are some things that you might tell us that we CANNOT promise to keep confidential. If you tell us about child abuse or neglect, about a crime you or others plan to commit, or about harm that may come to you or others, we are required to report these things.

Invitation for Questions

If you have questions about this study, please ask the researcher before you sign this consent form. If you have questions at any time regarding your rights as a participant, any concerns regarding this project, or any dissatisfaction with any aspect of this study, you may report them—confidentially, if you wish—to the executive secretary, Human Research Committee, 26 UCB, Regent Administrative Center 308, University of Colorado at Boulder, Boulder, CO 80309-0026 or by telephone to 303-492-7401.

Authorization

I have read this paper about the study, or it was read to me. I know the possible risks and benefits. I know that being in this study is voluntary.

_____ yes _____ no I agree to let Marki and her research team record information about my activities in meetings and activities at the school.

_____ yes _____ no I agree to participate in an interview with Marki or a member of her research team.

_____ yes _____ no I would like to wait a while to see how the research process unfolds before I agree to participate in an interview. I understand that Marki will ask me about an interview at a later date.

If I choose to be in this study, I know that I can withdraw at any time. I have received, on the date signed, a copy of this document, which contains four pages.

Name of Participant (printed) _____

Signature of Participant _____

Date _____.

(Also initial all previous pages of the consent form.)

Interview Invitation Note

Dear _____,

   The research team studying the development of the program at Manhattan School of the Arts would like to invite you to participate in an interview to help us better understand what's happening at the school and with your own teaching. We think that it's important to talk to everyone in the school, regardless of the subject(s) that they teach, because we want to get as broad a picture of the school's climate and personnel as possible.

   If you would be willing to be interviewed, would you please record below the times when it would be convenient (though we know that there's NO convenient extra time in the schedules of teachers!) for us to talk with you for about an hour? If there's a special place where you'd like to be interviewed, let us know that as well. We'd prefer a place that's also quiet, so our tape recorder will function well!

   Or, if you would prefer, you can call or email Marki to schedule your interview in person. You can reach her at Margaret.lecompte@colorado.edu or 303-492-7951.

   When you have filled out this invitation, please put it in Marki's mailbox in the main office at Manhattan School.

NAME: _____

_____ I DO NOT WISH TO BE INTERVIEWED

_____ I COULD BE INTERVIEWED AT THE FOLLOWING TIMES:

DAY OF THE WEEK	DATE	TIME	PREFERRED PLACE

_____ I PREFER TO CONTACT MARKI TO SCHEDULE AN INTERVIEW.

EXAMPLE THREE

Child Assent for Students Aged Ten to Fourteen Involved in "Imagining the Future, Creating the Present: The Impact of Arts Education on Achievement and Identity in Arts Focus"

   This consent form was used for public school middle school participants in the study of Arts Focus, an arts-intensive supplemental program, conducted by LeCompte and her graduate students. It preceded the project described in Example Two above. A similar and more detailed form was sent as well to the parents or guardians of each child; both parents and children had to sign the forms(s) in order for the child to participate. Children were asked to indicate both their own name and the name of their parent or guardian, since many times these may not be identical.

CONSENT TO PARTICIPATE IN ARTS
FOCUS RESEARCH PROJECT

We want to invite you to help us in our study of the Arts Focus Program because you are a student in that program. We are Marki LeCompte, a faculty member at the University of Colorado, and Debra Holloway, a graduate student at the University of Colorado. This will be our third year of studying the impact of the program on students. If you ever want to talk to either of us about this project, you may contact us at the University of Colorado, School of Education, Campus Box 249, Boulder, CO, or you can contact Marki at Margaret.lecompte@Colorado.edu or at her office at 303-492-7951.

For the past two years, we have evaluated the Arts Focus Program for Base Line Middle School. We believe it is important to include your own experiences as an Art Focus student in our studies. This year, we want to continue studying the program and its influence on you. We are interested in what you are learning in the Arts Focus Program and how the Arts Focus Program influences you personally and academically.

We may observe you during your Arts Focus classes and on field trips. During these occasions, we will take notes on the ways students and teachers talk to each other and on their activities. We also would like to include your standardized test scores, semester grades, and portfolios in our study. No student included in the study will be identified by name. Mr. Myers (the principal) and Mrs. Wheeler (the assistant principal) will assign code numbers to each student's academic record. These coded records will be followed while you're at Base Line Middle School to see how the Arts Focus Program affects achievement. Mr. Myers will keep the master code list in his possession in the building at all times so that no one will be able to see your grades and test scores.

We also would like to talk to you about your experiences in the Arts Focus Program and tape record our conversations. The interview should take approximately forty-five minutes to an hour, depending on how much you have to say. We will be tape recording our conversations with you to make sure that we remember exactly what you said, but once we have completed the project, we will erase your tape. We will make sure that no one, not even your teacher, sees or hears your interview, and we will use codes on the interviews instead of your name.

We do not believe that there are any risks to you if you participate in this project. However, we believe that your input will help improve the program. You may think about why you have been successful and/or frustrated in the program as you talk with us. You may also enjoy contributing to the improvement of the program.

Your participation in this study is voluntary, and you have the right to stop participating at any time. You also can refuse to answer any question(s) for any reason. In addition, we will use pseudonyms (fake names) to disguise the identity of all participants in any written or published material resulting from this study.

If you have any questions or concerns about participating in this project, or any unhappiness with any part of the study, you may talk to us, or write in confidence to the executive secretary, Human Research Committee, Graduate School, Campus Box 76, Regent Hall 308, University of Colorado, Boulder, CO 80309, or call 303-492-7401 and speak directly to the executive secretary.

Please sign both of these assent forms below. The one on the back of this page is for you to keep, and the other is for our records. Please sign the next page and return it **along with your parent's signed consent** in the attached self-addressed envelope.

Assent Form for "Imagining the Future, Creating the Present": For Students Involved in the Arts Focus Program

I understand the above information and agree to participate in the study titled "Imagining the Future, Creating the Present: The Impact of Arts Education on Achievement and Identity in Arts Focus."

Signature _____

Date_____

Please print your name _____

Please print the name of your parent(s) or guardian(s)

_____

EXAMPLE FOUR

Consent Form for "Enhancing HIV Prevention through Multilevel Community Intervention to Promote Women-Initiated Prevention Options"

This consent form was submitted for an Institute for Community Research study of female condom use to prevent HIV and STDs. Note the considerable attention paid to issues of confidentiality, including that the researchers obtained a Certificate of Confidentiality from the US Office of Health and Human Services. In addition, note that the researchers distinguish between benefits and compensation. They are not the same. Compensation is given to respondents in exchange for their time and the inconvenience of participating in the study. It is a fee for service, not a benefit.

Survey Consent Form

Invitation to Participate. You are invited to be in a research study about the availability, accessibility, and support for the use of the female condom (FC). You have been chosen because you are at least sixteen years of age and live in the targeted geographical area. We ask that you read, or have someone read to you, this entire form. Please do not hesitate to ask researchers any questions you have before agreeing to take part in this study.

Participation. During the one-hour interview you will be asked questions about HIV risk behaviors, and your knowledge, attitudes, and use of the FC. We also will ask for your contact information, including your local address. After the survey, you will be asked to refer up to three people you know who would want to participate in this project. Please know that you must provide an official form of identification with your photo and date of birth to confirm your identity and age before you can be included in this project.

Participation in this study is voluntary. This means that it is up to you to decide whether or not you want to be in the project. Your decision whether or not to participate will not affect your chances of being in other studies at the ICR. In addition, if you choose to participate and certain questions upset you or make you uncomfortable, you do not have to answer them. You can also drop out of this study at any time.

Confidentiality. Your participation in this project will be kept strictly confidential within the Multilevel Female Condom study team and the AIDS Research Team at the Institute for Community Research. This means that information from our different AIDS research projects might be shared between projects. An ID number, not your name, will be used on the information you share with us during this interview. However, your name will appear on this consent form and the participant information form, which will be kept in a locked file cabinet, separate from other project materials. All project documents will be kept in locked file cabinets, and all computerized information will be kept in password-protected files.

We will ask you to give us your current residential address as part of the data collected for the study. Addresses will be used only to determine the neighborhood you live in and to measure the distance between your residence and Hartford service locations. No address data or maps of your individual address or your individual neighborhood will be published or shared with anyone outside of the project team.

Project staff will never recruit people into the study directly upon referral from a participant. Referral of anyone into the study will be done by the participant herself or himself. No information that you give us about your personal contacts or people you are close to will be shared with them without your permission. Their names and all information about them will be kept strictly confidential. We will not release any information to a third party even if that person is also in the study.

Minors. In the state of Connecticut, minors may obtain testing and treatment for reproductive health without the consent of their parents or guardians. Therefore, parental consent is not required, and no information will be provided to them.

Certificate of Confidentiality. To help protect your privacy, this research is covered by a Certificate of Confidentiality issued by the federal Department of Health and Human Services. This Certificate will protect the researchers from being forced to release any data in which you are identified, even under a court order or subpoena, without your written consent.

Limits to Confidentiality. Despite our best efforts to protect your identity and the information you share with us, there are limits to confidentiality. For example, we must report sexual or physical abuse of a child, elderly, or disabled person; threats to hurt yourself; or threats to hurt others, even though this project has a Certificate of Confidentiality. If any staff member has this information, they will report it to the appropriate agencies.

Risks and Discomforts. Even though all project staff are trained to take care to maintain confidentiality, there is a possibility that some of the information you give us might accidentally be revealed. You also might feel upset or uncomfortable when discussing sensitive and personal information. To reduce these risks, 1) all project staff are trained and monitored to maintain confidentiality under the supervision of the Institute for Community Research; 2) no identifying information will be included in the survey; 3) all project materials will be kept in locked file cabinets or locked computerized data files at the ICR and will be used only for project purposes by authorized staff; 4) no individual address or neighborhood information will be published or shared with anyone outside of the project team; 5) we will not use your name or any other information that could personally identify you in project data to be presented to the public. Therefore, you will not be identifiable in any presentations or publications based upon this research.

Benefits. Benefits to you include HIV/AIDS and STD education and prevention materials like condoms; referrals to health and social services, including those related to prevention and care; and the opportunity to speak and think about your experiences with a project staff member who cares about you. In addition, the results of this study may help researchers understand more about the availability and use of the female condom for use in HIV/STD prevention.

Compensation. You will receive $25 for completing this interview. In addition, you will receive $10 for each eligible person you recruit into the study who completes the survey interview (up to three people). You can drop out of the project at any time without losing the payment or other benefits for the parts of the project you have completed.

Termination of Participation. We may ask you to leave this study if you become ineligible to participate, are disruptive, uncooperative, or too drunk or high to answer questions. If we end your participation in this study, it does not necessarily mean that you will never be allowed to join another study here in the future.

If You Have Questions. If you have questions about the project, you may contact Margaret Weeks, PhD, principal investigator, at 860-278-2044. If you have any questions about your rights as a participant in a research project you may call David Roozen, PhD, chairperson of the Institutional Review Board at the Institute for Community Research, at 860-509-9546.

I have read, or someone has read to me, the above information, and I voluntarily give my consent to take part in this research study. I understand that I may refuse to participate or stop my participation at any time without penalty. I also understand that the investigator may stop my participation in this study.

Participant's Name (please print): _____

Participant's Signature: _____

Date: _____

Interviewer's Signature: _____

Date: _____

EXAMPLE FIVE

Request for Review, "Translation of the Risk Avoidance Partnership (RAP) for Drug Treatment Clinic Implementation: Project RAP-Clinic," Submitted June 2012

OTHER CONTACT (OC) CONSENT FORM

Invitation to Participate: You are invited to participate in the RAP (Risk Avoidance Partnership) Clinic Project, a three-year collaborative study of the Institute for Community Research (ICR) and the Hartford Dispensary (HD), funded by the National Institute on Drug Abuse. The purpose of this study is to adapt a successful HIV/hepatitis/STI risk reduction project, conducted among not-in-treatment active drug users, for use among clients in drug treatment clinics. You have been chosen to be a participant in this study because you are an active drug user who is not in treatment at this time. We ask that you read, or have someone read to you, this entire form. Please do not hesitate to ask researchers any questions you have in regard to this study before agreeing to take part in this study.

Participation: Your participation in the study includes the following:

- A survey that asks about your drug use, sexual practices, health, and experiences with different HIV prevention programs, and
- It includes questions about the people who are close to you; that is, your personal network. This interview takes about one-and-a-half hours to complete.

Participation in this study is voluntary. There is no penalty if you decide not to participate. You are also free to refuse to answer any questions during any interview without penalty or loss of benefits to which you would otherwise be entitled. You can leave the study at any time. However, you will only be compensated for those interviews that you complete. Your decision whether or not to participate will not affect your chances of being in other studies at the ICR or the HD. In addition, if you choose to participate and certain questions upset you or make you uncomfortable, you do not have to answer them.

Confidentiality. The records of this project will be kept private. An ID number, not your name, will be used on all surveys and project data. Your name will be used on this consent form, as well as on documents used for follow-up activities. This means that your name can be associated with the information you give us. However, this identifying information will be stored separately from other project data. No information that you give us about your personal contacts or people you are close to will be shared with them without your permission. Their names and all information about them will also be kept strictly confidential. All project documents will be kept in a locked file cabinet, and all computerized data will be located in hidden files and are password protected. Any information from the study that we share outside the project will have all names removed. At the end of the project we will delete your digital photo from our files.

Certificate of Confidentiality. To help protect your privacy, this study has a Certificate of Confidentiality given to us by the National Institute for Health. Having this Certificate means that even if there is a court order or subpoena, we cannot be forced to release any information about you to anyone, unless you give your written consent.

Limits to Confidentiality. Despite our best efforts to protect your identity and the information you share with us, there are limits to confidentiality. For example, we must report sexual or physical abuse of a child, elderly or disabled person, threats to hurt yourself, or threats to hurt others, even though this project has a Certificate of Confidentiality. If any staff member has this information, they will report it to the appropriate agencies.

Risks and Discomforts. Even though all project staff are trained to take care to maintain confidentiality, there is a possibility that some of the information you give us might accidentally be revealed. You might also feel upset or uncomfortable when discussing personal information or exploring your own and your peers' HIV risks. To reduce these risks: 1) all project staff are trained to keep the information you share private and respond to your concerns, under the supervision of the Institute for Community Research and the Hartford Dispensary; 2) you will be identified only by a code number or pseudonym; 3) all project materials will be kept in locked file cabinets or locked computerized data files at the ICR and HD, and will be used only for project purposes by authorized staff; 4) no identifying information (name, address) will be published or shared with anyone outside of the project team; 5) we will not use your name or any other information that could personally identify you in project data to be presented to the public. Therefore, you will not be identifiable in any presentations or publications based upon this research.

Benefits. Direct benefits that come from taking part in this project include HIV/AIDS, hepatitis, and STI education and prevention materials, like condoms, bleach kits, crack kits, and informational brochures upon your request, and the opportunity to speak and think about your experiences with a project staff member who cares about you. In addition, this project offers the benefits to you and the community of the HIV prevention program that we will conduct in partnership with your peers.

Compensation. You will receive $30 for completing this survey. You can drop out of the project at any time without losing the payment or other benefits for the parts of the project you have completed.

Termination of Participation. We may ask you to leave this study if you become ineligible to participate, are disruptive, uncooperative, or too drunk or high to answer questions. If we end your participation in *this* study, it does not necessarily mean that you will never be allowed to join another study here in the future.

If You Have Questions. If you have any questions about the RAP-Clinic Project, you can contact Margaret R. Weeks, PhD, principal investigator, at 860-278-2044. If you have any questions about your rights as a participant in a research project, you can contact David Roozen, PhD, chairperson of the Institutional Review Board of the Institute for Community Research, at 860-509-9500.

I have read, or someone read to me, the above information and voluntarily give my consent to participate in this research study. I understand that I may refuse to participate and discontinue my participation at any time without penalty. I also understand that my participation in this study may be terminated by the investigator.

Participant's Name (please print): _____

Participant's Signature: _____

Date: _____

Interviewer's Signature: _____

Date: _____

EXAMPLE SIX

Consent Form for a Life History Interview
(Ms. Maestas)

This interview was requested of an eighty-six-year-old woman who had been a teacher and the wife of a teacher in New Mexico before its statehood. Mrs. Maesta knew the researcher, because she and her granddaughter were friends. Notwithstanding, Angela Johnson, the graduate student researcher, needed to obtain Mrs. Maesta's consent to participate in the study. Because of Mrs. Maesta's age and because she had some difficulty in English, she in some ways was considered to be a vulnerable subject. However, because she was well educated and understood research processes, the researcher simply "translated" the letter from the technical and academic language in which they usually are framed, and she occasionally translated a word or so into Spanish. Mrs. Maestas was very pleased to be asked to participate in this project. Furthermore, because she was very proud of her family's educational attainments, which reach well back into the 1800s, she wanted her own and their real names used. Note that Johnson did not include her home telephone in the consent form; students and most researchers are urged never to use their home telephone number as a contact in consent forms for research participants.

October 15, 1996

Dear Mrs. Maestas,

I am a graduate student in education at the University of Colorado. I am doing a project for a class I'm taking at the University of Colorado on the history of schools in New Mexico. This class is being taught by Dr. Ruben Donato; his telephone number is 303-

492-1000, and you can call him if you have any questions about the project. You also can reach me at the university at 303-492-6973.

I would be very interested in learning about your educational experiences in New Mexico and the education of your family. I would like your permission to tape record you when you tell me what you remember about going to school, what you learned, and what it was like to be a teacher. I will use the tapes of your interview to help me write my paper; after I'm done, I will return the tapes to you and your family, along with copies of the paper I write and transcripts of the tapes.

I am very excited about doing this project. Not many people realize that the Spanish American people in Northern New Mexico were graduating from high school and becoming teachers so long ago—even before the Anglo-Americans arrived from the East. I think it is very important that more people know your stories. If I do a good job on this paper, I hope to present it at conferences and maybe even submit it for publication in a journal or magazine for teachers and researchers in education.

If you would prefer, I can use a pseudonym or a fake name to protect your identity and the identity of your family members. If you have any more questions about this project or about the University of Colorado's policies about research on people, you can contact me at 417-2000 or Mary Ellen Ancell at the University of Colorado at 492-3000. Mrs. Ancell is the executive secretary of the Human Research Committee at the University of Colorado, which oversees all research projects involving people. You can report your concerns or ask your questions without fear that the Committee or Mrs. Ancell will tell anyone else that you called.

If you give your permission for me to interview you and to use the information in your interview for my paper, please read the statement of understanding below and sign on the line below it so I can show this form to the university.

Thank you for helping me.

Sincerely yours,

Angela Johnson

I understand the purpose of Angela Johnson's research project on the history of education in Northern New Mexico and I agree to be interviewed with a tape recorder for this project. I understand that I don't have to answer any questions that I don't feel like answering, and that I can end the interview any time that I wish. I understand that Angela will return the tape recordings and the paper itself to me when she has completed it.

Signed: _____

Date: _____

REFERENCES

Abu-Lughod, L. 1991. Writing against culture. In *Recapturing anthropology: Working in the present*, edited by R. G. Fox. Santa Fe, NM: School of American Research Press, 137–62.

Adams, L. G. 2014. Putting together a scientific team: Collaborative science. *Trends in Microbiology* 22 (9). doi: http://dx.doi.org/10.1016/j.tim.2014.05.001.

Adler, P., and P. Adler. 1995. Dynamics of inclusion and exclusion in preadolescent cliques. *Social Psychology Quarterly* 58 (3): 145–62.

Adler, P., and P. Adler. 1996. Preadolescent clique stratification and the hierarchy of identification. *Sociological Inquiry* 66 (2): 111–42.

Adler, P., and P. Adler. 1998. *Peer power: Preadolescent culture and identity.* New Brunswick, NJ: Rutgers University Press. Published in NetLibrary.com, 2000. Published digitally with Questia Media, Inc., 2001.

Agar, M. H. 1982. *The professional stranger: An informal introduction to ethnography.* New York: John Wiley & Sons.

Aguilera, D. E. 2003. *Who defines success?* Unpublished doctoral dissertation, Boulder, CO: School of Education, University of Colorado-Boulder.

Annas, G. J., and M. A. Grodin. 1992. *The Nazi doctors and the Nuremberg Code: Human rights in human experimentation.* London: Oxford University Press.

Aronson, R. E., A. B. Wallis, P. J. O'Campo, T. L. Whitehead, and P. Schafer. 2007. Ethnographically informed community evaluation: A framework and approach for evaluating community-based initiatives. *Maternal and Child Health Journal* 11 (2): 97–109.

Barrett, R. J., and D. B. Parker. 2003. Rites of consent: Negotiating research participation in diverse cultures. *Monash Bioethics Review* 22 (2): 9–26.

Bartunek, J., and M. R. Louis. 1996. *Insider/outsider team research.* Thousand Oaks, CA: Sage.

Baumslag, N. 2005. *Murderous medicine: Nazi doctors, human experimentation, and typhus.* New York: Praeger Publishers.

Benatar, S. R., and P. A. Singer. 2000. A new look at international research ethics. *British Medical Journal* 321 (7264): 824–26.

Benson, P., and K. Lewis O'Neill. 2007. Facing risk: Levinas, ethnography and ethics. *Anthropology of Consciousness* 18 (2): 29–55, American Anthropological Association, retrieved from www.anthrosource.net.

Bernard, H. R. 1994. *Research methods in anthropology*, second edition. Newbury Park, CA: Sage Publications.

Bernard, H. R. 1995. *Research methods in anthropology: Qualitative and quantitative approaches*, second edition. Walnut Creek, CA: AltaMira Press.

Blake, D. D. 2001. We wanted to include him: Personhood in one Hispanic family's experience of the genetic illness and loss of their son. In *Illness, Crisis & Loss* 9 (4) (October): 323–36.

Bloom, L. R. 1990. *Under the sign of hope: Feminist methodologies and narrative inquiry.* Albany, NY: State University of New York Press.

Bolton, R. 1995. Tricks, friends and lovers: Erotic encounters in the field. In *Taboo: Sex, identity, and erotic subjectivity in anthropological fieldwork*, edited by Don Kulick and Margaret Willson. London: Routledge.

Borofsky, R. 2005. *Yanomami: The fierce controversy and what we can learn from it*, volume 12. Berkeley, CA: University of California Press.

Boulton, M., and M. Parker. 2007. Informed consent in a changing environment. *Social Science & Medicine* 65 (11): 2187–98.

Boutin-Foster, C., E. Scott, J. Melendez, A. Rodriguez, R. Ramos, B. Kanna, and W. Michelen. 2013. Ethical considerations for conducting health disparities research in community health centers: A social-ecological perspective. *American Journal of Public Health* 103 (12): e1–e5. doi: 10.2105/ajph.2013.301599.

Braroe, N. L. 1971. *Indian and white: Self-image and interaction in a Canadian Plains community.* Stanford, CA: Stanford University Press.

Briody, E., T. M. Pester, and R. Trotter. 2012. A story's impact on organizational-culture change. *Journal of Organizational Change Management* 25 (1): 67–87.

Brosted, J., J. Dahl, A. Gray, H. C. Gullov, G. Hendriksen, J. B. Jorgensen, and I. Kleivan. 1985. *Native power: The quest for autonomy and nationood of indigenous peoples.* Oslo, Norway: Universitetsforlaget AS.

Brydon-Miller, M., D. Greenwood, and P. Maguire. 2003. Why action research? *Action Research* 1 (1): 9–28.

Buchholz, T. G. 1984. Margaret Mead and Samoa, by Derek Freeman. *Commentary.*

Burdick, J. 1995. Uniting theory and practice in the ethnography of social movements: Notes toward a hopeful realism. *Dialectical Anthropology* 20 (3–4): 361–85. doi: 10.1007/bf01298535.

Burgess, R. G. 1985. In the company of teachers: Key informants and the study of a comprehensive school. In *Strategies of Educational Research: Qualitative Methods*, edited by Robert G. Burgess. London: Falmer Press, 79–100.

Burnett, J. H. 1974. On the analog between culture acquisition and ethnographic method. *Anthropology and Education Quarterly* 5 (1): 25–29.

Cannon-Bowers, J. A., and E. Salas. 1998. Team performance and training in complex environments: Recent findings from applied research. *Current Directions in Psychological Science* 7 (3): 83–87.

Cargo, M., and S. L. Mercer. 2008. The value and challenges of participatory research: Strengthening its practice. *Annual Review of Public Health* 29:325–50.

Chenhall, R., K. Senior, and S. Belton. 2011. Negotiating human research ethics: Case notes from anthropologists in the field. *Anthropology Today* 27 (5):13–17. doi: 10.1111/j.1467-8322.2011.00827.

Clifford, G., and G. Marcus. 1986. *Writing culture: The poetics and politics of ethnography.* Berkeley, CA: University of California Press.

Clinton, W. J. 1997. Apology for the study done in Tuskeegee. The White House, Office of the Press Secretary, May 16. Retrieved from http://Clinton4.nara.gov/textonly/New/Remarks/fr.19970516-898html.

Cole, M., and P. Griffin. 1987. An embedded context framework. In *Contextual factors in education: Improving science and mathematics education for minorities and women.* Laboratory for Comparative Human Cognition, Wisconsin Center for Education Research, School of Education, Madison, Wisconsin, 6.

Commission for the Protection of Human Subjects of Biomedical and Behavioral Research. 1978. *The Belmont Report.*

Cooke, N. J., J. A. Cannon-Bowers, P. A. Kiekel, K. Rivera, R. Stout, and E. Salas. 2000. Improving teams' interpositional knowledge through cross training. *Proceedings of the Human Factors and Ergonomics Society Annual Meeting* 44 (11): 390–93. doi: 10.1177/154193120004401116

Critchfield, R. (1978). *Look to suffering, look to joy: Robert Redfield and Oscar Lewis restudied, Part 1.* Austin, TX: American Universities Field Staff.

Cromley, E. 2013. Mapping spatial data. In *Specialized ethnographic methods: A mixed methods approach*, volume 4, edited by J. J. Schensul and M. D. LeCompte. Lanham, MD: Rowman & Littlefield, AltaMira Press.

D'Andrade, R. 1995. Moral models in anthropology. *Current Anthropology* 36 (3):399–408.

Davidson, A. L. 1996. *Making and molding identity in schools.* Purchase, NY: State University of New York Press.

Denzin, N. K., and Y. S. Lincoln. 2011. *The SAGE handbook of qualitative research.* Thousand Oaks, CA: Sage.

Dewey, J. 2004. *Democracy and education.* New York: Courier Dover Publications.

Deyhle, D. M. 1986. Break dancing and breaking out: Anglos, Utes, and Navajos in a border reservation school. *Anthropology and Education Quarterly* 17:111–27.

Deyhle, D. M. 2005. Journey toward social justice: Curriculum change and educational equity in a Navajo community. In *Narrative & experience in multicultural education*, edited by J. Phillion, M. F. He, and F. M. Connelly. Thousand Oaks, CA: Sage.

Deyhle, D. M. 2009. *Reflections in place: Connected lives of Navajo women.* Tucson, AZ: University of Arizona Press.

Deyhle, D. M., G. A. Hess, and M. D. LeCompte. 1992. Approaching ethical issues for qualitative researchers in education. In *The handbook of qualitative research in education*, edited by M. D. LeCompte, W. Millroy, and J. Preissle. San Diego, CA: Academic Press, 597–643.

Deyhle, D. M., and M. D. LeCompte. 1994. Conflict over child development: Navajo culture and the middle schools. *Theory into Practice* 23 (3): 156–67.

Dobrin, L., and R. Lederman. 2010. Human subjects research protections: Enhancing protections for research subjects and reducing burden, delay, and ambiguity for investigators. ANPRM, 76 FR 44512. http://www.aaanet.org/issues/policy-advocacy/upload/AAA-Ethics-Code-2009.pdf.

Edelman, M. 2001. Social movements: Changing paradigms and forms of politics. *Annual Review of Anthropology* 30:285–317.

Erickson, F. 1985/1986. Qualitative methods in research on teaching. In *The handbook of research in teaching*, 3rd edition, edited by M. C. Wittrock. New York: Macmillan, 119–61.

Fals Borda, O. 1992. Social movements and political power in Latin America. In *The making of social movements in Latin America: Identity, strategy, and democracy*, edited by A. Escobar and S. E. Alvarez. New York: Westview Press, 303–16.

Fang, F. C., R. G. Steen, and A. Casadevall. 2012. Misconduct accounts for the majority of retracted scientific publications. *Proceedings of the National Academy of Sciences* 109 (42). doi: 10.1073/pnas.1212247109.

Firth, R. 1936. *We, the Tikopia: A sociological study of kinship in primitive Polynesia.* New York: American Book Co.

Flicker, S., R. Travers, A. Guta, S. McDonald, and A. Meagher. 2007. Ethical dilemmas in community-based participatory research: Recommendations for institutional review boards. *Journal of Urban Health* 84 (4): 478–93.

Foley, D. E. 1994. *Learning capitalist culture: Deep in the heart of Tejas.* Philadelphia: University of Pennsylvania Press.

Foley, D. E. 1995. *The heartland chronicles.* Philadelphia: University of Pennsylvania Press.

Freeman, D. 1983. *Margaret Mead and Samoa: The making and unmaking of an anthropological myth.* Cambridge: Harvard University Press.

Friel, S., M. Marmot, A. J. McMichael, T. Kjellstrom, and D. Vågerö. 2008. Global health equity and climate stabilisation: A common agenda. *The Lancet* 372 (9650): 1677–83.

Frisby, W., P. Maguire, and C. Reid. 2009. The "f" word has everything to do with it: How feminist theories inform action research. *Action Research* 7 (1): 13–29.

Galman, S. C. 2007. *Shane, the lone ethnographer: A beginner's guide to ethnography.* Lanham, MD: AltaMira Press.

Geertz, C. 1973. *The interpretation of cultures.* New York: Basic Books.

Geertz, C. 1989–1990. *Works and lives: The anthropologist as author.* Stanford, CA: Stanford University Press.

Gibson, M. A. 1985. Collaborative educational ethnography: Problems and profits. In *Applying educational anthropology*, special issue of the *Anthropology and Education Quarterly* 16 (2) (Summer): 124–48.

Gibson, M. A. 1988. *Accommodation without assimilation: Punjabi Sikh immigrants in an American high school.* New York: Cornell University Press.

Goffman, E. 1959. *The presentation of self in everyday life.* Garden City, NY: Doubleday.

Goffman, E. 1960. *Asylums: Essays on the social situation of mental patients and other inmates.* New York: Doubleday Anchor Books.

Goodwin, J., J. M. Jasper, and F. Polletta. 2009. *Passionate politics: Emotions and social movements.* Chicago: University of Chicago Press.

Greaves, T. (Ed.) 1994. *Intellectual property rights for indigenous peoples: A sourcebook.* Oklahoma City: Society for Applied Anthropology.

Greaves, T. 1996. Tribal rights. In *Valuing local knowledge: Indigenous people and intellectual property rights*. Washington, DC: Island Press, 25–40.

Grignon, J., K. Wong, and S. Seifer. 2008. *Ensuring community-level research protections*. Paper presented at the Proceedings of the 2007 Educational Conference Call Series on Institutional Review Boards and Ethical Issues in Research. Seattle, WA: Community-Campus Partnerships for Health.

Gubrium, A. C., A. L. Hill, and S. Flicker. 2013. A situated practice of ethics for participatory visual and digital methods in public health research and practice: A focus on digital storytelling. *American Journal of Public Health* 104 (9): e1–e9. doi: 10.2105/ajph.2013.301310.

Hagstrom, R. M., S. R. Glasser, A. B. Brill, and R. M. Heyssel. 1969. Long term effects of radioactive iron administered during human pregnancy. *American Journal of Epidemiology* 90 (1): 1.

Haney, C., W. C. Banks, and P. Zimbardo. 1973. Interpersonal dynamics in a simulated prison. *International Journal of Criminology and Penology* 1 (1): 69–97.

Harding, S. G. 2002. Rethinking standpoint epistemology: What is "strong objectivity"? *Knowledge and inquiry: Readings in epistemology*, edited by K. B. Wray. New York: Broadview Press, 352–84.

Harding, S. G. 2004. *The feminist standpoint theory reader: Intellectual and political controversies*. New York: Psychology Press.

Hartsock, N. C. 1983. The feminist standpoint: Developing the ground for a specifically feminist historical materialism. In *Discovering reality: Feminist perspectives on epistemology, metaphysics, methodology and philosophy of science*, edited by S. Harding and M. Hintikka. Boston, MA: Reidel.

Heath, S. B. 1996. Postmodern narrative and its consequences in knowledge transition. Lecture 1, School of Education, University of Colorado, September 30.

Henry-Waring, M. S. 2004. Moving beyond otherness: Exploring the polyvocal subjectivities of African Caribbean women across the United Kingdom. *Hecate* 30 (1): 31–41.

Hopper, K. 1990. Research findings as testimony: A note on the ethnographer as expert witness. *Human Organization* 49 (2): 110–13.

Horowitz, C. R., M. Robinson, and S. Seifer. 2009. Community-based participatory research from the margin to the mainstream: Are researchers prepared? *Circulation* 119 (19): 2633–42. doi: 10.1161/circulationaha.107.729863.

Horton, R., R. Beaglehole, R. Bonita, J. Raeburn, M. McKee, and S. Wall. 2014. From public to planetary health: A manifesto. *The Lancet* 383 (9920): 847.

Humphreys, L. 1970a. *The tearoom trade: Impersonal sex in public places*. London: Duckworth.

Humphreys, L. 1970b. Tearoom trade: Impersonal sex in public places, in *Transaction* (January): 10–26.

Ioannidis, J. P. A. 2011. An epidemic of false claims: Competition and conflicts of interest distort too many medical findings. *Scientific American* 304 (6).

Israel, B. A., E. Eng, A. J. Schulz, and E. A. Parker (Eds.). 2005. *Methods in community-based participatory research for health*. San Francisco: Jossey-Bass Publishers.

Israel, B. A., E. Eng, A. J. Schulz, and E. A. Parker. (Eds.). 2013. *Methods for community-based participatory research for health.* San Francisco, CA: Jossey-Bass.

Johnson, T. E., and D. L. O'Connor. 2008. Measuring team shared understanding using the analysis-constructed shared mental model methodology. *Performance Improvement Quarterly* 21 (3): 113–34. doi: 10.1002/piq.20034.

Johnston, B. R., & H. M. Barker. 2008. *Consequential damages of nuclear war: The Rongelap Report.* Walnut Creek, CA: Left Coast Press.

Jones, J. 1993. *Bad blood: New and expanded edition.* New York: Simon and Schuster.

Kalichman, S. C. 2009. *Denying AIDS: Conspiracy theories, pseudoscience, and human tragedy.* New York: Springer.

Keating, N. 2012. Spirits of the forest: Cambodia's Kuy People practice spirit-based conservation. *Cultural Survival Quarterly, 40 Years of Advocacy* 36 (2) (June).

Kelley, A., A. Belcourt-Dittloff, C. Belcourt, and G. Belcourt. 2013. Research ethics and indigenous communities. *American Journal of Public Health* 103 (12): e1–e7. doi: 10.2105/ajph.2013.301522

Kennedy, B. 2012, November. I am the river and the river is me: The implications of a river receiving personhood status. *Cultural Survival Quarterly, Free Prior and Informed Consent,* 36–40.

Khan, F. 2008. The human factor: Globalizing ethical standards in drug trials through market exclusion. *UGA Legal Studies Research Paper* (08-007).

Kimmelman, J. 2008. The ethics of gene transfer. *Nature Reviews|Genetics* 9 (March): 239.

Klein, N. 2007. *The shock doctrine: The rise of disaster capitalism.* New York: Henry Holt and Co.

Krugman, S., and R. Ward. 1961. Infectious diseases of children. *The American Journal of the Medical Sciences* 242 (2): 128.

Lambek, M. 2010. *Ordinary ethics: Anthropology, language and action.* New York: Fordham University Press.

Langhout, R. D. 2011. Facilitating the development of social change agents. *Human Development* 54 (5): 339–42.

Laska, S., and K. Peterson. 2011. The convergence of catastrophes and social change: The role of participatory action research in support of the new engaged citizen. *Journal of Applied Social Science* 5 (1): 24–36.

Lather, P. 1986. Research as praxis. *Harvard Educational Review* 56:257–77.

Lather, P., and C. Smithies. 1997. *Troubling the angels: Women living with HIV/AIDS.* Boulder, CO: Westview Press.

LeCompte, M. D. 1974. *Institutional constraints on teacher styles and the development of student work norms.* Unpublished PhD dissertation, Department of Education and the Social Order, University of Chicago, Chicago, Illinois.

LeCompte, M. D. 1993a. The loss of community culture in the culture of school reform: Teaching Navajo culture vs. teaching culturally Navajo. Paper presented at the American Anthropological Association Meetings, Washington, D.C.

LeCompte, M. D. 1993b. Controlling the discourse of culture: School reform as an obstacle to reform in an American Indian public school district. Paper presented at the American Educational Research Association Meetings, Atlanta, Georgia, April 12–16.

LeCompte, M.D. 2004. Using complementary research methods in education: Field methods. Round table discussion, American Educational Research Association, San Diego, CA, April 13.

LeCompte, M. D. 2008a. Secondary participants. *SAGE Encyclopedia of Qualitative Research Methods.* Newbury Park, CA: Sage Publications.

LeCompte, M. D. 2008b. Negotiating exit. *SAGE Encyclopedia of Qualitative Research Methods.* Newbury Park, CA: Sage Publications.

LeCompte, M.D. 2015. Ethics in interpretation. In *International handbook of interpretation in educational research methods*, edited by P. Smeyers, D. Bridges, N. C. Burbules, and M. Griffiths. Dordrecht: Springer.

LeCompte, M. D., and D. McLaughlin. 1994. Witchcraft and blessings, science and rationality: Discourses of power and silence in collaborative work with Navajo schools. In *Power and method: Political activism and educational research*, edited by A. Gitlin. New York: Routledge, 147–66.

LeCompte, M. D., and J. Preissle. 1993. *Ethnography and qualitative design in educational research.* San Diego, CA: Academic Press.

LeCompte, M. D., and J. J. Schensul. 1999. *Designing and conducting ethnographic research*, Book One of the *Ethnographer's toolkit.* Lanham, MD: AltaMira Press.

LeCompte, M. D., and J. J. Schensul. 2010. *Designing and conducting ethnographic research: An introduction*, Book 1 of the *Ethnographer's toolkit*, 2nd edition. Lanham, MD: AltaMira Press.

LeCompte, M. D., and J. J. Schensul. 2013. *Analysis and interpretation of ethnographic data: A mixed methods approach*, Book 5 of the *Ethnographer's toolkit*, 2nd edition. Lanham, MD: AltaMira Press.

LeCompte, M. D., and J. J. Schensul, with M. Weeks and M. Singer. 1999. *Researcher roles and research partnerships*, Book 6 of the *Ethnographer's toolkit*, 1st edition. Lanham, MD: AltaMira Press.

Leeuw, S. D., E. S. Cameron, and M. L. Greenwood. 2012. Participatory and community-based research, Indigenous geographies, and the spaces of friendship: A critical engagement. *Canadian Geographer/Le Géographe canadien* 56 (2): 180–94. doi: 10.1111/j.1541-0064.2012.00434.x.

Lévesque, M. C., S. Dupéré, C. Loignon, A. Levine, I. Laurin, A. Charbonneau, and C. Bedos. 2009. Bridging the poverty gap in dental education: How can people living in poverty help us? *Journal of Dental Education* 73 (9): 1043–54.

Levinas, E. 1981. *Otherwise than being: Or, beyond essence*, trans. by Alphonso Lingis. Hague: Nijhoff.

Levine, R. J. 1988. *Ethics and regulation of clinical research.* New Haven, CT: Yale University Press.

Levine, R. J. 1998. The "best proven therapeutic method" standard in clinical trials in technologically developing countries. *IRB: A Review of Human Subjects Research* 20 (1): 5–9.

Lewis, O. 1966. *The children of Sanchez: Autobiography of a Mexican family.* New York: Random House.

Liebow, E. 2003. *Tally's corner: A study of Negro streetcorner men.* Lanham, MD: Rowman & Littlefield.

Lurie, P., and S. M. Wolfe. 1997. Unethical trials of interventions to reduce perinatal transmission of the human immunodeficiency virus in developing countries. *New England Journal of Medicine* 337:853–56.

Macaulay, A. C., L. E. Commanda, W. L. Freeman, N. Gibson, M. L. McCabe, C. M. Robbins, and P. L. Twohig. 1999. Participatory research maximises community and lay involvement. [10.1136/bmj.319.7212.774]. *BMJ* 319 (7212): 774–78.

Macklin, R. 2004. *Double standards in medical research in developing countries*, volume 2. London: Cambridge University Press.

Magaña, M. R. 2010. Analyzing the meshwork as an emerging social movement formation: An ethnographic account of the popular assembly of the peoples of Oaxaca (APPO). *Journal of Contemporary Anthropology* 1 (1): 5.

Maguire, P. 2001/2006. Uneven ground: Feminisms and action research. In *Handbook of action research: Concise paperback edition*, edited by P. Reason and H. Bradbury (eds). London: Sage, 60–70.

Mahon, M. 2000. The visible evidence of cultural producers. *American Review of Anthropology* 29:467–92.

Malacrida, C. 2007. Reflexive journaling on emotional research topics: Ethical issues for team researchers. *Qualitative Health Research* 17 (10): 1329–39. doi: 10.1177/1049732307308948.

Manderson, L., M. Kelaher, G. Williams, and C. Shannon. 1998. The politics of community: Negotiation and consultation in research on women's health. *Human Organization* 57 (2): 222–29.

Mangual Figueroa, A. 2013. La carta de responsabilidad: The problem of departure. In *Humanizing research: Decolonizing qualitative inquiry with youth and communities*, edited by D. Paris and M. T. Winn, 129–46. Thousand Oaks, CA: Sage Publications.

Marcus, G., and M. Fischer. 1986. *Anthropology as cultural critique: An experimental moment in the human sciences*. Chicago: University of Chicago Press.

Marshall, P. A. 1992. Research ethics in applied anthropology. *IRB: Ethics and Human Research* 14 (6): 1–5. doi: 10.2307/3563851.

Marshall, P. A., and C. Rotimi. 2001. Ethical challenges in community-based research. *The American Journal of the Medical Sciences* 322 (5): 241–45.

McDonald, K. E., and D. M. Raymaker. 2013. Paradigm shifts in disability and health: Toward more ethical public health research. *American Journal of Public Health* e1–e9. doi: 10.2105/ajph.2013.301286.

McKee, M., D. Schlehofer, and D. Thew. 2013. Ethical issues in conducting research with deaf populations. *American Journal of Public Health* e1–e6. doi: 10.2105/ajph.2013.301343.

McMichael, A. J. 1995. The health of persons, populations, and planets: Epidemiology comes full circle. *Epidemiology* 6 (6): 633–36.

Mead, M. 1928. *Coming of age in Samoa: A psychological study of primitive youth for Western civilization*. New York: Murrow.

Medicine, B., edited with S. Jacobs. 2001. *Learning to be an anthropologist and remaining "Native."* Champaign, IL: University of Illinois Press.

Metz, M. H. 1978. *Classrooms and corridors: The crisis of authority in desegregated secondary schools.* Berkeley, CA: University of California Press.

Mikesell, L., E. Bromley, and D. Khodyakov. 2013. Ethical community-engaged research: A literature review. *American Journal of Public Health* 103 (12): e1–e8. doi: 10.2105/ajph.2013.301605.

Milgram, S. 1963. Behavioral study of obedience. *Journal of Abnormal and Social Psychology* 67 (4): 371.

Minkler, M., and N. Wallerstein. 2010. *Community-based participatory research for health: From process to outcomes.* Hoboken, NJ: John Wiley & Sons.

Moolchan, E. T., and R. Mermelstein. 2002. Research on tobacco use among teenagers: Ethical challenges. *Journal of Adolescent Health* 30 (6): 409–17. http://dx.doi.org/10.1016/S1054-139X(02)00365-8.

Nastasi, B. K., J. J. Schensul, M. W. A. deSilva, K. Varjas, K. T. Silva, P. Ratnayake, and S. L. Schensul. 1998–1999. Community-based sexual risk prevention program for Sri Lankan youth: Influencing sexual-risk decision making. *International Quarterly of Community Health Education* 18 (1): 139–55.

Nielson, J. M. 1990. *Feminist research methods: Exemplary readings in the social sciences.* Boulder, CO: Westview Press.

Newman, S. D., J. O. Andrews, G. S. Magwood, C. Jenkins, M. J. Cox, and D. C. Williamson. 2011. Peer reviewed: Community advisory boards in community-based participatory research: A synthesis of best processes. *Preventing Chronic Disease* 8 (3).

Noe, T. D., S. M. Manson, S. C. Croy, H. McGough, J. A. Henderson, and D. S. Buchwald. 2006. In their own voices: American Indian decisions to participate in health research. In *The handbook of ethical research with ethnocultural populations and communities,* edited by J. E. Trimble and C. B. Fisher. Thousand Oaks, CA: Sage.

Parker, M. 2007. Ethnography/ethics. *Social Science and Medicine* 65:2248–59.

Pearson, J. P., and M. D. LeCompte. 1986. Cultural transmission in a prison school setting: The construction of identity. Paper presented at the American Anthropological Association, Philadelphia, Pennsylvania, December.

Pelto, P. J., and G. H. Pelto. 1978. *Anthropological research: The structure of inquiry,* 2nd edition. Cambridge, England: Cambridge University Press.

Peshkin, A. 1988. Discovering subjectivities: One's own. *Educational Researcher* 17 (7): 17–21.

Petryna, A. 2007. Clinical trials offshored: On private sector science and public health. *BioSocieties* 2 (1): 21–40.

Pierce, J. R., and J. Writer. 2005. *Yellow jack: How yellow fever ravaged America and Walter Reed discovered its deadly secrets.* New York: John Wiley and Sons.

Portalewska, A. 2012. Free prior and informed consent: Protecting indigenous peoples' rights to self-determination, participation and decision-making. *Cultural Survival Quarterly* 36 (4) (December).

Postma, J. 2008. Balancing power among academic and community partners: The case of El Proyecto Bienestar. *Journal of Empirical Research on Human Research Ethics* 3 (2).

Powdermaker, H. 1966. *Stranger and friend: The way of an anthropologist.* New York: W. W. Norton & Company, Inc.

Quinn, S. C. 2004. Health policy and ethics forum. Ethics in public health research: Protecting human subjects: The role of community advisory boards. *American Journal of Public Health* 94 (6): 918–22. doi: 10.2105/ajph.94.6.918.

Radda, K. E., and J. J. Schensul. 2011. Building living alliances: Community engagement and community-based partnerships to address the health of community elders. *Annals of Anthropological Practice* 35 (2): 154–73.

Ragin, C. C. 2014. *The comparative method: Moving beyond qualitative and quantitative strategies*. Berkeley, CA: University of California Press.

Redfield, R. 1956. *The little community*. Chicago: University of Chicago Press.

Roman, L. G. 1988. Intimacy, labor and class: Ideologies of feminine sexuality in the punk slam dance. In *Becoming feminine: The politics of popular culture*, edited by L. G. Roman, L. Christian-Smith, and E. Ellsworth, 148–70. London: Falmer Press.

Roman, L. G. 1992. The political significance of other ways of narrating ethnography: A feminist materialist approach. In *The handbook of qualitative research in education*, edited by M. D. LeCompte, W. L. Millroy, and J. Preissle, 555–94. San Diego, CA: Academic Press.

Roman, L. G. 1993. Double exposure: The politics of feminist materialist ethnography. *Educational Theory* 43 (3): 278–309.

Rosen, L. 1977. The anthropologist as expert witness. *American Anthropologist* 79 (3): 555–78.

Rothman, D. J. 1982. Were Tuskegee and Willowbrook "studies in nature"? *Hastings Center Report* 12 (2): 5–7.

Rothstein, M. A. 2013. Ethical research and minorities. *American Journal of Public Health* 103 (12): e1. doi: 10.2105/ajph.2013.301390.

Ryle, G. 1949. *The concept of the mind*. London: Hutchinson.

Rylko-Bauer, B., M. Singer, and J. V. Willigen. 2006. Reclaiming applied anthropology: Its past, present, and future. *American Anthropologist* 108 (1): 178–90.

Said, E. W. 1978. *Orientalism*. New York: Pantheon.

Said, E. W. 1989. Representing the colonized: Anthropological interlocutors. *Critical Inquiry* 15:205–25.

Said, E. W. 1994. *Culture and imperialism*. New York: Vintage.

Sandoval, C. 2000. *Methodology of the oppressed*. Minneapolis, MN: University of Minnesota Press.

Schensul, J. J. 2002. Democratizing science through social science research partnerships. *Bulletin of Science, Technology & Society* 22 (3): 190–202.

Schensul, J. J. 2009. Community, culture and sustainability in multilevel dynamic systems intervention science. *American Journal of Community Psychology* 43 (3–4): 241–56.

Schensul, J. J. 2010. 2010 Malinowski Award Presentation Talk. Engaged universities, community based research organizations and third sector science in a global system. *Human Organization* 69 (4): 307–20.

Schensul, J. J., N. Diaz, and S. Wooley. 1996. Measuring activity expenditures of Puerto Rican children. In *The Proceedings of the Second Annual Conference of the National Puerto Rican Studies Association, San Juan, Puerto Rico*.

Schensul, J. J., and M. D. LeCompte. 2012. *Specialized ethnographic methods: A mixed methods approach*. Book 4 of the *Ethnographer's toolkit*, 2nd edition. Lanham, MD: volume 4. AltaMira Press.

Schensul, J. J., and M. D. LeCompte. 2013. *Essential ethnographic methods: A mixed methods approach*. Book 3 of the *Ethnographer's toolkit*, 2nd edition. Lanham, MD: AltaMira Press.

Schensul, J. J., and M. D. LeCompte. (forthcoming 2015). *Ethnography in practice: A mixed methods approach*. Book 7 of the *Ethnographer's toolkit*, 2nd edition. Lanham, MD: AltaMira Press.

Schensul, J. J., Margaret D. LeCompte, G. Alfred Hess, Bonnie K. Nastasi, Marlene J. Berg, Lynne Williamson, Jeremy Brecher, and Ruth Glasser. 1999. *Using Ethnographic Data: Interventions, Public Programming, and Public Policy*. Lanham, MD: AltaMira Press.

Schensul, J. J., K. Radda, E. Coman, and E. Vazquez. 2009. Multi-level intervention to prevent influenza infections in older low income and minority adults. *American Journal of Community Psychology* 43 (3–4): 313–29.

Schensul, J. J., S. Schensul, and M. D. LeCompte. 2013. *Initiating ethnographic research: A mixed methods approach*. Book 2 of the *Ethnographer's toolkit*, 2nd edition. Lanham, MD: AltaMira Press.

Schensul, J. J., S. Singh, K. Gupta, K. Bryant, and R. Verma. 2010. Alcohol and HIV in India: A review of current research and intervention. *AIDS and Behavior* 14:1–7.

Schensul, S. L. 1973. Action research: The applied anthropologist in a community mental health program. In *Anthropology beyond the university*, edited by A. Redfield. *Southern Anthropological Society Proceedings* (7). Athens: University of Georgia Press.

Schensul, S. L., and J. Schensul. 1978. Advocacy and applied anthropology. In *Social scientists as advocates: Views from the applied disciplines*, edited by G. Weber and G. McCall. Beverly Hills, CA: Sage.

Schensul, S. L., J. J. Schensul, M. Singer, M. Weeks, and M. Brault. 2014. Participatory methods and community-based collaborations. In *Handbook of methods in cultural anthropology*, edited by R. Bernard and L. Gravlee, 185–214. Lanham, MD: AltaMira Press.

Scheper-Hughes, N. 1995. Primacy of the ethical. *Current Anthropology* 36 (3): 409–20.

Shankman, P. 2009. *The trashing of Margaret Mead: Anatomy of an anthropological controversy*. Madison: University of Wisconsin Press.

Sherman, R. R., and R. B. Webb. 1988. *Qualitative research in education*. New York: Taylor & Francis.

Shore, N., R. Brazauskas, E. Drew, K. A. Wong, L. Moy, A. C. Baden, and S. D. Seifer. 2011. Understanding community-based processes for research ethics review: A national study. *Journal of Information* 101(S1).

Shore, N., E. Drew, R. Brazauskas, and S. D. Seifer. 2011. Relationships between community-based processes for research ethics review and institution-based IRBs: A national study. *Journal of Empirical Research on Human Research Ethics: An International Journal* 6 (2): 13–21. doi: 10.1525/jer.2011.6.2.13.

Shore, N., K. A. Wong, S. D. Seifer, J. Grignon, and G. Vanessa Northington. 2008. Introduction to special issue: Advancing the ethics of community-based participatory research. *Journal of Empirical Research on Human Research Ethics: An International Journal* 3 (2): 1–4. doi: 10.1525/jer.2008.3.2.1.

Sieber, J. E. 1993. The ethics and politics of sensitive research. *Sage Focus Editions* 152: 14.

Sieber J. E. n.d. Laud Humphreys and the tearoom sex study. WebMissouri.edu, http://web.missouri.edu/~bondesonw/Laud.html.

Sieber, J. E., and M. B. Tolich. 2013. *Planning ethically responsible research*, volume 31. Thousand Oaks, CA: Sage.

Silva, K. T., S. Schensul, J. Schensul, A. de Silva, B. K. Nastasi, C. Sivayoganathan, J. Lewis, P. Wedisinghe, P. Ratnayake, M. Eisenberg, and H. Aponso. 1997. *Youth and Sexual Risk in Sri Lanka*. Phase II Report.

Singer, M. 1997. Needle exchange and AIDS prevention: Controversies, policies and research. *Medical Anthropology* 18 (1): 1–12.

Singer, M., D. Himmelgreen, M. R. Weeks, K. E. Radda, and R. Martinez. 1997. Changing the environment of AIDS risk: Findings on syringe exchange and pharmacy sales of syringes in Hartford, CT. *Medical Anthropology* 18 (1): 107–30.

Sivayoganathan, C., J. Lewis, P. Wedisinghe, P. Ratnayake, M. Eisenberg, and H. Aponso. 1997. *Youth and sexual risk in Sri Lanka*. Phase II Report.

Spivak, G. C. 1988. Can the subaltern speak? In *Marxism and the interpretation of culture*, edited by C. Nelson and L. Grossberg, 271–313. Basingstoke: Macmillan Education.

Spradley, J. P. 1979. *The ethnographic interview*. New York: Holt, Rinehart & Winston.

Spriggs, M. 2004. Canaries in the mines: Children, risk, non-therapeutic research, and justice. *Journal of Medical Ethics* 30 (2): 176–81.

Sumsion, J. 2014. Opening up possibilities through team research: An investigation of infants' lives in early childhood education settings. *Qualitative Research* 14 (2): 149–65. doi: 10.1177/1468794112468471.

Tolich, M., and M. H. Fitzgerald. 2006. If ethics committees were designed for ethnography. *Journal of Empirical Research on Human Research Ethics* 1 (2) (June): 17–18.

Trimble, J. E., and C. B. Fisher. 2006. *The handbook of ethical research with ethnocultural populations and communities*. Thousand Oaks, CA: Sage.

Turnbull, C. 1987. *The mountain people*. New York: Touchstone.

Voithofer, R. 2005. Designing new media education research: The materiality of data, representation and dissemination. *Educational Researcher* 34 (9): 3–14.

Wax, R. 1971. *Doing fieldwork: Warnings and advice*. Chicago: University of Chicago Press.

Weber, M. 1949. *The methodology of the social sciences*, translated and edited by E. Shils and H. Finch. New York: Free Press.

Weber, M. 1968. *Economy and society: An outline of interpretive sociology*, edited by Guenter Roth and Claus Wittich. Berkeley, CA: University of California Press.

Weeks, M. R., J. Li, E. Coman, M. Abbott, L. Sylla, M. Corbett, and J. Dickson-Gomez. 2010. Multilevel social influences on female condom use and adoption among women in the urban United States. *AIDS Patient Care and STDs* 24 (5): 297–309.

Weller, S. C., and A. K. Romney. 1988. *Systematic data collection. Sage university paper series on qualitative research methods*, volume 10. Beverly Hills, CA: Sage Publications.

Werner, O., and G. M. Schoepfle. 1987. *Systematic fieldwork*, volumes 1 and 2. Newbury Park, CA: Sage Publications.

Whiteford, L. M., and R. T. Trotter, III. 2008. *Ethics for anthropological research and practice*. Long Grove, IL: Waveland Press.

Whiting, B. B., and J. Whiting. 1963. *Six cultures: Studies of child rearing*. New York: John Wiley and Sons.

Whyte, W. F. 1991. *Participatory action research*. Newbury Park, CA: Sage.

Whyte, W. F. 1991, 2012. *Street corner society: The social structure of an Italian slum*. Chicago: University of Chicago Press.

World Medical Association. 2015. *WMA Declaration of Helsinki: Ethical Principles for Medical Research Involving Human Subjects*. http://www.wma.net/en/30publications/10policies/b3/index.html.

Zimbardo, P. 2007. *The Lucifer effect: Understanding how good people turn evil*. New York: Random House.

INDEX

Note: Page numbers in italics refer to figures and tables.

AAA (American Anthropological
  Association), 74–76, 159, 193, 196, 210
abortion studies, 62, 106
absent presence, 4
abuse, 27, 66, 199–200
adornment, personal, 152–53
adverse events, 105, 108, 206. *See also*
  harm
advisory bodies, 84–87, 177, 197–99
advocacy, 6–8
affiliations, 157–58, 162–65, 227, 229
Afghanistan, 225
Africa, 6, 44–45, 146, 210
African Americans: adolescent sexual
  risk studies, 85; cultural imitation
  and criticism, 154; dental care studies
  and class disparaties, 155; hiring
  decisions and perceptions, 162–63;
  researcher's ethnicity and racism risks,
  149; researcher's ethnicity impacting
  research on, 152; syphilis studies on,
  37–39
age, as personal characteristic, 137,
  143–45, 151
Aguilar, Jemel, 60
Alabama syphilis studies, 37–39
alcohol studies, 83–84, 86, 184–85, 186
Altice, Richard, 60
Alzheimer's disease studies, 133–34
American Anthropological Association
  (AAA), 74–76, 159, 193, 196, 210
American Bar Association, 49

American Folklore Association, 210
American Indians. *See* Native Americans;
  Navajo Nation
American Medical Association, 49
American Psychological Association, 210
American Sociological Association, 210
ancestors, as living entities, 11–12
anonymity, 10–11, 30, 68, 70–71, 95, 224
Anthropology Newsletter, 159
antibiotics, 190
arrests, 29–30, 61, 137, 146, 188
arsenic poisoning, 232–33
assent letters, 54–55, 60–61, 103, 317–28,
  333–35
asthma, 169–70
attractiveness, 146–47, 148
audiovisual data, 100, 101
audits, 205–6
authorities: coercion as undue influence
  of, 67; field identities linked to, 131;
  obedience studies, 46–47; risk of
  retaliation from, 48, 54. *See also* illegal
  activities; legal risks
authority obedience experiments, 46–47
authorship, 76–81, 91

Bangladesh, 232–33
Barker, Holly M., 7
beauty, 146–47, 148
Belmont Commission, 50
Belmont Report (Code of Federal
  Regulations, Title 45, Section 46):

coercion issues, 66–68; confidentiality concerns, 68–71; consent process, 53–55, 218; enforcement of, 50, 97; overview and description, 50–51; principles of, 51–53, 206; researcher's reflection on guidelines of, 260–62; risk potential disclosure guidelines, 55–57; social science exclusion in, 208–10; on vulnerable populations, 58–66, 61–66

beneficence, principle of, 52, 97, 206, 248, 250, 260

benefits, 52, 56–57, 66, 225–26

biases: corporate special interests research, 82; disciplined subjectivity awareness to avoid, 255–60; historical views on, 4; stereotypical views of, 20, 22; value orientations, 22–23, 25–26, 89

biographical alterations, 68, 95, 224

Blessing Way ceremonies, 239, 240

Bowen, David, 66

brainwashing studies, 41–43

Braroe, Nils, 138–39, 157–58

bribery, 31

Burdick, J., 88

Bureau of the Census, US, 151

burial sites, 14, 16–17, 231, 254–55

Burnett, Jacquetta, 120

CABs (community advisory boards), 84–87, 177, 197–99

Cambodian tree-living spirits, 14

Cameron, Ewen, 42–43

Cargo, M., 198

carta de responsabilidad, 160–61

CBPR (community-based participatory research, or participatory action research, PAR), 88–89, 192–96

cell phones, 225, 235

Centers for Disease Control (CDC), 38, 40, 76, 261

Central Intelligence Agency (CIA), 42–43

Certificate of Confidentiality, 29, 65, 69, 95

CFR (Code of Federal Regulations), 50–51, 92–93, 208

change intervention, 6–7, 8, 25–26, 178

characteristics of researchers: age, 137, 143–45, 151; clothing and adornment, 141, 152–54, 163; culture, 154–55; education levels, 122–23, 154–55; gender, 137, 138–43, 145, 149; overview, 123, 136, 137–38; physical features, 128, 137, 145–52, 163; religion, 146; as researcher persona component, 116; self-reflection on, 258; sexual orientation, 146; social class, 122–23, 139, 154–56

chikungunya, 190

children: activity expenditure studies, 122–23; adolescent sexual risk studies, 85; age of researchers and data collection, 144, 151; consent guidelines for, 54–55, 60–61, 103, 317–28, 333–35; consent violations, 36, 41; hepatitis studies and violations, 41; IRB review level requirements involving, 99, 100; lead abatement studies and violations, 43–44; parent deportation and financial responsibility for, 160–61; risk potential assessments, 49; as vulnerable population, 41, 58–59, 60, 65, 67

Chile observatories, 254

China, 106, 166–67

chromosomal abnormalities, 232

CIA (Central Intelligence Agency), 42–43

CICATS (Connecticut Institute for Clinical and Translational Science), 215

CITI (Collaborative Institutional Training Initiative), 182

Citizens United, Appellant v. Federal Election Commission, 12, 241

class, social, 122–23, 131, 143–44, 154–56

Clinical Translation Science Award (CTSA), 193–94

clinical trials, 183, 184, 210–11

Clinton, Bill, 39
clothing, 141, 147–48, 153–54, 163
coauthors, 76–81
Code of Federal Regulations (CFR),
    50–51, 58, 92–93, 208, 209. *See also*
    Belmont Report
coercion: compensation as, 57, 67, 175,
    210; data collection obtained through,
    31; military interrogation studies,
    42–43; overview, 66–68; situational
    vulnerability due to, 62, 65, 66–68,
    225–26; threats of retaliation as, 41,
    52, 62, 65, 66, 67–68; voluntarism
    versus, 49, 52, 54
cold spots, 256–57, 259
collaboration: field identity construction
    for, 134; in history, 4, 5, 20, 31, 32;
    and insider-outsider perspectives,
    240–48; interdisciplinary teams
    and community of study, 192–96;
    as modern research practice, 7,
    31–32; multiple IRBs with, 109–10;
    reciprocity as acknowledgment for,
    175–76; researchers across disciplines,
    32; and research value issues, 7–8. *See
    also* interactions; interdisciplinary
    (transdisciplinary) teams
Collaborative Institutional Training
    Initiative (CITI), 182
collective risks, 231–33, 243, 261–62
Colombian social movement studies, 88
commercial sex workers (CSWs), 40
Commission for the Protection of
    Human Subjects of Biomedical and
    Behavioral Research, 50
communication. *See* interactions
communities of identity, 157, 200–201
communities of study: benefits of
    research accrued to, 52; consent
    of, 52–53, 218–24; data ownership
    and dissemination agreements, 77;
    familiarity impacting interaction with,
    125–26; field identity development
    for understanding, 132; identifiable

data usage restrictions, 10–11;
    interdisciplinary research and
    relationship guidelines with, 192–96;
    interdisciplinary research and risk
    protection strategies, 196–201;
    representation issues, 4, 5–7, 31–32,
    245–46, 248; results feedback and
    disclosure, 52, 94, 118, 119, 176–77;
    risk potential and collective harm,
    231–32, 261–62; risk potential of
    interaction with, 98; secondary
    subjects within, 53, 66, 95–96, 222–24;
    value of research results to, 8, 118. *See
    also* culture
community advisory boards (CABs),
    84–87, 177, 197–99
community-based participatory research
    (CBPR, *or* participatory action
    research, PAR), 88–89, 151, 170–71,
    192–96
compensation: as coercion, 57, 67, 175,
    210; disadvantages of, 31, 57; financial,
    30–31, 56–57, 175; as voluntarism
    incentive, 37. *See also* reciprocity
competence, 147
confidentiality: and data collection
    methods, 10–11, 30, 68, 70–71, 95, 224;
    definition, 68; exceptions and waivers
    to, 68–71; federal legal protection of,
    29, 39, 65, 95; as IRB concern, 98; IRB
    proposal application information on,
    102; requirements for, 3, 30, 49, 52; as
    research study disclosure requirement,
    52; of secondary subjects, 53, 66,
    95–96, 222–24; of sensitive topics,
    64–66, 70–71; team research and
    community protection of, 199–201;
    technology and information
    retrievability issues, 234–36. *See also*
    confidentiality breaches
confidentiality breaches: consequences of,
    48, 55, 56, 106, 227–29; data collection
    methods causing, 233–34; and data
    disposition, 107, 178, 231; data

interpretation dissemination resulting in, 243–44; safety intervention and risk of, 28–29, 171; of team research, 199–200

Connecticut Institute for Clinical and Translational Science (CICATS), 215

consent: coercion for, 41, 66–68; of communities, 52–53, 218–24; cultural information changes and modification of, 56; early use of contracts for, 37; exceptions to, 39; exceptions to written, 62–63, 69–70, 74–75, 104; long-term processes of, 54, 74; participant inconvenience and negotiations for, 217–18; for recording device usage, 124; requirements and guidelines for, 3, 14–15, 36, 39, 52–55, 217; research study risk disclosure for, 57, 101; of secondary subjects, 53, 66, 222–24; violations of, 39, 40, 41, 42, 43, 45, 46–48; as voluntarism component, 52; vulnerable populations and, 58–61. See also consent forms

consent forms: content requirements, 103; examples of, 317–41; as IRB proposal application component, 103; record keeping violations for missing, 104–5; requirement of, 54–55; for vulnerable populations, 59–61; waivers for, 62–63, 69–70, 74–75

consenting unit, 52

contexts, embedded, 116–19, 117

contraception studies, 85–86, 106, 233, 335–37

contractual (formal) responsibilities: funding agencies, 89–91; governmental and nongovernmental agencies, 91–92; IRBs and ethics committees, 92–112; reflection on, 260–62; of team research, 181

control groups, nontreated, 44, 45

coresearchers. See interdisciplinary (transdisciplinary) teams; team research

corporations, 12, 14–15, 77, 82, 241

counseling, 187

critical theorists, 25, 26

CTSA (Clinical Translation Science Award), 193–94

cultural brokering, 214

cultural relativism, 24

culture of community: age, views on, 143–44; belief system awareness, 11–17, 231, 254–55; clothing and adornment as identity of, 152–53; communication differences, 123, 124–25, 138–39, 146; and consent challenges, 69; familiarity changing interaction, 125–26; gender and sexuality, 138–39, 141, 146, 150; historical research practices and views of, 4–5, 231; imitation impropriety, 153–54; as operational context, 117, 118; representation issues, 5–7, 245–46; researcher's behavior expectations in, 114; researcher's personal characteristics and role in, 128, 137, 154–55; risk potential associations with, 227–29, 230–33; risks to, 230–31; situational vulnerability due to prohibitions of, 225; value conflicts and empathic positions, 24

data: authorship/ownership of, 76–84, 91; categories of, 18; de-identifiable/anonymous, 10–11, 30, 68, 70–71, 95, 224; disposition of, 27, 52, 91, 107, 177–78, 231; falsifying, 170–71; identifiable private or personal, 8, 10; protection of, 27, 29, 65, 69, 96; validation and verification of, 7, 32, 240–42, 250. See also data collection; data collection methods; data dissemination; data interpretation

data collection: age of researcher impacting, 137, 143–45, 151; compensation for, 30–31, 57, 175–77; gender of researcher impacting, 137,

138–43; learning roles facilitating, 120–23; physical features of researchers impacting, 137, 145–52; social class of researcher impacting, 122–23, 139. *See also* data collection methods

data collection methods: for confidentiality, 10–11, 30, 68, 70–71, 95, 224; confidentiality compromised by, 233–34; empathetic engagement, 23–24, 126, 144; field notes, 124; as IRB evaluation component, 101–2; participant observation, 22–23; recordings, 100, 101; situational vulnerabilities created with, 225. *See also* interactions

data dissemination: and authorship issues, 76–81; Belmont principles protecting, 52; community-based participatory research and guidelines for, 195; community sensitivities and public presentation of, 201; early, incomplete, or misleading results, 82; emic versus etic voice of, 246–47, 263; fame resulting from, 82, 175–76; media coverage and publicity responsibilities, 81–84; participant negotiations on, 118, 119, 175–77; results disagreements and, 167–69, 176, 243–44; vulnerability risks caused by, 233

data interpretation: compensation impacting, 31; consequences of, 241–42, 249–50; disagreements on, 77–78, 167; emic versus etic approaches and challenges to, 204, 240–48, 263–64; good, criteria for, 237–40; historical methods of, 4, 5, 31; as leadership role, 118; methodology of, 31–32, 236–37, 244–45, 248–49; reflection during, 264; researchers' biases impacting, 22

Declaration of Helsinki (DoH), 36, 49

Declaration on the Rights of Indigenous Peoples (United Nations), 14

dental care studies, 155, 185

Department of Health and Human Services, US, 50, 92

deportation, 48, 56, 62, 65, 160–61

depression, 27, 42, 187

Deyhle, Donna, 6, 144

Diaz, Nitza, 122–23

Dimba reproductive studies, 132–33

disciplined subjectivity, 257–62

disclosures: researcher's value orientations, 26; of research results, 52, 94, 119, 176–77; of team members' work-related health issues, 187. *See also* confidentiality breaches; research study disclosure

discrimination: due to data dissemination, 201, 232–33; racial, 25, 146, 149, 151–52; sexual orientation, 146; social status, 151

diseases, infectious, 190–91

DNA studies, 9, 64, 100, 107, 178, 231

DoH (Declaration of Helsinki), 36, 49

dress, 141, 147–48, 153–54, 163

drinking competitions, 166–67

drug (pharmaceutical) studies, 44–45

drug use studies: community consent challenges, 221; consent forms for, examples, 338–40; data de-identification for, 70–71; field identities for, 128; high-risk sites and safety protocols, 188, 189; IRB proposal applications for, examples, 310–16; observation versus intervention conflicts, 28–29, 171; researcher's personal characteristics impacting, 137; risk situations and team member support, 169–70; situational vulnerability of, 62, 63; team research reflective decision making for, 261–62; trustworthiness tests, 168

Earth, as living entity, 13–14, 15–16

education: ethics training for researchers, 22, 72, 181–86; illiteracy as vulnerable characteristic, 39, 61, 69, 224; of IRB members on ethnographic research process, 110–12, 211–13, 227; of participants and consent challenges, 41, 45, 70; of researcher impacting research, 154, 155

education studies: affiliations in, 164–65; coercive risk examples in, 67–68; consent guidelines, 60–61, 102, 329–35, 340–41; data interpretation disagreements in, 78, 168–69, 239–40; field identity modifications for, 130; IRB proposal applications for, 298–303; IRB review level requirements involving, 99; legal risk potential of, 48; multiple IRBs delaying, 109; romances during, 142–43; situational vulnerability in, 62, 64–65

emic (insider) perspectives, 24, 240–48

emotional risks, 27, 47–48, 186–88, 228–29

empathy, 23–25, 126, 144

enforcement of codes, 49–50, 74–76, 104–8. See also Belmont Report; Institutional Review Boards; oversight, federal

Eng, E., 194–95

environmental concerns, 6, 13–14, 15, 82, 232–33

epistemologies, 204, 215–16

equity, 51, 97–98

ethics, research, overview; definition and description, 2–3; formal, procedural, or institutional, 26–27, 29–30; in history, 3–9; informal, ordinary, or everyday, 27–30; qualitative versus quantitative research comparisons, 17–19; researchers' fieldwork guidelines for, 2–3; in social science research, 5–8

ethnicity: researcher's affiliation with community's, 157–58; research impacted by researcher's, 128, 137, 145, 149–52; stereotypes associated with, 148; as vulnerability characteristic, 39

ethnographers. See researchers

ethnographic presence, 4, 231

ethnography, overview: Belmont Report exclusion of, 208–10; experimental research compared to fieldwork of, 17–19; historical research procedures of, 4–8; IRB members and education in, 110–12, 212–14, 227; process description and challenges of, 212; stereotypes and limitations to, 20–22. See also related topics

etic (outsider) perspectives, 5–7, 17, 240–48

Everest, Mt., 15

exempt reviews, 99–100

exit negotiations, 172–75

expedited reviews, 100

experimental research, 17–19, 20–21, 21

exploitation, 13–16, 87, 217

Fals Borda, O., 88

fame, 82, 175–76

Federal Election Commission, Citizens United, Appellant v., 12, 241

feedback, 119, 174, 175–77

feminist researchers, 25, 26

field identities (introductory scripts): challenges to, 130–34; for collaborative relationships, 134; definition, 127; guidelines for, 129; overview and purpose, 126–29; undercover versus, 135

field notes, 124, 224

fieldwork: ethics guidelines in, 2–3; exit negotiations, 172–75; preliminary planning for international, 107; as qualitative research, 17–19; reflections on, 259; stress of, 188

financial risks, 55, 228

Firth, Raymond, 6

food, 166, 190–91

foreign relations, 106
forest, as living entities, 14
formal ethical responsibilities. *See* contractual responsibilities
Foster-Bey, Colleen, 185
fracking, 15, 82
Free Prior Informed Consent (FPIC), 14–15, 217
free will, 53–54
friendships, 143, 156–58, 161, 172–74
funding agencies, 76–77, 89–91, 181

Galman, Sally Campbell, 180
Garcia, Jose, 225
gardening, 146, 226–27
gatekeepers, 262
Geertz, C., 246–47
gender: consent challenges and patriarchal roles of, 218–19, 221–22; research impacted by, 137, 138–43, 145, 149; situational vulnerability of studies on, 64
gene transplant experiments, 105
Gibson, Margaret, 78, 167
glasses, eye, 146–47
global climate change, 14
Goffman, Erving, 153
going native, 4, 144, 154
gonorrhea studies, 40–41
Gonzalez, Elsa, 64–65
government, as operational context, *117*, 118
governmental agencies, 91–92
governmental monitoring. *See* oversight, federal
grants, 90–91, 93, 98, 181, 260
group-based research. *See* communities of study
groups, as operational context, *117*, 118
guardianship, legal, 54, 60, 69
Guatemalan studies, 40–41, 191, 267–98, 317–28
Gupta, Kamla, 86, 184
Guttman scale, 243–44

hair color and style, 147, 153, 163
handicapped people, 36, 58–59, 61
Harding, Sandra, 256
harm: adverse events of, 105, 206; amelioration protocols, 47, 102, 108; categories of, 48; collective, 231–33; failure to participate resulting in, 52; guidelines for minimizing, 2–3, 18, 26–27, 49, 50, 51; justifiable, 94; medical research causing, 36, 37, 38–39, 40, 42–43, 44, 211; reporting requirements, 108; representation issues as, 6; risk categories of, 55; risk disclosure requirements, 53, 101; social science research causing, 45–49, 95. *See also* risk(s)
Hartford, Connecticut (research site): affiliations as beneficial, 158, 165; drug use studies, 128, 169; medical student placement programs, 163; needle exchange programs, 221; prisoners studies, 60; senior housing vaccination studies, 85; situational vulnerability risks, 225; women's studies, 162, 170–71
Hartsock, Nancy, 256
Havasupai Indians, 107, 178, 231
Hawaiian volcanoes, 255
health risks: diseases and illnesses, 190–91; environmental contamination, 232–33; high-risk research sites and safety protocols, 188–89; researcher's personal, 169–70; work-related stress, 186–88
Heath, Shirley Brice, 144, 153
height, as personal characteristic, 146
hepatitis studies, 41
HIV/AIDS studies: advisory boards for, 86; confidentiality procedures for, 70; consent challenges, 221; consent forms for, examples, 335–37; cultural sensitivity of, 150; data interpretation disagreements, 243–44; high-risk research sites and safety issues,

189; infectious disease risks, 190; observation versus interference, 28–29; researcher's personal characteristics impacting, 144; risks of, 27, 44–45, 56, 188, 200, 227; situational vulnerability of, 63–64; team member's lack of training in, 186; team research and reflection, 261–62; unethical examples of, 44–45

Holloway, Deborah, 60–61

homosexuality, 48, 135, 146, 147, 227, 228

hospitality requests, 191

hot spots, 256–57, 259

hozho, 239–40

Huebner, Christina, 171

human remains, 11, 14, 16–17, 231, 254–55

human research, 8–17

human subjects, defined, 8–17. *See also* communities of study; participants; *specific types of human subjects*

Human Terrain Program (US military), 75–76

Humphreys, Laud, 48, 135

hunches, 22, 253, 259

hustling studies, 9–12

hydraulic fracturing, 15, 82

hygiene, personal, 155

ICR. *See* Institute for Community Research

identities, 135, 152–53, 157–58, 200–201. *See also* confidentiality; confidentiality breaches; field identities

Ik tribal studies, 6

illegal activities: arrests and prosecution as risk of, 29–30, 61, 137, 146, 166, 188; deportation as risk of, 48, 56, 62, 65, 160–61; federal certificates for legal protection, 29, 65, 69, 95; IRB review levels for, 101; risk potential, 55, 229; situational and informational risks in, 226–27; as situational vulnerability,

61–63, 62; undercover identities for, 135; written consent waivers for, 54

illiterate people, 39, 61, 69, 224

illnesses: cultural risks provoking, 231; field site environmental contamination causing, 232–33; food-related, 190–91; infectious diseases, 190–91; researcher's personal health, 169–70; as situational vulnerability, 61; stigmatizing, 101

immigrants, undocumented: relationship boundaries, 160–61; risks to, 48, 55, 56, 62, 65, 160–61, 226, 229; as situationally vulnerable category, 61, 65

Immigration and Customs Enforcement, US, 160

incarcerated people, 40, 58–60, 67, 107

India, 86, 190, 210–11, 221–22

indigenous communities: adornment as cultural identity, 152–53; consent guidelines, 14–15, 217, 219; cultural beliefs awareness, 11–12, 13–16, 254–55; cultural risks to, 230–31; field identities for access to, 128; gender roles and social practices, 138–39; researcher's cultural identification with, 157–58. *See also* Native Americans; Navajo Nation

infanticide studies, 106

influence, undue, 67

insider (emic) perspectives, 24, 240–48

Institute for Community Research (ICR) studies: advisory boards, 86; affiliation advantages, 165; consent forms, examples, 335–37; drug risk study consent forms, 338–40; field identity challenges, 133–34; informal research ethics, 28–29; interdisciplinary teams with, 185; IRB proposal application examples, 303–10, 310–16; media partnerships, 83–84; publication agreements of, 79–81; team member risk and reporting, 189; work-related stress, 187

Institutional Ethics Committees. *See* Institutional Review Boards
institutionalized people, 41, 58–60. *See also* prisoners
Institutional Review Boards (IRBs) (*or* Institutional Ethics Committees, IECs): adverse event reports, 108; annual reviews, 108; approval determinations, 96–97; auditing of, 205–6; Belmont Report on, 50; communities of study representatives on, 199; compliance failure consequences, 104–6; consent requirements, 218; criticism of, 203–11; education studies and coercion solutions, 68; epistemological perspectives of, 204, 215–16; ethnographic research education for members of, 110–12, 212–14, 227; exception to rules, 49; human versus nonhuman research assessments, 8–9; of indigenous communities, 219–20; for international research sites, 106–8; issues of concern to, 97–98, 206; lead abatement study approvals, 43; management of multiple, 108–10; membership experiences on, 214–15; overview, 92–96; proposal applications, 97, 101–4, 213, 229–30, 267–316; reflection on requirements of, 260–62; researcher's not seeking approval of, 209, 210; review levels, 98–101; risk potential and benefits assessments, 56; sensitive topics and situational vulnerability assessments, 64; undercover identities, 135; vulnerable populations and expertise representation guidelines, 29–30, 59; written consent waivers, 70, 213
institutions, as research partners: approval letters of, 102; multiple IRBs management, 108–10; as operational context, *117*, 118; research partnership with, 118, 119

integrity, disciplinary, 17–18
intelligence, 146–47
interactions: challenges to, 24–25, 136, 186–88; for change intervention, 6–7, 8, 25–26; as collaborative research practice, 7, 31–32; community-based participatory research and guidelines for, 192–96; confidentiality risks and guidelines for, 23, 30, 200, 233; cultural awareness requirements for, 123, 124–25, 218–19; as data collection strategy, 22–23; empathetic engagement building rapport, 23–24, 126, 144; familiarity impacting, 125–26; field identities facilitating, 128, 130–31; gender and gender roles influencing, 138–41, 146, 149, 218–19; historical practice of, 4, 5, 20, 31, 32; learner-focused suggestions for, 123–24; qualitative versus quantitative research comparisons in, 17; researcher's personal characteristics influencing, 137, 143–55; situational vulnerability due to social prohibitions on, 225. *See also* participant observation; participatory action research; relationships
interdisciplinary (transdisciplinary) teams: community of study protection strategies, 196–201; contractual obligations of, 181, 185; definition, 179–80; health and safety protection of, 186–91; independent research compared to, 180, 191, 196–97, 261; intragroup relationships in, 118, 119, 182–84, 192; relationships with community of study, 192–96; skills requirements, 180–81; training for, 181–83, 184–86
International Ethical Guidelines for Biomedical Research Involving Human Subjects, 36
International Institute for Population Sciences, 86

International Labour Organization Convention 159, 14

international research: compliance requirements, 45, 106–8; cross-institutional collaboration and multiple IRBs, 109–10; data ownership issues and research partners in, 77; ethics violations and foreign relations consequences, 106; local voluntary organizations for, 87; site-related risks, 27, 48, 98, 146, 227, 229–30; US oversight circumvention, 40–41, 44–45, 210–11

Internet, 8–9, 32, 234–36, 248

interrogation studies, 42–43

intervention research, 6–7, 8, 25–26, 178

interviews: compensation for, 31, 57; confidentiality of, 30, 234; consent forms for life history, 340–42; gender of researcher impacting, 140–41; local meanings understood through, 24; memory retention statistics, 124

introductory scripts. See field identities

invisibility, 136, 137

IRBs. See Institutional Review Boards

Israel, B. A., 194–95

Japanese internment studies, 130

Japanese mercury poisoning, 233

Johns Hopkins University, 43

Johnson, Angela, 340–41

Johnson, Barbara Rose, 7

journalism, 96

journals: personal, 259; professional, 72, 78–81, 195

justice, principle of, 51, 97, 206

juvenile prisoners, 60, 67

Kennedy Krieger Institute, 43–44

key informants (community experts, cultural consultants): allegiance conflicts, 29; authorship credits, 76; compensation of, 30–31; confidentiality breaches, 106; definition and description, 28; for disciplined subjectivity and data authenticity, 260; exit negotiations with, 173–74; feedback procedures, 176; fieldwork importance of, 28; historical roles and descriptions, 5, 31; illegal activity risks, 29–30; observation roles versus interventions, 28–29; relationships with, 5, 28–29; researcher's knowledge as data collection impediment, 121

Klingner, Janette, 109

Kuy people, 14

language, 52, 53, 54, 61, 146, 227

Laobe studies, 133

Latina/Latino studies, 64–65, 122–23, 133–34, 261–62

lawsuits, 12, 39, 77, 104

lead abatement studies, 43–44

Lead by Example (campaign and film), 84

leadership roles, 117, 118–19, 196

learner roles, 120–26

LeCompte, Margaret D.: affiliations and associations, 164–65; clothing and cultural perceptions, 153; confidentiality breaches, 233; consent guidelines for student-based studies, 60–61; data interpretation disagreements, 168–69, 239–40; field identity modifications, 130–31; IRB membership experiences, 214–15; IRB proposal applications, examples, 298–303; racism as access impediment, 152; rapport building experiences, 23, 126; Somalian beauty standards, 148; spirits of the dead beliefs, 16–17; subjectivity identification, 256–57

legal risks: arrests, 29–30, 61, 137, 146, 188; federal certificates for protection from, 29, 65, 69, 95; personal characteristics as, 146; of political affiliations, 48, 227, 229; as risk category, 55, 229; as situational

vulnerability, 61; and trustworthiness tests, 167
letters: assent, 54–55, 60–61, 103, 317–28, 333–35; deportation risks and child care responsibility, 160–61; for disciplined subjectivity, 239; institutional approval, 102. *See also* consent forms
licensing, 49–50
Likert scales, 19
linguistic capabilities, 52, 53, 54, 61, 227
listening skills, 123
living alliance model, 86–87
living arrangements, 141
lobby groups, 82
local voluntary associations (LVOs), 87
low-income populations, 39, 40–41, 43–45
Ludwig, Sheryl, 191, 267–98, 317–28

Mangual, Ariana, 160–61
Manhattan School of the Arts study, 298–303, 329–33
Maryland lead abatement studies, 43–44
mathematics studies, 64
Mauna Kea (volcano), 255
Mauritius, studies in, 150, 201, 243–44
McGill University, 42–43
McIntyre, James, 67–68
Mead, Margaret, 145
media, 81–84
medical research: oversight codification for, 36; oversight origins in, 26, 35–36, 49; private clinical trials lacking oversight, 210–11; with situationally vulnerable participants, 61–65; violations in, 18, 35–45. *See also specific types of medical research*
Medina, Zahira, 185
mentally handicapped people, 36, 58–59, 232
mentally ill people, 27, 40–43, 54, 58–59
Mercer, S. L., 198
mercury poisoning, 233

migrant worker studies, 160–61
Milgram, Stanley, 46–47
military, US, 42–43, 75–76
mission creep, 203, 205–8
Modern Red School House (education model), 168
morale, 170
Mosher, Steven, 105–6
Mother Earth, 13–14, 15–16
The Mountain People (Turnbull), 6
mountains, 15, 254–55

NAGPRA (Native American Graves Protection and Repatriation Act), 11
National Institute of Dental and Cranial Research, 185
National Institutes of Health (NIH), 76–77, 182, 211
National Research Act, 40
National Teen Action Research Center, 151
Native American Graves Protection and Repatriation Act (NAGPRA), 11
Native Americans: age facilitating data collection, 144; cultural beliefs awareness, 11; data disposition and confidentiality breaches, 107, 178, 231; data interpretation disagreements, 168–69; as partnership organizations, 109; representation and advocacy for, 6–7; social class sensitivity, 156; written consent waivers for, 69–70. *See also* indigenous communities; Navajo Nation
natural resources, 13–16, 87, 217
Navajo Nation: affiliations and negative stereotypes, 164; cultural beliefs awareness, 16–17; data interpretation disagreements, 239–40; racism as access impediment, 152; representation and advocacy for, 6–7; researcher's personal characteristics impacting studies on, 137, 152–54
Nazis, 18, 35–36, 46–47

needle exchange programs, 221
network research, 96, 223–24
neutrality, scientific, 22, 23–24, 25
New Zealand rivers, as living entities, 13
Nielsen, Joyce, 256
nongovernmental agencies, 91–92, 211
nonhuman entities, 11–17, 219, 231
nonparticipant observation, 4, 5, 20,
    31, 32, 136. *See also* participant
    observation
nuclear displacement studies, 7
Nuremburg Code, 36, 49

obesity, 146, 147, 148
objectivity, 4, 7, 20, 22–25, 263
observation, nonparticipant, 4, 5, 20,
    31, 32, 136. *See also* participant
    observation
Office for Protection from Research Risks
    (OPRR), 69
Office of Extramural Research (OER),
    182
Office of Human Research Protection
    (OHRP): certificates of protection,
    29, 65, 69, 95; creation of, 50;
    institutionalized people, protection
    of, 107; IRB audits of, 205–6; prisoner
    participants review unit of, 59–60;
    record keeping citations, 104–5
ontologies, 215–16
operationalization, 19
OPRR (Office for Protection from
    Research Risks), 69
orphans, 58–59
"other," concept of, 6, 242, 245–46,
    263–64
outsider (etic) perspectives, 24, 240–48
oversight, federal: clinical trials and
    lack of, 210–11; federal regulations
    for, overview, 50–51, 92–93; origins
    and development of, 26, 35–36, 49;
    research sites selected for lack of,
    40–41, 44–45; social science exclusion
    and rejection of, 208–10; treatment

protocols requirements, 45; US
    compliance requirements, 45, 106–8.
    See also Belmont Report; Institutional
    Review Boards

Paiute people, 15–16
PAR (participatory action research),
    88–89, 151, 170–71, 192–96
Parker, E. A., 194–95
parole, 47, 59, 107
participant observation: with community
    engagement, 88–89, 192–96; as data
    collection strategy, 22–23; intervention
    during, 28–29, 171, 261; for social
    movement studies, 88. *See also*
    interactions
participants (individuals): consent
    negotiations and power shift, 217–18;
    data disposition negotiations, 27, 52,
    107, 177–78, 231; exit negotiations
    with, 172–75; formal and informal
    research ethics protecting, 26–30;
    historical research and roles of,
    4–5, 20, 31, 32; human subjects
    certification training for working
    with, 72, 181–82; insider perspectives
    of, 240–48; as live human subjects,
    definitions, 8–17; with marginalized
    status, 156–57, 174; modern
    research practices with, 7, 31–32;
    as operational context, *117*, 118;
    participation withdraw rights, 46–47,
    52; perspective of, 3–4, 204, 216, 218,
    240–45; recruitment equity, 51, 97–98;
    results disclosure and feedback to, 52,
    119, 175–77; results dissemination
    negotiations, 175–76, 177. *See also*
    communities of study; *specific types of
    participants*
participatory action research (PAR),
    88–89, 151, 170–71, 192–96
patriarchy, 218–19, 221–22
Pearson, James, 59
peer reviews, 4, 17, 22, 31

Pelto, Pertti, 190
penicillin, 37–39
Permanent Commission on the Status of
    Women studies, 170
Peshkin, Alan, 256
pharmaceutical studies, 44–45
physical features of researchers, 128, 137,
    145–52, 163
physically handicapped people, 61
Pino, Raul, 190
political risks, 48, 227, 229–30
positionality: of consent negotiations,
    217–18, 219; data interpretation and
    dissemination, 5–7, 17, 204, 216,
    240–48, 263–64; directorship hiring
    and neutrality of, 163; in history,
    3–7; reflection on, 262–63; researcher
    responsibilities of, 216; social class and
    status disparities, 122–23, 139, 154–56
positivism, 4, 5, 20, 242–43
poverty, 39, 40–41, 43–45
Powdermaker, Hortense, 152
pregnant women, 41, 44–45, 58, 59, 61–63
press conferences, 82–83
Prey Lang forest, as living entity, 14
prison environment experiments, 47
prisoners, 40, 58–60, 67, 107
prison school studies, 59
privacy protection. See confidentiality;
    confidentiality breaches
probation, 58, 60, 107
Program Announcements, 90
prostitutes, 40
pseudonyms, 68
psychological risks, 27, 47–48, 186–88,
    228–29
publication. See data dissemination
public figures, 69
publicity, 81–84
Puerto Rican community studies, 122–23,
    133–34
Puerto Rican researchers, 138, 144, 225
pulque (drink), 190
Punjabi Sikh community studies, 78

qualitative versus quantitative research,
    17–19, 20–21

race. See ethnicity
racism, 137, 149, 151, 152, 168–69
Radda, Kim, 86, 185
RAP (Risk Avoidance Partnership) Clinic
    Project, 338–40
rape accusations, 141, 152
rapport, 23–24, 126, 144
reciprocity, 30–31, 126, 175–77, 222
Recombinant Eight (Rec8), 232
record keeping violations, 104–5
recruitment, 51, 97–98
recursivity, 252
Reed, Walter, 37
reflection: cultural sensitivity and,
    254–55; during data analysis and
    interpretation, 264; definition
    and description, 251; on formal
    requirements, 260–62; on openness
    to "other," 263–64; on positionality,
    262–63; self-, 253–54; subjectivity
    identification and discipline, 255–60;
    systematic processes of, 251–53
reflexive accounts, 259
reflexivity, 252
regular reviews of IRBs, 101
relationships: coresearchers', 119, 169–
    72; interdisciplinary research and
    intragroup, 118, 119, 182–84, 192;
    with media, 84; risks associated with,
    227–28; romantic/sexual, 140–43.
    See also relationships, researcher-
    participant
relationships, researcher-participant:
    boundaries, establishing, 160–61;
    collaborative, 7, 31–32; cultural
    interaction expectations building,
    125–26; exit negotiations, 172–75,
    173–75; friendships, 142, 156–58,
    161, 173–74; in history, 4, 5, 20,
    31, 32; interdisciplinary team with
    community of study, 192–96; with

key informants, 28; as leadership role and responsibility, 118, 119; long-term, 159–60; maintaining good, 165–69; rapport building for empathetic engagement, 23–24, 126, 144; reciprocity and feedback, 30–31, 126, 175–77; romantic/sexual, 140–43; trustworthiness tests, 166–67. See also interactions

religion, 48–49, 146, 201, 227–28, 229–30
repatriation, 11
representation, 4, 5–7, 31–32, 119, 245–46, 248
Requests for Applications (RFAs), 90
Requests for Proposals (RFPs), 90
research, overview: definition, 96; ethics in, 2–3; historical procedures of, 3–8; historical standards of, 17–18; qualitative versus quantitative, 17–19, 20–21; stereotypes of, 19–22
researchers (ethnographers): behavioral expectations of, 113–14; contact information for, 49, 98, 102; historical versus modern descriptions of, 31–32; independent versus teamwork, 76, 180, 191, 196–97, 261; personae of, 116; perspectives of, 5–7, 17, 240–46, 244; qualifications assessments, 102; reputations of, 104, 170, 171; scientific stereotypes and limitations to, 21–22. See also characteristics of researchers; roles of researchers
research results: authorship issues, 76–81; biases impacting interpretation of, 22; contractual agreements on use of, 91; feedback and disclosure of, 52, 94, 119, 176–77; historical practices, 4, 5–7, 20, 31, 245–46; stereotypical limitations of, 22; use of, 27, 52, 91, 107, 177–78, 231; value to participants, 8, 118. See also dissemination
[...] compliance requirements [...]onal, 45, 106–8;
[...]al concerns at, 6, 13–14,

15, 82, 232–33; exit negotiations, 172–75; experimental research and stereotypical, 20–21; high-risk, 27, 75–76, 98, 188–91; oversight avoidance in international, 40–41, 44–45
research study disclosure: community-based participatory research and guidelines for, 192–93; consent forms including, 103; deceptive practices and lack of, 46–47, 48, 49; disciplinary professional associations on, 75; guidelines for, 3, 44, 49, 52; for informed consent, 39, 53; medical research and lack of, 37, 38–39, 41, 42, 43; of risks, 52, 55–57, 106; risks of, 45; and secondary subjects, 66, 96; team research and information consistency for, 192; as voluntarism component, 52
respect, principle of, 52–53, 97, 206
retaliation, 41, 52, 62, 65, 66, 67–68
review panels, 260
RFAs (Requests for Applications), 90
RFAs (Requests for Proposals), 90
risk(s): and beneficence, principle of, 52, 56, 97, 206, 248, 250, 260; categories of, 55–56, 225–30; collective, 196–201, 231–33, 243–44; contractual agreements on, 91; cultural, 230–31; definitions, 52, 100; expectations of, 51, 57, 65; failure to disclose, 37, 38–39, 41–43, 46–49, 106; as IRB concern, 97, 98; IRB review levels and, 99, 100, 101; of research sites, 27, 75–76, 98, 188–89, 188–91; to secondary subjects, 53, 66, 95–96; of social science research, 45–49, 213; team research and safety protocols, 27, 98, 119, 171–72, 186–91; trustworthiness tests and situations of, 167. See also confidentiality breaches; harm
Risk Avoidance Partnership (RAP) Clinic Project, 338–40

Ritchwood, Tiarney, 85
rivers, as living entities, 13, 14–15
roles of researchers: affiliations
    influencing, 164–65; contexts and,
    116–18, *117,* 196; definition, 116; field
    identities and, 126–36; friendships,
    156–58; as learner/student, 120–26;
    multiplicity of, 115–16; as researchers'
    personae component, 116. *See also*
    characteristics of researchers
Roman, Leslie, 144
romances, 141–43

sacred objects and sites, 231, 254–55
sadism, 36
safety risks: high-risk sites and protocols
    for, 27, 98, 188–89; leadership
    responsibilities for, 119; team research
    and responsibilities for, 169–70, 171–
    72, 186–91. *See also* health risks
sampling methods, 223–24
Sandoval, C., 245
sanitation, 191
Schensul, Jean J.: advisory groups formed
    by, 86; affiliation advantages, 165;
    age and "passing," 144; friendships
    with participants, 158; living alliance
    models, 86; sexual attraction,
    unwanted, 141; social class disparities,
    155; team research, 172, 184–85, 187,
    189; trustworthiness tests, 166–67
Schensul, Stephen L.: clothing
    contradicting negative stereotypes,
    163; field identities and role
    modifications, 131; personal
    friendships with participants, 158;
    social movement study methods, 88;
    team safety and problem solving, 172
Scheper-Hughes, N., 263
Schoepfle, Mark, 28
Schulz, A. J., 194–95
scientific advisory groups, 84
scripts, introductory. *See* field identities
secondary subjects, 53, 66, 95–96, 222–24

secondhand information, 199–200
self-reflection, 253–60
Senegalese studies, 132–33, 137
sensitive topics: age of researchers and
    data collection alterations, 151;
    counseling for researchers of, 187;
    ethnicity of researchers impacting
    culturally, 150; IRB approval
    challenges, 96; IRB review levels and,
    99, 100, 101; situational vulnerability
    defined by, 63–66; written consent
    waivers for, 54
sexuality, 140–43, 145, 152, 233
sexuality studies: and data interpretation
    disagreements, 243–44; field identity
    conflicts in, 132–33; researcher's
    personal characteristics impacting,
    137–40, 150, 151; training
    methodology for, 184–85
sexually transmitted disease studies,
    37–41. *See also* HIV/AIDS studies
sexual orientation, 48, 135, 146, 147, 227,
    228
sexual predation, 143, 228
Shane (Galman), 180
Sherpas, 15
Short Grass Indians studies, 128, 138–39
shunning, 48, 227–28, 233
Silva, Amarisiri de, 172
Singh, S. K., 86, 184
situational risks, 226–27, 229–30
situational vulnerability, 29–30, 61–68,
    224–26
skin color. *See* ethnicity
skinwalkers, 16–17
social media, 88, 235
social movements, 88–89, 229
social risks, 227–28
social status, 122–23, 131, 143–44,
    154–56
soldiers, 37, 40, 41–43
Somalian beauty standards, 148
SOPs (Standard Operating Procedures),
    206

spirits, as living entities, 11–12, 14, 16–17, 231
sponsors and sponsoring agencies, 76–77, 89–91, 181
Spradley, James, 121
Sri Lanka, 125, 139–40, 147–48
Standard Operating Procedures (SOPs), 206
standpoints, 25–26, 256
Stanford Prison experiments, 47
stereotypes, 19–22, 146–48, 153, 163–65
stolen goods (hustling) studies, 9–10
strategic alliances, 84, 85
stress, 186–88
subjectivity: of researchers, 25–26, 255–60; of research process, 5, 6, 18
surveys, anonymous, 70
syphilis studies, 37–41

TAGs (technical advisory groups), 84, 86
team research: authorship credit, 76; definition, 180; health and safety protection of, 27, 98, 119, 169–72; reflective decision making with, 261–62; relationship situations in, 119, 169–71; selection and hiring for, 144. See also interdisciplinary (transdisciplinary) teams
The Tearoom Trade study, 48
technical advisory groups (TAGs), 84, 86
technology, 182–83, 184–86, 234–36
teenagers, 65, 85, 144, 151
telescope observatories, 254–55
tests, trustworthiness, 166–67
Tikopia studies, 6
tobacco studies, 188–89
TOR network studies, 8–9
torture, as ethics violation, 42–43
training, 22, 72, 181–86
transdisciplinary teams. See
⟩linary teams
See research study

treatment protocols: denial of, 38–39, 43, 45; federal guidelines for, 45; threat of denial, 41, 62, 65, 66
trust, 70, 135, 166–67, 217
tuberculosis, 190
Turnbull, Colin, 6
Tuskegee Study of Untreated Syphilis (TSUS), 37–39
twin studies, 104–5
typhoid fever, 190

undercover identities, 135
United Nations, 14, 36
universities, as funding agencies, 77, 93, 94, 109, 215
University of Connecticut Health Center (UCHC), 215
US military, 42–43, 75–76
US Public Health Services studies, 37–41
Ute tribal studies, 6–7

vaccination studies, 37, 85, 303–10
value orientations, 22–23, 25–26, 89
Van Gerven, Dennis, 9
video data recordings, 100, 101
virginity, as cultural value, 150, 243
voice amplitude, 146
voluntary participation (voluntarism), 3, 37, 46–47, 52, 60–61. See also consent
vulnerable populations: categories by definition, 58–63; definitions, 58, 224; federal government certification for use of, 65; guidelines for, 27, 51, 52; international research and lack of oversight, 210; as IRB concern, 98; IRB review levels for, 101; medical research violations on, 39–41, 43–44; as secondary subjects, 96; sensitive topics defining, 63–66; situationally, 29–30, 61–68, 224–27

war zones, 27, 63, 75–76, 98, 225, 230
Wax, Rosalie, 130

We, the Tikopia (Firth), 6
Weber, M., 245
Weeks, Margaret, 28–29, 189
weight, as personal characteristic, 146, 147, 148
Werner, Oswald, 28
Whanganui Iwi people, 13
Whanganui River, 13, 14–15
whistleblowers, 170–71, 228
WHO (World Health Organization) studies, 166–67
Willowbrook hepatitis studies, 41
withdrawal, study, 46–47, 52
women: change intervention as priority for, 25; diversity and hiring practices, 162–63; gender and sexuality, 140–43, 145; gender roles and communication practices, 138–39, 146, 149, 218–19; Guatemalan studies on, 267–303, 317–28; patriarchal communities and consent challenges, 218–19, 221–22; pregnant, as vulnerable population, 41, 44–45, 58, 59, 61–63; researcher's characteristics impacting research, 140–41, 143–44, 145; women's rights studies and data falsification, 170–71
World Health Organization (WHO) studies, 166–67
World War II medical research violations, 18, 35–36
Writ of Protection (Certificate of Confidentiality), 29, 65, 69, 95

yellow fever vaccination studies, 37

Zimbardo, Philip, 46, 47

ABOUT THE AUTHORS

Margaret LeCompte received her BA from Northwestern University in political science and, after serving as a civil rights worker in Mississippi and a Peace Corps Volunteer in the Somali Republic, earned her MA and PhD from the University of Chicago. She then taught at the Universities of Houston and Cincinnati, with visiting appointments at the University of North Dakota and the Universidad de Monterrey, Mexico, before moving to the School of Education at the University of Colorado–Boulder in 1990. She also served for five years as executive director for research and evaluation for the Houston Independent School District. She is internationally known as a pioneer in the use of qualitative and ethnographic research and evaluation in education. Fluent in Spanish, she has consulted throughout Latin America on educational research issues. Her publications include many articles and book chapters on research methods in the social sciences, as well as her cowritten (with Judith Preissle) *Ethnography and Qualitative Design in Educational Research* (1984, 1993) and coedited (with Wendy Millroy and Judith Preissle) *The Handbook of Qualitative Research in Education* (1992), the first textbook and handbook published on ethnographic and qualitative methods in education. Her collaborative work in research methodology continues with this second edition of the *Ethnographer's Toolkit*. Dr. LeCompte is deeply interested in the educational success of linguistically and culturally different students from kindergarten through university, as well as reform initiatives for schools and communities serving such students. Her books in these areas include *The Way Schools Work: A Sociological Analysis of Education* (1990, 1995, and 1999) with K. DeMarrais and *Giving Up on School: Teacher Burnout and Student Dropout* (1991) with A. G. Dworkin. Her diverse interests as a researcher, evaluator, and consultant to school districts, museums, communities, and universities have led to publications on dropouts, artistic and gifted students, school reform efforts, schools serving American Indian students, and the impact of strip mining on the social environment of rural communities. Her most recent research involves explorations in the politics and f of public universities. Winner of the Council on Anthropology and Education's 2011 Spindler Award for lifetime contributions to educational anthropology, she is an elected Fellow of the American Educational Research Association, the American Anthropological Association, and the Society for Applied Anthropology, and has been president of the Council on Anthropology and Education of the American Anthropology Association and editor of the journals *Review of Educational Research* and *Youth and Society*. A founding member and the first president of the University of Colorado–Boulder chapter of the American Association of University Professors, she also served as vice president of the Colorado Conference of the AAUP and was active in faculty governance at the University of Colorado. As professor emerita, she continues to use action research strategies in the service of improving the intellectual life in higher education.

Jean J. Schensul, founding director, and now full-time senior scientist, Institute for Community Research, Hartford, is an interdisciplinary medical/educational anthropologist with a lifelong commitment to the conduct and use of research to address social justice issues. Born in Canada, she completed her BA in archeology at the University of Manitoba and her MA and PhD in anthropology at the University of Minnesota. From 1978 to 1987, as deputy director and cofounder of the Hispanic Health Council in Hartford, Connecticut, she built its research and training infrastructure. In 1987, she became the founding director of the Institute for Community Research, an innovative, multi-million-dollar community research organization, conducting collaborative and participatory applied research and intervention in health, education, cultural studies, and folklore in the United States, China, Sri Lanka, and India. Dr. Schensul's research cuts across the developmental spectrum, addressing contributions of ethnography to disparities and structural inequities in early childhood development, adolescent and young adult substance use and sexual risk, reproductive health, and chronic diseases of older adulthood. She is the recipient of more than twenty National Institutes of Health research grants, as well as other federal, state, and foundation grants. In addition to conferences, workshops, over eighty peer-reviewed journal articles, many edited substantive special issues of journals including *Anthropology and Education Quarterly*, *AIDS and Behavior*, *American Bel* ntist, and the *American Journal of Community Psychiatry*, her rk in research methodology is reflected in a book (with Don aborative Research and Social Change, the widely celebrated ries, the *Ethnographer's Toolkit* with Margaret LeCompte, les and book chapters on ethnography and advocacy, community building, and sustainability of interventions. Dr. Schensul has served as reviewer on various NSF, NIH, and other federal committees, and is an appointed member of iSMOC, the committee of the National Children's study (NIH/NIDCR) that monitors ethics and adverse events. She has served as president of the Society for Applied Anthropology and the Council on Anthropology and Education, is an elected board member of the American Anthropological Association, elected treasurer of the Association on Anthropology and Gerontology, and appointed member of the AAA Committee on Applied and Practicing Anthropology. In recognition of her work as a scholar-activist she has been awarded two senior anthropology awards, the Solon T. Kimball Award for anthropology and policy (with Stephen Schensul) and the 2010 Malinowski Award for lifetime contribution to the use of anthropology for the solution of human problems. She has been active in other professional organizations including the Society for Prevention Research and the American Public Health Association, where she has organized oral and poster sessions on diverse topics including multilevel interventions, tobacco use, and oral health. Dr. Schensul holds an adjunct faculty position as Research Professor, School of Dental Medicine, and is director of Qualitative Research and Ethnography, Interdisciplinary Research Methods Core, Yale Center for Interdisciplinary Research on AIDS.